Portrait painted by Paul Trebilcock

WINTHROP W. ALDRICH
Ambassador to the Court of St. James's — 1956

WINTHROP W. ALDRICH

Lawyer, Banker, Diplomat

Arthur M. Johnson
Professor of Business History
Harvard University

DIVISION OF RESEARCH
GRADUATE SCHOOL OF BUSINESS ADMINISTRATION
HARVARD UNIVERSITY
BOSTON 1968

FOREWORD

The Harvard Business School, from the time of its founding in 1908, has been dedicated to the proposition that business is a profession and, as such, has responsibilities to society that transcend as well as embrace those commonly associated with economic decisions. On the occasion of the dedication of the School's new campus at Soldiers Field in 1927, Owen D. Young made a memorable address in which he underscored these responsibilities as an important part of the businessman's obligations and opportunities. At no time in the history of the School or of American business history has the challenge of meeting these responsibilities been greater or the opportunities more numerous than today. This book is a contribution to a better understanding of this challenge and its opportunities for constructive business contributions.

For many years the Harvard Business School has maintained an archives devoted to manuscript collections illuminating the history of business and business leadership. These valuable and virtually unique resources were enriched in 1965 by Winthrop W. Aldrich's gift of his papers. This book grew out of an investigation of these papers as a project in the School's wide-ranging research program to shed light on business problems, past, present, and future. The project itself was financed by an allocation of funds given to the School by The Harvard Business School Associates. It was coincidence, but a happy one, that the primary documentary sources for this study should come from a man and a family who have had a long association with Harvard and this School.

The distinguished career of Mr. Aldrich as a lawyer, banker, and diplomat exemplifies a concern for a high level of professional performance coupled with imaginative participation and significant accomplishment in civic, social, and public service fields that are, and must increasingly become, the province of professional business leadership and responsibility. It is for these reasons that it is particularly appropriate for the Harvard Business School to publish this biography.

GEORGE P. BAKER
Dean

Soldiers Field
Boston, Massachusetts
September 1968

PREFACE

Writing the biography of a living person is the launching of a perilous voyage for the author. He is quite likely to antagonize both friends and critics of the subject, and he cannot ignore the danger to objectivity resulting from lack of time perspective. If, as in this case, he has had any extended contact with the individual about whom he is writing, the danger of bias is further increased. These are risks not accepted lightly by a professional historian, but in this case the risk-taking seems warranted.

This book came directly out of my concern with the role of business and businessmen in history and the unexpected availability of unusual manuscript materials for studying this role. In early 1965 Mr. Winthrop W. Aldrich, former chairman of The Chase Bank of New York City, son of Senator Nelson W. Aldrich, and himself a past Ambassador to the Court of St. James's, deposited his papers in the Baker Library of the Harvard Graduate School of Business Administration. I first met Mr. Aldrich when he visited the School that summer to confer on some of the details of housing his papers. As a result of that meeting, I became interested in the extent and character of the Aldrich collection. The further I investigated, the more apparent it became that this collection offered a promising source of information about many facets of American history and the role of businessmen in it since World War I.

Mr. Aldrich had a prominent part in many of the activities and events that have shaped the environment of business and banking and of this country's international relations over an extended period of time. It seemed to me, therefore, that a biography of Mr. Aldrich, based largely on his papers, could provide a potentially valuable record of a prominent leader in recent American banking. Equally important, such a biography could show how the perception of an individual's opportunities and responsibilities at many levels can affect a wide and significant spectrum of professional, public, and social service activities.

Mr. Aldrich agreed to my free use of his papers and promised his full cooperation, subject to only one condition — that I would include nothing that reflected adversely on any other living person. I accepted this as a regrettable but reasonable condition of writing contemporary biography. Mr. Aldrich has been fully cooperative in our many interviews, and I have talked with more than two dozen of his colleagues from many areas and eras of his career. Combining these interviews with material from the Aldrich papers, supplemented by background research in secondary sources, the following record of his career has been compiled.

I have tried to make clear where Mr. Aldrich stood on major issues, why he took the positions that he did, and how his stands compared with those of others. Basically, my approach has been to present the events of his varied career in terms of his perceptions at the time as nearly as I could ascertain them — and in his own words where possible. The resulting significance of his decisions and actions is reflected in their results, which I have attempted to treat more on a factual than a value judgment basis.

In his legal, banking, civic, public service, and philanthropic activities, as in his internationalism, Mr. Aldrich expressed his convictions about the role and responsibilities of the private individual and businessman. Whether or not one agrees with the positions Mr. Aldrich took on specific issues, one cannot examine the record of his interests and accomplishments without recognizing that his field of activity was awesomely extensive, his dedication to his basic principles unswerving, and his efforts to discharge responsibilities of a high order unrelenting. Above all, he was not afraid to put his prestige on the line for causes in which he believed. In these respects I feel Mr. Aldrich's career provides a worthy example for present-day business leaders. Commitment to forthright positions based on principle and implemented with courage seems to me a *sine qua non* of any continued leadership role for the private sector.

The span of Mr. Aldrich's interests and the length of his career would challenge the understanding and resources of the most competent historian. Whatever merit this book may have, therefore owes a great deal to the contributions of many people besides the author. The concept of the "vital link" was suggested to me by Mrs. Laura Goldhar, who did much of the background research. The sheer magnitude of the Aldrich collection was itself a major challenge, but it yielded to the combined efforts of Miss Catherine Ellsworth, Mrs. Meg Burbank, and Mrs. Goldhar. Of course, the cooperation of Mr. Aldrich was invaluable in reconstructing a number of important episodes. Mrs. Aldrich and a number of Mr. Aldrich's colleagues also gave freely of their time and added new perspectives to the study.

I am especially indebted to Messrs. John J. McCloy, Robert Murphy, David Rockefeller, and Crawford Wheeler who read the manuscript from the standpoint of their association with Mr. Aldrich, and to Professors William Leuchtenberg of Columbia University, Herman Kross of New York University, Ross Robertson of Indiana University, and Ruhl Bartlett of the Fletcher School of Law and Diplomacy, who gave me the benefit of their expertise in their various specialties without in any way endorsing my interpretation of their criticisms and suggestions as reflected in this book.

To Mr. Aldrich's secretary, Miss Alice Whitney, who lent every assistance, to Mr. Robert Lovett of the Baker Library Manuscript Division, to Professor Bertrand Fox, Director of Research at the Harvard Business School, and to Professor Ralph Hidy, who made many helpful editorial and substantive suggestions, I am most grateful. Finally, without the assistance of Miss Susan Foley, who handled ably a number of things that normally impinge on an author's time, as well as typing the manuscript, the appearance of this book would have been delayed by a year or more. As always, however, the final responsibility lies with the author, and I am solely responsible for the errors of omission or commission contained in the following pages.

ARTHUR M. JOHNSON

Boston, Massachusetts
October 1968

CONTENTS

TABLES

WINTHROP W. ALDRICH

LAWYER, BANKER, DIPLOMAT

CHAPTER I

The Formative Years

IN 1885 Providence, Rhode Island, capital of the nation's
smallest state, was a thriving industrial city with over 1,200
manufacturing establishments employing more than 26,000
persons. Founded in the 17th century by strong-minded men
seeking to escape the religious conformity demanded of them
in the Massachusetts Bay Colony, Providence had grown to
mercantile greatness in the 18th century. Merchant capital
had in turn contributed to the revolution in textile manufacture that had marked the beginning of the American industrial revolution. Though textiles had remained important in
the city's economy, a more varied industrial base underlay its
bustling activity in the mid-1800s.

Providence was clearly in the process of entering yet another era of change. Nestled at the head of Narragansett Bay,
the city had good railroad connections to such points as New
York, Worcester, Hartford, Springfield, and Boston, but
steamboats and sailing vessels still carried a substantial amount
of the passenger and cargo traffic to coastal points in Rhode
Island and down the seaboard as far as New York and Phila-

delphia. From "College Hill" on the east side of Providence, where the buildings of Brown University stood, the haphazard development of industrial Providence was revealed by the irregular patterns of smoke from factory chimneys in various parts of the city. The smells, noise, and dirt of iron foundries, machine and textile shops, soap, rubber, and assorted manufactories assailed the nose and assaulted the ears of the visitor to Rhode Island's industrial showplace.

The Aldrich Family

Rhode Island's industrial progress was already a consuming concern of Nelson Wilmarth Aldrich, whom the legislature had elevated to United States Senator in 1881. Yet in 1885 the products of modern technology that were shortly to transform industry, communication and transportation were still new to Providence. Horsecars, different colored kerosene lights on the vehicles indicating their destination, still rattled past the Aldrich house on Broad Street on their way to and from downtown Providence. Electric lights were still a novelty, and the streets were mostly lit by gas. In Providence, as in the United States as a whole, rapid social and economic change based on new technology, large-scale business organization, and expanding domestic and international markets was beginning to make itself felt; yet in 1885 the old was still highly visible in Rhode Island's capital city.

A leader in the generation that was to complete the nation's economic transformation in the 20th century and then shape its response to the consequences in depression, world war, and world responsibilities was born on November 2, 1885, when Senator and Mrs. Nelson Aldrich welcomed a new son to their family in an unpretentious house at 565 Broad Street. They decided to name him Winthrop Williams. It is family legend that his mother intended to name him Roger Williams but at the last moment decided that John Winthrop, son of the first governor of Massachusetts Bay and himself governor of Connecticut, held a higher place in her esteem. In any case, it is abundantly clear that this child was a son of New England and that his parents hoped that this inheritance, embracing both the conscientious Puritan values of a Winthrop and the independence of spirit and judgment that had led Roger Williams to leave Massachusetts and found a new settlement on Narragansett Bay, would be perpetuated in their new son. Although they did not live to know his accomplishments, their hopes were more than fulfilled by Winthrop Aldrich's career as a lawyer, as president and then chairman of the world's largest bank, as a leader in outstanding civic, philanthropic, and war relief activities, and as Ambassador to the Court of St. James's at a particularly critical time in Anglo-American relations.

The newest Aldrich came from a family that had been in New England from its early days. The first Aldrich to come to America was a native of Derbyshire, England. Born in 1605, George Aldrich migrated to New England in 1631 and settled at Dorchester near Boston. After living in Boston and Braintree, he moved inland to Mendon, Massachusetts, in 1663 and died there in 1683. The next generation established itself at Smithfield, Rhode Island, where the succeeding four generations lived. Winthrop's grandfather, Anan Aldrich, however, moved to Killingly, Connecticut, where Nelson W. Aldrich was born in 1841. Nelson's mother, Abby Ann Burgess, provided the connection with the Williams family, for her mother, Phoebe Williams, was a direct descendant of Roger Williams.[1]

Despite descent from a leading family of colonial America, Nelson Aldrich, the future Senator from Rhode Island, was a farmer's son and had to make his own way. Educated at Providence Seminary, East Greenwich, Rhode Island, his first job was as a clerk in a wholesale grocery concern in

[1] Reference footnotes will be found at the end of this book beginning on page 485.

Providence. After Civil War service in the 10th Regiment of Rhode Island Infantry, he returned to the grocery business and became a partner in the firm of Wightman & Aldrich in 1865. The following year he married Abby Pearce Chapman, a descendant of Elder William Brewster of Plimouth Plantation. Her ancestor on the paternal side, Captain Israel Morgan, served in the Revolutionary War and married Elizabeth Brewster (1756–1826), a direct descendant of Elder Brewster.[2]

The Nelson Aldriches raised a large family, though they also lost two children. In September 1867 Nelson W. Aldrich, Jr., was born at the family's first home at 31 Lockwood Street, Providence, where he died in July 1871. The next child, Lucy Truman, was born at Lockwood Street October 23, 1869, the year that her father was elected to the Common Council in Providence. Edward Burgess Aldrich followed on September 28, 1871, and Abby Greene Aldrich, the future wife of John D. Rockefeller, Jr., on October 26, 1874. Meanwhile, the family had moved to 122 High Street, Providence.

The Aldriches remained on High Street only a short time, but Stuart Morgan Aldrich, the next son, was born there in August 1876. Four years later William Truman Aldrich was born at Washington, D.C., where Nelson Aldrich's political career had carried him to Congress. Another child, Emma Louise, was born at Broad Street, Providence, in October 1882 but died in June 1884, just a few months after Richard Steere Aldrich was born at the family's new Washington residence, 1311 New Hampshire Avenue. Winthrop Williams Aldrich was born at the Broad Street house on November 2, 1885, and the final member of the family, Elsie, was also born there on August 20, 1888.[3]

The conflict and tensions of industrial Providence were remote from 110 Benevolent Street, where the Aldriches moved in the early 1890s. It was there, on College Hill near Brown University, where Winthrop Aldrich spent his carefree early years in a big house surrounded by other imposing ones belonging to the old mercantile and new industrial elite of Providence.

Built in the early 19th century, the Benevolent Street house was a large wooden structure, surmounted by a cupola. The western boundary line of the spacious grounds was dominated by an ancient elm said to have been the marker for the original proprietor's grant that ran down to the harbor, just visible from the corner of the next street. The spacious high-ceilinged rooms downstairs were graced by marble mantelpieces. The first floor was divided into two parlors, library, dining room and kitchen. The girls and their parents slept on the second floor and the boys on the third, which was heated by Franklin stoves. In the library was a fine collection of books, for Senator Aldrich loved reading and book collecting. The Providence house reflected a secure, affluent, but not ostentatious, way of life, and to it the Aldrich children would return throughout their lives. For Lucy and Winthrop, especially, it was "home."

The Aldrich children were taught by two English ladies named Tetlow. Miss Asenath Tetlow had had primary responsibility for the older children. By the time Winthrop came along, Miss Fanny Tetlow was in charge of the Benevolent Street schoolroom with an occasional assist from her sister. They found an apt and eager pupil in young Winthrop, who at the age of six took obvious pleasure in writing to his older sister Abby: "You had to [*sic*] mistakes in your letter but I don't remember what they were. Please excuse me for saying that but I thought I better tell you. Because you might do it again." [4] A few years later he was writing extended letters in a flowing hand about all manner of childish interests, ranging from the predatory activities of the family cat to his own frustrating efforts to seize the brass ring on a merry-go-round.

Literary allusions began to mark even this youthful correspondence, and his interest in books was reflected and encouraged by the acquisition of a library card.[5]

To inculcate the virtue of thrift, Nelson Aldrich, as he did for the other children, opened a savings account for Winthrop at the age of eight. But young Aldrich was not then or later particularly interested in money which, first by virtue of his birth and later by dint of his own professional success, never constituted one of his personal problems. However, he was always interested in getting full value for money spent, whether his own or others'. Thus, in the letter just cited, he reported to Abby that the only fun on the merry-go-round at the Rocky Point Amusement Park was to have an outside seat where there was a chance at the brass ring. Accordingly, he had declined to pay for staying on when the outside seats were full.

The material objectives that kindled the ambitions of most enterprising Americans of his generation were to be relatively meaningless for Winthrop Aldrich. Far more important was the problem of living up to his New England inheritance by activity that would be satisfying to him, worthy of his family, and useful to society. In shaping these vague goals into meaningful decisions, Winthrop had the warm encouragement of his older sisters, Abby and Lucy. They apparently felt a special responsibility toward the youngest son in a large family where the mother suffered from ill health, and a bond of sympathetic understanding that lasted a lifetime developed between the brother and his sisters.

This was a matter of some significance in determining the specific direction in which Winthrop's career would finally take him. In 1901 Abby was to marry John D. Rockefeller, Jr., who, as heir to the greatest American fortune created by the new industrial era, had to shoulder unique burdens by virtue of his birth. In meeting this challenge he was eventually to find a staunch and able ally in Winthrop Aldrich.

Nelson Aldrich's ascent to a leading place in the United States Senate, of course, provided his youngest son with one possible model for his own career. After only three years in the Rhode Island House, where he served for a time as Speaker, the elder Aldrich had been elected to Congress. He occupied this seat from 1878 to 1881, when he was elected to the Senate. He retained this seat until 1911 and came to be recognized as a leader of the conservative wing of the Republican Party in Congress. His biographer states that Senator Aldrich wanted Rhode Island business "to see that he was, first of all, the businessman in politics. His aim was to bring business and politics together. Especially, he stood for manufacturing, for a cautious union between manufacturers and workmen." [6]

Nelson Aldrich had cast his political lot with the industrial Providence that lay at the foot of College Hill, and he became identified with the protective tariff and sound money policies that eastern Republicans opposed to the growing agrarian demands of the West. In this spirit, for example, he had opposed passage of the Interstate Commerce Act because its long and short haul provisions threatened the possibilities of eastern manufacturers making terms with the railroads to offset the geographical disadvantage of shipping inland from the seaboard in competition with other areas.[7] On the other hand, a few years earlier he had also opposed raising the tariff on sugar as a costly concession to a special interest.[8] But first and last, true to his constituency, his own inclinations, and his appraisal of where the underpinnings of industrial growth lay, he took the side of the manufacturing interest.

Although his wife had brought money to their marriage, Nelson Aldrich was not content to rely on her resources. In addition to his experience in the wholesale grocery business, he had been a director of the Roger Williams Bank in Providence and president of the First National Bank there before entering Congress. But a Senator's salary was not impressive, while a Senator's expenses in maintaining establishments in Washington and Providence for a growing family were large. Rhode Island businessmen sensed his financial need, appreciated his political influence, and respected his business ability. Accordingly, he was asked in 1892 to join his talents with theirs in developing the electric traction systems that were to form the new mode of urban and interurban passenger transportation.[9] The traction revolution was already under way in Providence, for the preceding year clanking trolley cars, deriving their power from overhead electric wires, had replaced the swaying horse-drawn conveyances that passed Winthrop Aldrich's birthplace on Broad Street.

Traction opened the path to wealth for Senator Aldrich. He and his associates obtained a controlling interest in two street railways in Providence and one in neighboring Pawtucket. This stock was shortly transferred to the United Traction and Electric Company, of which the senior Aldrich was president until 1902.[10] These interests eventually extended to traction systems in a number of states and the District of Columbia, and the profits — combined with other shrewd investments, of which American Tobacco was the most notable [11] — eventually made Nelson Aldrich a millionaire several times over.

All of these changes in his family's fortunes did not mean too much to young Winthrop Aldrich. He led the life of a typical American boy of his day, coasting on the hill near his home, playing practical jokes on the Misses Tetlow, taking violin lessons, and attending Sunday School under a certain amount of duress. More unusual, of course, were the trips and extended stays in Washington, where he visited the Capitol, met his father's colleagues in the Senate, and gained acquaintance with a cosmopolitan way of life that was different from that in Providence.

The Aldriches' new wealth made the most difference to Winthrop when it permitted acquisition of a magnificent piece of waterfront land at Warwick Neck, ten miles below Providence, where the Providence River joins Narragansett Bay. At this time he was in his early teens, an age when swimming and sailing, tennis and riding, at Warwick Neck were most pleasurable.[12]

The land had been owned by the Hoppins, a leading Providence family with a governor to their credit. Acres of manicured green lawns sloped gently to the water's edge from the crest of a ridge that afforded a magnificent, unobstructed view across the Bay toward Bristol on the far shore. As the Aldriches found it, the main residence was a plain, square, wooden house, its mansard roof punctuated with dormer windows and the ground floor surrounded by the inevitable broad piazzas of 19th century country places. Eventually it would be replaced by a vast stone structure, with its east wing especially designed to house Senator Aldrich's large library devoted particularly to economics, banking, and finance, but also spanning such diverse fields as agriculture, fine arts, and religion, plus an outstanding collection of books relating to Rhode Island.[13]

The central feature of the half-mile waterfront was the "Boathouse" with its long pier extending out into the Bay. Of wood and stone construction, the Boathouse was almost as large as the main house and afforded excellent accommodations for entertaining. Its porch made a fine place to watch the water activities of the Aldrich children in assorted small craft. Farther out, the Senator's handsome steam yacht lay at its mooring, ready for a leisurely cruise "Down East" or to the Senator's fishing retreat on the Moisé River in Canada.

Leading public figures, from the President of the United States down, were guests at Warwick Neck, and it was here that Winthrop Aldrich learned to sail and then to race. First in small boats and then in larger cruising boats owned by his brothers he learned the discipline of the sea and discovered the exhilaration of competition under sail. The attention to detail required in racing suited him, and the challenge of navigating a cruising boat fascinated him. He discovered a lifetime avocation on the waters of Narragansett Bay, and it would eventually carry him to participation as manager and navigator of the yacht *Enterprise*, in the supreme test of American yachting: defense of the America's Cup.

With the coming of fall, the carefree delights of Warwick Neck inevitably gave way to schoolboy routine. Nelson Aldrich believed in a democratic education for his sons. Therefore, instead of attending one of the private preparatory schools for which New England was famous, Winthrop in 1899 entered the Hope Street High School in Providence. At that time it was brand new and represented one of the first products of the city's decision to build schools only of brick. Located opposite Hope Reservoir not far from Benevolent Street, the building had a center section containing assembly room, offices, and library, flanked by two classroom wings with basement gymnasiums and lunch rooms. It was, in short, typical of the architecture of high schools in a growing number of cities throughout the land.

The Senator's son, who had acquired "Kit" for a nickname, was a good student, but he found keen academic competition among his classmates. At the top of his class stood Zechariah Chafee, Jr., son of a distinguished Providence family and later a distinguished professor at the Harvard Law School. Winthrop Aldrich struggled hard for second place against George Hurley, who went on to become a Rhodes Scholar; Claude Branch, later a prominent Boston lawyer; and a young lady named Huntsman, who subsequently became editor of a notable British weekly.[14]

Although young Aldrich enjoyed sports, he preferred games like tennis, and later golf, where individual skills rather than team play were paramount. Furthermore, his slender build and average height gave him no advantage for contact sports. Accordingly, while he played football and baseball in high school, he was always on the second team.

He took an active part in other high school activities. In his senior year he was an editor of the *Blue and White*, the class book. He made his first public speech on the occasion of the planting of the class tree in Roger Williams Park, and he took part in the class play.

Meanwhile, he had become increasingly enamored of music. His violin playing had progressed to the point where he even dreamed of a career as a professional musician.[15] But amateur talent and professional competence were two different things, he discovered. When it was pointed out to him that his fingers were too short to enable him to aspire to become a first-rank violinist, his dreams came back to earth. The immediate problem was where to go to college.

College Years

If Winthrop Aldrich had followed in his brothers' footsteps, he would have gone to Yale, which his brother Richard attended, or Brown, where Edward had been a football star. William had also started at Brown but then transferred to MIT preparatory to an outstanding career as an architect. But if Winthrop lacked the physique to become a football star like Edward, he also lacked the mathematical inclinations that won a Gold Medal for William at MIT.

His sisters Lucy and Abby knew Harvard, and they encouraged their youngest brother to consider this possibility. Even more influential, however, was a young lawyer and neighbor at Warwick Neck, Frederick Hoppin.[16] He became for Winthrop a model of what he himself would like to become. Aware of the judges and other public officials in his own family's background, young Aldrich now set his sights on becoming a federal judge, perhaps even in one of the higher courts. He had also decided that, whatever the future held, Harvard College was the place to start preparing for it.

Harvard College had been founded only a few years after the first Aldrich had come to America. It had provided training for generations of New England ministers, had its bout with Unitarianism, and under the guidance of President Charles Eliot, who entered that post in 1869, had been transformed into a major university with expanding graduate faculties. Along with educational advances, including an elective system, intercollegiate athletics had gained growing recognition at Harvard. When Winthrop Aldrich arrived in Cambridge in late September 1903, a great new stadium was nearing completion across the Charles River at Soldiers Field. The new freshman class numbered 556 while the college had a total enrollment of 2,073.

In later years Winthrop Aldrich was to say that Harvard was the most important influence on his life. He was undoubtedly thinking not only of his professors and program of study but also of classmates who became lifelong friends. Men like Harold Vanderbilt, O'Donnell Iselin, Harrison Tweed, George Whitney, and many others who later moved in the top business and legal circles of the nation were to be his intimates in the years to come. But initially young Aldrich, coming from Hope Street High School in Providence, had a lonely time in the large university. The situation was not improved by the fact that he roomed alone in Claverly Hall.[17]

To become known, he was determined to be active in undergraduate affairs. Accordingly, he signed up for the orchestra and the undergraduate paper, the *Crimson*. However, he had hardly established himself in his new surroundings when he was struck down by black diptheria. This forced him to drop out of college and to spend the rest of the academic year recuperating at the Aldrich home in Washington. With tutoring he was able to return to Cambridge and rejoin his class in September 1904.[18]

He soon became a member of the Institute of 1770, the oldest club at Harvard as suggested by its name. Only about 20 percent of the sophomore class was chosen for membership in this social organization, and the procedure was for the first ten selected to pick the next ten and so on until the class membership quota was filled. These groups automatically became members of D.K.E. In their junior year, members of the Institute of 1770 were taken into the Hasty Pudding Club and participated in its annual show.

One of the few mentions of Aldrich's extra-curricular activities records the fact that he was in the cast of Hasty Pudding's production of "The Lotus Eater," where he appeared as a Spanish dancer from L'Operetta di Castilio.[19] He was also a member of the Zeta Psi Club, known as the "Spee," which was one of the so-called "final clubs" at Harvard. Although membership in these various social clubs brought him into contact with other young men of similar background, he appears to have found no particularly congenial outlet in them for his interests.

Judging from the surviving record, the same was true for most other undergraduate activities. For example, the Union Dance was the major event for each junior class, but Winthrop Aldrich's name is missing from the list of boxes shared by members of '07. In his senior year, Claverly Hall won the bumping races and was named the best rowing house, but he was apparently not involved in these accomplishments.

The bout with diptheria, of course, discouraged active participation in athletic events of this kind.

But young Aldrich had not come to Harvard to be recognized as a socialite nor to be developed as an athlete but to get a thorough grounding for a career of public service. In this connection the elective system, which enabled a student to select his own course sequence, was particularly attractive. In his sophomore year, Winthrop was turning increasingly to history, English, and government. Like other undergraduates involved in these areas, he found special stimulation and inspiration in Professor Archibald Carey Coolidge.

Coolidge had joined the Harvard faculty in 1893 as a history instructor. His success as a section-man in History 1 led to his elevation to head of that formidable course, and from there his influence and activities spread rapidly. Although he was a specialist in the history of Russia and the Near East, Coolidge backed the introduction of courses in Far Eastern and Latin American history. He took the view that young men should know something about the major nations on the globe and that this knowledge should embrace not only past international relations but contemporary events.[20] This philosophy was quite in keeping with Winthrop Aldrich's own maturing ideas, reenforced by the example of his family's interests and travels. In addition to Coolidge, Dean Le Baron Russell Briggs made a particularly strong impression on Aldrich, who in his senior year received an "A" in Briggs's course on Browning.

Senator Aldrich made a practice of introducing his children to their cultural heritage by taking them to Europe, where they toured museums, libraries, galleries, and cathedrals, as the Senator sought an antidote to the rough-and-tumble of Washington politics. Winthrop had made two such trips before he entered college, and in the summer after his sophomore year he joined his brother Richard on a European tour which they themselves planned.[21]

Aware that this journey marked parental recognition of his maturity, he decided to keep a diary of day-to-day events. It opened with a record of the ocean voyage, which included inspection of the ship's wireless station, a recent product of technological progress, and a distant glimpse of the fleet bearing the remains of John Paul Jones back to the United States for burial at the Naval Academy. After recording the first two days on the Continent, however, Aldrich found the pace of sightseeing so strenuous that he gave up on the diary. It ends abruptly with this tantalizing entry: "Today has been one of the most interesting as well as one of the most tiring that I have ever spent." [22]

In full maturity Winthrop Aldrich would astonish his traveling companions by his resiliency and capacity for both work and play on grueling trips, but in 1905 he had not yet learned to pace his activities. However, he had already developed an interest in and appreciation of the Old World that would in the future draw him across the Atlantic with increasing regularity.

Outside the classroom, Harvard offered a liberal education for one with Winthrop Aldrich's interests. For example, during his Junior year, ex-Secretary of the Treasury Lyman Gage spoke to an open meeting on "The Proposed Changes in Our Banking Laws." As the son of the chairman of the Senate Finance Committee, whom incidentally Gage did not mention, Winthrop Aldrich should have been in the audience, though we have no record of it. It is far less likely that he would have attended the series of lectures by the eccentric but brilliant Thorstein Veblen of the University of Chicago on "Post-Marxian Development of Socialistic Theory." [23] During Aldrich's senior year, marked by the Longfellow Centenary, the Harvard community was treated to presentations

by other notables. Secretary of the Treasury Shaw spoke on
"The Evolution of Self-Government." On a Saturday in February 1907, President Theodore Roosevelt addressed the
Harvard students on their responsibilities to society and recalled his own undergraduate days. In April they heard Henry
Lee Higginson, the Boston investment banker and benefactor
of Harvard and the Boston Symphony Orchestra.[24]

On June 23, 1907, Winthrop Aldrich's Harvard class
gathered for the last time as undergraduates and then received
their diplomas. He was one of the group that shared responsibility for the class "spread" or buffet at Beck Hall. But as
he and his classmates packed to leave Cambridge, there was
little in his undergraduate record or extra-curricular activity
to suggest that Harvard had produced another son who would
leave an imprint on history and be honored as a "great American."

Superficially, the college experience did not seem to have
changed Aldrich, who appeared to be merely one more young
man of good family and good intelligence destined for a life
of comfortable obscurity. But the Cambridge years had, in
fact, quickened his awareness of change as a contemporary
phenomenon and as a historical process, deepened his determination to help shape the future in some meaningful way,
and confirmed the correctness of his decision to shun business
or politics as a means to this end.

Although during his undergraduate career he had been invited on two different occasions to serve as secretary to Ambassador to Italy Henry White of Rhode Island, a friend of
Senator Aldrich and father of one of Winthrop's classmates,
young Aldrich had determined to enter law school at the first
opportunity and he declined the Ambassador's offers without
regret.[25] Graduation from the College was not therefore a
goodbye to Cambridge but a temporary leave-taking until
the Harvard Law School opened its doors to a new class in

the Fall of 1907. In the interim, he again toured Europe with his brother Richard, who was then a Law School student, and enjoyed the experience of living with a French family in Tours.[26]

These broadening experiences reinforced rather than challenged Winthrop Aldrich's outlook as an upper class New Englander who felt strong ties to his region and to the values inherited from its earliest days, but recognized their debt to the culture of Western Europe. As reflected in his given names, this was his heritage and this had been his undergraduate experience. It was reflected in his public secondary school education combined with the best that Harvard College could offer in terms of social opportunity and intellectual challenge. Equally important, Senator Aldrich had exerted an increasingly stronger influence on his youngest son as he matured. Winthrop had been well schooled in the lessons that privilege demanded acceptance of personal responsibility, the exercise of informed and independent judgment, and adherence to uncompromising standards of self-discipline and performance in discharging one's obligations to society, family, and self. These homilies, as much a part of a New England heritage as the sacred cod, had been given added point for the young Rhode Islander against the wider backdrop of European history as interpreted by Coolidge, the history of religions as presented by Professor G. F. Moore, and English literature as seen by professors like Bliss Perry and Dean Briggs.

Exaggerated adherence to conservative "New England values" could have been stultifying, but young Aldrich was too full of life, too interested in what was going on around him, to be unduly sobered by his heritage. Instead, his interest in the challenge of serving a society that industrialization and urbanization were changing rapidly had been strengthened. The next step was to acquire professional training in the law.

CHAPTER II

The Seasoning Years

ALDRICH began his professional career in an era of transition for the United States and for its place in world affairs. He entered Harvard Law School in the year that financial panic underlined the need for revision of the nation's monetary and banking systems, eventuating in establishment of the Federal Reserve System. He achieved a partnership in a leading New York law firm as the country was being drawn into involvement in world war, and he served in the Navy throughout the United States' participation in the conflict. These were, for him, the seasoning years; for the country they brought a complex new era of world power and industrial maturity with problems of corresponding magnitude.

Harvard Law School

In September 1907 the Harvard Law School admitted a class of some 250 aspiring young lawyers, among them the son of Rhode Island's senior senator. They came to an institution that owed much to Dean James Barr Ames, who had entered that post in 1895 after serving on the faculty since 1877. Although close to the end of his active and productive career, he had lost none of his zeal for the development of his school or his desire that faculty-student relations should be close.

The faculty was also distinguished, and none more so than John Chipman Gray and Samuel Williston. Gray taught Evidence in the second year, where Winthrop Aldrich enjoyed his pithy remarks, including such observations as "Constitutional Law is not law but politics," and "Evidence is the bastard of the law." [1] Williston taught Contracts in the first year along with Bruce Wyman, and in that course Winthrop Aldrich received the highest grade of his law school career. He struck his nadir in Ames' third-year course on Equity Jurisdiction and Procedure. In later years, however, Aldrich recalled that Ames, Gray, and Williston had made the greatest impression on him, and from the record it appears that this influence was most felt in his second year when he had all three men.

Like many other students at the Law School, Aldrich had to arrange for his own living accommodations. He found them at the Misses Witheys' on Brattle Street, a tree-shaded Cambridge avenue graced by large mansions. The Withey house was large enough to accommodate six to eight students, and Aldrich's roommate there was A. Perry Osborne, whose outstanding record brought him a place on the *Harvard Law Review* in 1908–1909.

Among Aldrich's classmates were Irving S. Olds, later chairman of the board of United States Steel Corporation; Isaiah Sharfman, who became a distinguished student of public utilities and leading authority on the Interstate Commerce Commission; and Ernest Gruening, whose career was to be closely entwined with the growth to statehood of Alaska. One of Aldrich's closest friends, and a classmate from college days, was Harrison Tweed.[2] Grandson of William M. Evarts, President Rutherford Hayes' Secretary of State, and the son of a lawyer, Tweed's ability won him a place on the *Harvard Law Review* in 1909–1910. In the years to come his legal career fulfilled its early promise and was to be closely allied with Winthrop Aldrich's.

Although he knew the members of Harvard '07, like Tweed, who went on to the Law School with him, Aldrich quickly saw that there was little opportunity at the school to meet socially with graduates of other colleges. With the students living in various parts of Cambridge in rooming houses, there was also the practical problem of finding a place to have meals. Accordingly, Aldrich, his brother Richard, Harrison Tweed, and other friends in 1908 formed an eating club which they named Lincoln's Inn.³ Aldrich's roommate, Perry Osborne, was the first president of the organization, and Aldrich was assistant treasurer. Among the first members were Irving Olds, Gordon Auchincloss, Samuel Weldon, and Benjamin Moore, all of whom became lifelong friends.

Winthrop Aldrich was also invited to join the Choate Club, a student organization that participated in the Moot Courts where fledgling lawyers pitted their skill against one another before practicing lawyers and judges. As one of Aldrich's classmates recalled, the Choate Club was *the* student organization of its kind.⁴ It was here that Aldrich first emerged from obscurity in his class, and eventually he was elected president of the Club.

For as long as he could remember, Aldrich had wanted to practice law in New York City, where lawyers at the apex of corporate practice dealt with the manifold legal problems of a complex industrial system. He had achieved a record short of the requirements for the *Law Review*, but marking him as a most promising young lawyer. Accordingly, when he left Cambridge, he had earned the opportunity to test his skills in the city and law firm of his choice.

The total Harvard experience left an indelible mark on

Aldrich. He had come in close contact with some of the greatest professors of a great university, and it was in his understanding and appreciation of the varieties of human striving and experience that Aldrich had been most broadened by the educational experience. His undergraduate course in the History of Religions, for example, meant far more to him than the one he took on Municipal Corporations in his last year at Law School.

His interest in natural law, awakened in his courses at Harvard College, was rekindled at law school. He became fascinated with the basic principles of equity, their development and exposition by the great chancellors of England, and their descent in unbroken sequence to 20th century America. Throughout his life he continued to read in this area and always enjoyed the challenge of applying the principles of equity to practical problems. In his approach to such problems he was also very much influenced by his father, whose activities at this very time were laying the groundwork for revision of the banking system into one where Winthrop Aldrich would later have to make some of the most difficult decisions of his career.

REVISION OF THE BANKING SYSTEM

The Panic of 1907

In October 1907, as Winthrop Aldrich was settling down to his law studies, a panic hit New York's financial district like a line squall and then spread to other money markets. Despite its relatively short duration, the financial panic of 1907 held unusual significance for both Aldriches — for the father because it led to his campaign to revise the monetary and banking systems, for the son because his father's work not only shaped his own lifelong ideas about monetary and financial matters but also introduced him to financial leaders with whom he would later face the great banking crisis of the early 1930s.

Beginning with a run on New York's Knickerbocker Trust Company on Monday, October 21, 1907, that earlier panic fed on itself. The next day the Knickerbocker had to close its doors. Wall Street call money went to 70 percent and stock prices tumbled. From Pittsburgh came news that the Westinghouse companies had failed, and the Pittsburgh stock exchange had been closed.

A major crisis of confidence in the nation's monetary and banking systems was painfully evident. Relief was dependent on the availability of cash,* which the panic was driving into hiding. There was no central banking system to channel funds into banks whose assets were good but whose cash was exhausted. President Theodore Roosevelt was on a hunting trip in Louisiana, and Secretary of the Treasury Cortelyou was initially loathe to release government funds to New York banks.** The initiative therefore lay with private bankers, and J. P. Morgan took the lead in calling for their support.[5]

Day after day and night after night of that long week, Morgan guided the strategy that was to prevent complete collapse. With some aid from Secretary Cortelyou but much more from leading New York bankers, Morgan stemmed a threatening run on the Trust Company of America. But stock prices continued to plummet, and brokers found call money

* Currency in circulation consisted of the same forms of money (e.g., national bank notes) that constituted the ultimate reserves against deposit liabilities. The attempt to turn deposits into currency therefore drained bank reserves.

** On October 24 Cortelyou authorized the deposit of $25 million with the chief central reserve city banks in New York, but by this time the panic was well started. The authoritative study of the crisis is by O. M. W. Sprague, *History of Crisis Under the National Banking System* (Washington: Government Printing Office, 1910).

virtually unavailable. On Thursday, October 24, 1907, the New York Stock Exchange was faced with the imminent danger of having to close its doors, but on short notice Morgan was able to assemble $27,000,000 with which to counter this threat.

The next step, adopted after a long night-time conference of bankers at the Morgan library, was resort to clearing-house certificates. However, the certificate would be accepted by other member banks in settlement of obligations due them. This device met the problem of illiquidity, and the certificates were retired as the borrowers were able to "unfreeze" their collateral. From the onset of the 1907 emergency to the end of that year, some $97,000,000 worth of clearing-house certificates were issued, but this still represented only about 5 percent of total bank deposits.[6]

Senator Aldrich saw a need and an opportunity for change in these developments. He had sold his traction interests to Charles S. Mellen of the Morgan-backed New York, New Haven, and Hartford Railroad in 1906 and therefore weathered the Panic of 1907 with no personal difficulty.[7] However, as chairman of the Senate Finance Committee, as well as majority leader of the upper house, the Rhode Island Senator was especially sensitive to the need for banking and monetary reform. With the 1908 presidential election in the offing, he also believed that the Republicans would benefit from taking the initiative to deal with these problems.

Up to this time the Senator had not been an advocate of a flexible currency nor had he favored centralization in the American banking system.[8] These were ideas held by a younger generation, and their most articulate advocate was a brilliant young German emigré, Paul M. Warburg, a partner in the investment banking firm of Kuhn, Loeb & Company. Warburg's views on the unsophisticated nature of American banking compared to Europe, where reserves were centralized, note issues elastic, and commercial paper the primary source of quick bank assets, were already in print when the 1907 Panic occurred.[9] They had also met a cool, if not hostile, reception from most New York bankers. However, the banker's criticisms of American practice received new attention when the Panic underlined the costs of employing surplus funds primarily in the call-loan market rather than in the discount market and when the lack of a central reserve organization and elastic note issue contributed to banking collapse.

In Congress there were two rather well crystallized positions on these issues. One position, endorsed by Senator Aldrich at this time, held that currency should be bond-secured. In an emergency, the Treasury could step in with its deposits as long as they were available. As a last resort, clearing-house certificates could be employed to meet liquidity crises.[10] Another major group favored an asset-currency plan. Commercial assets, reflecting the state of economic activity and therefore the demand for money, would in this plan underlie note circulation. Rather than centralizing this issue, individual banks would be permitted to issue notes against their assets. Without adequate safeguards, however, the value of such notes could vary widely.[11] To meet this problem the asset-currency plan advanced in the House in 1908 by Representative Charles N. Fowler involved a guarantee of deposits, a proposal that was not to be enacted until 1933 when Winthrop Aldrich first became involved with national banking legislation.

Warburg felt that bond-secured currency was inadequate and that the decentralization involved in the asset-currency plan was dangerous. Accordingly, at the height of the 1907 crisis, Warburg published a paper proposing a plan for a modified central bank.[12] It was to be owned equally by the government and the banks. Such a central bank would establish a general rate of interest and would advance money at this rate against clearing-house certificates. In addition, it would be empowered to purchase three-months paper, provided it bore three signatures, one of them a bank's.

Warburg published this proposal in November 1907 and, by chance, the day after Christmas he first met Senator Aldrich.[13] Aldrich had dropped in at Kuhn, Loeb & Company seeking information about the German Reichsbank and the issue of a certain type of German currency. The senior partner, Jacob Schiff, introduced young Warburg as being well informed on the points in question. Warburg was well aware of the Senator's views on bond-secured currency, and as soon as the visitor left, he asked Schiff if it would be permissible to send Aldrich a personal letter on the disadvantages of "national bank currency issued against government bonds." His senior partner reportedly replied: "If you do, he will never look at you again." [14]

Senator Aldrich had discussed with Warburg not only government-bond secured national bank notes but also the possibility of authorizing national banks to issue notes against clearing-house certificates. Encouraged by this discussion, Warburg sent the Senator a copy of the modified central bank plan and followed it with an extended letter urging the need for a central clearing house in preference to decentralized national bank issues.[15]

When Congress reconvened early in 1908, it had before it an important bill introduced by Aldrich. The Rhode Island Senator proposed the creation of a national monetary commission to study monetary and banking problems and to make recommendations with respect to them. Pending the results of this investigation, Aldrich also proposed replacing the clearing-house certificates still outstanding. An emergency supply of national bank notes was to be issued on the security

of state and municipal bonds and also — a significant innovation — certain high-quality railroad bonds.

The rock on which the Aldrich bill stuck was western
opposition to inclusion of railroad bonds in the list of approved securities. Just as fiery Senator Robert M. La Follette
of Wisconsin was about to deliver a major attack on this provision, Aldrich withdrew it. His amended bill then passed the
Senate on March 27, 1908, by a vote of 42 to 16.[16]

The Aldrich-Vreeland Act

Meanwhile in the House, Representative E. B. Vreeland
of New York had advanced a currency bill. In April it was
agreed by Aldrich, Vreeland, and Speaker Joe Cannon to
substitute the House measure for Aldrich's. It passed the
House on May 14, but when it reached the Senate, Aldrich
substituted his bill for Vreeland's, and the Senate endorsed
the change, 47–20. Further compromise then took place,
leaving open the question of whether currency issues should
be backed by bonds or commercial paper. This version passed
the House on May 27, 1908. Despite a filibuster in the Senate led by La Follette, the bill passed that body on May 30
by a vote of 43 to 22, and was signed by the President on the
same day.[17]

The Aldrich-Vreeland Act was a milestone in the evolution
of an asset currency and a step toward the practices later
institutionalized under the Federal Reserve System. Although
virtually no use was made of the Aldrich-Vreeland Act before it expired,* it signalized the new acceptability of basing
currency on evidence of commercial transactions rather than
simply on an inelastic supply of government bonds to which
national bank notes had been tied since the Civil War. Most
important in terms of further change, the Aldrich-Vreeland

---

* The Act was intended as an interim measure and was invoked only
once, in 1914, before it expired June 30, 1915.

Act authorized the establishment of a National Monetary Commission to be composed of nine Senators and nine Representatives. Its charge was to develop suggestions for revising the monetary and banking systems if investigation showed that changes were desirable.

Genesis of the Aldrich Plan

It was a foregone conclusion that Aldrich would be chairman of the Monetary Commission and Vreeland his vice chairman. Since Aldrich proposed an extensive investigation of European central banking practices, he was most anxious to obtain a competent advisory group and its selection concerned him much more than the composition of the formal membership of the Commission.

The advisory group reflected a combination of practical and theoretical interests. Senator Aldrich had met and liked a young partner in J. P. Morgan & Co., Henry P. Davison, and he was asked to join the group as an advisor on banking as then practiced in New York.[18] To obtain further advice and support in this area, Aldrich asked G. M. Reynolds, president of the American Bankers Association, to join the group in Europe. For help on banking theory, Aldrich asked President Eliot of Harvard to nominate an expert from the faculty, and in this manner A. Piatt Andrew, at that time an assistant professor and one of Winthrop Aldrich's undergraduate instructors, became a special assistant to the Commission. These men provided the nucleus of the working group that visited central banks in England, France, Germany, and Austria during the summer of 1908. For the next four years, they and other investigators continued to study the monetary and banking systems of the world.

The stenographic transcript of the Commission's hearings, plus monographs prepared on banking practices at home and abroad, were published in 23 volumes and presented to Congress on January 8, 1912.[19] Banks and banking received much more attention than money, to which only one of the volumes was specifically assigned. The findings were varied, technical, complex and confusing. One of the most important results, however, had been the conversion of Senator Aldrich to the asset-currency idea. Reynolds pinpointed the time and place specifically by recalling that Aldrich had told him at the Hotel Adlon in Berlin in 1908 that he now accepted the commercial asset idea.[20]

By the fall of 1910, when his youngest son had just commenced his New York law apprenticeship, Nelson Aldrich was pondering what kind of bill he might propose to deal with the nation's banking ills. Davison appreciated the delicacy and complexity of the problem, and it was apparently this new Morgan partner who suggested that a small group tackle it in seclusion.[21] For this purpose Senator Aldrich; Professor Andrew; Arthur Shelton, the secretary of the Monetary Commission; Davison; Frank A. Vanderlip, vice president of the National City Bank; and Thomas Lamont, another Morgan partner, retired to the privacy of the Jekyl Island Club in November 1910. At the end of a hard week's work, they had produced what came to be known as the Aldrich Plan.

During this period Warburg had his first good opportunity to study the Senator, and he was impressed. In his words: "While I had approached Senator Aldrich with a good deal of prejudice and suspicion, I soon became convinced that the only object he had in mind was to establish in the United States, as a final monument to his long service in Congress, the best banking system that political and economic circumstances would permit." [22]

The Aldrich Plan was made public on January 17, 1911, just as delegates to a monetary conference called by the National Board of Trade were gathering in Washington. At this conference the principles of the Plan were endorsed in response to resolutions offered by the Chamber of Commerce of the State of New York, the Merchants' Association of New York, and the New York Produce Exchange.[23] The Plan called for a national association to act as a bankers' bank with an elastic note issue privilege based on gold and commercial paper and with supervisory power over rediscount operations of member banks. The organization of such a system would proceed from local associations of banks to 15 district associations, which in turn would elect a national board of directors for a "National Reserve Association." [24]

While some groups criticized the Plan as a "Wall Street" program, others like the American Bankers Association felt that it did not adequately protect the proposed reserve association against political control. The Aldrich Plan, they believed, gave more than necessary recognition to the government in providing that the Secretary of the Treasury, the Secretary of Commerce and Labor, and the Comptroller of the Currency serve as ex officio members of the Board of Directors of the Reserve Association.* This objection was strengthened by the fact that the executive officers, consisting of a governor and two deputy governors, were to be appointed by the President of the United States from a list submitted by the board of directors.[25]

In October 1911 Senator Aldrich presented a revised plan that called for the governor of the National Reserve Association to be appointed by the President of the United States but for the deputy governors to be elected by the board of directors.[26] He then undertook an educational campaign to win the support of financial leaders across the country. On

* Many years later the ABA, with Winthrop Aldrich as one of its spokesmen, would again express opposition to such ex officio representation of the executive branch on the Federal Reserve Board. It was eliminated in the Banking Act of 1935. See Chapter VIII.

November 21, 1911, Senator Aldrich addressed the American Bankers Association's annual convention in New Orleans and gained its endorsement.[27] The revised plan, however, did not satisfy those protesting the power of Wall Street. Thus, before the revised Aldrich Plan was presented to Congress, on January 8, 1912, further changes were made. One of the most important provided that where 40 percent of the stock in two or more banks of a local association was directly or indirectly held in common, such banks would be considered a unit and entitled to only one vote.[28]

Action on the Aldrich proposals became deeply mired in the changing political picture. The Republican party had been split between the Conservative element, with Aldrich in the leadership, and the Insurgents, who chafed at the constraints of this leadership. The rift had been painfully apparent in the battle over the Payne-Aldrich tariff of 1909, which was Senator Aldrich's last great fight, aside from the monetary issue. In 1910 he reached the decision not to seek reelection; he was past 70 and his health was beginning to fail.

By the time the Monetary Commission's report reached Congress, it was a presidential election year. Theodore Roosevelt had broken with his one-time protégé and presidential successor, William Howard Taft, and decided to try to recapture the office on the Progressive ticket. That party's platform adopted August 7, 1912, specifically condemned the Aldrich Currency Bill "because its provisions would place our currency and credit system in private hands, not subject to effective public control." The regular Republican platform refrained from endorsing the Aldrich Plan, perhaps out of fear that endorsement would make it a party measure and thereby further aggravate criticism. The Democrats' platform flatly rejected the Aldrich Plan.[29]

The outcome of the 1912 elections, with the elevation of Woodrow Wilson, the Democrats' candidate, to the Presidency and the shift of Congressional control to the Democrats sealed the fate of the Aldrich Plan as such. The initiative in framing the legislation that was to become the Federal Reserve Act in 1913 passed to Carter Glass of Virginia, chairman of the House Banking and Currency Committee, and to Robert L. Owen of Oklahoma, chairman of the corresponding Senate committee.

Subsequently, Carter Glass * claimed that the substance of the Federal Reserve Act owed little or nothing to the Aldrich Plan.[30] Dr. H. P. Willis, technical adviser to Glass, made a similar claim.[31] Paul Warburg, however, after making a detailed comparison of the two measures came to a different conclusion. In his words: "For our part we believe the evidence adduced from these comparisons will warrant the conclusion that there is a very distinct relationship between the two bills and that, instead of differing in 'principle, purpose, and processes,' they are surprisingly akin." [32]

The Federal Reserve Act

The Federal Reserve Act, which governed the operation of the banking system in which Winthrop Aldrich later gained prominence, was the product of numerous compromises but the key elements were clear. A Federal Reserve Board of seven members, including the Secretary of the Treasury and the Comptroller of the Currency, was to supervise the system. The other five members were to be appointed by the President. The country was divided into 12 districts, each with its own Federal Reserve Bank. Each of these banks had three classes of directors representing banking, business, and

---

* Since Glass was a Democrat and the Federal Reserve Act was passed by a Democratic Congress, his reluctance to credit Republican Aldrich and the National Monetary Commission appointed by a Republican Congress seems to have had a political origin. See Milton Friedman and Anna Jacobson Schwartz, *A Monetary History of the United States, 1867–1960* (Princeton, N.J.: Princeton University Press, 1963), p. 171 n59.

the general public. The district chairman was appointed by the
Federal Reserve Board, but the actual operating head, or
so-called "governor," of each Reserve bank came to be a
selection of the district board, since the post itself had no
statutory basis.

Each district bank was empowered to issue Federal Reserve notes secured by 100 percent commercial paper and
a 40 percent reserve in gold or gold certificates. It was required to maintain a reserve of 35 percent in "lawful money"
against member bank deposits and was permitted to rediscount
commercial paper for member banks. Each district bank
could buy and sell government obligations under rules and
regulations of the Federal Reserve Board. All national banks
were compelled to become members; state banks might voluntarily join. Member banks were classified as reserve city, city,
and country banks, each with a differing reserve requirement.
A Federal Advisory Council, of which Winthrop Aldrich was
later a member, was composed of one member from each
district. Its function was to advise the Board on banking
and monetary policies in the light of current business conditions. The system was also to provide check-clearing facilities and each district bank could act as fiscal agent for the
government.

Each of these provisions was to be tested over time, and
expectations of 1913 were to be changed, modified or disappointed, as well as fulfilled, in the years ahead. As head of
the world's largest bank two decades later, Winthrop Aldrich
was to be closely involved in some of these changes, and he
would always approach them with the knowledge of what his
father had contributed to the pre-World War I reform of the
monetary and banking systems.

The cry of banker control was heard in 1913, intensified
by the investigation of the "money trust" led by Congressman Pujo,[33] but the fact was that the Federal Reserve System

in its early years was a weakling. It had corrected the glaring deficiencies of the national banking system with respect to inelastic currency, pyramiding and immobilizing of reserves, and inefficient and expensive check clearance. On the other hand, as then conceived against a widely held belief in the automatic operation of the gold standard, the System did not exert a major influence on national monetary policy. The rediscount rate, which was expected to be a major instrument for affecting the money market, proved a weak counter-cyclical weapon. If banks could make money by borrowing, even a high rediscount rate could not stop them; conversely, if they could not make loans, a low rediscount rate was no inducement to borrow from the "Fed." The System's buying and selling of government securities to affect the reserves of member banks and therefore their lending capacity was a much later development and proved a powerful force.

As a young lawyer, Winthrop Aldrich, of course, had no foreknowledge that his career would eventually take him into banking, make his views on monetary policy and banking matters of national and international interest, and give him a prominent role in the revision of the Federal Reserve Act in the 1930s. His only direct contribution to the work of the Monetary Commission had been to suggest his Law School contemporary, Samuel Weldon, as an assistant to his father. However, the younger Aldrich's ideas about banking and monetary policy were deeply influenced by his father as they discussed together the problems of the Aldrich Plan, the Federal Reserve Act, and more generally the relations between business and government. These discussions influenced Winthrop Aldrich's later decisions as a banker fully as much as any of his formal education or early training in the law.

As the result of his father's important position and work, the son also had an unparalleled opportunity to make the acquaintance of America's financial leaders. Thus, when he was later unexpectedly catapulted into the leadership of a great New York bank at a critical time in its fortunes and those of the nation, he had the benefit of a wide acquaintance in the financial community dating back to these pre-World War I days. It proved an asset of substantial value in meeting his new responsibilities.

STARTING HIS LAW CAREER

Winthrop Aldrich's legal training at Harvard had sharpened his natural inclination toward precision in logic and expression, and it had confirmed his lack of interest in becoming a legal technician. Questions of strategy, the equities of a complex situation, the broad roles of law in protecting hard-won personal and property rights appealed strongly to Aldrich. Nevertheless, he had first to demonstrate his technical competence to his seniors before he could move on to the problems that interested him most. Recognizing the importance of this apprenticeship period, he picked the New York law firm of Byrne, Cutcheon & Taylor as the place to spend it and landed a job there on his own initiative.[34]

At that time James Byrne, the head of that firm, was reputed among the undergraduates of the Law School to be the leading technician in financial law at the New York bar. He was also known as the most demanding taskmaster. Any man who could become his personal assistant and survive the ordeal successfully was looked upon with awe by his contemporaries. Aldrich made up his mind that if he could accomplish this feat he would have proved to himself that he was capable of having a successful career as a New York financial lawyer. If it should not prove to be possible for him to do this, the sooner he found it out the better.

His classmate, Harrison Tweed, recalls that Aldrich was

at this time a very self-confident young man with a knack for "carrying off" roles that would have challenged men of more mature years.[35] To Tweed, Aldrich's direct and successful approach to and acceptance at a leading New York law firm was an example of this quality.

Of course Aldrich did not immediately work directly for Mr. Byrne, but after a year or two of apprenticeship with the junior partners, including a most fruitful association with Mr. Cutcheon, he realized his ambition of working directly with Mr. Byrne. James Byrne demanded a high level of intelligence in and initiative from his assistants. He would tell them what he wanted done and leave it completely up to them to do it. Since much of his practice involved complicated railroad and other corporate reorganizations, Byrne's delegation of responsibility created many challenges and opportunities for his subordinates. Winthrop Aldrich learned Byrne's lessons well and later put them to good use in his own law firm.

One interesting occurrence which throws some light upon the relations that came to exist between Aldrich and Byrne occurred in connection with the reorganization of the Seaboard Air Line Railway corporation, which took place in the Court of Chancery in New Jersey. The occasion was the presentation to the court of the final papers. Aldrich had worked as assistant to Byrne in these proceedings, and Bryne asked Aldrich to accompany him to New Jersey. As they left the office, the older man handed a bag to his companion with instructions to guard it carefully. Assuming that he had been entrusted with some of the key papers in this case, Aldrich took his assignment very seriously.

As Aldrich tells the story, when he and Byrne arrived in the courtroom Aldrich saw that there was a large group of lawyers behind the rail of the courtroom before the judge. They included a very famous lawyer from Philadelphia, and other men who had been prominent in the reorganization proceedings. He therefore decided to sit down outside the railing of the court among the spectators. Suddenly, to Aldrich's amazement, he realized that Byrne was in the most formal manner presenting his "associate in these proceedings" to the court. There was nothing that Aldrich could do at the moment but rise from his seat and, still carrying the bag, come up to the railing and bow to the judge. When the presentations were over, Aldrich sat down beside Byrne inside the railing and Byrne, laughing, said: "I was in the midst of my presentation when I looked around to find you and could not see you. But I at last found you 'arising from the proletariat.' Did you not know that as counsel you should sit inside the railing?" Aldrich, still clutching the all-important bag, admitted that he had not realized that he was considered associate counsel.

When the day's business was concluded without Byrne asking for the bag, Aldrich asked what it was that he had been safeguarding so carefully. Byrne replied, "It is a pair of shoes. My cobbler is over here and I wanted to be sure that I did not forget to leave the shoes with him before we went back to New York." Of course Byrne was delighted to have played this little joke on his "associate," and many years later Aldrich still recalled this episode with relish.[36]

It was not long before Byrne was entrusting his assistant with complex and demanding tasks. As counsel for Blair & Co., Byrne inherited many railroad organizations in the wake of the 1907 Panic. One involved the Chicago & Eastern Illinois Railroad, which had a very complicated financial structure. One day he called Aldrich in and asked him to set up the accounts for that company. Winthrop Aldrich had never taken an accounting course, but this didn't matter to Byrne. He expected his young men to have the ingenuity to deal with any problem that he assigned them. And, of course, this was the reason Aldrich had wanted to work for the firm. Accordingly he set to work enthusiastically and eventually produced a scheme that seemed to place all the company's varied mortgages and other elements of its financial structure in proper relationship to one another.

Byrne was pleased with the results but skeptical that they were without flaws. He therefore instructed Aldrich to spread out all the documents on the floor of his office, and the two men went about on their hands and knees verifying by physical evidence the correctness of the younger one's work. It passed inspection and thenceforth Winthrop Aldrich enjoyed the full confidence of his mentor.[37]

Aldrich got along with the senior partners in a way that was the envy of his contemporaries, and he was soon representing the firm in other lawyers' offices and with client companies. It was clear that his apprenticeship would not last much longer. In fact, it ended in 1916 when, six years out of law school, he became a partner in the firm.

Other young men whom Aldrich had known at Harvard joined him at Byrne, Cutcheon & Taylor. His close friend Harrison Tweed specialized in estate work and also became a partner in 1916. Lawrence Bennett, Harvard Law '12, joined the firm after his graduation as top man in his class. It was, in short, an able group of young men that came down from Cambridge, as well as a socially compatible group.

Aldrich, for all his seriousness of professional purpose, loved a good time.[38] He had seemingly boundless energy and thought nothing of staying up half the night, or more, at parties and then putting in a full day's work. Tweed recalls that on one such occasion he and Aldrich played roulette all night in Philadelphia, ending up in the cold dawn with only the train fare back to New York. Tweed put up his watch as security with the bartender in return for the money with which to pay the hotel bill. Although the young lawyers appeared late at the office that morning, they escaped censure. Nevertheless, this sobering experience decided them to give up games of chance in favor of less expensive activities.[39]

Nearing 30 years of age, Winthrop Aldrich was a most eligible bachelor. Of medium height and slender build, he dressed well and possessed all the social graces. On meeting this trim young lawyer, one was likely to be struck most by his pale blue eyes. They could sparkle with amusement, inviting companionable laughter, or they could turn cold and expressionless, showing unmistakable disapproval.

Although he was in great demand at parties, Winthrop Aldrich somehow gave certain young ladies the impression that he was shy. Among them was Miss Harriet Alexander, whom he met at various house parties and also at Tuxedo Park, where her parents had a home and where Aldrich went with increasing frequency to go riding.

Marriage

Among his resolves, the young lawyer had promised himself not to marry until he became a partner in his firm and therefore could afford to maintain a household out of his own resources.[40] That resolve was not shaken by the fact that his father, who died in 1915, left him $8,000 a year plus an equal share with the other Aldrich children in his estate.[41]

The partnership condition that Aldrich had imposed on himself was met in 1916, and the announcement of his engagement to Miss Alexander on September 2 of that year came as no surprise to those who knew them both well. The event was celebrated at Warwick Neck, where a gala clambake was held on the broad lawns of the Aldrich estate overlooking Narragansett Bay.

Harriet Alexander was the eldest daughter of New York lawyer Charles B. Alexander, a trustee of Princeton and the descendant of a long line of distinguished Presbyterian preachers. The Alexander progenitor who moved to this country was a Scotch-Irishman, Archibald Alexander. Like many of his countrymen in that time, he settled first in Pennsylvania. From there, around 1747, he moved to Timber Ridge, Virginia. His grandson, Archibald III, married Janetta Waddell, daughter of James Waddell, the famous "blind preacher." Janetta was named for her grandmother, the daughter of Colonel James Morgan of Virginia who had married into the family of William Henry Harrison.[42]

Harriet Alexander's mother was Harriet Crocker, daughter of Charles Crocker of the California "Big Four." Crocker, born at Troy, New York, in 1822 rose from poverty to a commanding position in California. Arriving in the wake of the first gold rush, he had engaged in the more profitable but less glamorous task of supplying the newcomers' needs. From that venture he had gone on to become a member of the group that built the Central Pacific Railroad to a connection with the Union Pacific Railway in 1869, thus completing the first transcontinental railroad.

Crocker was a restless, active individual. He sold out of the Central Pacific but soon came back to it and expanded his investments. These interests came to embrace the Southern Pacific Railroad, San Francisco real estate, railroad subsidy lands in the San Joaquin Valley, the Crocker-Huffman Land Company at Merced, coal lands, and other enterprises. As befitted his status, Crocker built a mansion on Nob Hill in San Francisco near those of his partners Leland Stanford and Mark Hopkins.[43]

In 1886 Charles Crocker had purchased a house on West 58th Street, New York City, and the following year he presented it to his daughter when she married Charles Alexander. The Alexanders spent the summer months in Seabright, New Jersey, and it was there that Harriet Alexander, the future wife of Winthrop Aldrich, was born on July 3, 1888.

One of the stipulations made by Harriet Crocker when she married Charles Alexander was that she should visit California every year. She made the first such trip only six weeks after her daughter Harriet was born. Mrs. Aldrich remembers other childhood trips when she visited the Crocker mansion on Nob Hill and the Del Monte, a huge and fashionable resort hotel on the Monterey Peninsula, created by the Southern Pacific and a project of great personal interest to Charles Crocker.[44]

Harriet Alexander's interests were as varied as her fiancé's. For one thing she loved the sea, and the Alexanders' yacht had cruised the same waters that were familiar to the Aldriches. She liked the same kind of individual sports, like hunting and riding, that appealed to Winthrop Aldrich. Also, while she had made the conventional debut expected of daughters of leading New York families, she found genuine satisfaction in the charitable and social welfare work that was part of such training. Before her engagement, she had participated in a successful exhibition and sale for the benefit of the American Ambulance Hospital in Paris, engaged in numerous charitable activities, served as First Vice President of the Junior League, which sought to promote such interests, and also as its President for several terms. The wedding, which took place on December 7, 1916, therefore united representatives of two leading American families who shared many common interests and a mature outlook on their new responsibilities.

Service in World War I

Woodrow Wilson had just been returned to the White House. Despite the Democrats' campaign slogan, "He kept us out of war!" the imminent possibility of active American involvement in the European hostilities seemed very real to Aldrich, as it did to many of his contemporaries. Accordingly he took steps to prepare himself to serve where he felt he could do the most good. For him this naturally meant service at sea.

Aldrich's favorite avocation had equipped him well for naval service. His early interest in yachting had remained keen, and one of the first clubs that he joined upon arriving in New York had been the famed Seawanhaka-Corinthian Yacht Club. Many of his closest friends, among them his college classmate Harold Vanderbilt, shared his sailing enthusiasms. When a training camp for citizen-soldiers was established at Plattsburgh, New York, a naval counterpart, Naval Plattsburgh, quickly followed. Under this program, yachtsmen like Vanderbilt planned to offer their boats for patrol duty and to accompany them on active service.

This idea had immediate appeal for Winthrop Aldrich, and he quickly took appropriate action. He switched from a brief affiliation with a National Guard unit to the Naval Reserve. Next, he organized a syndicate composed of his brother-in-law John D. Rockefeller, Jr., his law partners Carl Taylor and James Byrne, his brothers Richard and Edward, Jay Gould, and himself.[45] This group contracted with the famous Herreshoff yacht builders of Bristol, Rhode Island, for construction of a naval patrol boat. To complete his own preparation for service Aldrich enrolled at Uttmark's Nautical Academy in Brooklyn for an intensive course in navigation. Perhaps he prepared too well. In any event, when the United States declared war on Germany in April 1917, Winthrop Aldrich was not called to duty with Naval Plattsburgh but was sent to Newport, Rhode Island, and was shortly placed in command of a training regiment for Naval Reservists.

That he should have become a commanding officer in his first active duty assignment surprised no one more than Lieutenant (j.g.) Winthrop Aldrich. In his new capacity as Regimental Commander, he found himself engaged in such

unaccustomed tasks as policing Newport's bawdy houses and
making disciplined sailors and officer candidates out of assorted civilians* His job was complicated by the fact that
the men of the training regiment were initially quartered in
rented houses all over Newport. In fact, he and Harriet were
also living in such quarters at 13 Old Beach Road.

The situation was not improved when the regiment was
put into hastily erected barracks on the Naval Base, for they
were located next to the naval hospital for contagious diseases.
An epidemic of spinal meningitis was sweeping Newport,
and Lieutenant Aldrich's great concern was that some of his
men might be forced, as the result of this very serious and
often fatal illness, to end their Navy careers before they had
really begun. Accordingly, he ordered a barbed wire fence to
be erected between the barracks and the hospital and posted
armed guards to maintain a constant patrol along the length
of this fence to prevent any close contact between the patients
in the hospital and the occupants of the barracks.

As Aldrich recalls it, his next step was to bring higher
authority to bear on the situation. On his initiative, Assistant
Secretary of the Navy Franklin D. Roosevelt visited the base
to assess the situation, and the Rockefeller Institute was asked
to send contagious disease specialists to investigate the medical
problem. In the end, it was decided that the boundary zone
and the patrol established by Lieutenant Aldrich were adequate to protect the naval reservists from contagion.[46]

The assignment to Newport had placed Aldrich in familiar
territory. His father's Warwick Neck estate, "Indian Oaks,"
now occupied by his mother and his sister Lucy, was just up
the Bay, and the Benevolent Street house was within easy
reach. But he had not entered naval service to watch the

---

* As the Navy went on a war footing, staid Newport became such a
hotbed of immorality that the Rhode Island governor went to Washington
to seek aid to combat it (*New York Times*, July 9, 1917).

progress of the war comfortably from the sidelines. Accordingly, he waited impatiently for an answer to his application for sea duty. Meanwhile, men under his command, selected to be officer candidates, moved on to Annapolis and final training for just such an assignment as he desired.

As the summer of 1917 dragged by, he had the satisfaction of seeing the completion of the patrol boat for which his syndicate had contracted. He also had the pleasure of piloting her down Narragansett Bay from her builder's yard at Bristol to the Newport Base, where she was commissioned as Section Patrol No. 1218. Although this vessel was a contribution to the war effort, and the credit for conceiving it belonged to him, a boat represented a financial commitment rather than personal involvement in the war effort. Only sea duty would satisfy his concept of involvement.

In September 1917 his turn came. He was ordered to join the U.S.S. *Niagara*, a converted 2,600-ton yacht that had belonged to the Goulds. Her captain was Commander E. G. "Ted" Larimer, U.S.N., and Aldrich became his navigation officer.

The *Niagara* was slated to be flagship of the yacht patrol squadron off Brest, and months passed while she was being prepared for this assignment. Finally she was outward bound for France in June 1918. Before the ship had cleared Montauk Point, however, a wireless message informed Commander Larimer that the *Niagara's* orders were cancelled and he was being transferred to the U.S.S. *New Orleans*, 4,000 tons, assigned to convoy duty. Since Larimer had developed confidence in his young yachtsman-navigator, he requested Aldrich's transfer to the *New Orleans*. As a result, Lieutenant Aldrich became Assistant Navigating and Communications Officer of Larimer's new command.[47]

It turned out to be a dull assignment. The *New Orleans* worked out of various Atlantic Coast ports, shepherding slow and rusty merchantmen across the sea to Europe but turning back tantalizingly short of a landfall. The monotony of these months was broken only once when a German submarine was believed to be stalking the convoy, but even this proved to be a false alarm. Therefore, Aldrich had special reason to welcome the Armistice of November 1918 that shortly ended his disappointingly routine sea duty. In the interim he had been promoted to a full Lieutenant and had been selected for Lieutenant Commander, an appointment that was confirmed shortly after he was released to civilian life.

At the age of 33 Aldrich had proved his competence as a New York financial lawyer, and he had served his country from the start of its involvement in the late conflict to its end. With his return to civilian life, he confronted a situation that called for decisions of major importance in resuming his legal career.

CHAPTER III

The Later Law Years, 1919-1929

W HEN Aldrich returned to New York late in 1918, he found that his old law firm had fallen apart. Byrne had practically retired, and Cutcheon was practicing by himself. Therefore, after less than a month of inactivity, he joined the firm of Murray, Prentice & Howland at the suggestion of John D. Rockefeller, Jr. During the next decade he became the leader in this firm, developed an outstanding team of lawyers, and in the process established a major New York law firm that continued to grow in size and prestige.

Murray, Prentice & Howland

George Welwood Murray, the senior partner in the firm when Aldrich joined it, had been brought to this country from Scotland at the age of two, but his Scottish background was reflected in his rigorous and stern approach to the law. A graduate of the Columbia Law School in 1876, he was made a partner in 1888 of a firm which became Anderson, Howland & Murray in 1892. At this time his career began to embrace work for John D. Rockefeller, Sr., in connection with the latter's extensive investments in the Mesabi iron range and allied railroad and shipping interests. As the relationship developed, Murray handled an increasing variety of Rockefeller legal affairs.

When the Rockefellers purchased a substantial interest in the Equitable Trust Company of New York in 1911, Murray became the bank's general counsel, and his firm was reorganized to become Murray, Prentice & Howland. E. Parmalee Prentice was a son-in-law of John D. Rockefeller, Sr., and Charles P. Howland's father had entered the predecessor firm at the same time as George Murray. The fourth partner when Aldrich entered the firm was William Roberts.

The age and diverse interests of the principal partners were shortly to give Aldrich an opportunity to become the active head of the firm. During the first few months in his new position, however, he chafed at the routine nature of his assignments. It would have been far more interesting and exciting, he wrote a friend in 1919, to be participating in the Peace Conference.[1] But, instead of helping to shape the postwar world, he found himself dealing with federal boards and legal technicalities.

This situation changed very shortly. Charles Howland retired in 1920, and E. Parmalee Prentice increasingly indulged his classical interests which, among other things, involved translating *Treasure Island* into Latin.[2] Despite his relative youth, Winthrop Aldrich began to exert active leadership in the firm. His first step was to recruit a group of bright young lawyers to rejuvenate the practice developed by the distinguished but aging partners at 37 Wall Street. From his old colleagues at Byrne, Cutcheon & Taylor he drew his close friend and classmate, Harrison Tweed, as well as Lawrence Bennett and Arthur Gammell. Tweed's cousin, William M. Evarts, and William D. Embree, formerly an Assistant District Attorney of New York County, also joined the firm, which became Murray, Prentice & Aldrich on New Year's Day, 1921.[3]

Murray, Prentice & Aldrich

The leading client of the new partnership, as of the old, was the Equitable Trust Company, whose legal affairs now became Aldrich's primary responsibility. Tweed handled the legal side of the bank's trust and estate work, while other members of the firm participated in the areas where their specialties were of most value. Evarts, for example, made the problems of the Equitable's foreign department his chief concern. Embree was the litigator. Bennett was a specialist in corporate problems and became an expert on public utilities. In the six partners and ten associates the Equitable could call on a varied pool of legal talent. Aldrich had assembled a good, young "team" whose members had confidence in his leadership.

In his legal work for the Equitable, Aldrich was in close and constant contact with the Trust Company's senior officers. Among them were Alvin W. Krech, president; Arthur W. Loasby, who succeeded to this position; Lyman Rhoades, head of the Trust Department; F. W. Black, head of the Foreign Department; Robert C. Adams of the Bond Department; and Henry Cooper and Herman Cook, senior vice presidents. When Aldrich later took over leadership of the bank, he was not only familiar with its operations but also knew well many of its key personnel.

The Equitable's legal problems posed varied and interesting challenges. One of the first to come Aldrich's way involved the effort of some American sugar buyers, who had borrowed several million dollars from the Equitable, to avoid repayment of these loans when the post-World War I sugar boom collapsed. The letters of credit issued in connection with their sugar buying in the Far East had contained an arbitration

clause. Aldrich therefore decided to institute arbitration proceedings in a test case and to obtain firsthand evidence with
which to refute the claims of the sugar buyers as to the transactions in question, particularly with respect to the bills of
lading involved. For this purpose he dispatched Talbot Malcolm, an associate in the law office, to Java, where Malcolm
obtained affidavits and documents to support the bank's case.
The surprised sugar buyers then asked the court for an order
to take their own depositions in Java. On appeal to the Appellate Division, Aldrich successfully countered this move.
Having won the test case on a strategy devised by Aldrich,
the Equitable collected from the other recalcitrant sugar
buyers.[4]

The short-lived boom in sugar had also led to increased
production in Cuba, much of it financed by New York banks.
With the downturn of 1921, many sugar mills were taken
over by their creditors who reorganized, refinanced, and
modernized these facilities. The increased output, however,
only led to further difficulties and deeper bank involvement.
The Equitable had participated in some of these loans, and
Aldrich went to Havana from time to time as counsel to
reorganization committees.

Still another problem grew out of the Equitable's foreign
business. The bank had made some large loans to two dealers
in foreign exchange who could not meet their commitments
when European currencies were sharply eroded in value by
the postwar inflation. In addition, the Equitable itself had
made foreign exchange contracts with customers who were
now trying to extricate themselves from these obligations.
Aldrich and his partner, William M. Evarts, were charged
with handling the legal side of these difficult situations. In
the end, some $5 million had to be written off by the Equitable
as losses on the foreign exchange operations.[5]

About this time Aldrich became involved in a case in which

virtually every major law firm in New York had a part. It involved the will of Jay Gould, the famous railroad promoter. When he died in 1893, his will had divided his estate among his six children, four of whom served as executors and trustees. The oldest son, George Gould, took the lead in administering the estate, but his activities in this connection were challenged when an accounting action was instituted in the Supreme Court of New York County in 1916. The result was a celebrated and long-lived legal controversy. Corporate fiduciaries, among them the Equitable Trust Company, were substituted in 1922 for George Gould,[6] and the estate, previously administered as a unit, was at last divided into the six parts stipulated by Jay Gould's will. At this point the Aldrich firm was brought into the case, and Aldrich personally acted for Lady Decies, a daughter of George Gould.[7] Gould's death in 1923 further confused an already complex situation, and the action initiated in 1916 dragged on until 1927 when it was finally settled by a stipulation of compromise.

A somewhat similar case came to Aldrich from Mrs. Benjamin Moore, the wife of a close friend from college years. She was the daughter of John J. Emery, a wealthy resident of Cincinnati, Ohio. His estate included a large amount of valuable real property in that city and in New York City. A Philadelphia trust company had been named trustee under his will. When an accounting of the trusteeship was filed, Aldrich was retained to represent the Emery children.[8] Among the questions to be resolved were whether the trustee had power to make permanent improvements on the real estate and to form a corporation to manage it. These issues were satisfactorily resolved, and Aldrich thenceforth represented the Emery children in the development of their valuable New York property.

Another trusteeship case in which Winthrop Aldrich became involved made a significant contribution to the New

York law of trusts. In 1917 John D. Rockefeller, Sr., had created trusts for his two daughters, Alta Rockefeller Prentice and Edith Rockefeller McCormick. In each instance the Equitable Trust Company was named trustee. Several issues involving the trusts were litigated, among them the question of whether stock dividends paid into the Prentice trust and allocated by the trustee to principal, pursuant to the trust agreement, violated the statute of unlawful accumulations. Aldrich and Tweed represented the Equitable in this action.[9]

Both parties to the case agreed to submit the issues to a referee, who ruled that allocation of stock dividends to principal violated the New York statute. The trustee and remaindermen decided to appeal this decision, and again Aldrich's initiative proved important in the outcome. He had learned that the referee, a retired judge, was planning a Caribbean vacation. Aldrich decided that the appeal record should be printed and signed by the referee before he left the city. To accomplish this result, printers had to work around the clock to get the record out. It was signed by the referee just before he boarded his ship. Within a week he had died aboard the cruise ship at Havana, but, due to Aldrich's fast work, this unfortunate turn of events did not delay the appeal.[10]

The Appellate Division reversed the referee and held that stock dividends could be assigned to principal without violation of the law. Upon further appeal, this decision was upheld by Justice Cardozo of the Court of Appeals in a landmark decision.[11]

Meanwhile, as counsel to the Equitable, Aldrich became engaged in two controversies involving the unglamorous fiber, sisal, used for binder twine. Sisal was grown in the state of Yucatan, Mexico, under the control of a government agency; the largest purchaser of the sisal was International Harvester. The Equitable Trust Company, the Royal Bank of Canada, the Interstate Trust Company of New Orleans, and the Continental Bank of Chicago made large loans in Yucatan, secured by sisal, and they had formed the Eric Corporation to handle sisal sales.[12]

Trouble developed when the Yucatan government was overthrown in 1922. International Harvester's resident agent was forced to grant the revolutionary government a letter of credit for $480,000, which was quickly spent on arms and ammunition. When the revolutionists were in turn ousted, the government disowned the notes issued to cover the letter of credit. Subsequently, International Harvester attempted to pay for sisal purchases from Eric Corporation with these notes, and Eric brought suit to compel payment in more acceptable tender. The case was heard in federal district court, with Aldrich and William Embree appearing for the Eric Corporation.[13] The outcome hinged on whether it could be proved that the Yucatan government agency had actually promised to accept its discredited notes in payment for sisal. International Harvester's resident agent testified that this was the case. The government agency's representative in the episode was believed to be unavailable so his side of the story was not presented.

Although the jury decided for International Harvester, the judge set this verdict aside as contrary to the evidence. In preparing for a further contest, Aldrich supervised a successful hunt for the government's agent. He was found and brought to New York, where he was ready to testify that he had promised to accept the controversial notes in payment for sisal. Other witnesses were located who were also willing to testify in support of the Eric Corporation. With these strong resources at hand for a second trial, Aldrich entered into negotiations with International Harvester and the case was settled without further resort to the legal process.[14]

This was not the end of the Equitable's, or Aldrich's, connection with sisal. Sisal Sales Corporation, like Eric Corporation, was organized by banks that had made loans to the Yucatan government agency. When the loans were foreclosed, the banks, including the Equitable Trust Company, found themselves to be the owners of a large amount of unsold sisal in the United States. A complicated series of maneuvers followed. The government agency that had handled the sisal sales was succeeded by an export commission which was given a monopoly of the sale of all sisal grown in Yucatan. This commission then took over the sisal owned in the United States by Sisal Sales and made that company its exclusive selling agent. Sisal Sales in turn made a contract with commission brokers to dispose of the sisal. Since these arrangements covered the supply of the fiber in this country, they were attacked by the Justice Department as a violation of the antitrust laws.

In the federal district court, the defendants won. The court in this instance relied on a Supreme Court decision that a contract made beyond the boundaries of the United States was beyond the reach of the American antitrust law.

Upon the government's appeal to the Supreme Court, this decision was reversed. The Supreme Court held that the antitrust law did apply to the Sisal Sales case because all the acts involved took place in the United States, except for the Yucatan law granting the initial restraint. Aldrich argued the case for Sisal Sales before the United States Supreme Court, and Harold Medina, later a distinguished federal judge, appeared for the commission brokers, who had also been named as defendants.[15]

Aldrich handled numerous other cases during this period. For example, the Equitable Trust Company was a major creditor of the Green Star Steamship Corporation when it went into receivership, a situation complicated by the fact that each of its ships was subject to mortgages in different ports.[16] Aldrich supervised the unscrambling of the various claims, sale of the vessels, and liquidation of the company. In 1924, as counsel to the reorganization managers of the Habirshaw Electric Cable Company, he helped to settle a controversy with creditors which involved a successful appeal to the federal circuit court.[17] Two years later he negotiated successfully with J. P. Morgan & Company for air rights over a wing of their building at the corner of Broad and Wall Streets. This agreement, a novel one at the time, permitted the Equitable to build over rather than around the Morgan wing in constructing a new building with its main entrance at 15 Broad Street.[18]

In 1925 Aldrich took the initiative in advocating adoption of a uniform promissory note to be used by New York banks. To this end he sponsored a series of luncheons for leading bank lawyers, who eventually hammered out a form that was acceptable to them. Unfortunately, however, the banks were not equally interested, because they feared that the wording of the uniform note might alienate customers.[19]

Aldrich also participated in the drafting of the Settlement of War Claims Act of 1928. The purpose of this Act was to set a schedule of priorities for payment of German obligations to American creditors. The Equitable's interest in it came from hopes of recovering a large deposit that it had in a German bank prior to American involvement in World War I. The Mixed Claims Commission had already allowed the Equitable's claim for over $1,000,000 plus interest, and under the 1928 statute the principal and most of the accumulated interest were ultimately recovered.[20]

A different kind of assignment came to Aldrich in 1923 when he was asked to represent one of the owners of the New York Yankees in the sale of that baseball club to Colonel Jacob Ruppert.[21] Considering his lack of interest in that sport, his

role in this transaction was evidence of his increasing prominence as a lawyer.

Lawyer for John D. Rockefeller, Jr.

In his legal work for John D. Rockefeller, Jr., Aldrich
won not only the respect and confidence of his brother-in-
law but of the latter's professional staff. Among this group
were Colonel Arthur Woods, a close advisor; Bertram Cutler,
who managed financial matters; and Charles O. Heydt, who
handled Rockefeller's real estate interests.

Aldrich's native intelligence and professional competence
won him his place in the inner group of Rockefeller advisors.
He participated, for example, in the selection of John D.
Rockefeller, Jr.'s personal counsel, Thomas Debevoise. Although Debevoise coordinated the varied legal assignments
arising from his principal's varied interests, Aldrich was always
consulted on any major move.

Apparently the first legal work that Aldrich handled personally for the junior Rockefeller was in connection with
apartment house projects undertaken as a philanthropic enterprise. The objective was to make good housing available to
low-income families who would pay for their apartments over
a long period of time by installments that were the equivalent
of rent. The first such project was the Thomas Garden Apartment in the Bronx, and it was followed by the Paul Laurence
Dunbar * Apartment in Harlem. In neither case were the
tenants required to make a down payment before taking up
occupancy, and the resulting difficulties indicated a need for
revising this policy. Drawing on this experience, a third
apartment project in Tarrytown met with more success. Al-

---

* Dunbar was a distinguished Negro author, poet, and journalist. The
Rockefeller interest in this project was an imaginative antecedent of contemporary private efforts to improve conditions in the "ghetto" areas of
large cities.

drich supervised the legal details of this pioneering experiment in cooperative apartment buildings.[22]

By 1928 John D. Rockefeller, Jr.'s, varied interests in philanthropic, civic, and educational projects were expanding rapidly. Aldrich and his law firm found themselves intimately involved in the legal side of some of the most important of these undertakings, including Colonial Williamsburg, Rockefeller Center, and consolidation of the Laura Spelman Rockefeller Memorial with the Rockefeller Foundation.

Williamsburg

The restoration of Williamsburg, Virginia's colonial capital, was a tribute to the persistence and enthusiasm of the rector of Bruton Parish, Dr. William A. R. Goodwin, and the enthusiastic sharing of his vision by Mr. and Mrs. John D. Rockefeller, Jr. Dr. Goodwin had served in Williamsburg early in the century and returned there in 1923. The sleepy town still retained much of its colonial flavor, since America's industrial progress had touched it lightly and unevenly. Dr. Goodwin was captivated by the early greatness and historical inheritance of the town, and he determined to find the means to recapture them. Only a person of great wealth could do what he felt had to be done, and he found little interest among the prospects that he selected until he came to the junior Rockefeller.[23]

In November 1927 John D. Rockefeller, Jr., committed himself completely to the restoration, and a long, complex process of recreating the colonial town began. He had already authorized Dr. Goodwin to purchase buildings that might fit into such a plan. At this point secrecy was essential; yet Rockefeller's interests had to be protected. Thomas Debevoise looked after the overall legal problem, but direct responsibility fell on the Aldrich firm. As the project progressed, contracts had to be made with architects, contractors, the city of Williamsburg, and the Association for the Preservation of Virgina Antiquities. A young associate in the Aldrich office, Francis T. Christy, handled many of these assignments under the supervision of Winthrop Aldrich.[24]

Rockefeller Center

While engaged in restoring a colonial town, Rockefeller also unexpectedly found himself transforming a run-down residential area of New York City into a major complex of modern office buildings. This development grew out of a search for a new site for the Metropolitan Opera Company. It was thought that land owned by Columbia University between Fifth and Sixth Avenues and 48th and 51st Streets would be suitable, and John D. Rockefeller, Jr., was brought into the discussions. Aldrich, Thomas Debevoise, Colonel Arthur Woods, and other Rockefeller associates participated in the arrangements that culminated in a long-term lease of the Columbia property to the Metropolitan Square Corporation, owned by Rockefeller.[25] Aldrich became a director and vice president of this new corporation.

The Rockefeller interest did not extend to building the opera house in addition to acquiring the land on which it was to stand. His contribution was to facilitate the leasing of the land needed by the Opera Company and to provide a suitable plaza which he planned to present to the city. The Metropolitan's backers, however, encountered difficulties in raising the money necessary to carry out their part of the plan. For one thing, the cost of buying out tenants with long leases was greater than anticipated. For another, the stock market crash of October 1929 contributed to the steepness of the leaseholders' demands while making it even more difficult to raise the money with which to satisfy them.

Debevoise and Aldrich were active on behalf of Rockefeller in these matters, and one of his advisors recalls that a showdown came on a day when he happened to be having lunch with John D. Rockefeller, Jr., in a private dining room downtown. As he remembers it, there was a knock on the door and when it was opened, Aldrich was standing there. Rockefeller beckoned his brother-in-law to a seat. "John," Aldrich said, "I've just come from a meeting of the directors of the Metropolitan Opera Company and their whole attitude is: You've got the money and therefore there's no reason why you shouldn't do this [pay half the cost of the opera house]." Rockefeller instantly replied: "Winthrop, go back and tell them that I am no longer interested." [26] Already committed to providing a plaza that would cost some $2,400,000, he did not feel that he should do more.

Further negotiations with the Opera Company failed to change this decision, and on December 4, 1929, it was publicly announced that the cooperative plan for a new opera site was dead. This development left Rockefeller with a commitment to pay Columbia University at least $3.3 million annually for a period of 24 years; [27] yet there were no currently productive assets of significance on the property and few prospects of any in a deepening national depression.

Part of the original plan had been to develop some attractive commercial buildings in connection with the opera house. There was now no alternative other than to go ahead with this project using available (i.e., Rockefeller) resources. The Metropolitan Square Corporation's directors therefore resolved to create "a commercial center as beautiful as possible consistent with the maximum income that could be developed." [28] From these beginnings the present Rockefeller Center grew. Since Aldrich had moved into banking by this time, he was not closely associated with the travails that accompanied this work. However, he served for a number of years on the board of directors of Rockefeller Center, which succeeded the Metropolitan Square Corporation in 1932.

The Rockefeller Foundation

At the same time that he was active in the Metropolitan Square Corporation, Aldrich was engaged in yet another Rockefeller matter. The Rockefeller Foundation, intended to promote human welfare throughout the world, had been established before World War I by John D. Rockefeller, Sr. In 1918 he had also endowed the Laura Spelman Rockefeller Memorial in the memory of his wife, and this organization sponsored useful work in the social sciences and social technology. In 1928 it seemed desirable to combine the two charitable corporations, and Aldrich and Debevoise presented the resulting petition to the New York Supreme Court, where it was approved in January 1929.[29]

The consolidation involved the transfer of large amounts of stock from the old corporations to the new one. A ruling was sought and obtained from the New York State Tax Commission that the transfer was not taxable, and federal authorities followed suit. However, the State's Attorney General had second thoughts on the matter, and the favorable ruling was reversed, with the federal government again following this example. Although it appeared for a time that the Tax Commission might settle for payment of a token tax and grant a refund on the remainder, this possibility failed to materialize. Aldrich and Debevoise considered the tax issue worth litigating. The Rockefeller Foundation therefore went to court, and the New York Court of Claims in 1932 held that the transfer was not taxable. The federal tax authorities thereupon relinquished their claims.[30]

The Ousting of Colonel Stewart

These legal activities, however varied and interesting, were not the kind to bring the name of Winthrop Aldrich before a very large public, but this situation was to change very shortly as the result of a bitterly contested fight to oust

Colonel Robert Stewart as chairman and director of the Standard Oil Company (Indiana). Indiana Standard had been organized before the turn of the century to operate the world's largest oil refinery at Whiting, Indiana, fed with crude from the Lima-Indiana field and later from the Mid-Continent. As a result of the successful 1911 antitrust action against Standard Oil Company (New Jersey), the parent holding company of the Standard Companies, Indiana Standard was left as a refining and marketing company without its own sources of crude or transportation. In an industry that was largely integrated from the well to the distributor of petroleum products, Indiana Standard found itself increasingly at a disadvantage. Therefore, under the leadership of Colonel Stewart, it had purchased a half interest in the pipeline system and crude-oil purchasing affiliate of the integrated oil company created by Harry Sinclair. In the constant search for crude, Indiana Standard became in effect a partner of Sinclair. And out of this relationship came the difficulty that led to the ousting of Colonel Stewart.

A favorable purchase of crude by the two oil companies in the Mexia, Texas, field in the early 1920s involved a short-lived intermediary company whose function, investigators later said, was to funnel an unearned commission to key oil company officials, including Colonel Stewart. The issues of ethics and legality were brought to light in the controversy over the Teapot Dome leases acquired by Harry Sinclair's Mammoth Oil Company. Court action and congressional investigation followed.[31] As these matters developed, Stewart assured John D. Rockefeller, Jr., that he had taken no action contrary to the best interest of the company.[32] Rockefeller accepted these assurances, but he was already beginning to be criticized by papers like the *New York World* for not taking an active part in clearing up the cloud of suspicion that was settling over the Indiana Company.[33]

The Rockefeller interests in the company were substantial but by no means adequate to confer control. Later testimony showed that the junior Rockefeller personally held about 4.5 percent of the company's capital stock; the Rockefeller Foundation had about 5 percent; the Rockefeller-endowed University of Chicago about a third of one percent; and the Equitable Trust Company, as trustee for the two Rockefeller daughters mentioned earlier, about 6 percent.[34] Nevertheless, the Rockefellers were popularly believed to have the power to dominate the company.

In January 1928 the United States Senate adopted a resolution to investigate the Continental Trading Company, which was the intermediary in the Mexia oil purchase. The inquiry was entrusted to the Senate Committee on Public Lands and Surveys. Meanwhile, Stewart had left the country with the assurance that he would not be needed until March or April as a witness in the government's court case against Harry Sinclair. When the Senate investigation got under way in late January, Stewart showed no disposition to return home. Only after he had received a wire from Rockefeller that his appearance was indispensable to justify the confidence of his friends and business associates, did Stewart return to this country.

In his appearance before the Senate Committee, Stewart appeared blustery when he was not evasive. Rockefeller was now thoroughly caught between his desire to be loyal to the Colonel, who had done so much for Indiana Standard, and his desire that mounting criticism of Stewart, of the company, and of him be met by forthright testimony. In an interview with Rockefeller in New York in February 1928, Stewart affirmed once more that he had done nothing wrong, and Rockefeller believed that he had Stewart's assurance that he would resign at Rockefeller's personal request.[35]

Further developments soon put this belief to the test. At the company's annual meeting, Rockefeller and the Rockefeller Foundation refrained from voting for Colonel Stewart's reelection to the Indiana board, but he was elected anyway. When the second Sinclair trial ended with Harry Sinclair's acquittal, Stewart was free to testify before the Senate Committee on matters covered by the trial. This time he acknowledged receipt of Liberty bonds which represented his share of the Continental Trading Company's profits, but he also made it clear that he had not touched them personally.[36] Instead, he said that he had made them the subject of a trust which he had terminated when he revealed his role in the affair to his directors on April 20, 1928. The bonds had then been turned over to the company. In view of his earlier testimony, the possibility that Stewart had committed perjury existed in many minds.

John D. Rockefeller, Jr., was aghast at this turn of events. On April 27, 1928, he asked for Stewart's resignation on the basis of the promise that he thought the Colonel had given him earlier. At a dinner at the Rockefellers' New York house on May 8th, Stewart declined to resign, and the following day Rockefeller made his request public.[37]

The Stewart affair by this time had reached the stage of legal inquiries. The question of the possible liability of participants in the Continental Trading Company to Indiana Standard had been called to the attention of the company's directors by Rockefeller in March.[38] Receiving no reply, he submitted the question to the Aldrich firm, then known as Murray, Aldrich & Roberts. Their reply, on April 17, was that all the participants were jointly and severally liable for damages as the result of a conspiracy.[39] Accordingly, Winthrop Aldrich was well briefed on the developing situation before Rockefeller decided to force a showdown with Colonel Stewart.

After the Indiana directors refused either to ask for Stewart's resignation or to call a stockholders' meeting to consider it, Debevoise and Aldrich emerged as the strategists of the Rockefeller side. While Stewart was standing trial for contempt of the Senate and for committing perjury, the Rockefeller lawyers were quietly gathering all the evidence they could get their hands on to force his resignation from Indiana Standard. When Stewart was acquitted in both trials, his position was greatly strengthened and he determined to seek reelection as a director of the Standard Company in March 1929. The Rockefeller group was determined to gain enough proxies to oust Stewart at that meeting. Accordingly, on January 2 a proxy committee composed of John D. Rockefeller, Jr., Winthrop Aldrich, and his law partner, William Roberts, sent a letter to all stockholders asking for their proxies to vote against Stewart's reelection. The president of Indiana Standard and his board came to Stewart's support.[40]

Such proxy fights were an innovation in those days, and the nature of this one intrigued many observers. The *Chicago Tribune* delightedly commented that the fight would have startled an earlier generation: "No one would have believed that a Rockefeller would be engaged in such a struggle [appealing for public support to control a Standard Company] and fighting on the side of a more scrupulous business morality."[41]

The Aldrich law offices became the headquarters for the solicitation of proxies. As one of the young lawyers in the office recalled it: "Mr. Aldrich was like General Eisenhower conducting a campaign for the invasion of Europe. There were, you might say, auxiliary commanders, there were auxiliary troops; we were all assigned certain things; and I can remember distinctly that they assigned to me what they would call the large proxies."[42] His job was merely to collect the proxies, for the advance work involving telephone calls and other contacts by Aldrich, Debevoise, or other members of the senior group had already been done. This group included Bertram Cutler, Rockefeller's financial advisor; William Roberts, Aldrich's law partner; Ivy Lee, a public relations expert; and Raymond B. Fosdick, of the Rockefeller office. Rockefeller himself had departed for Egypt in January 1929 and was not therefore in a position to direct the strategy of the contest that he had initiated.

The campaign plan, as indeed it was called by the participants, focused on 24 of the largest cities in the country. Stockholders with more than 500 shares were systematically canvassed in each city, and voluntary committees of such stockholders were formed to insure wide coverage. Lawyers and law firms across the country were also pressed into service.[43]

Meantime, Stewart rallied his forces. His directors stood by him and were active in the counter-campaign, as were sales representatives of the Indiana Company. Stewart had many friends and his record of achievement for the company was well known; he further emphasized it when the directors voted an extra cash dividend and a stock dividend in February 1929. Public interest in the tide of battle became so great that the capture of a major proxy by either side became a newsworthy item.

As the contest grew hotter, the Rockefeller campaign committee issued a 72-page brochure, signed by Winthrop Aldrich, and sent it to the Indiana Company's stockholders. It contained excerpts and testimony from the Senate hearings on the Continental Trading Company. The Stewart forces condemned this tactic as unfair, deceptive, and unworthy of John D. Rockefeller, Jr. However, Rockefeller praised the brochure when he received a copy, and newspaper comment was very much in his favor.[44]

The Rockefeller committee's emphasis on large stockholders paid off. By January 15, 1929, it had secured proxies for nearly 26 percent of the stock. On February 7, Aldrich announced publicly that the figure had reached 51 percent;

by early March it was 59 percent.[45] Barring some totally unexpected and improbable development, the battle had been
won and won decisively. However, the decision had yet to
be announced.

A private car carried Aldrich, Roberts, Debevoise, and
others of their group to Chicago on the night of March 3,
1929. Accompanying them were 17 steel filing cases filled
with proxies. Colonel Stewart, either out of fear for what
might happen or with a fine sense of the dramatic, apparently
arranged for armed guards to meet his opponents and escort
them to their hotel.

The annual meeting took place on March 7. In view of the
interest in the event, arrangements were made to hold it in
the Whiting Community House. Shortly after noon the
Rockefeller group took seats in the front of the hall, and
Stewart mounted the stage to conduct the proceedings. Faced
with the knowledge of certain defeat, he never faltered in
his conduct of the meeting. At one point, however, he gave
Aldrich a start by entertaining a motion suggested by a small
stockholder that the board be reelected and two additional
seats filled — one by a representative of stockholders with
less than 500 shares and one by a representative of those with
more. Aldrich was quickly on his feet to protest that the
motion was out of order, but Stewart played to his audience
and the suggestion was put to a vote. Since the Rockefeller
forces voted against it, there was no question but that it would
be lost. Stewart, however, savored the moment before announcing "The 'noes' seem to have it." When the vote on the
board of directors came, the Rockefeller forces won decisively. Their slate received 8,465,276 votes, while Stewart
received only 2,954,986, which was almost identical with the
vote for another director whom the Rockefeller group had
determined to oust because of his activities on behalf of
Stewart.[46]

The proxy fight was waged on an ethical issue of the type that Winthrop Aldrich believed should be raised, but the decision to fight in this instance was not his responsibility. Participation in the conferences between Rockefeller and his advisers preparatory to that decision, however, left a deep impression on him. Aldrich witnessed his brother-in-law's private anguish over the necessity of publicly challenging an executive in whom he had placed full confidence and whom he had publicly endorsed. Furthermore, the decision to oust Stewart had to be made in the absence of a sure means to make it effective. It would have been far easier to have dodged the issue by simply voting the Rockefeller shares against Stewart as a sign of disapproval, as was done in 1928. These lessons on how John D. Rockefeller, Jr., and his most trusted advisors regarded their responsibilities and those of executives in companies where the Rockefellers had substantial interests were of more than passing importance to Winthrop Aldrich, who would find himself within a few months heading a bank where these interests were strongly represented.

Rockefeller's decision to leave the country on the eve of the proxy fight brought criticism from some who otherwise approved his course of action. Whatever his motivation for absenting himself from the scene of action, he clearly trusted the group headed by Debevoise and Aldrich. In his skillful mobilization of the Rockefeller forces and his systematic campaign for proxies, Winthrop Aldrich just as clearly gave new evidence of his capacity to lead.

This capacity for leadership had already been demonstrated beyond question to the members of Aldrich's law firm. By Wall Street standards the office was still small in its number of partners and lawyers. As a result, everyone put in long hours and frequently worked right through the weekend. Aldrich, as the leader of the firm, worked as hard as his subordinates but always kept evenings and weekends free for his family. His preference for problems that involved major strategy, plus his aversion to pleading, led to his avoidance of personal involvement in day-to-day trial work. He enjoyed and did his best court work on appeals of the type reviewed earlier in this chapter.

In many respects his method of assigning responsibility was similar to that of James Byrne, from whom he had learned so much. In the words of a lawyer who served in Aldrich's office as a young man during the 1920s: [47]

> His method was amazing. He always took it upon himself to decide whether a person could do something, and he dumped it in your lap. He never asked you what you were doing; he never asked you how you did it. He only expected you to perform. And when you performed, he was not given to lavish praise. He might say in a quiet voice: "Fine," or "That was well done." It was always in an undertone, but you knew he meant it. The greatest tribute you felt was that he gave you the job.

If a young lawyer failed to produce, there was no reproof. He simply did not get another assignment from Aldrich. As the lawyer recalled: [48]

> That was the sign of his disfavor, because you must remember that Mr. Aldrich, by background and training, achieved an attitude which, to the outsider, might seem one of aloofness. But I attribute that to, you might say, environment. But underneath that aloofness, there was a warm personality, there was a considerateness, there was — you know — a feeling for people. And certainly in his family life, I found, all the warmth that his exterior here would not register.

CHAPTER IV

Family and Yachting Years

W INTHROP ALDRICH found time in these busy years to enjoy his growing family and his favorite sport, yachting. From the beginning of his law career, he had resolved not to let his professional interests and obligations deprive him of an opportunity to engage in the social, sporting, and public service activities that he found stimulating and satisfying. Family, and family life, were especially important to him.

Family Life and Activities

Tragedy struck the Aldriches in February 1921 when their first-born, Winthrop Williams Junior, died, but less than a month before, their first daughter, Mary, had been born. Three more daughters — Harriet Crocker, Lucy Truman, and Elizabeth Brewster — were added to the family before another son, Alexander, was born in March 1928. With five small children in the household, the Aldriches' family life was a busy one.

The pattern of family life reflected the changing seasons. In the winter the Aldriches lived in New York City; in the spring and fall and on weekends they could usually be found on Long Island. In the summer they might be on Long Island, in Maine, or cruising and racing in coastal waters. Interspersed with these activities was usually a trip to Europe and, during the winter, a few weeks in the South.

During this period the Aldriches lived in various houses. From 1919 to 1925 their New York City residence was at 23 East 73rd Street. In the spring and fall they leased "Linden Farm," the Syosset, Long Island, estate of R. High Carleton. In 1923 the Aldriches decided to buy land and build a house of their own on Long Island. This decision led them to Wheatley Hills in Roslyn. There they developed an outstanding estate on Cedar Swamp Road, and occupied the main house for the first time in April 1926. After selling their 73rd Street house, they lived for the next several winters in various leased houses, including Kermit Roosevelt's at 29 East 69th Street and Mrs. Rodman Wanamaker's at 11 East 74th Street. In 1927 they purchased a home at 15 East 78th Street.

Yachting was Aldrich's favorite avocation, and he found in it a congenial challenge to his competitive drive. In 1919 Aldrich acquired his first boat in partnership with a lawyer-friend, William A. W. Stewart, and in the late summer of 1920 they contracted for a new "S" boat. Before it was well along, however, he and Stewart decided to enter the first international races for 6 meter sailing yachts * to be held at Cowes, England, in the summer of 1921. Accordingly the "S" boat was transferred to Winthrop's brother, William, and Aldrich and Stewart joined forces to build the 6-meter sloop *Montauk*. They raced the new boat at Oyster Bay in the spring of 1921 before she and three others were shipped to England. In July the Aldriches crossed the Atlantic and established their headquarters for the races at "Hardwicke," in the Cowes yachting center.

---

* These were the first American yachts built to the International Rule, which still governs construction of the America's Cup contenders.

The contest for the British-American cup involved four American and four British boats, and the conditions were trying. On the first day, July 29, a gale was blowing and only two American boats, one of them the *Montauk*, were able to start. Despite good handling, the *Montauk*'s performance was disappointing, for she had too much sail for the turbulent winds and waters of the Solent. Nevertheless, the Aldrich-Stewart boat finished second among the American entries in the series, though she placed sixth among all the boats. More important, in the course of the campaigning, Aldrich formed friendships with British yachtsmen who many years later would welcome him back to their country as American Ambassador.

Aldrich's appetite for yachting was further whetted by his summer in England, and early in 1922 he purchased the beautiful schooner *Flying Cloud*, formerly the *Radiant*. She was over 90 feet long, carried 5,000 square feet of sail, and, of course, required a professional crew. At this time Aldrich joined the venerable New York Yacht Club. It gave him much satisfaction that his private signal was the same as the one that had flown from Nelson Aldrich's yachts.

That first summer, the *Flying Cloud* participated in all the races of both the New York and Eastern Yacht Club cruises. In the schooner class besides the *Flying Cloud* were Carll Tucker's *Ohonkara*, Harold Vanderbilt's *Vagrant*, E. Walter Clark's *Irolita*, and N. F. Ayres's *Queen Mab*. With their lofty spars and billowing sails, they stood out among the more than 100 yachts that gathered at Newport on August 1, 1922, for the New York Yacht Club cruise. From there they raced each day to a new port. The Aldrich schooner won the squadron run three times out of five and was first in her class with only one exception.

While the *Flying Cloud* lay comfortably in Fyfe's shipyard at Glen Cove during the winter of 1922–1923, the Aldriches resumed their normal routine. They moved back to the city late in the fall. In January 1923 they visited Cuba in connection with Aldrich's job as counsel to the reorganization committee of the Central Sugar Corporation. On their crowded social calendar in February was the Trust Companies Section dance of the American Bankers Association, which the Aldriches attended annually. In the same month Aldrich added to the long list of his club memberships by joining the Creek Club, a new golf club whose membership list virtually duplicated that of the New York Yacht Club and included Vincent Astor, George F. Baker, Jr., J. P. Morgan, and Marshall Field.

As far as Aldrich was concerned, sailing and yacht racing took precedence over golf and tennis, though he enjoyed both the latter sports. As he once told a reporter, yacht racing ". . . gets one out of one's self. The fresh air, the fine points of the competition and the thrills make it the great game it is, although the dull spots when the wind fails are not any too enjoyable." [1]

With this kind of enthusiasm, it was natural that the Aldriches should spend their vacations by the sea. In the summer of 1924 they leased Mrs. Dixon's cottage at Dark Harbor, Maine. Located on an island in Penobscot Bay opposite the wooded Camden Hills, Dark Harbor had attracted a number of leading American families. Mrs. Aldrich had visited the island before her marriage on cruises aboard her father's yacht, and her uncle Maitland Alexander, a minister in Pittsburgh, had a summer place there. This fact was probably decisive in the Aldriches' selection of Dark Harbor for their own summer home. They had decided that fashionable Bar Harbor was not the place for their children, and they were unable to find a suitable house at Seal Harbor or Northeast Harbor near the Rockefellers' summer home.

The Aldriches became such consistent visitors at Dark Harbor that they finally decided in 1934 to purchase their own summer place there. It became a much-beloved retreat, and the constantly changing play of light and shadow on the waters of Penobscot Bay and the distant Camden hills later furnished Winthrop Aldrich with one of his favorite scenes for painting, an avocation in which he proved quite proficient.

Expanding Commitments

When growing up in Providence, Aldrich had attended the Round Top Congregational Church, and he continued to do so when he visited there. In 1926, at the urging of the Rockefellers, he began attending the Park Avenue Baptist Church in New York City where Harry Emerson Fosdick, a brother of one of the Rockefeller lawyers, was minister. When the Riverside Church was completed with the aid of the Rockefellers, Dr. Fosdick became its minister, and Aldrich became a member and eventually a trustee.

His interests and responsibilities outside his law firm increased very rapidly in these years. In connection with his legal work he served on the boards of several railroads, including the Denver & Rio Grande and the Western Pacific. In addition, he served on the boards of several banks, various companies, and such organizations as the Legal Aid Society, the Council on Foreign Relations, and numerous philanthropic groups. He was an officer of the New York Yacht Club and a trustee of the Seawanhaka-Corinthian. His memberships in various social clubs frequented by men in the top echelons of New York's financial, business, and legal life also grew steadily, for Aldrich felt some compulsion to honor the suggestions of his friends that he join "their" club.

In 1919 Aldrich made the first of a lifetime's contributions to Harvard by agreeing to serve on the New York Committee for the Harvard Endowment Fund, headed by Thomas Lamont of J. P. Morgan & Company. His continuing interest in the university was demonstrated not only by his own substantial financial contribution and work in fund-raising but also by his annual attendance at the Harvard-Yale boat race and the Harvard-Yale football game. These gala occasions brought together many of his college and law school friends, while the annual gatherings of the 1907 Dinner Club assembled members of his class like Francis Appleton, George Whitney, O'Donnell Iselin, Harrison Tweed, and Harold Vanderbilt for evenings of conviviality and reminiscence.

As 1919 turned into 1920 and the fruits of the Peace Conference became an issue in the impending national elections, Winthrop Aldrich had added work for the Republican party to his growing list of activities. Both he and Mrs. Aldrich became members of the 15th Assembly District Republican Organization, whose members included such well known individuals as Edward L. Harkness, Ogden Mills, and Chauncey Depew. Soon Aldrich was chairman of the Committee on Speakers and Meetings. The Aldriches attended the 1920 national Republican convention that nominated Warren Harding for President, even though earlier Aldrich had contributed $25 to a premature campaign to nominate Herbert Hoover. As he later recalled, he was "not above water politically at that time." [2] During that summer the Aldriches contributed chairs and rugs for the Republican Club of the 15th District, and in the fall they worked enthusiastically as election district captains for the Republican ticket that won. In November Aldrich continued to be active in Republican affairs. However, although he was urged to run for Congress and was also sounded out by President Coolidge concerning his interest in a federal judgeship,[3] he preferred his active and growing legal practice to either elective or appointive office.

Meantime, Aldrich had received his baptism in major fund raising at the request of John D. Rockefeller, Jr., who was a leading supporter of the mushrooming Interchurch World

Movement. This project had been inspired by the success of service groups in working with American troops during World War I and was conceived as a vehicle for Protestant denominations in North America to undertake a worldwide missionary effort of broad scope. Such a vast interdenominational effort appealed strongly to the junior Rockefeller, who enthusiastically endorsed a campaign to raise nearly $337 million for the Movement and the 31 denominations affiliated with it. Mr. Rockefeller himself spent a fortnight traveling to more than a dozen cities in April 1920 to promote the Movement, and he naturally turned to his brother-in-law for aid in the fund-raising drive. On April 10, 1920, Aldrich agreed to serve on the General Committee of the Interchurch World Movement of North America.

Unfortunately the expectations of the promoters of the Movement, including Mr. Rockefeller, had far exceeded the realities. As it turned out, allegiance to denominational giving outweighed the attractions of giving to the interdenominational organization. As a result, while the associated denominations raised $176,000,000 for their needs in the 1920 fund-raising campaign, the Interchurch World Movement received only $3,000,000, and one-third of this came from the Rockefeller family.[4] Although an additional effort was made to remedy this showing, it, too, failed and the Movement was liquidated. Though success or failure was not Aldrich's responsibility, the experience of participating in the fund raising drive was chastening and valuable. As head of a comparably large but successful undertaking during World War II, he showed that he had learned the lessons of the 1920 fiasco well.

During this period he also became interested in the East Side Branch of the YMCA and served as chairman of its Collections Committee. It became an annual custom for him to contribute to Mrs. John D. Rockefeller, Jr.'s Girl Scouts

while she in turn sent him a check for "his" YMCA. With
his own interest and example, it was not too difficult for him
to find financial support for the East Side Branch year after
year, though on one occasion he was rebuffed by such re-
doubtable figures as George F. Baker, Sr. and Jr., on the
grounds that the "Y" discriminated against Unitarians.[5]

The junior Bakers were among the Aldriches' closest
friends. Yachting interests provided one common bond, and
Baker had endorsed Aldrich for membership in the New
York Yacht Club. Mr. Baker's father, head of the First National Bank of New York, had made a significant contribution to Harvard for housing its Graduate School of Business
Administration, and Aldrich was invited to attend the dedication ceremonies in June 1927. He was unable to be present,
but he and his brothers and sisters gave Senator Aldrich's fine
personal library to the School and provided suitable housing
for it in a room that was dedicated in the fall of 1928. Many
years later, Aldrich returned from his Ambassador's post in
London to speak at the dedication of the first major additions
to the Harvard Business School campus, one of them named
for his father.

Defense of the America's Cup

Although Aldrich's interests and commitments expanded
rapidly, he still found time for yachting. Harold Vanderbilt
had been a friend since college days and during the New
York Yacht Club cruise of 1926 he and Aldrich discussed the
desirability of building a new class of sloops which would be
better for racing and less expensive to operate than the schoon-
ers with their large crews. The idea appealed to Aldrich because *Flying Cloud* cost some $20,000 a year to operate; yet
he could only use her for short periods. As the first step
toward acquiring a new racing sloop, he decided to sell the
beautiful schooner after the 1926 sailing season. The buyer

was Seward Prosser, chairman of the Bankers Trust Company. While plans for the new boat were maturing, the Aldriches, together with their friends Mr. and Mrs. Benjamin Moore, leased "Yester Hall," an estate near Edinburgh, Scotland, and grouse shooting and golf took the place of sailing for the summer of 1927.

Flying Cloud was replaced in 1928 by an M-Class sloop, which Aldrich named *Valiant* and raced in for the next several years. She proved to be a fast boat and took several first prizes during the 1928 Larchmont Race Week. Escorting *Valiant* the next summer was the 104-foot long motor yacht *Wayfarer*, built for the Aldriches by George Lawley's famous yard at Neponset, Massachusetts.

The experience with *Valiant* was valuable preparation for Aldrich's participation with Vanderbilt in the America's Cup defense of 1930 aboard the J-Class sloop *Enterprise*. The America's Cup is the most prized trophy in yachting, dating back to 1851 when the American yacht *America* won it in English waters. Over the succeeding years one British challenge after another was accepted by the New York Yacht Club, which held the cup, and each time the trophy was safely returned to its place of honor in the New York Yacht Club House. The most consistent challenger was the genial Irish tea merchant, Sir Thomas Lipton, who made repeated, vain efforts to recapture the trophy with his handsome sloops named *Shamrock*. In early 1929 his challenge was renewed once more, and at a meeting at the Broad Street Club in May of that year it was accepted on behalf of the New York Yacht Club.

By this time Winthrop Aldrich had risen to the post of Vice Commodore, and he agreed to head a syndicate to build a boat to defend the cup. Members of his syndicate included his friends Vincent Astor, George F. Baker, Jr., Floyd L. Carlisle, E. Walter Clark, Harold S. Vanderbilt, and George Whitney. Aldrich selected the name for the syndicate's new boat, *Enterprise*. A second syndicate headed by Rear Commodore Junius Morgan was to build another contender.

E. Starling Burgess, a noted yacht designer, was selected to draw up designs for the Aldrich boat, which Vanderbilt suggested should be modeled on the M boats that he and Aldrich had pioneered only a year before. She was to have a waterline length of 80 feet compared to the 50 to 54 feet of the M boats. Like Aldrich's SP 1218 of World War I, *Enterprise* was built at the Herreshoff yard in Bristol, Rhode Island, where her keel was cast on October 5, 1929, only a few weeks before the catastrophic stock market collapse of that month. Aldrich's chief connection with the boat during that busy winter was raising the money to pay for her, by no means as easy a task as had been anticipated when the British challenge was accepted.

On April 13, 1930, Mr. and Mrs. Aldrich, several other members of the syndicate, and E. Sherman Hoyt, who was to sail in the boat, joined Vanderbilt on his yacht *Vara* at City Island. After inspecting the spars of *Enterprise* there, they steamed across Long Island Sound and up Narragansett Bay to Herreshoff's yard. They arrived at 7 a.m. on April 14, and shortly thereafter Mrs. Aldrich christened the potential cup defender as it slipped down the ways.[6]

Business responsibilities prevented Aldrich from participating fully in the hard round of campaigning and tune-up that preceded the selection of *Enterprise* as the actual defender of the cup. This testing period lasted from May to August and involved numerous other possible cup defenders such as the *Weetamoe*, *Yankee*, and *Whirlwind*. Since Aldrich had never lost his interest in navigation acquired during World War I, he had been assigned this job. When he was absent, Burgess performed these duties. Aldrich was aboard *Enterprise*, however, when she and *Yankee* in a trial race broke the old record for the 30-mile course around Vineyard

Sound lightship. "I think that probably was the greatest race of its kind ever sailed," he said later.[7]

Enterprise embodied so many technical innovations that she was a novelty. Among other things, instead of a conventional wooden mast, she sported a duraluminum one manufactured by the Glen L. Martin Company. In addition, she had an unusual boom designed to improve the curvature and therefore driving power of her huge mainsail. In honor of Vanderbilt, who approached such matters very scientifically, it was called a "Park Avenue boom."

A combination of careful and imaginative engineering plus skillful handling finally brought the selection of *Enterprise* as the cup defender on August 27, 1930. Since the races with Lipton's *Shamrock V* were to be held off Newport, Rhode Island, the Aldriches leased Ogden Mills's house in the yachting center as their headquarters.

The contest got under way on September 13. Aldrich's job was to keep the log book, start the watches, carry out the formula which would put the *Enterprise* across the starting line with the starting gun, and to navigate while keeping an eye on the *Shamrock*. His "office" was a small compartment between one where a portly British observer was comfortably ensconced, and the wheel, where Vanderbilt officiated.

The races showed that all the thought and money and skill that had gone into *Enterprise* had not been wasted. She went through the series in four straight wins, though on the third one *Shamrock* contributed to the ease of the American victory by breaking down. In the final race, *Enterprise* sailed 30 miles at an average speed of 9.45 knots to break the America's Cup record.

This triumph was very satisfying to Winthrop Aldrich, but it was only a brief interlude in a demanding life where events seemed to be crowding in with greater insistence and acceleration. During the very time that he had been preparing

for the cup defense, a completely unexpected development
had altered his legal career — temporarily, he thought; permanently, it proved. While *Enterprise* was hauled out on the
shore to await her fate at the hands of junk metal dealers,
Aldrich returned to New York to face the problems of directing a great bank in the midst of a deepening national depression.

CHAPTER V

The Fateful Year, 1929-1930

IN DECEMBER 1929 Winthrop Aldrich became president of the Equitable Trust Company, a financial institution with over $1 billion in assets. It was a position that he had not sought and one that he did not expect to retain. Before another six months had passed, however, a further merger, with the Chase National Bank, made him president of the world's largest bank. This abrupt change of roles was accidental as far as Aldrich was concerned, but he found himself at the top level of commercial banking as a generation of bank mergers reached their climax in the institution of which he became president. Furthermore, his involvement came as disaster overtook the New York financial community and threatened the system of private initiative that had produced these mergers.

The Equitable Trust Company

The Equitable's history went back to 1871 when the Traders Deposit Company was organized. The Equitable name itself dated from 1902 when the immediate predecessor company was reorganized. At that time the number of trust companies in New York was growing rapidly because state law conferred broad powers on them. To take advantage of this fact, the Equitable Life Assurance Society, one of the country's major insurance companies, acquired a controlling interest in the renamed Equitable Trust Company.[1] Originally chartered to make loans on life insurance policies, the bank was empowered to do a general banking business and to engage in trust activities.

The opportunity to carry on these dual functions free from insurance company control resulted from the 1905 Armstrong investigation in New York State and subsequent legislation designed to end abuses in the life insurance investment business. As part of this remedial legislation, the New York law forbade insurance companies to hold more than 5 percent of a bank's stock and limited representation of such interest to one board member.[2] This law forced Equitable Trust Life to reduce its holdings in the Equitable Trust Company by December 31, 1911, and this in turn led to John D. Rockefeller, Sr.'s interest in the bank.[3] As previously noted, the Rockefeller connection brought the firm of Murray, Prentice & Howland into the bank's legal affairs, while the Rockefeller representative on the board was reported in 1911 to be Henry Cooper, later a vice president of the bank for many years.[4]

Mergers helped the Equitable increase its resources from about $35.6 million in 1908 to over $98 million in 1912.[5] Those mergers involved the Bowling Green Trust Company (March 1909), the Madison Trust Company (June 1911), and the Trust Company of America (February 1912). Thereafter growth was very rapid. By 1920 the Equitable had over $254 million in deposits and ranked eighth in the country by this measure, just behind George F. Baker's First National Bank.[6] At that time, it will be recalled, Aldrich became involved in the bank's legal affairs as counsel.

In 1923 a further merger, with the Importers and Traders National Bank, increased the Equitable's capital to $23 million. Alvin Krech moved up to chairman of the board and Arthur W. Loasby, who had joined the Equitable as a vice president in 1920 and handled the latest merger, became the new president.[7] Meantime, the bank had expanded overseas

TABLE V-1

Growth of the Equitable Trust Company
1923–1929

Year Ending December 31	Capital	Surplus and Additional Profits	Deposits	Total Resources
1923	20,000,000	9,798,393	325,924,539	394,022,605
1924	23,000,000	11,057,465	447,011,085	511,066,777
1925	23,000,000	13,356,789	418,881,258	489,238,468
1926	30,000,000	22,425,651	430,972,351	544,068,581
1927	30,000,000	24,721,707	478,852,295	607,320,638
1928	30,000,000	27,098,866	530,843,928	672,360,297
1929	50,000,000	63,611,005	765,344,701	1,013,970,799

SOURCE: Equitable Trust Co., *Annual Reports; Poor's Financial Reports*, 1925–1930

with the formation of the Equitable Eastern Banking Corporation to facilitate trade in China and with the Orient. Winthrop Aldrich supervised the incorporation of this affiliate and became a director.

The Equitable Trust Company was housed in a building at 37 Wall Street, which was also the address of the Aldrich law firm, but in 1924 Aldrich began the work of obtaining the old Mills building, fronting on Broad Street, as the site for a new Equitable building. It was in this connection that air rights were obtained so that the new building could be built over a portion of the Morgan building at the corner of Broad and Wall Streets. In addition to the legal interest of this arrangement, one practical consequence was that no additional stories could be added to the Morgan structure. When Arthur Loasby drove the final rivet (a gold one) in the structure in August 1927, Winthrop Aldrich was on hand to witness the ceremony.[8] The new building with its entrance opposite the New York Stock Exchange was occupied the following year.

By the end of 1927 the Equitable had assets of over $600 million.[9] This growth had been achieved by a rapid expansion of the bank's services, since no further mergers took place after 1923. The variety of these activities is suggested by the roster of departments in the bank: Trust, Foreign Banking, Bond, Credit, New Business, Loan and Discount, Transfer, Registration, Reorganization and Coupon, Industrial, and Real Estate. Special investment services were offered, and the Equitable pioneered in an insurance trust department which coordinated the interests of the underwriter, client, lawyer, and estate.[10] Throughout the decade the Equitable had continued to improve its trust services and to expand its foreign activities, the two leading areas of its rapid growth

In the opinion of Winthrop Aldrich, the bank was too deeply involved in current loans to Germany and he was concerned about earlier ones to Russia.[11] The serious German inflation of the 1920's, the complex interrelationships of war debts, reparations, and allied loans, plus the collapse of one international effort after another to find a solution to these post-Versailles problems, gave ample basis for his concern. For him they added up to the possibility — indeed the probability — of a future war and major losses to the Equitable. His legal work on the Equitable's foreign claims after World War I had impressed him with the serious consequences such a development could bring, and he wanted the bank's exposure to such risks reduced.

The death of Alvin Krech in May 1928 deepened Aldrich's concern. Krech had guided the Equitable with a sure hand for 25 years, but just as the giant institution that he had helped to create faced new problems generated by its very size, he was taken from the scene. Without denying the ability of his successors, prudence dictated that the Equitable's lead-

TABLE V-2

SUMMARY OF FOREIGN BOND ISSUES IN WHICH THE EQUITABLE TRUST COMPANY PARTICIPATED IN THE ORIGINATION AND/OR MANAGEMENT AND PARTICIPATED UNDER MANAGEMENT OF OTHERS

	Originated and/or Managed (1921–1930)			Participations with Others (1917–1931)			Total Principal Amount of Originations and Participations with Others	Total Gross Profits
	Principal Amount	*Retired*	*Gross Profit*	*Principal Amount*	*Participations*	*Gross Profit*		
Equitable Trust Co.:								
Canada	376,200,000	162,400,000	270,000	—	—	—	376,200,000	270,000
Latin America	3,000,000	3,000,000	120,000	431,472,000	56,351,031	1,071,528	434,472,000	1,191,528
Germany	50,000,000	25,506,000	295,000	169,500,000	25,430,428	327,887	219,500,000	622,887
Other European	—	—	—	57,000,000	8,366,666	128,157	57,000,000	128,157
Miscellaneous	50,000,000	2,283,500	149,000	—	—	—	50,000,000	149,000

SOURCE: 72 Cong., 1 Sess., "Sale of Foreign Bonds or Securities in the United States," *Hearings before the Committee on Finance, United States Senate* (Washington, 1932), p. 419.

ership be strengthened in every way possible. As the bank's counsel, Aldrich was scarcely in a position to take any direct action himself, but his personal relationship to one of the bank's major stockholders and the obvious trust placed in his judgment, exemplified by his role in the Indiana Standard proxy contest, gave his opinions weight in very influential circles. Although there is no specific documentation that Winthrop Aldrich was more alarmed about the Equitable's foreign position than other Rockefeller advisers, there is no question that he took every opportunity to emphasize his concern.

Otto Kahn, the German-born partner in Kuhn, Loeb & Company and a trustee of the Equitable Trust Company, was impressed by Aldrich's assessment of the foreign situation. To test informed reaction to the lawyer's interpretation, Kahn arranged a dinner in October 1929 and invited Winston Churchill, the British statesman turned lecturer, as guest of honor. Aldrich recalls that his presentation on the possibilities of another world war within a decade or two met no disagreement from Churchill. Brendan Bracken, a member of the future Prime Minister's World War II cabinet, attended that dinner and years later remembered that he had taken notes of the discussion.[12]

BACKGROUND OF THE EQUITABLE-SEABOARD MERGER

The Seaboard National Bank

By the time of the Kahn dinner, steps had already been taken to reduce the Equitable's exposed position abroad. A merger with the Seaboard National Bank had just been completed. To interested observers this meant two things. First, the leading stockholder interests of the Equitable considered Chellis Austin, Seaboard's president, and the team that he had assembled, to be outstanding bankers, capable of giving the

Equitable a new direction.* Second, the extensive foreign business and large trust department of the Equitable were to be balanced by the predominantly domestic and commercial orientation of the Seaboard. Together the institutions represented resources of over $850 million and a full line of bank services. In Austin's words, the merger of the two banks would "substantially multiply the measure of service they can perform separately." [13]

The Seaboard National Bank was deeply rooted in the oil business. In fact, it was the first "oil bank" in New York City. Its principal promoter had been Samuel G. Bayne, an Irish immigrant who had entered the Pennsylvania oil fields in their early days and found success both as an oil operator and as a supplier of oil-field equipment. In 1880 he had helped to organize the First National Bank of Bradford, Pennsylvania, located in the town where the first great flush field in the American oil industry was discovered. Bayne conceived the idea of establishing a bank in New York City to specialize in oil finance, especially on the basis of pipeline certificates which were negotiable evidences of ownership of oil. The Seaboard National Bank, located at 18 Broadway next to the Oil and Produce Exchanges, opened in 1883. From these beginnings the Seaboard grew gradually and expanded its activities to embrace a general commercial banking business.[14]

In 1922 the Mercantile Trust and Deposit Company was merged into the Seaboard National Bank, and to this merger Winthrop Aldrich later owed many of his most able associates. The Mercantile had been created in 1917 because at that time national banks were not allowed to perform trust functions, and the Chase National Bank under the leadership of

---

* As Aldrich recalled it in 1966, neither John D. Rockefeller, Jr. nor any of his advisers, except Bertram Cutler who was a director of the Equitable, took part in the discussion of the merger. He attributed a leading role to Howard Bayne of the Seaboard National.

Albert H. Wiggin wanted to participate in this business. Other interested parties in the organization of the Mercantile Trust were Seward Prosser of Bankers Trust and Henry P. Davison of J. P. Morgan & Company, the late Senator Aldrich's close friend and advisor on banking reform. Chellis A. Austin, a virtually unknown young banker, was hand picked by Wiggin to head the new bank.[15] Fate was to intertwine the careers of both these men with Winthrop Aldrich's emergence as a banker.

Austin was born in West Berkshire, Vermont, in June 1876, but his first five years were spent in Canada. Then the family moved to Canton, New York, where Chellis' father opened a dry goods store. After two years at St. Lawrence University, young Austin entered Columbia University. Always more interested in athletics than in academic studies, he left Columbia at the end of two years with insufficient credits for a degree.[16] His subsequent career was a classic success story.

After working for two railroads in minor posts, Austin turned to banking in New York City. Through A. B. Hepburn, president of the Chase National Bank and a former neighbor of the Austins in Canton, he met the president of the Columbia Trust Company and was engaged in 1911 to solicit new business for that institution. In his new job Austin quickly demonstrated ability and initiative that won him rapid promotion. By devising a credit information system he won a place in the credit department. At the end of his first year in the bank he was an assistant treasurer. In four more years he was a vice president. Among his contributions was the development of effective bank advertising, at that time a real innovation.[17] Even more important was his unusual ability to pick able young men who developed into excellent executives.

When handling the estate of a boyhood friend who had

worked for the Chase National, Austin first met Albert Wiggin, who had succeeded Hepburn as the bank's president. Wiggin, who was then organizing the Mercantile Trust Company, recognized Austin's ability and asked him to head the new institution. In the short space of six years, Chellis Austin had moved from a routine railroad job to leadership of a new bank backed by some of the biggest names in New York financial circles. At the end of the first year's operations the new bank had over $13 million in deposits and had earned nearly $100,000.[18]

Even in his early days at the Columbia Trust Company Austin had made a practice of identifying men with whom he would like to work at some future time. One of them was H. Donald Campbell, who later served as president of the Chase National Bank under Aldrich. He had met Austin prior to 1917 when the New Yorker was in Seattle in connection with a bond issue. The two men immediately became friendly and before he left the West Coast, Austin told Campbell, "You know, if you're in the banking business, you ought to be in New York — that's the place to be." [19]

When Austin became president of the Mercantile Trust Company he offered Campbell the position of secretary of the new bank. Campbell recalled later: "In joining the Mercantile I became associated with a group of men of high character, and who were particularly congenial. This group worked together successfully, as a team, through the years." [20]

Austin, his officers, directors, and friends had an opportunity in 1921 to buy out the Chase interest.* This move was followed in 1922 by the Mercantile's merger into the Seaboard National with Austin as president and Samuel Bayne, the founder of the Seaboard, as chairman.

---

* A change in the national banking law enabled national banks to conduct the kind of business for which the Chase National had originally sponsored the Mercantile Trust Company.

In addition to its oil business, the Seaboard specialized in loans to stock brokers. On its board of directors was the son of the fabulous woman stock operator, Hetty Green. In fact, the Green estate carried such a large balance with the Seaboard that the bank's day-to-day operations had to be carried on with an eye to the possibility that the Green money might be withdrawn. Hetty's son, Colonel Green, was often more particular about small matters than those of greater importance. Donald Campbell recalls that at one time he had to advise the Colonel that due to changes in the Banking Act, the bank would no longer be able to pay interest on his deposits. Although the amount of interest was substantial, the Colonel was not disturbed and he continued to carry his usual balances.[21]

Austin was a man of ideals, and he inspired loyalty and faithful cooperation. The team that he had developed at the Mercantile gladly followed him to the Seaboard. In the words of John Traphagen, one of his officers and himself later a bank president: "The result was his institution stood for the very highest principles of banking, and his bank's employees felt a new interest in life and in the welfare of the institution with which they were connected." [22] Austin also found good officers in the Seaboard, including Percy J. Ebbott, later to be Campbell's successor as president of the Chase National.

The combined resources of the Mercantile and Seaboard were $80 million in 1922; by April 1929, on the eve of the Seaboard's merger into the Equitable Trust Company, they had reached more than $306 million.[23] In the interim there had been only one merger — the New Netherland Bank had joined the Seaboard in March 1928. Austin and his "team" had proved themselves outstanding bankers.

The Seaboard's success under Austin led to its being constantly approached as a partner in proposed mergers. An effort to merge with the Bank of Manhattan Company in 1927 failed,[24] and the path to merger with the Equitable Trust Company was far from smooth. Austin reported to his daughter in May 1929 that the Seaboard management was not "unduly concerned" about the prospect of managing a bank with assets of over a billion dollars, but that arranging the merger itself was an exhausting task. "Last week," he wrote, "it all looked impossible to me but I bucked into it and *made* it come through." [25]

Merger and its Aftermath

The Equitable-Seaboard merger was formally consummated September 16, 1929, little more than a month before the great Wall Street crash of October 24th. That disaster and its repercussions did not shake the Equitable Trust Company. So sound was its condition that it not only covered the $40 million that it owed in the Street but also absorbed $100 million in loans for others, as well as lending new money to hard pressed firms and individuals.[26]

Soon after the merger, Austin pushed for a reorganization plan that would add $45 million of new capital. In view of the stock market crash, some of the directors felt that this project should be deferred, but Austin insisted on moving ahead.[27] By early December, despite the adverse financial conditions, the new stock had been fully subscribed and the reorganization was complete.*

On Thursday, December 12, 1929, Chellis Austin delivered an address to the convention of the Association of Life Insurance Presidents. Among other things, he pointed out that loans on securities represented 45 percent of all loans reported by members of the Federal Reserve system in leading cities just prior to the crash. Such support of speculation interfered with the financing of industry and commerce, he

---

* A pool was formed to protect the stock at 87. However, it did not have to enter the market since the new stock did not sell for less than 90.

said, and he predicted a return to a proper emphasis on commercial banking. In his closing paragraph he declared: "I have
the utmost confidence that the banks will continue to advance
steadily through the coming years, not only in the size of
their resources but in what I may call the 'size' of the service
they render; and that, as our country grows in strength and
prosperity, they will fulfill ever more effectively the high
duties of national trust and responsibility which are vested
in them." [28] These were Chellis Austin's last words in public.
That night, at the age of 53, he died of a heart attack in his
Montclair, New Jersey, home.

The passing of the man was mourned by all who knew him.
There were still, in 1966, bank offices in New York City
where Chellis Austin's picture was prominently displayed
and where his death was mentioned as though it were only
yesterday. Such was the man, and the creation of a billion-
dollar bank had been predicated on his attaining a normal
longevity. To the principal backers of the Equitable-Seaboard
merger his untimely death was a catastrophic blow. Austin
had been the leader, and there was literally no one in the
bank as fully conversant with the details of the recent merger
as he was. There was, however, one man outside the bank
who had the equivalent knowledge from his role in handling
the legal intricacies of the merger — Winthrop Aldrich.

From Lawyer to Banker

Aldrich's law firm had been growing as its corporate and
banking clients grew in size and required a wider range of
services. Following the successful fight to oust Colonel Stewart from Indiana Standard in March 1929, William Roberts
had left the partnership, which then became Murray & Aldrich. This situation existed for only a short time. In May 1929
the firm of Webb, Patterson & Hadley was merged with
Murray & Aldrich, to become Murray, Aldrich & Webb.[29]

Vanderbilt Webb specialized in real estate and took over the legal problems of Colonial Williamsburg; Robert Patterson left the firm in 1930 to become a federal judge and later served as both Under Secretary and Secretary of War. Morris Hadley, the son of the former president of Yale University, was a lawyer of proven ability. Aldrich therefore headed a strong, profitable firm. His capacity for leadership and judgment had been tested repeatedly and within the year they had helped to win the Rockefeller contest with Colonel Stewart. Given his knowledge of the Equitable-Seaboard merger, he was a logical choice to fill the void left by Austin's death until it was possible to evaluate the best course of action for the long run.

Aldrich had no desire to become a banker; he had chosen the law for a career and he had had no reason to regret it. There was no gainsaying, however, that an emergency existed. John D. Rockefeller, Jr., and Thomas Debevoise urged him to take on the Equitable's presidency for a year, and it was with this understanding that he consented to move into Austin's office.[30]

It took a week to arrange this change in leadership. In the interim the Equitable's officers waited in suspense. At last Aldrich's election as president was announced and a meeting of all the bank's officers was called for 4 p.m. on December 17, 1929. Percy Ebbott remembers that scene vividly:

> When Mr. Aldrich came down . . . we had an opportunity to hear him and, in the parlance of the Street, size him up. He made an excellent impression. And I think one of the first things he said [was], 'No one needs to be disturbed. You will all stay in your present positions and continue doing what you have been doing, because I thoroughly approve of the administration of my predecessor, Mr. Chellis Austin, and I shall hope to continue the same type of administration which you enjoyed under him.'[31]

There was little else that the spruce, mustached lawyer of 44 could have said at that moment, but the way in which he said it and the obvious command that he had over a difficult situation left a lasting impression on those who saw and heard him that day.

Aldrich was deluged with congratulations from the rich and famous and from little known people who had crossed his path years before. Many of the letters showed that the writers had been friends of Senator Aldrich. Bernard Baruch, for example, wrote: "It is not often that I have the pleasure of seeing you, but I have an interest and pride in your accomplishments as a very old and dear friend of your father's necessarily must have." [32] Another writer declared: "My first feeling was that I wished your father might have had the satisfaction of knowing of your progress for it would have given him a tremendous amount of happiness and satisfaction." [33]

Albert H. Wiggin, chairman of the Chase National Bank, dispatched a hand-written note welcoming Aldrich "to the fraternity." "If there is anything that one of the old men in the Street can do that will be of any assistance at any time," he wrote, "command me." [34] Little did either man know in December 1929 how soon their careers would touch one another intimately. However, Wiggin was conscious of the unsought responsibilities that Aldrich was shouldering. "I appreciate that you must be making a sacrifice not only in your finances but in your personal comfort," he wrote.[35]

In several of his replies to congratulatory letters, the new president of the Equitable Trust Company made it clear that he had assumed his duties reluctantly. To Professor Manley O. Hudson of Harvard Law School he declared frankly: "I am sure that you will understand with what reluctance I am entering into duties which will prevent my giving all of my time to the practice of law, but the situation was such that it was utterly impossible for me to pursue any other course." [36]

To Thomas Lamont of J. P. Morgan & Company, he wrote: "It is an extraordinary thing how inevitable it appears to be that if one has the earnest desire to accomplish a given result, the burden of responsibility of accomplishing that result ultimately descends upon one's own shoulders." [37]

In his first remarks to the Equitable's officers, Winthrop Aldrich had stressed his approval of Chellis Austin's administration and he meant it. He was not taking over from a man unknown to him. They had worked closely together on the merger, but they had also been associated in public service activities for some time. Austin had recommended Aldrich for the Board of Managers of the State Charities Aid Society in 1926, and Aldrich succeeded Austin as vice president of that group in December 1929. Similarly, he replaced Austin as a member at large and trustee of the United Hospital Fund. Their personal relationship had led Austin to ask the lawyer to review what turned out to be his last speech, the address to the Life Insurance Presidents of December 12. It was therefore with genuine feeling that Aldrich wrote Lewis H. Brown, president of Johns-Manville Corporation, a week later: "It will be my ambition in performing the duties of my new office to follow as closely as I can the policies of Mr. Austin for whom I had the highest admiration and personal affection." [38]

Resources and Personnel

Austin had left his successor a strong and growing organization. The Equitable, enlarged by the merger with the Seaboard, ended 1929 with resources of well over $1 billion. It had four branches in New York City, two in London, one in Paris, and one in Mexico City. Through the Equitable Eastern Corporation, it had branches in Shanghai, Tientsin, and Hong Kong. The Equitable's securities business had been handled by the bank's bond department, but at the time of the merger it had been decided to form a separate corporation that would handle such matters and take over the assets of the Seaboard National Corporation. This decision led to the creation of the Equitable Corporation, of which Winthrop Aldrich also became president. In addition to these subsidiaries, there were also several separately incorporated safe deposit companies.[39]

The Seaboard National Corporation had scarcely begun to function when the Equitable-Seaboard merger occurred. The responsibility for launching its successor, the new Equitable securities affiliate, into the underwriting and distribution of securities fell largely on John Traphagen, an associate of Chellis Austin since 1919. Both he and Donald Campbell had a man in mind for active supervision of this operation — Edward Love.[40]

Love had started his career as a messenger boy for the Seaboard National Bank in 1912. He soon decided that he wanted to enter investment banking and after World War I joined Bonbright & Company, a large investment banking firm that specialized in public utility securities. After an apprenticeship there, Love helped to organize a small firm in this field, Love, Macomber & Company.[41] Shortly after the preliminary steps to the Equitable-Seaboard merger were taken, Love was approached by Traphagen and Campbell of the Seaboard with the proposition that he join them in the merged bank as of January 1, 1930.[42] His affirmative reply, given some time before the death of Chellis Austin, brought him to a vice presidency in both the Equitable Trust Company and the Equitable Corporation only a few weeks after Winthrop Aldrich assumed their presidencies. Love's expert competence in the field of public utility securities, as it turned out, was invaluable to the bank.

Another important officer who had been selected by Austin but joined the bank under Aldrich was Shepard Morgan. He became a vice president in April 1930, nearly a year after

Chellis Austin had asked him to join the combined Equitable-Seaboard. Morgan had been associated with the administration of the Dawes Plan for German reparations since 1924 and was Finance Director for the Reparations Payments Office in Berlin. It was there that Austin had addressed him in May 1929, pointing out: "Mr. John D. Rockefeller, Jr., who is the largest single stockholder in the Equitable, has for some time had a desire to make that institution one of the most outstanding banks in the country, first perhaps on the side of character and ability and, second, by means of its size. We are invited to give consideration to the question as to whether by merger we could be induced to assume the leadership in this larger picture." [43]

In a subsequent letter, Austin outlined what he had in mind: "I think most of the principal banks here, as we ourselves will be, are well equipped with first class technical heads of the foreign commercial business but I believe that no bank has yet tried to accomplish in a broad way what I have in mind. In other words, I should like to set up a general cabinet of a few senior officers under the president, who will be relieved of any detailed work but who can in their respective fields develop in the largest way as many of the possibilities which the years to come may bring forth. . . ." [44] Further correspondence made it clear that Austin had faith in Siegfried Stern of the Foreign Department but in addition wanted a very high-level officer with strategic responsibilities for development of the Equitable's world position. By the end of September 1929 he was reporting to Morgan, who was finding it difficult to clear away his existing obligations, that Charles Mitchell of the National City Bank had a comparable idea.[45]

The problem of the Equitable's German loans had been very much on Winthrop Aldrich's mind, and if anyone knew the German situation it was Morgan. Accordingly, on the day that he assumed the presidency of the Equitable, Aldrich wrote Morgan: "It has been my privilege as counsel for the bank to have been in very close association with Mr. Austin during the last two or three months and to know the plans which he had in mind. I want you to know that I am in hearty agreement with the plan which he had in mind in his correspondence with you and I hope that you will come to see me when you are in New York in February." [46] Since Morgan was deeply involved in the implementation of the recent Young Plan and the establishment of the Bank for International Settlements, it was March 1930 before he arrived in New York to accept the vice presidency for which negotiations had commenced nearly a year before.

Meantime, Aldrich had been examining various possible mergers that would strengthen the Equitable's management and allow him to return to the practice of law. In his words, "The understanding I had when I became President was that I would be authorized to negotiate with some other bank that would give first class management to the merged institution." [47] Other banks were, of course, aware of Aldrich's search for a suitable partner for the Equitable, and they sounded him out with respect to their institutions. Donald Campbell recalls that Winthrop Aldrich dropped into his office after one such conversation and mentioned it to him. Campbell said: "If we are going to merge again, let us consider one of the larger banks, and make one more merger," and he suggested the Chase.[48] This suggestion was a natural one for Campbell to make. He had come up through the Mercantile Trust Company with Chellis Austin, and the Mercantile had been organized at the instance of Albert Wiggin for the benefit of the Chase National Bank. As Campbell put it: "I knew Mr. Wiggin well; he had offered me two or three interesting jobs; and furthermore, as you know, Mr. Wiggin at that time was regarded as one of the top bankers in the country." [49]

While Campbell was probably not the first to suggest a merger with the Chase to Winthrop Aldrich, the Equitable's new president certainly shared Campbell's view of Wiggin. As Aldrich recalled many years later, "The Board of Directors — and I also — looked upon Albert Wiggin as *the* leading banker in New York, because he had been so courageous and so active in stemming the tide of the whole crisis that started in 1929." [50]

THE CHASE-EQUITABLE MERGER

Albert H. Wiggin and the Chase National Bank

There was no question that Wiggin had an outstanding record of banking accomplishments. Born at Medfield, Massachusetts, in 1868, he completed high school in 1885 and went to work as a clerk in the Commercial Bank of Boston. After serving as a national bank examiner, he became assistant cashier of the Third National Bank of Boston. In 1897 he was made a vice president of the Eliot National Bank. Two years later he moved to New York as vice president of the National Park Bank, and in 1904 he was elected a vice president and director of the Chase National Bank. [51]

The Chase National Bank of New York City had been organized in 1877, with the controlling interest held by John Thompson, a lottery dealer who was something of a legend on Wall Street. Thompson had been the author of Thompson's *Bank Note Reporter*, an authoritative source of information on state bank currency, and he was an admirer of Salmon Portland Chase, Lincoln's Secretary of the Treasury. During Lincoln's administration the National Bank Act was adopted, and Thompson and his son were the organizers of the First National Bank of New York City, the first institution to take advantage of the new law. Its welfare was appreciably advanced when Secretary Chase named it a government depository, and when Thompson sold out of the First National and organized a new national bank he named it for Chase.[52]

Thompson had been optimistic about the future of his newly organized bank. The worst of the aftermath of the Panic of 1873 had passed, and in his words: "Everything has touched bottom and got as low as it can. If there be any change at all it must be for the better. A bank which has no real estate, not a debt in the world, no law suits, and plenty of cash need fear nothing." [53] Some 60 years later Winthrop Aldrich was to find the state of economic affairs about the same, though the bank's position was much less favorable when he picked up from where Albert Wiggin left off. But in 1930, when the Equitable's merger with the Chase was being arranged, there was no indication that things would turn out that way.

Wiggin had joined the Chase at the invitation of George F. Baker, Sr., of the First National, a substantial stockholder in the Chase, and Henry P. Davison, at that time one of Baker's vice presidents.[54] In 1911 Wiggin succeeded A. B. Hepburn as president of the bank, and in 1918 he took over the chairmanship as well.

Under Wiggin, the Chase organized a securities affiliate in 1917 and, as noted earlier, backed the Mercantile Trust Company to extend its range of services. During the 1920s the Chase grew rapidly and impressively. From assets of less than $500 million in 1918, it grew by expansion from within, as well as by merger, to a bank with nearly $1.5 billion in assets by January 1929. Stockholders benefited handsomely. An investor who bought stock in January 1919 and held it for the decade would have received an average annual return of about 27 percent, including dividends and market apprecia-

tion.[55] About $4.00 of the annual $18.00 dividend was attributable to earnings of the Chase Securities Corporation. The
shares of this affiliate engaged in the underwriting and distribution of securities were printed back-to-back with those
of the bank, making a stockholder in the latter automatically
a stockholder in the affiliate. This relationship was to confront Winthrop Aldrich with some of his most serious problems as a banker, culminating in his decision to seek its prohibition by federal statute.

TABLE V-3

GROWTH OF THE CHASE NATIONAL BANK: 1920–1930

Year Ending	Capital	Surplus and Undivided Profits	Deposits	Total Resources
1920	$15,000,000	$24,990,300	$351,346,700	$534,938,100
1921	20,000,000	21,104,400	359,162,500	425,264,500
1922	20,000,000	22,057,400	466,349,900	528,342,300
1923	20,000,000	23,706,900	437,467,200	496,228,000
1924	20,000,000	25,461,600	570,787,200	641,715,700
1925	20,000,000	27,178,000	564,608,800	638,050,200
1926	40,000,000	38,204,500	852,456,100	968,967,300
1927	50,000,000	55,674,800	792,339,500	1,001,292,700
1928	60,000,000	77,498,400	1,126,781,600	1,430,308,200
1929	105,000,000	136,364,100	1,248,218,400	1,714,829,400
1930	148,000,000	213,523,927	1,852,295,045	2,432,434,809

SOURCE: Bond & Goodwin, Inc., 1930.

In 1929, however, these problems lay in the future, and
the tempo of expansion by the Chase quickened. In January
Wiggin's bank acquired the Garfield National Bank and in
August the National Park Bank, where Wiggin had started his
New York career. Meanwhile, Chase Securities had added
ownership of the venerable American Express Company.[56]
By early 1930 the only New York banks leading the Chase
in deposits were the National City and the Guaranty Trust.[57]
There were numerous changes in the top management of
the Chase during this period. Robert L. Clarkson became

president of the bank in 1928, succeeding John McHugh who had served only two years in that post. McHugh moved up to chairman of the executive committee, following Gates W. McGarrah who was appointed president of the new Bank for International Settlements. After the merger with the National Park Bank the following year, Clarkson became vice chairman of the Chase board, and Charles S. McCain, a native of Arkansas and previously a vice president of the National Park Bank, became president of the Chase National Bank. The presidency under Wiggin seemed to be almost a temporary assignment.

Negotiation and Outcome of the Merger

In the merger negotiations with the Equitable Trust Company, McCain and Wiggin acted for the Chase, and Campbell and Aldrich for the Equitable.[58] Among the law firms involved was Masten & Nichols, which had served the Seaboard. The senior partner, Albert G. Milbank, proved particularly helpful to Aldrich, and in March 1931 Masten & Nichols was merged with Aldrich's old firm,[59] which has served the Chase ever since.

Inevitably the news of the negotiations between the Equitable and the Chase began to spread in the New York financial district. On March 7, 1930, Milbank suggested that Aldrich and Wiggin confirm the negotiations publicly to avoid further speculation and to inform stockholders and other interested parties that the possibilities of merger were being explored.[60] *The New York Times* carried this news the following day.

Another important consideration in the decision to make this public announcement was the fact that it might aid the negotiations to include the Interstate Trust Company in the merger. This bank had been organized in 1926, and while its resources were small compared with the Equitable's and the

Chase's, they had been swelled by several mergers in the late 1920s. Following the Equitable-Seaboard merger, George Le Blanc, who had headed the Equitable's foreign department, left the merged institutions to head the Interstate Trust Company.[61] The planners of the Equitable-Chase merger were not, however, as interested in these facts as in the physical facilities of the Interstate. It had leased the old Equitable building with its entrance on Wall Street, a convenience which the other two large banks lacked.[62] Milbank felt that a public announcement of the Equitable-Chase negotiations would strengthen Aldrich's hand in dealing with the Interstate group.

One of the key decisions involved in the Equitable-Chase merger was whether it should follow the procedure of merging a federally chartered national bank into a state-chartered trust company, requiring the abandonment of the federal charter, or of maintaining the two types of banks under common control, as had been the case with the National City Bank and the Farmers' Loan & Trust Company.* Chellis Austin had merged the Mercantile Trust into the Seaboard National in 1922, but that bank had in turn been merged into the Equitable Trust Company in 1929. In each instance the management group that Austin had developed took over the key positions in the larger merged institution. The situation in 1930, however, was different. Because of the Chase National Bank's size and Wiggin's prominence, the decision was made that the Chase would be the survivor. This meant that top management would be composed largely of men who had come up under Wiggin. To preserve the other partner's name, a new Equitable Trust would be created and maintained for at least a few years.

* The merger pattern used in the Chase-Equitable-Interstate merger was compared with that used in other New York bank mergers in *The New York Times*, May 7, 1930.

The decision in favor of the Chase created the problem of how the Equitable's contribution to the merger would be recognized in the top echelons of Chase management. Since both institutions had been the product of numerous mergers, there were many officers as well as a staggering number of directors to accommodate. The delicacy of the situation was indicated when Lyman Rhoades and Donald Campbell of the Equitable were directed to cooperate with their opposite numbers in the Chase. It was specifically stated that there should be no titles assigned.[63]

Decisions on these problems were particularly relevant to Winthrop Aldrich's own position in the merged institutions. He had accepted the Equitable's presidency as an interim step, and he had regarded the merger with the Chase as the final step toward providing a strong management succession that would enable him to step out of the picture. In fact, his own goal at this point was to return to the practice of law, becoming general counsel to the merged banks.[64]. Until the trauma of merger was past, however, it seemed appropriate for him to assume the post of president of the Chase National in fairness to the Equitable's contribution and interests.

This arrangement necessarily called for a reshuffling of posts in the top echelons of the Chase. To give Albert Wiggin an appropriate place, the position of chairman of the Governing Board, copied from the Bank of England, was created. John McHugh remained chairman of the Executive Committee, and Charles McCain was elevated to chairman of the Board of Directors. Aldrich was the sole Equitable officer in the highest circles of the merged banks.[65]

Naturally there was a great deal of surprise at his appointment. There were some who predicted that Aldrich, who had only been a banker for six months, would not last a fortnight in his new position. However, he was not easily awed or intimidated, and he was confident of his ability to meet the challenge. As one who witnessed his adjustment to his new responsibilities recalled it: "Mr. Aldrich joined this crowd. I say 'crowd' because it seemed like a crowd — so many top executives. He was very quiet. He did not demand anything in particular. He took his place at a desk. He began to know just what was going on, and to take part in the discussion. It did not take them long to realize that they had a very able citizen as the new president of the bank." [66]

Aldrich's acceptance by the banking community was insured when George F. Baker, Sr., of the First National Bank of New York, gave a dinner for the new president of the Chase to which he invited leading bankers.[67] Andrew and Richard Mellon also gave a dinner in honor of Aldrich, and these expressions of confidence confirmed his acceptance as a member of "the fraternity" to which Albert Wiggin had welcomed him a few months before.

Aldrich was president of a mammoth institution. In terms of total resources the Chase surpassed The Midland Bank, Ltd., for many years the world's largest bank. Second place went to the National City Bank, followed by the Midland and Lloyds Bank of London, with the Guaranty Trust of New York in fifth place.[68] Before the merger, the Chase had 27 branches in New York City, the Equitable had 12, and the Interstate 11. These branches now came under common direction, and to the Equitable's overseas branches, the Chase added its offices in Cuba, the Panama Canal Zone, and the Republic of Panama. The Chase Securities Corporation, of which Winthrop Aldrich became vice chairman, had widespread operations and controlled the American Express Company with 34 domestic and Canadian offices and 66 overseas.[69]

At the end of the first month's operations of the merged banks, total deposits topped $2 billion.[70] The problems of managing a bank of this size in an era of national depression and worldwide financial chaos were unprecedented, but Aldrich had an experienced and able group of associates fully capable of meeting this challenge with his leadership and support. Neither he nor they, however, realized the full extent of the problems to which the merged banks would soon fall heir as the result of Wiggin's approach to banking.

CHAPTER VI

The Years of Revelation, 1930-1932

ALTHOUGH Winthrop Aldrich may have hoped to re-turn to the practice of law after the Equitable-Chase merger, his career had been profoundly altered by that development and he realized it. Writing to a friend in March 1930, he reported the merger plans and stated: "This latter event means, I think, that I will have enlisted permanently in the ranks of bankers." [1] His prediction proved true, partly because events over which he had no control soon left him with no acceptable alternative. By 1933 he had been cast in the role of spokesman for a new generation of bankers who had to reestablish banking's reputation for integrity, which bank failures and revelations of "insider operations" had severely tarnished in the public's view. In his own institution he found himself faced with the need to exert strong leadership to overcome problems that he did not dream existed when he had accepted the presidency of the Chase.

Aldrich had not sought these new roles, but he was well equipped to handle them. Above all, he was not personally tarnished by the banking practices that came under heavy fire in the early 1930s. Personal conviction had kept him from involvement in the speculative plunges of other top men in the New York banking community. His high position in the

TABLE VI-1

BANKS MERGED INTO
THE CHASE NATIONAL BANK OF THE CITY OF NEW YORK, 1921–1930

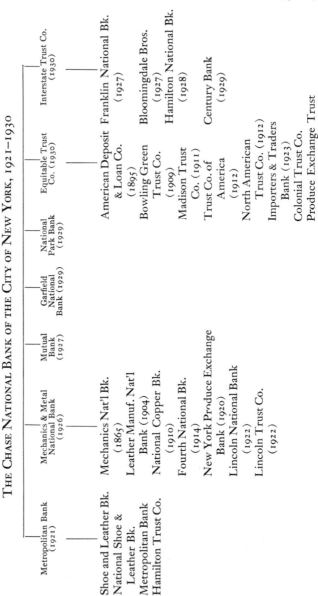

Metropolitan Bank (1921)
- Shoe and Leather Bk.
- National Shoe & Leather Bk.
- Metropolitan Bank
- Hamilton Trust Co.

Mechanics & Metal National Bank (1926)
- Mechanics Nat'l Bk. (1865)
- Leather Manuf. Nat'l Bank (1904)
- National Copper Bk. (1910)
- Fourth National Bk. (1914)
- New York Produce Exchange Bank (1920)
- Lincoln National Bank (1922)
- Lincoln Trust Co. (1922)

Mutual Bank (1927)

Garfield National Bank (1929)

National Park Bank (1929)

Equitable Trust Co. (1930)
- American Deposit & Loan Co. (1895)
- Bowling Green Trust Co. (1909)
- Madison Trust Co. (1911)
- Trust Co. of America (1912)
- North American Trust Co. (1912)
- Importers & Traders Bank (1923)
- Colonial Trust Co.
- Produce Exchange Trust Co.

Interstate Trust Co. (1930)
- Franklin National Bk. (1927)
- Bloomingdale Bros. (1927)
- Hamilton National Bk. (1928)
- Century Bank (1929)

Van Norden Trust Co.
City Trust Co.
New York Real Estate
  Guaranty Co.
Citizens Loan Agency &
  Guaranty Co.
International Banking &
  Trust Co.
American Bond & Mortgage
  Guaranty Co.

Seaboard National
  Corp.
Seaboard National
  Bank (1929)

Seaboard Bank (1883)
Mercantile National
  Bank (1922)
Mercantile Trust Co.
  (1922)
Mercantile Trust &
  Deposit Co. (1922)
New Netherlands
  Bank (1928)

SOURCES: Trust Companies Magazine, July 1925, pp. 45–46.
Chase National Bank, *Annual Reports.*
Aldrich papers.

Chase management and his reputation as an outstanding lawyer insured that his views on banking reform would receive
widespread attention. As a result, he was in an unusually good
position to speak frankly about banking ills, to insist that his
own bank and the banking community put their houses in
order, and — above all — to have credibility when he sought
public understanding and support for his recommendations.
Moreover, he could speak with special conviction as a result
of his own education in banking between 1930 and 1933.

Aldrich had assumed the presidency of the Chase National
Bank with little actual experience in banking as such and with
a surprising degree of naiveté about the conduct of some commercial and investment banking affairs. Although he sat on
the board of Chase Securities, he was not aware of the problems that its activities had been creating for its parent institution, the bank of which he was president. Only slowly
did he begin to perceive some of the underlying problems that
the Chase had brought to the merger that he had helped to
promote. Their full import did not become apparent until
Albert Wiggin was mercilessly grilled by the Pecora Committee in 1933. By that time Aldrich had succeeded to Wiggin's place in the bank and was charged with clearing up the
wreckage left in the wake of this investigation and with
building a new organization made up of men of his own choos-
ing. In 1930 any prediction that this would be his lot would
have sounded absurd to the lawyer who still had hopes of
returning to his chosen profession. In a literal sense, then, the
years 1930–1932 were years of revelation to Winthrop
Aldrich.

President of the Chase

When Aldrich moved his office from the Equitable's building on Broad Street to the new 36-story Chase home office

building on Pine Street in June 1930, he entered a new world both physically and figuratively. That short migration symbolized the fact that the Chase organization was dominant in the merger and that Aldrich would have to work through and within it. As counsel to the Equitable he had come to know and had had the opportunity to evaluate its officers, but he only knew the top Chase men and their organization by casual contact. His personal problem of integrating with them was only one facet of the larger problem of melding the two institutions and their staffs, totaling over 400 officers and 8,000 employees.

Officers of the Merged Banks

The Equitable's officers moved into the new situation without the loss of a man, but a few did not remain long. Among them was John Traphagen, who had come up the banking ladder under Chellis Austin. Although a vice president of the merged banks and, at the invitation of Mr. Wiggin, also a director, he had reservations about working in such a large institution. One reason Winthrop Aldrich had accepted its presidency was to protect the interests of the Equitable's personnel. Thus, when Traphagen approached the new Chase president with news that he had been offered the presidency of The Bank of New York, Aldrich was prepared. As Traphagen remembered it, Aldrich already knew about the offer and said: "It's an attractive job, but I think if you stay here a while longer you might feel differently about it." [2] However, there was no intimation of what the passage of time might bring, and Traphagen decided to accept the position at The Bank of New York. To lose him to the presidency of another New York bank was obviously a compliment to the calibre of the officers with whom Aldrich was associated.

The Equitable group found their opposite numbers in the Chase to be very competent bankers; Wiggin knew how to pick good men. They included Carl Schmidlapp and Sherrill Smith, senior loan officers, Joseph Rovensky of the Foreign Department, Reeve Schley and George Warren of the Trust Department, Maurice Ewer who had charge of bank loans, and Dr. B. M. Anderson, economist. In them, and others from the Chase group, Aldrich was to find loyal and able support.

As the frequent turnover of Chase presidents in the 1920s had shown, Wiggin had found less success in selecting the right individual to fill this key position.[3] This perhaps explains in part why Wiggin himself had taken such an active part in the bank's management. The merger with the Equitable offered him relief. While the Equitable's major stockholders had obvious reasons to want Winthrop Aldrich as president of the merged banks, this move also gave Wiggin a welcome opportunity to test a new man in a critical position. He soon put Aldrich to the test and indicated his confidence in the new president by departing for Europe in the summer of 1930, shortly after Aldrich had assumed his new duties.

Percy Ebbott, himself later president of the Chase, recalled how Albert Wiggin operated from the corner office on the fourth floor of the Chase building after the merger.

> . . . We had a loan meeting, every morning, and all the loans that were approved, or lines of credit that were approved at the morning loan meeting [were put on] a tissue sheet just as soon as that meeting was over, and that tissue sheet went to Mr. Wiggin's office. Mr. Wiggin, inasmuch as I was the head credit officer from the Equitable Trust Company, was very much in the habit of sending for me. And . . . here was some name we'd brought from the Equitable Trust Company, and he'd look at it and he'd say, "Ebbott, what's this?" — and the tone of his voice indicated he didn't think much of it. But it was largely because he didn't know it. He knew his own names [of borrowers] in the Chase National Bank, but he didn't know the Equitable.

Well, that went on for, oh, six months or a year, until he began to get some familiarity with our names, and then it was easier going.[4]

Wiggin had reason to know the Chase accounts well, because he had secured many of them himself. Moreover, for those who ran into trouble, his support was assured. In fact, the alacrity, steadfastness, and success with which he had conducted rescue operations in the backwash of the 1929 debacle was one of the attractions for the Equitable's merger with the Chase National. In the long run his courage and loyalty to the bank's customers also paid off. The companies that Wiggin aided thereafter looked to the Chase as "their" bank.

Going back to the days before World War I, when the Chase was still a small bank, Wiggin's developmental strategy had involved the selection of his directors from the top ranks of American industry. As early as 1915, for example, he had been able to add Guy E. Tripp, chairman of the board of Westinghouse Electric & Manufacturing Company, and Charles M. Schwab, chairman of the board of Bethlehem Steel Company, to his board of directors. In 1917 he brought in, among others, Newcomb Carlton, president of Western Union, and Frederick Ecker, at that time treasurer of the Metropolitan Life Insurance Company. Ecker subsequently became chairman of Metropolitan Life, and it was through Ecker's chance encounter with Thomas Debevoise at Wiggin's cottage on a plantation near Charleston, South Carolina, that the Metropolitan Life Insurance Company took a large share of the bonds issued to finance construction of Rockefeller Center.[5] In later years Ecker was a highly valued adviser to Winthrop Aldrich, particularly on real estate matters.

Complementing the selection of influential directors for the Chase was Wiggin's own service on other boards. He became a director of more than 50 companies, and the usual condition of his service was that they maintain an account with his bank.

Such personal contacts were given an institutional status with the formation of a New Business Committee, composed of Chase directors, which made industrial corporations and railroads capitalized at more than $10 million its particular targets.[6] Although the bank spent up to $2 million a year in seeking new business, most significant new accounts came from the efforts of directors and referrals by existing customers. For example, the systematic cultivation of such contacts, plus the flight of deposits from weaker uptown banks, added $11 million to Chase deposits between February and November 1930.[7]

The Board of Directors

On the board of the Chase National when the Equitable Trust was merged with it were many leaders of American business. They included Arthur G. Hoffman of the Great Atlantic & Pacific Tea Company; Alfred P. Sloan, Jr. of General Motors; H. W. Endicott of Endicott, Johnson Company; E. D. Babst of American Sugar Refining Company; and others equally prominent in American industry. To this group the Equitable added an equally prestigous group. They included Hugh Blair-Smith, treasurer of American Telephone and Telegraph; Walter Carpenter, Jr., vice president of E. I. DuPont de Nemours & Company; Howard Cole, vice president of Standard Oil of New York; Roy E. Tomlinson, chairman of National Biscuit Company; George Whaley, president of Vacuum Oil Company; Henry Whiton, president of Union Sulphur Company; plus a sprinkling of corporation lawyers and investment bankers like Charles Hayden of Hayden, Stone & Co., and Otto Kahn of Kuhn, Loeb & Co.

The roster of over 80 directors of the merged banks read like a "Who's Who" of American business and finance, but it was a completely unwieldy body. One of Winthrop Aldrich's early objectives was to cut it to a more manageable size without offending those who had to be dropped. However, the problem grew worse in the summer of 1930 because the number of directors was further increased when Chase Securities acquired the Harris Forbes Companies.[8]

Acquisition of Harris Forbes Companies

The Harris Forbes Companies owned the Harris Forbes operating companies with offices in some 50 cities in the United States and foreign offices in Montreal, London, and Paris. Acquisition of the companies was by a transfer of stock with Chase Securities, which of course made the former owners of these companies also substantial stockholders in the Chase National Bank. Four of them — Lloyd Waddell Smith, John R. Macomber, E. Carleton Granbery, and Henry M. Addinsell — became members of the bank's swollen board, while others associated with the Harris Forbes organization were added to the board of the Securities Company. In return, Albert Wiggin, Winthrop Aldrich, and five other Chase officers took places on the Harris Forbes board.[9]

The large Harris Forbes organization had its beginnings as the Chicago firm of N. W. Harris and Co. in 1882. Subsequently branches were opened in Boston (1886) and New York (1890). In 1907 the Chicago operation was reorganized as the Harris Trust and Savings Bank, while the eastern offices were incorporated with ownership vested in the eastern partners under the leadership of Allan Forbes. The Harris Forbes Companies remained exclusively in the bond business until 1929 when the Harris Forbes Corporation was established as a means of entering the stock distributing field.[10]

Acquisition of the Harris Forbes Companies added two important dimensions to Chase Securities' activities: a major distributing organization and a list of valuable clients. As pioneers in municipal and public utility bonds, the Companies had worked with two large investment trusts, United Founders Corporation and American Founders Corporation, each with extensive interests in public utilities.[11] This brought under common banking sponsorship a group of public utility companies with assets in excess of $5 billion.[12] Also, the Harris Forbes organization had been active in financing the American Telephone and Telegraph Company, a substantial operation in which Chase Securities had not been a participant.

The Harris Forbes Companies continued to operate under their separate executive management until July 1931 when a formal merger with Chase Securities Corporation created the Chase Harris Forbes Corporation.* Its nationwide network of offices was connected by private wire to the New York headquarters in the Chase National Bank building. The merged corporation was one of the world's largest engaged in the retail and wholesale distribution of securities.[13]

Banking Operations

As a result of the Equitable merger, the Chase National Bank's physical facilities were at this time spread all over New York's financial district. The Chase Trust Department moved in with the old Equitable's department at 11 Broad Street, making a total of some 70 officers and 1500 employees in this activity alone. Direction of this Department was shared by Lyman Rhoades, who came from the Equitable, and George Warren from the Chase.[14] A special trust committee, of which Winthrop Aldrich was a member, supervised this important activity.[15]

Although he was interested in all departments of the bank, the new Chase president took a special interest in the Foreign Department. This was natural because much of his legal work

* Only the Boston office chose to remain separate and became Chase Harris Forbes of Boston.

for the Equitable had involved its foreign accounts, and the Equitable's contribution to the merger with the Chase lay fully as much in this area as in the trust business. Furthermore, by far the largest element of Chase commercial loans involved foreign trade. Out of total commercial loans in excess of $502 million in 1930, some $186 million were in this category.[16] Therefore, not only personal inclination but the bank's existing, as well as potential, overseas commitments justified Aldrich's interest in this area.

To conduct its foreign business more effectively, the Chase National Bank in May 1930 had sponsored the organization of the Chase Bank under the provisions of the Edge Act of 1919.* This Act permitted a banking corporation, engaged primarily in financing trade overseas, to conduct its business with considerably more freedom than could an overseas branch of a domestic bank. After the merger, the Equitable's Paris office and the Equitable Eastern's offices in Hongkong, Shanghai, and Tientsin were assigned to the new Edge Act corporation, of which Winthrop Aldrich became president.

From his days as legal counsel to the Equitable Trust Company Aldrich was familiar with one of the major problems that confronted the Chase in 1930 as the result of its interest in foreign trade. This problem involved a shipment of $5 million in gold bars that the government of the Soviet Union had delivered in equal amounts to the Chase and the Equitable early in 1928 as security for Russian purchases of machinery and other capital goods in the United States. When the Bank of France learned of this shipment, it brought action against both banks to recover the gold, claiming that the Russians had unlawfully appropriated gold that the French had de-

---

* The first Edge Act corporation was the First Federal Banking Corporation, which received a permit in 1926. (Beckhart, *The New York Money Market*, Vol. III, pp. 273–274.)

posited in the State Bank of the Russian Empire during World War I. One of Aldrich's last legal assignments before taking over the presidency of the Equitable had been to set up a defense against this claim.[17]

The actual handling of the subsequent trial work fell to Embree and MacKinnon of Aldrich's old firm. They won the case by showing that the gold deposited in New York was not physically the same gold that the Bank of France had deposited in the State Bank at Petrograd.[18] The meticulous research to support this contention was very reminiscent of the strategy and procedure employed by Aldrich to win the Equitable's case against the recalcitrant sugar buyers following World War I.*

Visit to Overseas Branches

Although Aldrich had talked with the managers of the Equitable's London and Paris branches in New York prior to the merger, he wanted to see for himself the state of affairs in Europe and to review the progress of the London and Paris offices in the wake of the merger. Soon after Albert Wiggin returned from abroad and the completion of the 1930 America's Cup races, Mr. and Mrs. Aldrich, accompanied by Charles McCain, E. H. Gannon and Lynde Selden of the Foreign Department, boarded ship for an extended European visit. Starting in Berlin, they covered most of the Continent. As Aldrich later reported to a friend: "We had a very interesting trip in Europe where we visited every country except Russia, Poland, and the more easterly of the Balkan countries. As you can imagine we did not find a very cheerful situation. The whole world seems to be very much depressed these days." [19]

In Paris the Chase men found that the old Equitable office, newly placed under the Edge Act corporation, and the

* See Chapter III.

Chase National Bank branch were functioning smoothly, and they moved on to London. Under the direction of an able Scot, John M. Wallace, the Chase National had two London offices. One, at 10 Moorgate E.C. 2, was close to the Bank of England. The other, Bush House, Aldwych W.C. 2, was close to the Strand, hotels and shops. These offices were in effect complete banks in themselves, and part of the consultations between the home office representatives and Wallace concerned ways in which these facilities could be made better known to American corporations doing business abroad. Other topics discussed were coordination with New York and policies governing solicitation of deposits and investment of these deposits.[20]

When Aldrich paid a courtesy call on Montagu Norman, Governor of the Bank of England, his cool reception was testimony to his newness in the club of international bankers. In later years, however, Norman warmly welcomed Aldrich as a friend.

Although the Chase officers found many rumors in Europe about the difficulties of New York banks, the Chase ended 1930 in good condition. In November, for example, an investment advisory service compared the Chase with other New York banks and concluded that "its stock would seem to be selling in line with other New York bank stocks and at present prices (about $120) represents an investment opportunity." [21] In the Chase annual report, Albert Wiggin also took an optimistic view of the future. After explaining his view of the causes of the depression, including high tariffs, low money rates, and excessive credits, he declared: "I think we are approximately at the worst of the depression, and that the next important move will be upward. . . . I expect conditions at the end of 1931 to be a good deal better than they are at the end of 1930." [22] Unfortunately, his optimism proved to be ill-founded.

The German Problem

At the start of the new year Winthrop Aldrich was distinctly uncomfortable about the bank's foreign exposure, especially in Germany. In October 1930 the Chase had participated in a major loan to the German government,[23] and in December the bank's total German commitments had reached an all-time high of $147.5 million.[24] One purpose of his European trip had been to ascertain the possibilities of reducing such foreign commitments, and when he returned to New York this became one of his primary objectives.

Germany's financial problem was serious. The nation vanquished in World War I had suffered from an adverse balance of trade, but prior to 1929 foreign loans had made it possible for her to pay reparations to the victorious Allies. When the loans had stopped, Germany's budgetary problem became acute. Central to the solution of this problem was the fact that reparations called for about 16 percent of the country's budgetary outlay.[25]

Repayment of war debts by the Allies to the United States was largely contingent on their receipt of reparations payments from Germany. When general European financial collapse occurred in the spring of 1931, the weaknesses of these international financial relationships were fully revealed. By June 1, 1931, all lines of credit were closed to Germany.

Shepherd Morgan, the Chase vice president who had been close to the reparations problem for a number of years, was especially well equipped to handle the problems posed by this development. He spent some time in Germany early in 1931 and returned with firsthand information on the situation. Together with Dr. Benjamin Anderson, the bank's economist, Morgan worked out a proposal for dealing with the German problem.[26] The plan was for Winthrop Aldrich to place the proposal personally before President Herbert

Hoover, whom Aldrich had actively supported for high office since 1920. The date selected for their meeting was June 19, 1931. As the finishing touches were being placed on the presentation, however, the Chase officers learned that Hoover had made up his mind to propose a moratorium on interallied war debts. Since the Chase plan was no longer relevant, Aldrich's presentation to Hoover was canceled.

Hoover's announcement of the moratorium set a new train of events in motion. The president of the German Reichsbank wired suggestions on the handling of the situation, and the leading New York banks, commercial and private, decided to establish a committee to deal with the problem of short-term German credits. Albert Wiggin was asked to represent the banks at a conference in Basel, Switzerland, where German creditors from ten nations assembled on August 8. At that time Wiggin was elected chairman of the group, whose deliberations went on sporadically for the next two years. On August 17 he cabled home the text of a "standstill agreement" which would postpone the collection of German and Austrian short-term debts.[27]

By this time the Chase had significantly reduced its German position. With Aldrich's active initiative and support, the bank cut its German commitments in half compared to the year before. Of the $71 million remaining by November 30, 1931, only $46 million was subject to the standstill,[28] which had gone into effect on September 17. Eventually these loans were fully repaid and in the interim Aldrich served on various committees composed of bankers concerned with this problem.

Affiliates of the Chase

Meantime, steps had been taken to bring into a coherent organization the many-faceted activities of the Chase's varied affiliates. As previously noted, the securities-distributing business of Chase Securities Corporation and of Harris Forbes was consolidated under the name of Chase Harris Forbes Corporation in July 1931.[29] In December the general banking business of the American Express Bank and Trust Company, organized in April 1930 to capitalize on the American Express name and to supplement that company's services, was transferred to the Chase National Bank, while the affiliate's trust business was assigned to the new Equitable Trust Company created at the time of the Chase merger to protect the name and controlled through Chase Securities.[30]

Winthrop Aldrich had become a director of American Express in October 1930 and therefore was privy to the discussions relating to it. Almost 98 percent of the stock of this company was in the hands of Chase Securities, and in the early part of 1931 considerable thought was given to liquidating American Express and transferring its liquid assets to Chase Securities and its travelers check and letter of credit business to the Chase National Bank. The minority stockholders, however, did not favor such a plan. Their opposition proved decisive, since to move ahead required unanimous consent. The possibility that the minority could be bought out receded when the price of American Express stock rose in June 1931.[31] For the time being the company remained a Chase property.

A Legacy of Problems

In connection with American Express, Winthrop Aldrich began to appreciate more fully the problems that he had inherited as a result of the merger. The Clearing House Examiner's report to the Chase board, submitted on August 5, 1931, showed that Chase officers were borrowing from the American Express Bank and also from Metpotan Securities Corporation, securing their loans with Chase National Bank stock.[32]

Metpotan had been organized in 1921 following the merger

of the Metropolitan Bank with the Chase. Like American Express, it was another subsidiary of Chase Securities, and its original purpose had been to take over Metropolitan's mortgages that the Chase did not want.[33] Later Metpotan had been used to buy and sell Chase National Bank stock.[34] These activities, conducted partly with funds borrowed from Chase Securities, had helped to raise the price of Chase National Bank stock in the late 1920s.[35]

The revelation that bank officers were borrowing from subsidiaries of their own bank, a practice encouraged by Wiggin, alarmed Aldrich and the Rockefeller representatives on the Chase board. With Wiggin in Europe on the German standstill question, investigation of this new problem was specifically assigned to a committee of the directors. Aldrich also asked all officers for a statement of their position with respect to loans.[36]

At this time England was on the verge of abandoning the gold standard, and on September 14 Wiggin cabled Aldrich that he was concerned about the price of Chase National Bank stock and would be willing to take a one-third interest with a group in the purchase of 100,000 shares. It was Wiggin's custom to protect Chase stock in such a manner and to encourage his officers to do likewise. The following day Aldrich cabled back to London that he had only been able to form a group to take 30,000 shares and had put Wiggin down for 10,000 of them.[37] Presumably Aldrich took an interest himself, but unlike some of the other Chase officers he never borrowed from the bank to finance such purchases.

Aldrich still did not know of the close connections that existed between Chase Securities and its affiliates and investment companies that were controlled by Wiggin or his family, and which were thus given a direct pipeline into the bank itself. However, the Chase president had strong convictions about the inadvisability of banks themselves being directly involved with common stocks. In June 1931, for example, he had written to the president of a Wilmington, Delaware, trust company as follows: "I do not believe that as a matter of investment policy, banks should include common stocks of any kind in their portfolios." [38]

About this time Aldrich learned that the Chase was making large loans to a major investment banking firm without having access to its statement. When he approached the senior partner of the firm about the matter, he was informed that they did not give out statements. However, they were willing to make an exception for him personally. On this basis he was able to obtain statements, which he kept locked in his desk drawer. From them he discovered with amazement that the investment banking house held very substantial deposits and was in effect conducting a commercial banking business without the supervision that state and federal regulations imposed on commercial bankers. [39] This situation became a matter of increasing concern to him, and it was also now becoming clear that the great bank of which he was president might be entangled in arrangements that invited abuses of its fiduciary and moral responsibilities.

In addition to these problems there was the disturbing fact of the continued downward trend of the economy and the resulting danger to the bank's outstanding loans. One of the largest domestic loans had been made to Continental Shares, an investment trust created by Cyrus Eaton of Cleveland, Ohio, in the 1920s. This trust had bought up steel companies and had battled with Samuel Insull over his public utilities empire. A series of court fights growing out of some of these operations culminated in Eaton's retirement from Continental Shares in April 1931, and control was taken over by his friend George T. Bishop and the heads of four Cleveland banks. [40] The Chase had a stake of $30 million in Continental Shares, and in September 1931 Winthrop Aldrich urged that this indebtedness be reduced greatly when the loan came due the following April. Eventually it proved necessary to liquidate the company. In 1933, after the Chase acquired the collateral for its defaulted loan, the deficiency amounted to more than $4.5 million.[41]

In the fall of 1931, the Chase was also deeply involved in a complicated situation growing out of the misfortunes of the film empire created by William Fox. Fox had had a large theatre chain in the United States, with production facilities near Beverly Hills, California, and he was acquiring stock in Loew's, Inc., a domestic competitor, and Gaumont Pictures, an English film concern, when he ran into trouble in 1929.[42] Fox's difficulties interested Harley Clarke, a utilities man and friend of Wiggin, who had organized a company known as General Theatres Equipment, Inc., to supply the movie industry. When it became apparent that Fox was not going to be able to meet his financial commitments, Clarke became concerned. A collapse of this kind could adversely affect the industry and therefore his customers. He also scented an investment opportunity, since it seemed that an investment of about $38 million would meet the immediate problem and secure control of the potentially lucrative business.[43]

Halsey, Stuart & Co. were the Fox bankers, but Clarke worked out a joint financing operation, involving Chase Securities. The total amount of financing eventually amounted to $63 million, or almost double what had been originally anticipated.[44] A substantial amount of this additional money came from the Chase National Bank and Chase Securities in the spring of 1930.[45] Albert Wiggin and his personal investment company, Shermar Corporation, were also involved in some of the syndicates.[46] Subsequent to its merger with the Equitable, the Chase continued to make loans secured by stock in Fox Film and other Clarke enterprises. In April 1931 the balance outstanding stood at $19.7 million.

Fox Film was kept alive, but its movie business failed to prosper. The Fox production head seemed to prefer expensive epic productions which frequently did not repay their costs. Although the company's roster of stars included Will Rogers and Shirley Temple, whose pictures were uniformly successful and were produced on low budgets, these names were not enough to keep Fox Film in the black. In 1933 control of

TABLE VI-2

SUMMARY OF CHASE LOANS TO MR. HARLEY CLARKE
IN CONNECTION WITH FOX FILM FINANCING, 1930–1931

1930	Borrowed	Paid off	Balance owing
Apr. 7: Borrowed to make cash payment to William Fox for Film and Theatres, Class B	$15,000,000	—	$15,000,000
Apr. 18: Borrowed to raise funds to pay for Fox Class A and to retire Apr. 7 loan	27,000,000	$15,000,000	27,000,000
Apr. 30: Borrowed from Chase Securities Corporation	2,000,000	—	29,000,000
May 1: Paid off Apr. 18 note with proceeds from sale of $30,000,000 debentures	—	27,000,000	2,000,000
May 6: Borrowed from Chase National, paid off Apr. 30 loan from Chase Securities	2,500,000	2,000,000	2,500,000
May 7: Borrowed from Chase National	2,500,000	—	5,000,000
May 16: Part payment on May 6 loan	—	1,000,000	—
Oct. 10: Borrowed to retire May 7 loan, balance on May 6 loan, and to provide $6,000,000 new funds	10,000,000	4,000,000	10,000,000
1931			
Apr. 14: Borrowed to purchase 100,000 shares Film Securities Corp. preferred stock	9,700,000	—	19,700,000

SOURCE: 73 Cong., 1 Sess., "Stock Exchange Practices," *Hearings before the Committee on Banking and Currency, United States Senate* (Washington, 1934), 3442.

the property passed to the Chase National Bank. Hermann Place, a Chase vice president, was charged with following Fox matters, in which the bank then had a total interest of over $31 million.[47]

Still another loan that caused Aldrich concern resulted from Albert Wiggin's directorship in International Paper and its allied International Power Securities. Headed by able and aggressive A. R. Graustein, International Paper had received a $2 million loan from the Chase that was uncollateralized, while International Power Securities received $6.25 million which was collateralized.[48] Mr. Graustein also had extensive personal loans from the Chase, and in these troubled times he became a frequent visitor to Winthrop Aldrich's office.*

In yet another area of lending activity there was more serious trouble. The Chase National Bank through loans to Chase Securities, Pynchon & Co., and other investment bankers for syndicate operations, found itself caught up in the problems of the collapsing public utilities business. Through loans to Pynchon, the bank became involved in the affairs of the Washington Gas Light Co., Utilities Power & Light Co., American States Public Service Co., and others.[49] Through Chase Securities it became a party to the troubles of the Utility Equities Company, International Hydroelectric System (a Graustein enterprise), and Central States Power & Light Corporation, to name only a few.[50] The Harris Forbes affiliate was likewise deeply committed to public utilities financing. In 1931, for example, it participated in a syndicate with International Power Securities to purchase the Berlin (Germany) Electric Company.[51] When the complicated structure of

---

* It was reported in early 1937 that Mr. Graustein had turned over to the Chase a substantial amount of stock in International Paper (*Financial & Commercial Chronicle*, Feb. 13, 1937). The Chase already had a substantial interest in the company. Hermann Place shortly became a director and devised an imaginative plan to reorganize the company's capital structure. See Chapter IX.

utilities financing, built up in the 1920s, collapsed during the depression, the Chase National found itself placed in the position of a major public utilities holding company while trying to realize on its collateral.

Fortunately, in Edward Love the Chase had an expert in public utility financing. In the fall of 1931 Winthrop Aldrich told Love that he had decided to establish a Public Utility Department in the Bank.[52] Lawrence Bennett of the old Aldrich law firm had been working closely with Love on public utility problems, and at first Aldrich thought it might be good to have him physically in the new department. However, in the end Bennett remained outside the bank, though working closely and almost daily with Love. The new department was staffed with several engineers, and the Chase, making a virtue of necessity, became the best equipped bank in New York to handle the financing of public utilities. This functional approach to major areas of the bank's interest was a significant organizational innovation, and the utilities department was soon followed by others which overlaid the geographical zone system that had been brought over from the Equitable-Seaboard.[53]

Faced with mounting problems, Aldrich was more interested than ever in reducing the unwieldy board of directors to a manageable and useful size· The handsome board room on the Chase building's fourth floor, modeled after the room in the Sub-Treasury where Congress once met, could not even accommodate the full board. By December 1931 Aldrich was actively discussing how and when the number of directors should be cut.

The year had been a disappointing one at the Chase. Net write-offs totaled $77.2 million, or more than $10.00 a share, with a resulting earnings deficit of $5.37 per share.[54] Lack of business dictated the closing down of some regional offices, including even the important one in Chicago.[55] Although all

the losses for which provision had been made did not materialize, the picture was gloomier than what securities analysts
had forecast for the Chase a year earlier, or what Wiggin's
predictions for 1931 had been.

A WASHINGTON APPEARANCE

New Year's Day 1932 fell on a Friday and ordinarily
Winthrop Aldrich would not have gone near his Pine Street
office over the following weekend. But this weekend was dif-
ferent; he had been asked to appear on Monday before the
Senate Committee on Finance, which was investigating the
sale of foreign bonds and securities in the United States.
Therefore, he spent Saturday in his office preparing for his
Washington appearance.

The issues that interested the Senators were whether American securities companies and banks had misled American investors in the distribution of foreign bonds and securities, or
profited unduly through the arrangements for such distribution. Aldrich went to Washington with complete information
about the participation of the Chase National Bank and its
affiliates in foreign financing and with the resolution to make
these transactions a matter of public record. He had sounded
out other New York banks on their attitude and found them
equally prepared to reveal their participation.

In his presentation to the Senators, the Chase president gave
a brief dissertation on the nature of foreign financing, short-
term credits, and similar matters — particularly as they related
to the German situation. In the process he stressed the currently subordinated place of foreign loans in the Chase National's loan structure. "Eighty-four percent of the commercial loans which the Chase Bank makes are domestic loans,"
he said. Of the remaining 16 percent of foreign loans, ap-
proximately one-third were German.[56]

He defined the primary function of commercial banks in financing foreign trade as the extension of short-term credit. "We find," he said, ". . . that an important amount of such credit finances current shipments of cotton, which, of all commodities so financed, ranks first; then sugar, coffee, wheat, rubber, tobacco, wool, hides, copper, and so on." [57] And he reported that the total of short-term debt of German origin held by 100 leading American institutions was $415 million as of October 31, 1931.[58] The Chase itself held about $69 million.[59] He placed the full record of his bank, its affiliates and predecessors' foreign financing activities in the record.

When Aldrich reported that he had discussed disclosure of these foreign operations with other New York banks, the committee members pressed him hard for the banks' names and an estimate of their obligations. As a lawyer as well as banker, however, he declined to repeat "gossip" or reveal names.[60]

The Chase president made it clear that he had not personally been involved in the loans under discussion and, further, that he considered the manner in which some of them had been made was unfortunate. Competition had led to carelessness if not recklessness. In his words:

> Senator, I have been a banker only for about two years. One of the things I have been very much interested in in the past year is to see the cooperation that is in existence now to ascertain the facts as to the economy of a country to which the banks are making loans.

* * *

> . . . Obviously, in the past the banks have competed with each other in making these loans, and the banking houses, as well, without cooperation and without consultation. I think that has been a very harmful thing, because it has led

to overloaning. But I hope that that is a thing that is very much in the past.[61]

Although Aldrich was willing to testify on the foreign loans handled by Chase Securities and Harris Forbes, he said that he preferred to have representatives of those organizations testify from their firsthand knowledge. The activities in question had antedated his own connection with the bank, and his information would have had to come from the records or from these officers. Accordingly, he was excused and further testimony about these matters was provided by C. P. Anderson, Jr. and E. C. Granbery of Chase Harris Forbes Corporation.

MOUNTING PRESSURES AND PROBLEMS

As the Senators probed the area of foreign loans, the nation had not yet reached the bottom of the depression. To make things worse, England's departure from the gold standard the preceding September was still having serious international repercussions. The resulting problems constituted the chief agenda of Winthrop Aldrich's busy days in 1932.

Aside from stated meetings of the bank and its affiliates, which occupied a good part of each week, his calendar for 1932 shows his attendance at frequent meetings of the committees concerned with Fox Film financing and with public utilities problems, both direct legacies of the depression. He was also carrying a heavy load outside the bank, including service on the Executive Committee of the New York Salvation Army's Emergency Unemployment Relief Committee, work as treasurer of the Welfare Council which coordinated social service and health work in New York City, and active participation in the State Charities Aid Association. He was a trustee of Barnard College and in November 1932 was elected an Overseer at Harvard. The number and demands of these responsibilities grew so rapidly that something had to give. He decided that it had to be his post as Commodore of the New York Yacht Club, to which he had been elected in December 1930. Accordingly he served only two years of the usual three-year term.

As chairman of the governing board, composed of senior officers, Albert Wiggin was still the Chase's top executive. In May 1932, however, Aldrich became vice chairman of the board as well as president, a formal acknowledgement of his growing influence.

By inclination and of necessity, Aldrich kept aloof from the routine activities of the bank except as they impinged on basic strategy decisions. He conserved his time for coping with these larger issues and with major new problems. This was not an easy regime, since it frequently called for a full day in the office followed by an evening at some club, where business dominated the conversation. Fortunately, as numerous of his colleagues from this era testify, Aldrich had an unusual capacity for grasping quickly the essentials of complicated problems and a facility for concentration. The two combined enabled him to master the essence of complex issues in a minimum amount of time, but his absorption in whatever he had in hand made him the despair of secretaries charged with keeping his appointments on schedule.[62]

Aldrich recognized that periodic escape from the tensions of his job was important. Accordingly, he usually managed to keep his weekends free for his family, and in 1932 took a mid-winter holiday with them in Bermuda as well as a summer vacation abroad at The Hague.

It proved difficult, however, to escape from the affairs of an international bank by going abroad. The Aldriches had been in Holland for a fortnight in the summer of 1932 when a Chase vice president wrote: "I gather from our returned travelers that you started your holiday with no holiday at all. I hope that by now you have retired to your jonkheer's villa and contemplate nothing but the sea and the Dutch." [63]

Detached contemplation of the Dutch countryside and waterways was difficult amidst the ebb and flow of national and international politics and finance that were becoming increasingly important to the Chase's future and therefore to Winthrop Aldrich. For example, although President Hoover had called for a moratorium on payment of war debts to the United States, he had left undecided the long-term settlement of the matter. It seemed to some observers that the Republican president had missed an opportunity to insure his reelection. From a less partisan viewpoint his avoidance of the ultimate problem seemed equally unfortunate, because no further action toward a lasting settlement could be taken in a presidential election year. Such a course as forgiving the debtor nations their debts would hardly set well with an American electorate submerged in debt that private creditors would not voluntarily wipe off their books. Although the Democrats' 1932 campaign platform had declared against cancellation of war debts, their presidential candidate, Franklin D. Roosevelt, had not taken an active stand on the question. However, whatever position was taken by either political party, or indeed if no stand were taken, the Chase National Bank would be affected, and Winthrop Aldrich was appraising the various possibilities as he vacationed by the sea in the summer of 1932.

The Chase commitment in Cuba was also on his mind that busy summer. The sugar market, where the bank had long had an interest, was in the doldrums, and Cuba was in both economic and political trouble. Under a law of 1925 the Cuban government had undertaken a major public works program, including construction of a central highway the length of the island to connect the provinces with Havana. Between 1927 and 1930 the Chase National Bank and Chase

Securities, together with the National City Bank and Continental Illinois Bank & Trust Company of Chicago, handled loans to the Cuban government for a total of $81 million, secured by the pledge of specified revenues.[64] In June 1932, just before the Aldriches left for Europe, it became apparent that Cuban revenues were not going to be sufficient to cover interest and maturing principal. Therefore the bankers' group had to extend more credit to help the Cuban government over this crisis.[65] This supposedly short-term credit committed the Chase National for over $9.6 million.[66] In addition, it had in its own account $867,000 of Cuban serial certificates plus public works bonds worth about $3 million at par but less than $1 million in the market.[67] Like so many other of the bank's problems, this one was to come to a head in 1933 — in this instance when a new Cuban government renounced the obligations incurred by its predecessor.[68]

To the seemingly endless number of problems confronting the Chase and Aldrich was added the financial predicament of the City of New York. Under debonair Mayor Jimmy Walker, city expenditures had outstripped city income, and the city government had been kept afloat by short-term bank loans. While the bankers and various citizen groups called for economy in city government, the whole matter became entangled in city politics and power struggles.

The Chase National and the National City Bank had been the leaders in giving financial assistance to the city, but they conditioned their aid on hopes and promises of increased economy in its operations.[69] While Aldrich was abroad in the summer of 1932, charges and countercharges on the economy issue flew back and forth within the city administration. By the time Aldrich returned to his office in September, Walker had resigned as mayor, the financial crisis persisted, and the controversy over economy in city expenditures was as acute as ever. In October Aldrich and Charles Mitchell of the National City Bank held a series of conferences with City Comptroller Berry and finally offered a loan of $18.5 million to cover the city's needs for the month of November plus an additional amount for emergency unemployment relief.[70] The crisis continued while the mayoralty election was held. The proposed city budget for 1933 failed to ease the situation, and bankers' and citizens' groups questioned whether genuine economies were incorporated in it or merely some book-keeping changes.

Meanwhile, New York Governor Franklin D. Roosevelt's victory in the national presidential election gave his role in New York City's affairs unusual significance. He tried to escape involvement in the city's financial crisis and initially opposed calling a special session of the state legislature to change the salary laws and thereby permit reductions in this important element of the city's budget. Aldrich, Mitchell, and the president of the Board of Aldermen, trying to find a solution, conferred with Lieutenant Governor Lehman on December 1, 1932, but with disappointing results. The next afternoon Judge Samuel I. Rosenman, counsel to Roosevelt, was in Aldrich's office to discuss the matter, and for most of the following week Aldrich was occupied with it. Finally, Roosevelt agreed to call the legislature. It made the necessary changes in the salary laws, also meeting the bankers' demands that no time limit be placed on salary cuts.[71] New York's financial problems continued to be a matter of concern, but the worst was over.

WIGGIN STEPS DOWN

At this time, an important change relevant to the handling of these matters occurred at the Chase: Albert Wiggin decided to retire. The Wiggin family had a very substantial stock interest in the Chase, and Wiggin's bank salary for

1932 alone was authorized as $250,000, though this was re-
duced by a general cut of 10 percent in officers' salaries and
an additional 10 percent that he took voluntarily.[72] Wiggin
had been under considerable strain in connection with travel
and negotiations for the German "standstill" agreements and
he was close to his 65th birthday, which under bank policy
marked retirement age. In December 1932 he made known
his decision to step down.

The question of what compensation the bank might give
Wiggin in retirement became a subject of discussion between
him, Aldrich, and other directors.[73] This was no easy decision.
There had been a continuing deterioration of his official relations with Aldrich,[74] and apparently there was concern
among large stockholders that Wiggin's personal interests
might have unduly benefited by his connection with the bank.
In any event, Shermar Corporation, one of Wiggin's personal
investment companies, offered in December 1932 to pay
Chase Securities $1 million in settlement of its part in the Fox
Film financing of 1930. The resulting arrangement with
Shermar was made by Debevoise, Ecker, and Jeremiah Milbank on behalf of the Chase directors, with Aldrich sitting
in. Concurrently, or almost so, the bank's directors agreed
that Wiggin should be paid $100,000 annually on the condi-
tion that he be prepared and willing to consult with the active officers on matters pertaining to the welfare of the bank.[75]

Wiggin had excellent contacts with many of the Chase's
largest accounts, and his advice and assistance with respect
to them were regarded as major assets. This was undoubtedly
the dominant consideration in the size of his post-retirement
compensation, as well as gratitude for his many contributions
to the growth of the world's largest bank. As the unanimous
resolution of the Executive Committee on December 21, 1932,
phrased it, "The Chase National Bank is in no small measure
a monument to his energy, wisdom, vision, and character." [76]

Thus an era in the Chase National Bank's history came to an end — or so the directors apparently thought. Unfortunately, especially from Aldrich's viewpoint, an unhappy postscript was soon to be written. But in December 1932, Aldrich and the Executive Committee, although they may have had suspicions, apparently had no inkling of the real magnitude of the problems which Albert Wiggin was leaving behind, aside from those already enumerated. The years of revelation were not yet at an end.

CHAPTER VII

The Crisis Year, 1933

BY ANY test of historical significance, the year 1933 ranks as one of the most critical in the peacetime history of the United States. As the year opened, the country was struggling in the depths of unprecedented depression, the world economic picture was bleak, business leadership was discredited and unsure of itself, and millions were unemployed and desperate. The outgoing Hoover administration had tried in vain to stem the downward economic spiral, and the incoming Roosevelt administration had refused to commit itself to a course of action in advance of taking office. Before the year was out, however, action had taken the place of paralysis. The "New Deal" had initiated a variety of new approaches to the problems of depression, as well as adapting old approaches to new needs. It was by no means clear where the nation was heading. But that it had begun to move again was unquestionable.

Restoration of faith in the banking system received top priority in the Roosevelt program. To this end, emergency steps were taken immediately after Roosevelt's inauguration, and basic reforms to cope with the abuses that the financial collapse had highlighted took on a new urgency. To the surprise of the general public and the incredulity of many bankers, Winthrop W. Aldrich of the Chase National Bank took a leading role in publicly criticizing practices that had characterized his own bank and in suggesting restrictive legislation that would prevent their recurrence. In this national crisis his contribution to banking reform was as direct as his father's had been in an earlier day. Unlike his father, however, he was responsible for the management of an institution that would be affected in a major way by the reforms that he suggested.

TESTIMONY ON CAUSES OF THE DEPRESSION

During 1933 Aldrich spent much of his time in Washington. After Wiggin's retirement he had become chairman of the Chase's governing board while retaining his post as president. As head of the nation's largest bank, his views on economic and banking problems interested both legislators and the public. There was no popular expectation, however, that in his first Washington appearance in 1933 the Chase president would attack some of the economic policies of the outgoing Hoover administration and more especially the policies of the Federal Reserve. Dr. Benjamin M. Anderson, the Chase's economist, had been a critic of both, and Aldrich also adopted this position.

As part of a plan by the new Democratic leadership to obtain collective business judgment on the problems of depression, and, perhaps more important, to forestall action on innumerable remedial measures until the Roosevelt administration took office, 52 business leaders were invited to testify before the Senate Finance Committee in February 1933.[1] Aldrich was among them. His appearance before the committee came a year after he had first testified before that group. Where he had dealt in 1932 with a relatively specialized problem,* he now addressed a major national one.

Aided by the technical expertise of Dr. Anderson, Aldrich presented his analysis of the causes of depression and possible remedies. He opened his presentation by suggesting that improved communication between government and the financial community would prevent misunderstandings:

> Mr. Chairman: I am glad to appear before you in response to your invitation, not because I have any panacea to present, but because I think it eminently desirable that there should be frank interchange of opinion between those who are charged with responsibility for government and those who are charged with responsibility for finance and for other phases of the economic life of the country. It is in some ways unfortunate that the political capital and the financial capital of the country should be separated. Misunderstandings between the financial community and the Congress have created many needless difficulties. I feel sure that much of this misunderstanding would pass away and better cooperation would exist if we knew one another better personally and had the opportunity of talking more frequently and frankly with one another.[2]

Moving on, Aldrich suggested that the essence of the current economic problem was the imbalance between the agricultural and industrial sectors of the economy. Farmers who had expanded their activities to meet the demands of World War I found themselves in the postwar period without a domestic market that could absorb their output, while the export market, which could have done so, was restricted. This had come about, Aldrich argued, because of high tariffs that prevented imports, plus other government controls on inter-

* See Chapter VI.

national trade. As he saw it, the significance of the imbalance had been obscured during the 1920s by loans that maintained foreign trade. Domestically, he said,[3] the easy money policy followed by the Federal Reserve had contributed to the imbalance, agricultural prices had slumped relative to those of manufactured goods, and speculation was encouraged.*

This analysis was not substantially different from Albert Wiggin's as set forth in the Chase annual report for 1931, and Dr. Anderson undoubtedly contributed substantially to both. But Aldrich propounded it in open forum and defended it with vigor, making it clear that he was personally committed to the propositions he advanced.

For Aldrich, the trigger to business revival lay in the export sector. This, of course, meant reduction of tariffs in direct contrast to the policy that the United States had been following. Farm surpluses had been one of Hoover's greatest problems;[4] as part of a multifaceted attack on the problem he had favored tariff protection for farmers as well as manufacturers.** In reply to the expression of senatorial fears that repudiation of this protectionist approach would add to domestic unemployment, Aldrich argued that the

---

* For a summary and evaluation of Federal Reserve policy in the 1920s and its relation to speculation, see Paul Studenski and Herman E. Krooss, *Financial History of the United States*, 2d ed. (New York, McGraw-Hill Book Co., 1963), pp. 327–343. Although these authors concede that the Federal Reserve made "very serious errors," they doubt the effectiveness of monetary policy in that era to check speculation. They assign heavy responsibility to the Whit House and the Treasury for the tragedy of the decade. For a more detailed analysis of Federal Reserve monetary policy, see Elmus R. Wicker, *Federal Reserve Monetary Policy, 1917–1933* (New York, Random House, 1966). Wicker finds that Federal Reserve officials did not understand how open market operations could be used to combat recessions and depressions.

** While Hoover saw the tariff as a necessary protection for American farmers, his approach to the agricultural problem embraced a variety of remedies ranging from reduction of transportation rates to reorganization of the marketing system.

creation of income and demand in the agricultural sector *
would more than offset any decrease in other sectors due to
foreign competition.

The Gold Standard

Within this broad thesis, the New York banker dealt with
many allied topics. First and foremost, he stressed the importance of the government's maintaining its financial integrity. This meant, in his view, that a departure from the
gold standard was unthinkable. On this point he was especially
emphatic:

> I think the maintenance of the integrity of the Government
> and the gold standard, and the gold content of the dollar, are
> so important that I would deplore any legislation that would
> prohibit the entering into of such contracts in the future, and
> I cannot see that it would have any bearing on the present
> situation at all.

*   *   *   *   *

> . . . Personally, it is impossible for me to see how anybody
> can propose seriously a repudiation of the Government con-
> tract [to pay in gold] which is written on every bond and
> every piece of Federal Reserve currency that is outstanding.
> To me, it is simply incredible.[5]

In the banker's opinion, the financial integrity of the United
States government was one of the world's greatest capital
values. "Wantonly to destroy it, quite apart from the question of morality, would be an act of economic destruction
of fearful magnitude,"[6] he told the committee. Within a
few months, however, the "incredible" happened — the
United States abandoned the gold standard.

---

* When he entered the White House, Franklin D. Roosevelt also saw
agricultural prosperity as one key to industrial revival. Raymond Moley,
The First New Deal (New York: Harcourt, Brace & World, 1966), p. 525.

Among other things, the Hoover administration and the Federal Reserve had been trying to combat severe deflation by policies to expand credit through easy money, supplemented by emergency credit measures.[7] Aldrich had no faith in this approach. It would, he thought, destroy credit yet would not improve the farmer's position relative to the manufacturer, since the impact would be across-the-board rather than selective. Further, and even more important, this approach would do nothing to restore the export market for agricultural commodities which, in his opinion, was the key to the problem of economic revival.[8]

Governmental Austerity

The Chase president's domestic remedy endorsed the austerity side of the Hoover program: reduction of government expenditures and increases in taxation. The banker opposed veterans' claims for special assistance * and urged the reorganization and consolidation of government agencies at all levels in the interests of economy. In his view, "The Budget ought to be balanced in the sense that all ordinary expenses are covered by current taxes and that the borrowings for special and nonrecurrent purposes should be covered by additional taxes to the extent of current interest."[9] These views, orthodox for the time, were shared by Lewis Douglas, the incoming director of the Budget, and apparently even by Franklin D. Roosevelt.[10]

Reconstruction Finance Corporation

In his testimony Aldrich next turned to one of Hoover's emergency measures, the creation of the Reconstruction Finance Corporation which utilized $500 million of government

---

* In May 1932 Aldrich contributed $100 to the National Economy League which was opposing payments to veterans with nonservice-connected disabilities. (Aldrich papers.)

capital primarily to aid banks and other financial institutions. Initially the RFC had operated without public notice of its loans, and it had been charged that this practice encouraged favoritism in the lending process. Congress then required that RFC loans be made matters of public record. Aldrich stated that he approved of the RFC's aid in instances where financial difficulty was the result of slow but good assets. However, he opposed publicizing such loans. This publicity, he thought, might lead to withdrawal of bank deposits in the unwarranted fear that an RFC loan indicated that the recipient was in imminent danger of collapse.* He endorsed Senator James Couzens' proposed bill to meet this problem, and stated that the Chase National Bank itself had not resorted to RFC aid.[11]

In summary, Aldrich maintained that foreign trade was the key to the nation's current economic problems and that lowering trade barriers, plus conservative financial practice by government and selective aid to distressed sectors of the economy, would spur revival. Although some commentators thought Aldrich's views were the result of his conservative New England heritage, they actually seem to have been much more the reflection of his father's influence strengthened by his own experience in the law and banking.

Unemployment Relief

Aldrich acknowledged "the responsibility of the whole country for the suffering millions who, through no fault of their own, are victims of this great depression." [12] In meeting this responsibility he endorsed the Hoover program for federal aid to states to enable them, rather than the federal government, to give "direct unemployment relief." [13]

* Publicity for RFC loans was championed by Vice President Garner. There seems to be little doubt that some bank officials in the New York district felt the requirement had aggravated their difficulties. See Moley, *The First New Deal*, pp. 133–134.

Aldrich's Position in Retrospect

This was the first time that Winthrop Aldrich had appeared on the national scene in the role of business statesman. It was a difficult role to assume amidst business collapse but, invited to speak his mind, Aldrich did so. His endorsement of Hoover's policies came at a time when their inadequacy was evident to most Americans. Nothing that the Hoover administration had been able to do had seemed to stem the downward spiral of confidence, employment, prices, or bank liquidations. Explanation of the gargantuan collapse defied conventional economic wisdom and the remedies that it suggested. If, in retrospect, one can charge that Aldrich's prescriptions for the economic crisis of 1933 were inadequate and his insight on its causes clouded, one must also concede that he spoke frankly and offered as his best judgment propositions accepted by others with far more experience on the national scene.* Whether right or wrong, the depth of his conviction is evidenced by the fact that in the years to come he saw no reason to desert the principles on which his 1933 testimony was based.

Press coverage of Aldrich's testimony stressed the fact that he was the first New York banker to mince no words in his attack on the credit expansion policy of the Federal Reserve.[14] Before many months had passed, he would make bigger headlines by taking a public position that challenged the practices of major New York banks, including his own.

Aldrich's presentation to the Senate Finance Committee was prepared in pamphlet form [15] by the Chase and distributed to a selected list of recipients. The demand proved so great that the first printing of 100,000 copies was quickly exhausted

---

* Hoover, appealing to Roosevelt for reassurance of the public in mid-February 1933, made substantially the same points that Aldrich advanced in his testimony.

and 15,000 more had to be printed. Thereafter most of his addresses in his capacity as an officer of the bank were distributed in this form.

BANKING CRISIS

Even while Aldrich was testifying in Washington, the banking and monetary situation was growing worse. Monetary gold stock fell by $173 million in February 1933 alone. Bank failures had multiplied at such a rapid rate that one state after another had declared "bank holidays" in an attempt to halt the stampede of depositors to withdraw their funds. Moreover, Senate probers were casting serious doubt on the management of one of New York's greatest banks.

The Senate Committee on Banking and Currency, at the request of President Hoover, was conducting an investigation of stock exchange, banking and security market practices. Beginning in February 1933 Charles E. Mitchell of the National City Bank underwent extensive questioning, and the results were catastrophic. His bank had only recently been displaced by the Chase as the largest bank in the world, and the similarities of the two institutions in terms of securities affiliates were marked. The National City Company had "manufactured," in Mitchell's terms, between $1 billion and $2 billion worth of securities annually over the preceding decade.[16] It further developed that when the National City Company had been formed in 1911, the device — to enable a national bank to engage in the securities business — had been declared a violation of the National Banking Act by the United States Solicitor General, but this opinion had been buried in the files and had been disregarded.[17] Under questioning, Mitchell also admitted that he had sold stock to his wife in 1929 to avoid income taxes and had repurchased it at the same price in 1932.

Following these revelations, Mitchell resigned from the National City and was succeeded as chairman by James Perkins. A few months later the government instituted criminal action against Mitchell on tax-evasion charges, but he was acquitted. A civil proceeding found the sale of securities to his wife was not *bona fide* and produced a judgment in favor of the government for $700,000 in back taxes on the transaction.[18]

Mitchell's troubles were but a sample of what was yet to come for other New York bankers, but the immediate problem was to save the nation's banking system from complete collapse. The difficulty was exacerbated by the fact that Hoover and Roosevelt could not find a mutually acceptable basis for taking corrective action before the latter's inauguration.[19] Action was therefore deferred until the new administration took office. Meanwhile the banking community, especially in New York, waited with uncertainty hanging heavy over their every action.[20] Whether William Woodin, shortly to be named Secretary of the Treasury,* relayed any of the administration's plans when he visited Winthrop Aldrich on February 17 is not recorded.

The Bank Holiday

The inauguration was on Saturday, March 4, 1933. From the steps of the Capitol Building, Franklin D. Roosevelt declared: ". . . We must act, and act quickly." The first step was to meet the banking crisis. New York had just joined the list of states that had ordered banking holidays within their borders, and Roosevelt had under consideration a presidential proclamation declaring a national bank holiday and con-

---

* Roosevelt had asked Senator Carter Glass to become Secretary of the Treasury, but Glass declined on February 19. Woodin, president of American Car and Foundry Company and a director of the New York Federal Reserve Bank, was then named to the post.

trolling the export of gold under a World War I statute, the Trading with the Enemy Act. On the eve of the inauguration Senator Carter Glass of the Senate Banking and Currency Committee had remonstrated with the President-elect against issuing such a proclamation.[21] On inauguration day the final decision had yet to be announced.

Aldrich, like Glass, believed that a national bank holiday was unnecessary. Hoover had favored control of withdrawals of gold and currency from banks, and to meet any cash stringency that might result, one of the last acts of the outgoing administration was to prepare a joint resolution authorizing the clearing houses to issue scrip currency. Aldrich felt that this step was appropriate. As chairman of the New York Clearing House Conference Committee, he spent most of inauguration day at the Clearing House,[22] where the New York banks readied themselves for whatever might come.* Aldrich hoped, as did many other bankers, that the clearing-house certificate plan would be adopted, as it had been in the Panic of 1907. But this was not to be.

In Washington the new President was preparing the way for a national bank holiday and emergency banking legislation. He instructed Treasury Secretary Woodin to have this legislation ready when Congress was called into emergency session the following Thursday. On Sunday morning Woodin sounded out leading bankers and found they had no alternative plan of action. Late that evening the proclamations on the bank holiday and a special session of Congress were issued.

On Monday morning, March 6, Hoover's Secretary of the Treasury Ogden Mills and his assistant Arthur Ballantine, who had been battling the collapse without let-up, were

---

* Thomas W. Lamont of J. P. Morgan & Co. had telephoned Roosevelt on March 3 indicating that the leading New York bankers felt that the banks could reopen on Monday, March 6, if the inaugural address boosted public confidence. (Moley, *The First New Deal*, p. 149.)

working with the new Treasury officials. They were joined by George L. Harrison of the New York Federal Reserve Bank and George W. Davison of the Central Hanover Bank. This group turned down the clearing-house scrip idea in favor of a plan advanced by Dr. E. A. Goldenweiser of the Federal Reserve Board that would permit the issuance of Federal Reserve notes against bank assets.* Woodin accepted the idea, and he and Raymond Moley obtained Roosevelt's approval.[23]

Champion of Banking Reform

In this hour of crisis and uncertainty Winthrop Aldrich made the decision to call publicly for the prevention of banking abuses grounded in the relationship between commercial banks and securities affiliates. It was a momentous personal decision, since it meant repudiating the practices of his own bank, not to mention those of the banking community of which he was a member. But in his judgment, there was now no choice but to face facts, work for legislative correction, and accept the personal consequences whatever they might be. How far removed this stand was from that of most of his peers is suggested by the statement of the president of the American Bankers Association in January 1933. "What American banking needs," Francis H. Sisson said, "is the abolishment of special laws placing it under public regulation and supervision, rather than more statutes for its restriction and control.[24] Aldrich, based on his own experience, thought otherwise, and the time to say so publicly had arrived by March 1933.

Charles Mitchell's public revelations about the conduct of the National City Company's affairs had led not only to his resignation from the National City Bank but to the decision of its directors to divorce the securities affiliate from the bank.[25] This was precisely the step that Aldrich had come to

---

* As it turned out, the flow of cash and gold back into the banks as they reopened made this issue of Federal Reserve notes superfluous.

recognize as essential in the case of the Chase National. With Wiggin's views on such a move no longer a consideration, and with the news that the National City was moving in this direction, Aldrich decided to act. On the first day of the bank holiday, he informed the Chase directors of the need for severing the bank's ties with the securities affiliate. They concurred and a subcommittee of the Executive Committee was appointed to report on ways of bringing about the separation. On March 8, the day before Congress was to convene to discuss emergency banking legislation, Aldrich put himself and his bank on public record as favoring banking reform.

After noting with approval the decision of the National City to divorce its securities affiliate, Aldrich's statement declared: "It is impossible to consider the events which took place during the past ten years without being forced to the conclusion that intimate connection between commercial banking and investment banking almost inevitably leads to abuses." And, stating that the Chase National had resolved to take appropriate action in this regard, Aldrich went on to say: "I am entirely in sympathy with the divorcing by law of security affiliates from commercial banks." [26]

A legislative step to this end, sponsored by Senator Glass, was already under discussion in Washington. Among other things, the bill called for strict supervision of securities affiliates by the Federal Reserve Board and their complete divorce from commercial banks within five years. Aldrich did not think the Glass bill had gone far enough, and he said so. In his statement of March 8, 1933, he suggested four additional provisions: [27]

(1) No corporation or partnership should take deposits unless subjected to the same regulations and required to publish the same statements as commercial banks.

(2) No corporation or partnership dealing in securities should be allowed to take deposits "even under regulation."

(3) No officer or director of a commercial bank should be permitted to serve in either of those capacities in any enterprise engaged in the business of dealing in securities and *vice versa.*

(4) The number of directors on the board of a commercial bank should be limited to the point where the directors could be fully cognizant of the affairs of their banks and could properly discharge their responsibilities.

The basis for these recommendations in Aldrich's own experience has been outlined in the preceding chapter, but the proposals fell like a bombshell on the New York financial community. Aldrich, head of the largest banking institution of them all, was attacking relationships that existed in most of the large banks, including his own. To some it seemed that Aldrich was turning traitor. W. C. Potter of the Guaranty Trust stated the extreme reaction when he said that the proposals made by the Chase National's head were "quite the most disastrous [he had] ever heard from a member of the financial community." [28] Others depicted Aldrich's statement as a Rockefeller attack on the House of Morgan, an illusion that was fostered by J. P. Morgan's prediction that enactment of the proposal would limit his firm's ability to supply capital.[29]

Senator Glass welcomed the Aldrich statement and declared: "Of course, Mr. Aldrich is right in every proposition he lays down, and I am sure I would like to include all of his proposals in legislation by this Congress." However, Glass was careful to point out that some of Aldrich's ideas were incorporated in his original bill and had been eliminated as the result of opposition from "a number of bankers, including lesser officials of the Chase National Bank." [30]

Walter Lippmann made the Aldrich statement the subject of a column which appeared on March 10. Lippmann applauded the banker's contribution as demonstrating that those who abused moral responsibilities, as in the case of Charles

Mitchell, would no longer be protected by the silence and "easy-going tolerance" of the banking profession. Furthermore, the Aldrich statement proved to the public, the columnist said, that reforms would find active support in the banking community.[31] The *Wall Street Journal* made the same point: "The significant thing is that it can no longer be anywhere supposed that 'Wall Street' refuses to submit to a necessary major operation." [32] Newspaper comment was uniformly favorable, and the New York *World Telegram* took the opportunity to provide a feature biography on Winthrop Aldrich under the banner "W. W. Aldrich, First Challenger of House of Morgan." The writer characterized him as "the most approachable of leading bankers." In his words, the Chase president was "never jocose, he displays what is known as dry humor. But, most of all, he exhibits competence." [33]

Two letters commenting on his statement gave Winthrop Aldrich particular satisfaction. From the President of the United States came a note saying: "I want you to know that I appreciate your action in regard to the affiliate. What you and Jim Perkins [of the National City] have done will make for a better feeling in every direction." [34] From Ormond Beach, Florida, John D. Rockefeller, Jr. wrote:

> Your statement about the banking situation was sound, timely and courageous; it gave me further cause to be proud of you. You might have stopped after outlining what you thought your own bank should do. . . . But by stopping there you would have lost the chance to be the first to proclaim the only really sound principles upon which depositors' money can be sure to be safeguarded.

And the younger Rockefeller went on to say that if his brother-in-law could rise above criticism and adhere to his ideals, ". . . it is difficult to overestimate the extent of the service to business which you can render." [35] The San Diego

Tribune editorialized in the same vein when it said: "Mr. Aldrich speaks for business leaders of today — and tomorrow. From now on, unless present signs fail, banks are to be banks, and not sales offices. Promotion is to be left strictly to promoters." [36]

Unquestionably Aldrich had seized the right psychological moment to show private initiative in calling for a new departure in banking. The next move was up to the new administration in Washington.

At noon the day after the Aldrich statement, the 73rd Congress assembled to hear a presidential message which stated: "Our first task is to reopen all sound banks." The emergency banking legislation that was to accomplish this objective was ready, and even Carter Glass had enlisted to call for its enactment. While making it clear that some of the provisions were repugnant to him personally, the Virginia Senator nonetheless asked his colleagues to take prompt action in imitation of the House, which had adopted the bill unanimously.[37] The Senate responded by a vote of 73 to 7, and the bill introduced shortly after noon was on the President's desk for signature less than eight hours later.[38]

Two days later a Presidential proclamation announced that solvent banks would be opened progressively in the coming week. When these steps had been taken, banks holding some 92 percent of the nation's deposits were reopened.[39] Public fears had been considerably relieved and the President, who had initially contemplated dismissing Congress after the emergency banking legislation, was presented with an opportunity to capitalize on the momentum generated by that success to enact a wide-ranging legislative program.

The 100 Days

During the succeeding 100 days, the Democratic Congress adopted a staggering variety of legislation, including the

Agricultural Adjustment Act, the Tennessee Valley Authority Act, the Truth-in-Securities Act, the National Industry Recovery Act, and the Glass-Steagall Banking Act of 1933.[40]

It is an interesting commentary on the President's economic views at that time, however, that the first major measure to be passed on his initiative after the Emergency Banking Act was an Economy Act, designed to cut a half billion dollars from the budget by reorganizing and reducing veterans' pensions and by cutting congressional and other federal salaries.[41] This legislation fulfilled a campaign pledge and was presumably evidence of the administration's concern for government credit. The emphasis on economy was, of course, in harmony with one of Winthrop Aldrich's major recommendations in his testimony before the Senate Finance Committee the preceding February.

The day after passing the Economy Act, Congress also voted a modification of the Volstead Act to permit the sale of 3.2 beer. This legislation was also in line with Winthrop Aldrich's (and John D. Rockefeller, Jr.'s*) view that the Eighteenth Amendment was ineffective and pernicious.[42]

But these were minor victories for principles and policies with which Aldrich had associated himself compared to the staggering blow dealt to the underpinning of the whole economic system as he conceived it — the gold standard. In April an Executive Order took the United States off the gold standard; in May the President was authorized to reduce the statutory gold and silver content of the dollar by as much as 50 percent; and on June 5 the gold clause in public and private contracts was abrogated.[43] The very thing that Winthrop

* Rockefeller was a teetotaler and had hoped that Prohibition would succeed. However, the failure of this legislation and the lawbreaking that it encouraged changed Rockefeller's position on the experiment. Aldrich was in the group that met in May 1932 and backed Rockefeller's decision to call for repeal of Prohibition. (Raymond B. Fosdick, *John D. Rockefeller, Jr.*, pp. 254–257.)

Aldrich had publicly declared unthinkable in February had become very much a reality.

These steps were part of the inflationary policy that Roosevelt had come to feel was indispensable to recovery.* The international gold standard, if it worked as theorists held it should, adjusted trade imbalances by changes in domestic price levels. To maintain the currency on a gold standard abroad could, then, mean depression of prices at home, and there was no question in 1933 that prices were depressed. Aldrich's answer had been to increase exports; but even if this had been possible it would have taken time. Abandonment of the gold standard required little more than a flourish of the pen.

Aldrich's views on the gold standard were orthodox, and in holding them he was very much his father's son. But he was far from alone, even within the Roosevelt administration. Lewis Douglas, Director of the Budget, also believed that maintenance of the gold standard was the essence of governmental integrity. Both he and Aldrich made their views known to Roosevelt, and to their protests were added those of men like James P. Warburg, Herbert Feis, and Dean Acheson.[44] Roosevelt, however, was not swayed by these arguments, and there was a large body of public opinion, as well as important interest groups, that supported his course of action. Even J. P. Morgan was numbered in this element.[45]

Departure from the gold standard seemed to be a major step toward transferring the financial capital from New York to Washington, rather than bringing about a closer liaison of the political and financial capitals as advocated by Aldrich. Since he could not alter what he regarded as a disastrous public

---

* A factor in Carter Glass' decision to decline the Treasury post under Roosevelt was the Senator's fear of the President-elect's dedication to an inflationary policy. Learning of the Senator's concern through Raymond Moley, Roosevelt was emphatic that he would not abandon ideas "simply because they're labeled inflation." (Raymond Moley, *After Seven Years*, p. 119.)

policy decision, he adapted to it. In his family investments he switched from interest-bearing securities to equities, and he advised the heads of educational institutions with which he was associated to do likewise with their portfolios.[46] Later, he joined the Economists' National Committee on Monetary Policy, formed in November 1933 to combat soft-money doctrines.

During that hectic spring of 1933 Aldrich was a frequent Washington visitor in connection with legislative matters. At the end of March he was giving Roosevelt his views on the regulation of selling securities,[47] and on several occasions he had extended interviews with Carter Glass about the pending banking reform legislation.

Glass was formally head of the Appropriations Committee, but he also ran the Banking and Currency Committee as vice chairman under Senator Duncan Fletcher. The crusty Virginia Senator and Aldrich found themselves in basic agreement on many points. Following up the proposals of his March 8 statement, the New York banker even drafted the section of the Glass bill prohibiting firms dealing in securities from accepting deposits. Similarly, he was responsible for the provision limiting the number of directors of a national bank to not more than 25.[48]

In his collaboration with Glass, Aldrich was working at cross purposes with some New York bankers and seemingly even the chairman of his own bank, Charles McCain. When the Glass bill was before the Senate earlier in the year, McCain and other members of the New York financial community, according to Senator Glass, "Came down here and were positively offensive, some of them, in threatening members of the committee with the defeat of this bill, and in consequence of their efforts and of their opposition to the separation of affiliates there was a filibuster of 21 days in the Senate against the bill." [49] McCain later had an opportunity to challenge this allegation, as will appear subsequently, but he did not deny that he had opposed the divorcement of securities affiliates.[50]

The Glass bill became attached to a measure sponsored by Henry Steagall of the House Banking and Currency Committee to guarantee bank deposits. The combined measures, known as the Banking Act of 1933, became law on June 16. In addition to creating the Federal Deposit Insurance Corporation, the act forbade commercial banks to engage in securities underwriting and required them to divorce their securities affiliates. The powers of the Federal Reserve Board were strengthened and eligibility for membership broadened. In addition, other provisions sought to close the loopholes by which banks might grant credit for speculative securities operations or favor individual borrowers. Although Aldrich was pleased with the results, he still did not feel the law went as far as it should. Glass, however, was very proud of the act, and before the end of the year he and Aldrich were to have a spirited public debate on its strengths and shortcomings.

Liquidation of Securities Affiliates

A year was available in which to complete the divorcement of securities affiliates from commercial banks as required by the 1933 Banking Act. Several courses of action were open. J. P. Morgan, for example, decided to give up underwriting, whereas Kuhn, Loeb gave up commercial banking.[51] Having argued publicly for the separation of securities affiliates from commercial banks, Winthrop Aldrich felt himself under a pressing obligation to achieve this result in the Chase even before it was required by law. On April 5, 1933, he addressed a letter to Chase stockholders indicating the steps to this end that he proposed be ratified at a meeting on May 16. They included amendment of the certificate of incorporation of the Chase Securities Corporation to prohibit it from selling publicly or distributing securities, a change of name to the Chase

Corporation, a reduction of its directors from 30 to 10, a decrease in the par value of shares, liquidation of the business of the Chase Harris Forbes Corporation, and sale or liquidation of its underlying companies.[52] With the approval of these proposals by the stockholders, the Chase Corporation became a holding and liquidating corporation.

Disposal of the Chase Harris Forbes operation was expedited by the fact that its chairman, John R. Macomber, was a director of both the Chase National and the First National Bank of Boston, which under the new law also had to divorce its securities affiliate. The idea of combining the Chase affiliate with the First of Boston Corporation as an independent, publicly owned company grew out of the personal ties that existed between the Boston and New York banks. What the promoters of the merger wanted were not the tangibles of Chase Harris Forbes but the good will and expertise that it had built up in the underwriting field.[53] Whether the merger could be worked out, however, hinged on whether the necessary capital would be provided by the public.

By the end of 1933 the Chase had taken major steps to liquidate Chase Harris Forbes. Forty-one offices had been closed and personnel had been reduced from 100 officers and employees to 42. The only remnants of the organization were two Chase Harris Forbes Corporations, one chartered in New York, the other in Massachusetts.[54]

Meanwhile, promoters of the merger with the First of Boston Corporation had worked out the financing problem by dividing the capital stock of $9 million into three parts. Stockholders of the First National Bank of Boston were offered rights to 45 percent of the stock; another 45 percent was made available to stockholders of the Chase National; and the remainder was tendered to the officers of the new company, who included many of the top officers of Chase Harris Forbes.[55] In this manner, adequate financial support for the company was obtained, and the Chase Harris Forbes activity, acquired by the Chase under Wiggin, was phased out under Aldrich.

The final step in the Chase Securities divorcement came in June 1934. At that time the Chase Corporation, established the year before to handle the liquidation, was renamed the Amerex Holding Corporation.[56] The name of the newly formed holding company reflected the fact that its major asset was nearly 100 percent of the stock of the American Express Company. That company had for many years been engaged in the general business of foreign trade and travel, as well as selling travellers' checks. The fact that such checks are payable on demand created a potentially serious problem for Aldrich and the Chase, because the American Express Company was not a corporation. It was a joint-stock association (similar to a Massachusetts Trust), and one of the characteristics of a Massachusetts Trust is that the holders of its certificates of interest, or so-called shares of stock, unlike the holders of shares of stock of a corporation, are jointly and severally liable for all the debts of such a Trust. The Chase Securities Corporation would therefore have been liable for all the debts of the American Express Company if the latter had been unable to meet its obligations.

Aldrich had served as a director of the American Express Company since October 1930 and was its chairman from January to December 1933. During the period of financial crisis he was understandably concerned about the very large sum represented by travellers' checks outstanding (an amount referred to as the "float") and the possibility that a very high percentage of them would suddenly be presented for redemption. He found, however, that the assets of the American Express Company in which the float was invested could in all probability be quickly liquidated if a panic similar to that resulting in the 1933 bank closings should ever recur. The liquidity of the company's position made it possible for him to put into effect an unusually cautious investment policy of investing its float in nothing but short-term state and federal securities and of keeping a percentage of the float in cash as a reserve against withdrawals.

With respect to these matters, Winthrop Aldrich told the author the following in the summer of 1968:

> "The reason why this unusually cautious investment policy was deemed necessary was that some time in the past it had been held (as I remember it, by a Massachusetts court) that the sale of a travellers' check by the American Express Company was not a banking transaction and that the American Express Company by engaging in this business did not subject itself to the banking laws of the state and federal governments. As a result of this decision, the American Express Company was not subject to regulation by any banking authority. This, in my opinion, made it doubly necessary for it to refrain from investing in equity securities or anything of a speculative nature.
>
> "In carrying out the plan for the final liquidation of the Chase Securities Corporation's assets, I did not think it was advisable to distribute the stock in the American Express Company to the stockholders of the Chase National Bank and thereby subject them to unlimited liability for its debts and to the unrestricted investment policies of any new management which might come into power. Therefore, before the final distribution was made, the name of the Chase Corporation (successor to the Chase Securities Corporation) was changed to the Amerex Holding Corporation and its charter was amended so that it could not engage in the business of issuing and dealing in securities. After the disposition of all other assets except the American Express Company stock, the stock of the Amerex Holding Corporation was distributed to the stockholders of the Chase National Bank."

Thereafter, all relationships between the officers and directors of the Chase National Bank and the Amerex Holding Corporation came to an end. Some of the former officials of

Chase Securities, however, moved into Amerex, just as top men from Chase Harris Forbes remained with the new First of Boston Corporation.

At the Chase National Bank stockholders' meeting on May 16, 1933, which endorsed the liquidation of Chase Securities, it was also voted to reduce the number of the bank's directors from 72 to 36. This move not only produced a more compact board but gave concrete evidence of the separation of the bank from investment banking activities. Among the departing directors, for example, were Clarence Dillon of Dillon Read & Co., Charles Hayden of Hayden, Stone & Co., Frederic W. Allen of Lee Higginson & Co., Harold B. Clark of White, Weld & Co., Frank Altschul of Lazard Freres, and Henry S. Bowers of Goldman, Sachs & Co. With the subsequent passage of the 1933 Banking Act, the number of directors had to be further reduced to 25, a step completed by early 1934.[57]

A Change of Pace

The hectic pace of the first three months of 1933 was relieved for the Aldriches by a two-week sojourn in Bermuda in April, and after their return Winthrop Aldrich began slowly to resume his activities outside the bank. These responsibilities had necessarily been curtailed owing to the pressure of business and decisions that preceded and followed the Bank Holiday. Now he made some time for them. His yacht *Wayfarer* was in commission and he was even able to steal a few days afloat in mid-June before leaving for Chicago, where Chase chairman Charles McCain hosted a large dinner in his honor.

The purpose of the Chicago visit was to introduce the Chase president, whose recent activities had made him a national figure, to the Midwest's industrial and financial leaders. Among those present at the dinner were Charles G. Dawes of the City National Bank, several representatives of the

Continental Illinois Bank and the Harris Trust Company, with which the Chase had close relations, Philip L. Reed of Armour & Company, Robert E. Wood of Sears, Roebuck & Company, and George A. Ranney of Commonwealth Edison.[58] There is no record of what Aldrich said on this occasion, but his remarks undoubtedly included comments on the new banking legislation and the abandonment of the gold standard as viewed from his vantage point.

THE CRISIS ABROAD

A month later Mr. and Mrs. Aldrich departed for a two-month stay in Europe. The day before they left New York, the London Economic Conference had come to a disappointing end. Called to deal with international economic problems, it had been the subject of much preparatory work before the Roosevelt administration took office. Accordingly, there was strong hope in some quarters that the conference would deal affirmatively with the gold standard problem, reduce international trade barriers, and through cooperative action contribute to more healthy economic relationships between nations, all matters of great interest to Aldrich.

By the time the London Economic Conference convened in June, the United States had gone off the gold standard, and the resulting rise in prices of domestic commodities seemed to have justified the predictions of the inflationists. Although the countries still clinging to the gold standard hoped that the United States would agree to stabilize the dollar, they were dealt a shattering blow by Franklin Roosevelt. He cabled London that he did not propose to handicap his domestic program of creating a dollar with long-run purchasing power by indulging what he termed "old fetishes of so-called international bankers," or by temporarily stabilizing the dollar in terms of the pound or franc. Instead, he urged the Conference to get on with its basic mission of "curing fundamental economic ills." [59] But this was just what the Conference could not do, and it came to an end with little accomplished.

These were matters that Aldrich discussed at length with British and European bankers in August 1933. In London he lunched with the top officers of the National Provincial Bank and Lloyds Bank and called on the chairman of such leading institutions as the Midland Bank and Westminster Bank. When he moved on to Berlin, he followed the same procedure and unexpectedly found himself involved in remonstrating with Adolph Hitler, the new German leader.

An Interview with Hitler

Changes of great importance had taken place in Germany since the turn of the year. In March Hitler and his National Socialist Party had swept to power on a program that promised overthrow of the Versailles Treaty and the restoration of Germany's old glory. At the end of March the Reichstag had voted the government power to rule for the next four years by decree and had then adjourned indefinitely.

At a luncheon of German bankers assembled by Dr. Hjalmar Schacht of the Reichsbank, Aldrich spoke his mind about the German situation.[60] He had watched with concern the Nazi takeover. The possibility that it might result in another world war, with Germany and the United States as opponents, was one that he had had very much in mind in appraising the Chase position in Germany. At the luncheon he expressed frankly his views on this score, pointing out that continuation of the Nazi policies would in all probability force the Chase National Bank to cease making advances to German banks, and that the bank would have to take steps to liquidate existing loans as fully as possible.*

* Although the Chase's short-term German commitments had been substantially reduced since 1930, a sum of $34,949,331 remained outstanding at

Hitler's Minister of Economics, Kurt Schmitt, was at the luncheon, and Aldrich had scarcely returned to his room at the Hotel Esplanade when he received a call from Dr. Schacht saying that he and Schmitt would like to talk privately with the American banker at the Reichsbank. Upon his return there, Aldrich was ushered into a private office and was asked almost immediately if he would present the views that he had expressed at the luncheon to the Reich Chancellor at his mountain retreat at Berchtesgaden.

Schacht and Schmitt stated they had been impressed by what Aldrich had said. They thought it important that Hitler hear from the head of the largest bank in the world that Nazi policies were destroying Germany's credit. Aldrich agreed to their suggestion, provided he could be furnished with a plane to make an appointment in Amsterdam after the meeting with Hitler.

This conversation took place on the tenth of August, and the meeting was scheduled for Sunday the thirteenth. In the interim Aldrich reported his proposed interview with Hitler to American Ambassador Dodd, who heartily approved, and to Jewish bankers in Berlin who provided him with evidence that the Nazis' anti-Semitic campaign was even more severe than Aldrich had believed.

Aldrich traveled to Berchtesgaden on the 12th and met Mrs. Aldrich, who had been visiting in Munich. They spent that afternoon with Schacht, Schmitt, and "Putzi" Hanfstaengl. Putzi was a piano-playing Harvard graduate whom Aldrich had known in Cambridge many years before, and he was also Hitler's official interpreter. During a brief meeting with him in Berlin, the Chase president had found Putzi to be

---

the close of 1933. Of this total 33% represented loans to the German and Bavarian governments, while the remainder was on credit to banks and commercial and industrial concerns. (*Chase Annual Report*, 1933, pp. 13–14.)

violently anti-Semitic and this fact gave him considerable concern since he feared that it might flavor the translation of the interview. However, Schacht said there was no alternative to using Putzi, and he assured Aldrich that either he or Schmitt would interrupt if the interpreter failed to perform properly.

The appointment for 3:00 Sunday afternoon was postponed until 5:30 as the result of an automobile accident from which Hitler emerged unscathed but in which his secretary was nearly killed. Hanfstaengl, Schmitt, Schacht, and Aldrich ascended the mountain to Hitler's retreat along a road guarded by brown-shirted storm troopers who gave them the Nazi salute. Ushered onto the terrace of the chalet, they found Hitler waiting for them. To Aldrich's amazement, the Chancellor stepped forward quickly, raised his arm in salute, and said, "Heil Hitler."

Aldrich was spared the problem of opening the conversation, for immediately after the introductions had been made, Hitler addressed him through Hanfstaengl. "I am very glad to see you, Mr. Aldrich," he said, "because I am very indignant over the fact that the Jews in New York City, under the leadership of Mr. Untermyer, are attempting to boycott German goods entering into the United States in trade." To this the New York banker replied: "I am very glad that you are interested in that subject, because it is part of the general subject that I came here to talk to you about."

A general cabinet meeting had been temporarily adjourned so that the interview could be conducted in privacy. Therefore, after a brief exchange on the terrace, the little group went into the chalet and took seats around a small table set before a window with a view of the mountains.

At Hitler's invitation, Aldrich started to outline his views as expressed earlier in Berlin. The general thrust of the remarks, as he recalls them, was that if Hitler persisted in persecuting the Jews, the Führer would not only destroy Germany's credit but would create a situation that could lead to war with the United States. Before Aldrich had gotten far with his presentation, Hitler jumped to his feet and began walking rapidly around the room, gesturing with his hands and talking so loudly and rapidly that Putzi Hanfstaengl could not keep up with the translation. However, it did not take a complete translation to make it clear that Hitler was attacking the Jews and asserting the need and justice of dealing harshly with them for the protection of Germany.

The interview went on this way for about an hour. In the end Hitler quieted down and asked Aldrich why the United States government could not do something about the boycott of German goods in New York. This question called for a short dissertation on the nature of a democracy and Aldrich's suggestion that the way to modify or end the boycott was to stop persecution of German Jews. On this point, the interview ended just where it had commenced. On the way down the mountain, however, Schacht and Schmitt assured Aldrich that his effort had been worthwhile and might have some beneficial result.

Recalling the episode many years later, Aldrich said: "If I had known what kind of man he was, I perhaps wouldn't have been as bold as I was in saying exactly what I thought. But my attitude towards him at that time was that he was just another politician. It never occurred to me that he was going to sweep the Germans right off their feet in the way he did, and I personally thought at that time that what he was doing was so terribly bad that it couldn't continue to last."

Further visits to European capitals by the Aldriches were followed by a leisurely cruise with friends aboard a yacht in the Mediterranean. When Aldrich returned to his office in late September, however, he faced some of the busiest months of his entire career.

THE PECORA HEARINGS

Ferdinand Pecora, as counsel to the Senate Banking and Currency Committee, had been putting the leaders of American finance under the merciless spotlight of publicity as he questioned them in detail about their past activities. They had not come off well. Charles Mitchell of the National City Bank was only the first to feel the whiplash of the relentless probing. The Morgan partners had been next, with the final indignity for J. P. Morgan, the younger, of being photographed in the hearing room with a female midget in his lap. Nothing could have symbolized the fall of the mighty better than this publicity stunt arranged by a circus press agent.

It was inevitable, of course, that Albert Wiggin would be summoned before the Pecora Committee and that the Chase National Bank and its affiliates would receive the same searching scrutiny that other financial institutions had experienced during the investigation. Some, in fact, thought that Aldrich's statement of March 8 on securities affiliates had been designed to deflect the investigation from the Chase to J. P. Morgan & Company.[61] There is no evidence to support this inference, but the statement did clearly differentiate Aldrich's position from Wiggin's and gave the new Chase management an opportunity to disassociate itself publicly from the old policies.

At the time Aldrich apparently did not appreciate how critically important this distinction would become. Although he knew something about Wiggin's methods of operation and was aware of some of the problems that had resulted, he was still not prepared for the admissions that Pecora would draw from the former Chase National Bank chairman once he was in the witness chair. After these began to come out, Aldrich had to protect the bank and make absolutely clear that the conditions and policies associated with the Wiggin era no longer prevailed at the Chase. He could offer his actions and policies since Wiggin's retirement as concrete evidence that the bank had taken a new direction, but the final painful step involved virtual repudiation of the man whom he had succeeded.

On October 17, 1933, Albert Wiggin was sworn in by the subcommittee of the Senate Banking and Currency Committee investigating stock exchange practices. Among those present in the hearing room in addition to Wiggin and his lawyer were Winthrop Aldrich and counsel for the Chase National Bank and the Chase Corporation: Albert Milbank, William Embree, and A. Donald MacKinnon of Milbank, Tweed, Hope & Webb, the new name of Aldrich's old law firm.

In his opening statement, Wiggin, perhaps inadvertently, anticipated the thrust of his subsequent interrogation. After summarizing his banking career culminating in the creation of the largest bank in the world, he said:

> The bank has been under my general direction. I was the largest stockholder for many years. I haven't always been able to study all the details. But I have always wanted to take my full share of responsibility. I have always had entire confidence in all my associates. We have made mistakes. We must not look at things in the year 1933; we cannot look at them now as we did in 1929.[62]

But this was precisely what the subcommittee was doing: looking at the events of 1929 with the benefit of the perspective of 1933. In this light, Wiggin fared as badly as any of his predecessors in the Pecora investigation.

Under detailed questioning, Wiggin conceded that no one in the bank had greater power than he, "but there were several who had equal power so far as that went." Naming Aldrich, McCain and McHugh, he said, "they all had full authority to do business, to make decisions." But he conceded, "I presume I was the chief man." [63]

Questioning very quickly got around to the reasons for organizing Chase Securities. Senators Couzens and Adams suggested that it was a device to enable the bank to do something that it could not otherwise legally do, such as control corporations through stock purchases. Wiggin denied it, citing the fact that the Chase Securities Corporation had been owned by the bank's stockholders, not by the bank itself.* He subsequently stated that Chase Securities was organized to give those stockholders "the benefit of what we thought would be profitable business." [64]

In the midst of this interrogation Aldrich was sworn in to give brief testimony on the divorcement of the securities affiliate from the bank, since this development had taken place after Wiggin's retirement. He made a concise statement in which he emphasized that he considered separation of investment and commercial banking one of the most important topics before the committee. He reported that dissolution of Chase Harris Forbes and liquidation of Chase Securities were well advanced, and stated his view that the recent Glass-Steagall Act still had not gone far enough in separating investment and commercial banking.[65]

After the introduction into the record of Aldrich's letter to Chase stockholders of April 5, 1933, on these points, the questioning of Wiggin resumed. When he was asked whether he approved of the steps taken under the Aldrich regime, he tried to separate his attitude on policies from that toward the management that adopted them. On the one hand, he maintained that — at least up to the time he left the bank — he did not think it necessary to divorce securities affiliates; on the other hand, he declared: "I have absolute confidence in the management of the bank, and I am for them. When they

---

* Since evidence of ownership in the bank and the securities affiliate had been printed back-to-back on the same certificate, a stockholder in one was automatically a stockholder in the other.

decide it is the thing to do I vote with them." [66] It was quite clear, however, that Wiggin still did not share Aldrich's view on the necessity for separating securities affiliates from commercial banks.

The questioning of Wiggin ranged over a broad field of topics, and the answers illuminated the growth of the Chase National Bank, Wiggin's contributions to the bank, and his benefits from it. The record showed that he had been handsomely compensated by the bank and its affiliates, receiving a high of $75,000 from Chase Securities alone in 1930 and a bonus of the same amount from the bank in 1931, a year when his salary was over $200,000. In addition, he received compensation for service on the boards of numerous companies where he served, he said, in the interests of attracting their accounts to the Chase.[67]

The questioning obviously sought to highlight the size of the salaries of the bank's top officers, including Aldrich who received $135,556 during 1932, and to contrast unfavorably the officers' freedom to engage in activities outside the bank with the written statements required from bank employees that they would engage in no outside business without written permission from their employer. Wiggin defended the distinction on the grounds that the officers' associations with other enterprises "were of benefit to the bank." Subsequently, as the result of litigation, Judge Mahoney of the Supreme Court, New York County, endorsed Wiggin's claim. "In view of Wiggin's connections, his financial influence, and his usefulness to the bank, it is my opinion," the judge wrote, "that the salaries and additional compensation paid to him during these years were not excessive." [68]

Wiggin's relations with corporations that became Chase accounts had also led in some cases to personal loans to leading figures in these companies. In one such instance, Wiggin volunteered that these loans had been for "speculation," and he provided a definition that won widespread attention. "Investments that turn out wrong are speculations," he said.[69]

The key parts of Wiggin's testimony related to family corporations and their activities in Chase National Bank stock. The first of these, the Shermar Corporation, was formed in 1916. Wiggin explained its purposes in these words:

> In the first place it helped a great deal in detail. I did not have to mix up in bookkeeping or check signing or running it. I wanted my family to familiarize themselves with investments and the finance business. I also had the idea that perhaps does not work out, knowing that I would make a great many mistakes in life investments, that they would not be exposed to the public. I thought they were gone forever and would not show up in my estate. I hoped it would help on taxes.[70]

Subsequently, more family corporations were organized in this country and in Canada. The personnel of the latter consisted of a single employee of a Canadian law firm retained by Mr. Wiggin. A Canadian corporation could record stock transfers at market value rather than at cost, and this made it easy for an American to arrange a tax-free sale. Furthermore, when the stock was sold in Canada, it did not have to be reported for United States tax purposes. Wiggin conceded that his Canadian corporations had conferred this kind of advantage.[71]

The former Chase chairman's testimony on the activities of the Wiggin corporations showed that they had frequent participations with Chase Securities and with Metpotan, the Chase affiliates, and had dealt extensively in the stock of the Chase National Bank. Out of the latter operations, the Wiggin corporations made over $10 million between 1927 and 1932.[72]

Wiggin defended these activities as part of an effort to stabilize the market for the bank's stock. But the fact was that this stock rose from 575 in September 1927, when the first of these operations commenced, to the equivalent of 1415 in the fall of 1929 just before the market collapsed, and then dropped precipitously.[73] This did not suggest stability to Wiggin's questioners. Furthermore, a substantial part of the profit on the operations in Chase stock came in those disastrous last months of 1929 when the Wiggin interests were selling the bank's stock short — that is, selling against future delivery at a lower price. Some of this very stock was sold to the group sponsored by the Chase affiliates to maintain the market in the bank's stock; the Wiggin corporations also borrowed the money from Wiggin's bank with which to cover their short purchases. Finally, the arrangement was worked out in such a manner that no income tax had to be paid on the profits.[74]

The barrage of questions on these points left Wiggin staggering. Ferdinand Pecora pounded home his case in the following typical exchange:

MR. PECORA. Then you were using the machinery and personnel of the bank's affiliate in market operations for your private corporation that resulted in your private corporation making several millions of dollars of profit?

MR. WIGGIN. They were only used for their own benefit and protection, sir.

MR. PECORA. And the benefit and protection that they got — by "they" I mean the Chase Bank and its affiliate — was how much in dollars and cents, if there was a benefit in dollars and cents?

MR. WIGGIN. I don't know. I don't know how you would figure it.

MR. PECORA. You said that the bank received benefits from it. What were those benefits? What was the extent of them?

MR. WIGGIN. Did I say the bank received benefits?

MR. PECORA. Or the affiliate.

MR. WIGGIN. No; I said it was handled through them so that it would not interfere with their interests and what they wanted to do themselves.[75]

Wiggin was pursued relentlessly by his interrogators, who did not hesitate to push him into areas where any answer to their questions would leave him looking foolish if not culpable. It must have been an excruciating experience for the tired old man whom a leading New York banker had termed a "big, jovial, handsome boy" a scant three years before.[76] But, right or wrong, Wiggin refused to repudiate the principles that had guided his behavior and that of many of his contemporaries in the banking and industrial communities. If it was legal, it was acceptable in his book. Thus, questioned on the ethics of selling stock solely to avoid taxes and then repurchasing it, he replied: "I think that you are bound to have people save taxes where they can according to law. It is a simple matter to change law if it is a bad practice." [77] When questioned specifically as to whether a bank should make loans to officers or directors to enable them to engage in market operations in the stock of that bank, Wiggin did not hesitate to answer: "I think it is commendable for the officers of the bank to be interested in the institution for which they are working, and I think it is entirely commendable and proper for the bank, on proper collateral, to loan to its officers." [78]

Such statements as these ran directly contrary to Aldrich's philosophy, and he had to make it very evident to the Senators and to the public that Wiggin spoke for himself and perhaps for the old Chase but certainly not for Aldrich or the current management of the bank. Thus, wherever there appeared to be any danger of confusion on this point, the Chase president interrupted to make the record clear. One such statement ran:

Mr. Chairman, in order that there shall be no misunderstanding on the part of the present stockholders of the bank as to what the attitude of the present management of the bank is with regard to the participation by the affiliates of the bank in trading accounts in bank stock, I would like to state that it is absolutely opposed to such transactions.[79]

On the other hand, where Aldrich felt that the Senate probers were asking questions that he was better qualified to answer than Wiggin, he did not hesitate to break in and point this out.[80]

Unquestionably Wiggin felt that he had been deliberately isolated from the new Chase management. And this indeed appears to have been the case. He had his own counsel; the Chase had a different group. The public relations for the bank were being handled by Ivy Lee; [81] Wiggin had no one. If it seemed to Wiggin that the directors' resolution of December 21, 1932, praising him for his contributions to the Chase had been turned into a mockery, it must have seemed to Aldrich and the directors that Wiggin had sold them short, as well as the bank's stock. The embarrassing thing was that they had voted him $100,000 a year along with their thanks, and both they and Wiggin now had to explain that arrangement publicly.[82]

When the subject came up, Wiggin could not explain the origin of the proposal to pay him such a large amount, but he defended it in terms of the services that he had and could render in return. As to the possibility that it might have been a trade-off for a settlement of Shermar's participation with Chase Securities in the Fox Film syndicates, he pointed out that the $1 million involved in that settlement had been a voluntary offering.[83]

Less than a week after the interrogation about his retirement pay, Wiggin requested the Chase directors to terminate the arrangement. This was an honorable step, but it still left the directors, and more especially Aldrich, with the unpleasant task of explaining how they had come to vote such a generous stipend in the first place.

The question was put directly to Aldrich by Senator Glass when the banker took the chair before the Senate Committee on Tuesday, December 5, 1933. It was clearly a question that Aldrich had anticipated and wanted to handle on as impersonal a basis as possible. He made the point explicit in reply to Glass's question when he said: "It is somewhat embarrassing to me, because it brings up personal relationships between myself and Mr. Wiggin, which I had hoped to find unnecessary to discuss. But I will be very glad to do it if you desire." [84] Glass denied any interest in these relationships but insisted on an explanation, as well as charging that the arrangement had been illegal in any case. To this Aldrich replied:

MR. ALDRICH (interposing). If I may be permitted, I can only say that we were advised by counsel that it was a proper resolution to pass. And I can further say that it was the sincere belief of the board of directors at the time that action was taken, that it was for the best interests of the bank, and it was done in order that the bank might have the right to call on Mr. Wiggin at any time for his advice and services if they were needed in connection with the operation of the bank in the future.

SENATOR GLASS. Well, in view of recent disclosures I imagine it has somewhat aggravated the case.

MR. ALDRICH. There is no doubt at all that the board at the present time considers it was a mistake to have voted that resolution. But you must remember that a great many things have been brought out here that the board did not know about at the time when it passed that resolution.

SENATOR GLASS. Well, it seems to me that the board of directors should have known about them.

MR. ALDRICH. Well, I did not have the great number of investigators such as Mr. Pecora has.[85]

Thus passed one of the most difficult moments of Aldrich's

interrogation. He was clearly on the defensive — for him an unaccustomed and uncomfortable position.

Aldrich, Carter Glass, and the Banking Act of 1933

Senator Glass quickly showed that he was far more interested in the Chase president's criticism of the recent Banking Act than he was in Wiggin's retirement compensation. In a lengthy prepared statement submitted to the subcommittee on November 29, Aldrich had argued that the Banking Act of 1933 was not sufficiently restrictive or precise in some of its provisions.[86] The Virginia Senator was displeased that the New York banker should find any fault with the legislation, which he characterized as the product of "the most thorough banking investigation that was ever conducted by the United States Congress, or either branch thereof." [87] He questioned whether Aldrich's statement had any place in the investigation of stock-exchange practices. To this the banker responded that he had acted in good faith and felt that his critique was pertinent since he believed that "some of the practices disclosed here should be prevented by specific legislation." [88]

Senator Glass then proceeded to review the provisions of the act which Aldrich felt should be further tightened. Aldrich commented as the Senator went along. For example, Section 12 of the 1933 statute sought to prevent recurrence of a problem that had been highlighted in the testimony about Chase officers borrowing from the bank under Wiggin. The new law required that an executive officer of a member bank of the Federal Reserve System be prohibited from borrowing from his own bank and further required that he report in writing to the chairman of his own bank any personal loans from other member banks, including the amount, security, and purpose of such borrowing. Aldrich maintained that this provision should be extended to cover not only borrowing from member banks but also loans from a broker or private bank. He further advocated that the chairman of the board of any member bank should report his personal borrowing to his board.[89]

Aldrich also made the point that the definition of "affiliate" in Section 18 of the act was too broad. Glass concurred. He pointed out that the language of this section was so comprehensive that it had been applied to a newspaper, which was found to be a bank affiliate because two of its executive officers were also executive officers of a bank. Glass therefore agreed that this section should be amended and invited Aldrich to submit such a proposal to the Banking and Currency Committee.[90]

In discussing Section 20 relating to the divorcement of securities affiliates, Aldrich explained how he reached his decision that such a step was necessary. He declared that when he had first studied the matter he recognized the evils in the relationship, but believed that they could be eradicated by placing the affiliates under supervision of the Federal Reserve authorities. Addressing Glass, he said: "It was not until along toward the end of the year 1932 that I came fully to the conclusion that you were right on what you were trying to do in connection with affiliates, and from that time on I have taken the position consistently that you were right, and the Chase National Bank has taken a separate position on all these matters from any other bank in New York." [91]

The question of the constitutionality of paragraph 2 of Section 21, subjecting all banks — except private banks and financial institutions under regulation of state or federal law — to examination by the Federal Reserve or Comptroller of the Currency was also raised. Glass admitted that there was a real doubt concerning the constitutionality of this provision but said that abuses revealed in the banking system warranted its inclusion. Aldrich agreed that there was a significant legal question here and noted that he had submitted a brief on the point to Senator Glass. He further stated that to achieve such a unified banking system would probably necessitate a constitutional amendment, though in his opinion the situation had not yet reached that stage.[92]

Opposition to a unified banking system and to extending branch banking stemmed in large measure from the traditional American fear of concentration of money power. This fear was reflected in the chartering of banks by both state and federal authority, state restrictions against existing banks organizing branches which might eliminate the opportunity for creating another bank, and the very low bank capitalization acceptable in some states.

To unify the nation's banking system, as Glass hoped to do, it would be necessary to bring all state-chartered banks into the Federal Reserve System; yet the stringent requirements of the 1933 act not only discouraged such moves by state banks but gave some national banks already in the system an incentive to exchange their federal charters for state ones.

It was Aldrich's view that the absence of a unified banking system produced weak banks and had contributed to the difficulties that culminated in the Bank Holiday. He was too much a realist, however, to anticipate that banking reform could be achieved except through a series of gradual steps. Accordingly he proposed increasing the capitalization requirement for new banks and for the exercise of federal authority, overriding state law where necessary, to enable national banks to establish branches in cities where the main office was located and, under certain conditions, throughout a state.* [93] These views, of course, were loaded with political dynamite since they ran counter to the American tradition of

---

* The Banking Act of 1933 had permitted statewide branch banking by national banks only where state law allowed state-chartered banks to follow this practice.

"free banking." Aldrich was anxious to discuss this whole question but felt that another time and place might be more appropriate. Therefore the testimony passed on to other topics.

In the afternoon of that same day, December 5, there was some further discussion of other provisions of the Banking Act of 1933. Aldrich indicated that he felt it was unfortunate that the statute forbade payment of interest on demand deposits, since this tended to immobilize funds at their points of origin rather than permitting them to be drawn to central points where they could be used in legitimate trade. On the other hand, he acknowledged the validity of Senator Glass's position that payment of such interest led to unhealthy competition among banks seeking deposits and also contributed to the banks' use of these funds for speculation. Aldrich seemed to feel, however, that proper supervision by the Federal Reserve could remedy this problem.[94]

Subsequent questioning of the banker covered a number of these points in detail and introduced some new ones. Aldrich was quite specific in saying that he thought bank officers should be made dependent on their bank salaries except when authorized by their directors to engage in compensated activities outside the bank. He also reported to the committee criticisms of the new Securities Act as he had heard them from brokers and investment bankers, but he declined to take any position with respect to their validity.[95] In an exchange with committee counsel Pecora he advocated publicity for bank operations but questioned whether this publicity should go as far as Pecora suggested it might.[96]

When he finally rose from the witness chair, Aldrich had come off well. His numerous contributions to recent banking reform legislation had been publicly acknowledged by Glass, and under questioning he had handled himself with a lawyer's dexterity and aplomb. Except for occasional needling from

Glass, and a short-tempered comment or two from Senator Couzens, he had been handled with consideration by the subcommittee and its counsel. Pecora summed up his impression of Aldrich when he later wrote: "His whole attitude was as severely high-minded and as militantly imbued with the necessity for correcting banking abuses as Mr. Wiggin's was skeptical and unbending." [97] John D. Rockefeller, Jr. took a similar view. "You have availed of a great opportunity in a great way," he wrote Aldrich on December 1.[98] A commentary in the New York *American* of the same date pointed out that the Chase president had not made the mistake of organized banking lobbies in opposing all reform. Therefore, when Aldrich asked for modification of overly stringent reforms, "he was respectfully heard."

McCain's Testimony

Aldrich was followed to the witness chair by Charles McCain, chairman of the Chase National Bank. The proceedings quickly reverted to the same probing approach that had characterized the questioning of Wiggin. McCain admitted that he was indebted to the bank and that he had increased his own loan account to enable an Arkansas friend and Chase director, with whom he engaged in syndicate operations, to reduce his loan at the Chase.[99] He conceded that he had had some transactions with Wiggin's Murlyn Corporation and that he had participated in various syndicates which received loans from the Chase, though some of them originated prior to his connection with that bank.[100] McCain denied any participation in Metpotan's operations in Chase stock and stated that reports on these activities went to Wiggin but not to him.[101]

McCain denied that he was responsible for the filibuster against the Glass bill, which the Virginia Senator had earlier attributed to him. He admitted talking with Senator Huey

Long, who had conducted the filibuster, but said that he had been trying to stop rather than promote the Louisiana Senator's obstructive tactics. McCain also said that he had not originally favored separation of security affiliates from commercial banks and some other provisions of the Glass Bill, but "I afterwards changed." [102]

Glass, who had come into the hearing room during this testimony, refused to withdraw his earlier charges against McCain, but he also would not or could not substantiate them except by drawing inferences. McCain maintained that he had discussed the bill only with Glass himself; therefore he could not have been offensive to members of the Senator's committee, as Glass had charged.[103] The Senator accepted this explanation and soon withdrew with the parting comment: ". . . I wish to God these people would stop referring to me as the venerable Senator from Virginia and respecting me for my age." [104]

Outcome of the Pecora Hearings

McCain's testimony suggested that he had been the victim of the speculative spirit in much the same way as Wiggin, though on a smaller scale. He testified that he had not been kept fully informed about inside operations and had not thought to investigate them. He had engaged in practices which, though acceptable in the circles where he moved at the time, had now been attacked by Aldrich and exposed to adverse criticism and publicity by the Senate subcommittee. It was therefore virtually a foregone conclusion that McCain would have to leave the bank. Again it was a painful separation, but Aldrich was relieved of bearing the full brunt of its initiation. When Aldrich talked with President Roosevelt at the White House later in December, he recalls, Roosevelt made it quite clear that he could not passively accept the con-

tinuation of bankers in high places who had been so compro-
mised as McCain.[105]

The formalities of changing the bank's leadership were concluded at the meeting of the board of directors on January 10,
1934. At that time McCain's resignation was announced, as
was that of John McHugh, former chairman of the executive
committee. Both men went on to important jobs outside the
bank: McCain to the presidency of the United Light and
Power Company, McHugh to chairman of the Discount Corporation of New York. Winthrop Aldrich was elected chairman of the Chase board of directors and H. Donald Campbell
succeeded him as president.

Although a complete change had been made in top executive leadership, the full extent of the destruction wrought by
the hearings before the Senate subcommittee was just beginning to become clear. The long and arduous task of clearing
away the debris and restoring the bank's public image for
integrity was just beginning. In Thomas Debevoise's judgment, Aldrich had already displayed "great courage, initiative, resourcefulness and understanding of the banking problems." And, with an eye to the future, the Rockefeller lawyer
added: "I think now it should be recognized that the leadership which you want, the leadership which is worthwhile,
cannot come because we seek it for you, but only as a result
of your rendering a service of the highest and most enduring
character to the bank itself, to the community and to the
country." [106]

CHAPTER VIII

The Early Leadership Years, 1934-1935

W ITH his election as chairman of the board of the Chase National Bank, Winthrop Aldrich formally took over the leadership of the world's largest bank. The transition from law practice to this high position in commercial banking had taken place in less than five years; yet Aldrich found himself talking, acting, and being accepted as a spokesman for the banking community both in its inner councils and in those of the new Roosevelt administration. Even those who were amazed by his rapid ascent to power in the Chase could not deny his increasing influence outside the bank. The fact was that circumstances — the death of Chellis Austin and then Wiggin's fall — had given Aldrich an opportunity to demonstrate his leadership qualities in new areas. That he should have responded with enthusiasm and successful accomplishment was no surprise to those who knew him from his law days. The energy, imagination, decisiveness, and courage that he had brought to his law practice were transferred to banking and then to banking in a time of world crisis.

ALDRICH'S CONCEPT OF LEADERSHIP

Aldrich himself always believed that he practiced banking as a lawyer. His role in the Chase, defined in terms of self-image, was that of strategist, top-level decision maker, and marketer of bank services — entrepreneurial activities that turned his attention outward from the bank and most of its daily routine. Outside the bank he was recognized for civic mindedness and public service in keeping with the high levels of integrity and responsibility appropriate to an officer of a banking institution and particularly to one at the Chase. The fact that some officials of his bank had fallen short of their moral obligations gave him an added incentive as chairman to bend his every effort to repair the damage, and this task tested his leadership capacity to the full.

As John D. Rockefeller, Jr., had observed in connection with Aldrich's statement of March 8, 1933, on the separation of commercial and investment banking, Aldrich could easily have stopped short of advocating reform in the banking system itself. That he did not do so was an indication not only of his courage but also of his conviction that the obligations of leadership extended beyond any single institution if there was a need and an opportunity to discharge them in a larger sphere. Unquestionably Aldrich also saw benefits for the Chase from exercising such leadership in connection with banking reforms, but he seems to have been more pulled than pushed into his role as a spokesman for the banking community in Washington.

The years 1934 and 1935 saw him move quickly and purposefully into his new roles. On the one hand, he had to get the Chase moving in new directions; on the other hand, he chose to take a leading role in completing the banking reforms started in 1933.

Choosing a New President of the Chase

The immediate problem confronting Aldrich in January 1934 was to repair the damage done to the bank by the Pecora hearings and to further in any way that he could the changes in banking laws that he had advocated before the Glass sub-committee. Within the bank, his first step was to find a successor for the presidency so that he could be free, as chairman, to devote himself to these problems. He chose H. Donald Campbell.

Campbell was a very competent banker and an individual with whom Aldrich had worked closely. When Aldrich had succeeded Chellis Austin as president of the Equitable Trust Company in 1929, he was on first-name terms with Campbell within a week — a somewhat unusual occurrence for one as reserved as Aldrich.[1] It was typical of both men that Aldrich did not inform Campbell of his selection as the new president until the evening before the public announcement and that Campbell was genuinely surprised by the news.[2]

Shortly after this appointment, Aldrich left for a Florida vacation. When one of the directors questioned the advisability of his leaving New York with Campbell so new in his job, the Chase chairman assured the director that there was no problem. "We think alike," he said of the new Chase president. Campbell, who had been brought up in a strict Scotch family, shared this feeling. Of New Englander Aldrich he said, "I had the greatest confidence in his doing the right thing always."[3]

Public Relations and Legal Problems

The bank needed men of Aldrich's and Campbell's type to combat the effects of the adverse publicity emanating from the Pecora hearings, but the changeover in top management understandably created a tense atmosphere. The situation was not unlike the one at Indiana Standard in 1929 when Aldrich had led the forces that successfully ousted Colonel Robert Stewart. As in that earlier instance, Aldrich handled a difficult situation well. At the 1934 Chase annual meeting he spoke "with great tact, ability and complete and disarming frankness," according to one of his admirers.[4] Small stockholders who were present were also impressed and several took the trouble to write and tell the new chairman that they felt a new confidence in the bank because of his presence. One important element contributing to these expressions of confidence was Aldrich's announcement that a special committee of the directors had been appointed, with Elihu Root, Jr., as counsel, to investigate possible claims in the bank's favor arising out of the testimony during the Pecora hearings.

The directors' committee had been appointed on December 13, 1933, with Howard Bayne as chairman.[5] Its investigation of the conduct of the bank's affairs under Wiggin became entwined with stockholders' suits brought against the bank and its directors and officers for their alleged negligence and violation of trust in specified loans and other matters. These suits were eventually consolidated into an action known as the *Bookbinder* suit, named for one of the plaintiffs.[6] Years were to pass before this suit was finally settled.* And it was but one of many growing out of the Wiggin era at the Chase.

While coping with these legal problems, Aldrich and the bank's new top management also had to combat the actual and potential loss of business resulting from the Washington hearings. Fortunately most of the accounts actually withdrawn because of the hearings were small, personal ones, but at least one large industrial account was lost.[7] Long-established relationships with correspondent banks of major importance were also affected. In one instance, Campbell himself had a hard time convincing his opposite number in a

* See Chapter IX.

large midwestern bank that there was, clearly, no cause for apprehension.[8]

THE CHASE OFFICERS' WESTERN TOUR

The farther one got from New York and firsthand knowledge of the Chase National Bank, the more suspicion there was likely to be about the bank as the result of the Pecora hearings. To combat this suspicion, Campbell, who by upbringing, education, and early banking experience knew the West well, suggested in the fall of 1934 that the Chase's top officers tour the country. The potential of the idea intrigued Aldrich immediately, and a plan to implement it was soon worked out. James Perkins of the National City Bank had just completed a western trip and William C. Potter of the Guaranty Trust had taken a swing through the South. The Chase group proposed a more comprehensive and extensive investigation of banking problems and opportunities by covering the country east to west and north to south in a private railroad car, which, it turned out, was appropriately named for the explorer Roald Amundsen.

The party, consisting of the leading officers of the Chase,* accompanied by two secretaries, records of accounts, deposits, and problems, as well as lists of influential people in the cities to be visited, left New York on Sunday, November 18, 1934. In the ensuing weeks, the Chase group covered many of the major cities of the United States, ranging in a broad sweep from Chicago to Seattle and Portland in the Pacific Northwest, to San Francisco and Los Angeles in California, and to San Antonio, Houston, Dallas and Fort Worth in Texas.[9]

* The party included Aldrich; Campbell; Percy J. Ebbott, at that time vice president in charge of the bank's commercial business in the Midwest; Edward Love and Nelson Rockefeller of the Public Utility Department; Dr. Anderson; and Louis Jacoby, Chicago representative of the bank.

Aldrich's presence in these cities symbolized the new era of banking; New York was coming to the hinterland. To make the most of the undertaking, arrangements were made to give the Chase chairman the broadest possible exposure in each city visited. The format of each visit consisted of a heavy schedule of appointments during the day followed by one or more social occasions in the evening. Then, while the party slept, their car moved through the night toward the next destination. As the *Roald Amundsen* entered the various zones into which the Chase had divided the country, the zone vice presidents joined the party to brief the head office people on local problems and arrangements. It was an exhausting routine, but it was the kind on which Aldrich thrived.

Aldrich found the trip fascinating, for like many Easterners with his background he was less acquainted with the interior of the United States than with Great Britain or Europe. The response to his appearances further whetted his enthusiasm. Campbell recalled: "Business leaders and bankers were pleased that Aldrich was making this trip. It was a great trip. It gave me the opportunity to know Winthrop intimately. He is a wonderful man to travel with. If I were going to select a companion to travel around the world, with a view to business, and also for the enjoyment of the cultural side of the countries visited, I would certainly choose a man like Aldrich, who is quite unique in his interest in all phases of life." [10]

The 1934 tour had its lighter moments. The Chase's interest in the Fox Film Company, for example, brought the Aldrich party to the Fox Film studios in Hollywood, where the New Yorkers were entertained at a dinner presided over by the humorist Irvin S. Cobb. Will Rogers was one of the principal speakers. Aldrich knew that he was also expected to speak, and he was somewhat disconcerted by the prospect of matching his wit against Rogers'. But he proved himself equal to the occasion. The job was not made any easier when

Rogers, whose wit could be vitriolic on occasion, introduced the Chase chairman as the first eastern banker who had visited California since 1929 who had not been on his way to Alcatraz. Aldrich, however, replied by saying that he had come out to inspect the assets of the company in which the Chase had a large investment, that he found Will Rogers and Shirley Temple to be the principal assets, and that after listening to Rogers' introduction he was inclined to prefer the smaller to the larger asset. This sally brought down the house and Aldrich passed on to more serious business.

At the conclusion of the New York banker's talk, Shirley Temple, who had been sitting on her mother's lap, jumped down, trotted to the platform, made her way around the head table, and, using Aldrich's lap for a stepladder, climbed onto the table. Thereupon she threw her arms around the banker's neck and kissed him. This apparently spontaneous gesture again brought down the house and erased the noticeable tension that had accompanied the New Yorkers' visit to the studio.* Events such as these spiced an otherwise arduous and serious business trip.

Speaking Out on the New Deal

Among other things, the numerous stops gave Aldrich welcome opportunities to express his views on the state of the economy and his evaluation of the steps being taken by the Roosevelt administration to deal with it. In Milwaukee and Seattle, for example, he made cautiously optimistic estimates of the situation, citing an economic upturn whose beginning he placed at mid-September 1934. When the party arrived in San Francisco, he took the occasion of an appearance before

---

* The tension resulted from the fact that hostility still existed between the representatives of William Fox and General Theatres Equipment, Inc., through which the bank controlled Fox's former property. (New York *Evening Journal*, December 5, 1934.)

the Commonwealth Club on December 3 to deliver a speech that invited controversy and nationwide attention. Flanked at the head table by such leading western bankers as A. P. Giannini of the Bank of America and William Crocker of the Crocker National Bank, the New York banker spoke out on the New Deal.[11]

The first part of his Commonwealth Club address was typically optimistic in its tone. He reported that he had found business sentiment improved and business activity reviving. Further, he reported an encouraging rapprochement between the government and the banking community reflected at the fall meeting of the American Bankers Association in Washington. He was also encouraged by the lifting of foreign exchange restrictions and the progress being made toward the national and international stabilizing of currencies. But this was only a prelude to the main topic of his speech: the financing of unemployment relief, which he characterized as "the most important problem which confronts us at this time."

In approaching this topic, he reiterated and expanded on the principles that had guided his testimony before the Senate subcommittee investigating the causes of the depression in February 1933. His point of departure was clearly expressed in these words: ". . . I am taking for granted that no one in this room wishes to change the fundamental character of our institutions, so that we will be obliged to look to the central Government to take care of the people under any of the many forms of paternalism which have developed in other parts of the world." In this context, which acknowledged the importance of emergency action by the federal government but emphasized the primary importance of private initiative and enterprise in creating a sound economy, Aldrich examined the unemployment relief program in both economic and philosophical terms.

From an economic standpoint, the federal program would,

he thought, perpetuate an unbalanced budget with its attendant threat to government credit. Under these conditions he predicted that private capital would be hesitant to make long-run commitments. In his words, "The credit of the Government and the soundness of the currency are basic to that general confidence which is necessary for vigorous business activity, and, above all, for the making of long time commitments." * Thus, government borrowing to finance federal unemployment relief as it was currently being conducted would, Aldrich said, depress rather than stimulate business activity. He argued that the same was true with respect to government competition with private enterprise in the public utility field,** because it discouraged private commitments and this in turn decreased employment opportunities in the heavy industries catering to public utilities.

Aldrich was one of the first major American business or financial leaders to attack publicly the idea of "spending ourselves back to prosperity by the creation of public debt." This approach to reviving the economy seemed to him completely mistaken if the goal was to stimulate private business activity and investment. In taking this position he undoubtedly had in mind not only the large amount of excess reserves that the Chase and other banks could not put to work for lack of borrowers but also the threat, as he perceived it, to private interests and public fiscal responsibility of reliance

* It is interesting to compare Aldrich's views with those of Russell Leffingwell of J. P. Morgan & Co. Like Aldrich, Leffingwell stressed the importance of confidence, the lowering of trade barriers, and the dangers of inflation. However, he was more inclined to see the emergency monetary steps of 1933 as justified and was seemingly less concerned than Aldrich about the actual threat of inflation. See Russell Leffingwell, "The Gold Problem and Currency Revaluation," address before Academy of Political Science, March 21, 1934.

** This area was a matter of considerable concern to the Chase as the result of its involvement with public utility financing. See Chapter V.

on government deficit spending to stimulate economic activity.

Aldrich was not unsympathetic with the problems of the unemployed, and he recognized the need for emergency relief. Traditionally relief had been a local matter, in many instances privately sponsored. Aldrich himself was active in many such groups, including the New York State Charities Aid and the Citizens Family Welfare Committee. He was also a member of the Governor's Commission on Unemployment Relief for New York State. By belief and experience he was firmly attached to the idea that relief should be handled on a municipal or state basis. He questioned the extending of federal aid in the form of work projects, which he viewed as expensive compared to relief in the home, as inviting abuses that would be less likely to occur in home relief at the local level, and as the source of fiscal and monetary difficulties.

He pointed out to his San Francisco audience that unemployment was to be a continuing problem, and he emphasized the inadequacy of approaching it in terms of sweeping generalizations and easy answers. Facts, not theories, he believed, should be the first step toward intelligent action; yet, he pointed out, there were no studies of the unemployment problem in terms of the reasons for individual unemployment, reemployment possibilities, or the need for retraining of the unemployed. Similarly, precise data on the costs of different types of relief were unavailable, and much of the data and the recommendations based on them came from "professional welfare workers" whose humanitarian interests, in his opinion, outweighed their economic knowledge.

Aldrich made it a practice never to engage in criticism of governmental or business policies unless he could offer an alternative to them. Accordingly, in his San Francisco speech he suggested that one step in meeting the relief problem would be the creation of boards, modeled on the draft boards of World War I, to supervise and analyze the administration of relief on the local level. "My own feeling," he said, "is that such instrumentalities might well be created by action of the various States, so that, in every community, a better understanding would be created of the unemployment relief problem, a greater sense of community responsibility would be fostered, and the tendency now existing in so many parts of the country to lie down and wait for the Federal Government to come to the assistance of the locality would be combatted." [12]

In terms of national attention, the San Francisco visit was the high point of the trip. At subsequent stops in Arizona and in Texas, the same themes were sounded in Aldrich's more informal talks and interviews. At Fort Worth the entire party was presented with wide-brimmed western hats, and press coverage of the trip featured more the reunion of the Rockefeller brothers, Nelson and Winthrop, than what their uncle had to say. In fact, one Dallas reporter complained that instead of being granted an interview he had been handed a copy of Aldrich's presentation to the Senate subcommittee on the causes of the depression and a copy of his San Francisco address. [13]

Looking back on the western trip many years later, Aldrich felt that it had been "most fruitful." He believed that it had done a great deal to reestablish confidence in the Chase National Bank and in the New York banking community; it certainly established and cemented relationships of enduring value to the bank. [14] From a personal standpoint the swing around the country had also helped to confirm Aldrich's public image as a business leader. It had given him the opportunity to express his views on the New Deal before a national audience, and it had afforded him an unusual opportunity to test public and business sentiment about the program emanating from Washington.

WINTHROP ALDRICH AND JESSE JONES

Press coverage of the western trip occasionally identified Aldrich with the business and financial groups supporting the Roosevelt administration. In Texas, the home state of Jesse Jones, head of the Reconstruction Finance Corporation, the New York banker was asked for his views on Jones' recent address to the Bond Club which was critical of bankers and businessmen for their lack of interest in refinancing mortgage institutions. Aldrich replied that he was sure Jones' remarks reflected levity and good fellowship rather than criticism.[15] Undoubtedly this response was a sincere one, because he had come to know and respect Jones both as a banker and as a friend. Furthermore, Aldrich had been actively trying to remedy the very situation about which Jones was talking, at least as far as New York City was concerned.

The Great Depression had dealt New York real estate a paralyzing blow, with devastating consequences for small investors. During the 1920s participating certificates evidencing undivided interests in New York mortgages had been popular with many institutional and individual investors. Good past experience, however, proved a poor guide to New York real estate values once the depression of the 1930s swept across the land. Foreclosures multiplied, but even at low prices the market for even the best property was thin. Many holders of participating certificates found them worthless as collateral for loans, and the issuers found themselves not only in financial difficulty but the targets of hundreds of suits. To cope with this situation, Governor Lehman during his successful reelection campaign in 1934 had suggested formation of a Mortgage Certificate Loan Corporation to make loans to small holders of certificates who had exhausted conventional sources of funds. He had asked Aldrich to assist in mobilizing the private resources necessary to execute this project.[16] The

Chase chairman was successful in this endeavor, to which Jesse Jones' RFC also made a substantial commitment.

Aldrich had earlier been instrumental in helping Jones win commercial bankers' acceptance of RFC aid, and this had proved no small feat. In the aftermath of the banking crisis of early 1933, many bankers had feared that the government would try to take control of banking. Their fear of such control extended to the point of refusing aid from the RFC even where such assistance could have been vitally important to their banks' capital structures. The Roosevelt administration regarded this situation as dangerous and unacceptable from the standpoint of public confidence in the banks.

Under the Banking Act of 1933, banks participating in the federal deposit insurance plan, scheduled to go into effect January 1, 1934, had to be certified as sound by the Secretary of the Treasury. Member banks of the Federal Reserve System were required to join the plan, but there were numerous banks that had reopened after the 1933 Bank Holiday whose short-run situation was shaky. Try as he would, Jesse Jones had not been able to get these institutions to sell his agency preferred stock in order to add to their capital. Finally, in the fall of 1933, the New York Clearing House decided to initiate action. Three representatives of the Clearing House were appointed to discuss the alternatives with Jones and Roosevelt.[17] The log-jam was broken at last when, after a conference at the White House, the National City Bank asked for $50 million from the RFC. The Chase National followed suit early in 1934, issuing $50 million of preferred stock, of which the RFC took $46 million.[18] Since the Chase was in no danger whatsoever, the purpose of this move was primarily to set an example which Aldrich and Jones hoped other, smaller banks would follow.* And they did. Meanwhile, Secretary of the

---

* The Chase was enabled to revise its capital structure. It did not reduce the number of shares of common stock outstanding but rather reduced the

Treasury Henry Morgenthau was induced to certify even questionable banks on the basis of Jones' guarantee that the RFC would make them solvent, and the insurance deposit plan went into effect as scheduled.[19]

Jesse Jones and Winthrop Aldrich became close friends and found a number of common interests over the ensuing years. Each liked to use the other as a sounding board for his ideas. They served together on the Business Advisory Council and regularly exchanged views on fields as varied as banking and negro education. Like Aldrich, Jones became a trustee of Tuskegee Institute and was active in raising money for the United Negro College Fund. The RFC head and the New York banker found their cooperation productive and mutually satisfying even when other bankers regarded Jones' agency as the entering wedge of government in banking.

Aldrich and Roosevelt

There were other reasons for the press to identify Aldrich with the Roosevelt administration, despite his criticisms of its monetary and relief policies. In early 1934, for example, Aldrich met with President Roosevelt on two occasions, once to give his views on bank reform and the second time to discuss the proposed legislation to regulate the stock exchanges, which became the Securities Exchange Act of 1934.[20] Their discussion took place against a background of growing business discontent with the New Deal. The President attempted

---

par value of each share from $20 to $13.55 per share. The resulting change was as shown:

December 30, 1933		December 31, 1934	
Capital	$148,000,000.00	Capital-Preferred	$ 50,000,000.00
Surplus	50,000,000.00	Capital-Common	100,270,000.00
Undivided profits	9,187,898.62	Surplus	50,000,000.00
		Undivided profits	18,839,363.44

Source: Chase *Annual Reports*, 1933, 1934.

to allay some business fears by a Fireside Chat on September 30, 1934, when he referred to the importance of private initiative and the profit motive in terms that Aldrich could easily approve. This encouraging development was followed by Roosevelt's acceptance of an invitation to address the American Bankers Association in October. Aldrich was so pleased at this news that he phoned the White House to encourage the President to "rebuild the confidence of the public in the bankers." [21] As it turned out, Roosevelt was now prepared to make some general gestures in this direction.

President Roosevelt's 1934 Address to the ABA

When the President addressed an overflow ABA convention crowd in Washington's Constitution Hall, Aldrich was in the audience. He could especially appreciate the President's opening remark. "I have been seeing many of your members almost daily during the past year and a half," Roosevelt told the bankers, "and let me make it quite clear that in these meetings I have not done all the talking." To some listeners, however, it appeared that he had not done too much listening, for while Roosevelt stated that an objective of government was to encourage confidence in banks, he also stressed the overall leadership role of government and its responsibility to encourage "the confidence of the banks in the people." [22]

Although the bankers had hoped for a more conciliatory message,* Roosevelt clearly indicated that the administration

---

* Raymond Moley, Henry Morgenthau and Harry Hopkins drafted the President's speech. Moley later wrote that Morgenthau and Hopkins worked against the conciliatory tone that Moley favored. They especially objected to some parts of Jackson Reynolds' (First National Bank of New York) introduction of the President, though Reynolds was trying to be friendly. Reynolds finally agreed to delete the objectionable passages after Morgenthau almost caused the banker to cancel his appearance. These developments did not contribute to the kind of atmosphere or presidential mood that built rapport between Roosevelt and his banker audience. See Raymond Moley, *After Seven Years*, pp. 295–298.

did not intend to retreat from the power position that it had assumed in the critical days of 1933. Nevertheless, as he reported to his audiences during his western tour, Aldrich for one felt that the net effect of the President's ABA address had been favorable — a view reinforced by his interview with Roosevelt on October 25, 1934.[23]

Aldrich's visits to the White House were of the informal and personal type that Roosevelt seemed to prefer over the formal channel for communication between the administration and leading businessmen established by Secretary of Commerce Roper in 1933 and named the Business Advisory Council. Theoretically the President could have used the Council as a sounding board; in practice he appeared to lack interest in it.[24] Nevertheless, it was a formal mark of Aldrich's growing national stature that he was elected to the Council in November 1934.

Aldrich and The Banking Act of 1935

Owing to his place in commercial banking and his access to the administration, Aldrich was now recognized by the banking community as a valuable spokesman and adviser on legislation. In September 1934 he was appointed to the American Bankers Association's Special Committee on Proposed Revision of Banking Laws, later known simply as the Committee on Banking Studies. This turned out to be a very important appointment since once the fall elections were over, with very gratifying results for Roosevelt admirers, proposals for banking reform threatened to go considerably beyond the limits that Aldrich had contemplated.

In no small measure the new departure was attributable to Marriner Eccles, a Utah banker who was appointed to the Federal Reserve Board at Treasury Secretary Morgenthau's suggestion in the fall of 1934. Eccles made no secret of the fact that he believed the Federal Reserve System had been operated more for the benefit of private than for public interests and, more particularly, that it had been unduly responsive to the needs and wishes of the New York financial community.[25] With the aid of Lauchlin Currie, a young "braintruster" in the Treasury Department, Eccles prepared a memorandum on the subject and his proposed remedies. He submitted it to Roosevelt after the 1934 elections but before his own appointment to the Federal Reserve Board. The essence of his recommendations was that the Federal Reserve Board should be given increased power over (1) open market operations, which affected the level of member bank reserves, (2) appointment of the heads of individual Federal Reserve Banks, and (3) the nature of assets that could be rediscounted at such banks.[26] Eccles outlined to Roosevelt what would be involved in such a fundamental overhaul of the existing structure and functions of the Fed, and he received an enthusiastic response from the President followed by appointment to the Board.

Eccles' proposals were relevant not only to the place of private banking vis-à-vis the Fed, but to the whole question of financing the administration's work relief program. It had been common knowledge in November 1934, as the Chase group started its western trip, that Roosevelt would ask Congress in January for $4 or $5 billion dollars to finance a new relief effort and that it would have to be financed by government securities channeled by the Federal Reserve into the banking system. Eccles feared that with the existing structure of the System and with the hostility of powerful private interests, the work relief program might be hamstrung or its impact seriously diminished. He therefore decided to put his proposed reforms into legislative form as rapidly as possible. The Federal Reserve Board had assented to this strategy while Aldrich was still in the West.[27]

Changes in the Federal Reserve System

The resulting legislative proposals were introduced in the House by Congressman Henry Steagall on February 5, 1935, and in the Senate on the following day by Senator Duncan Fletcher. The legislation had been shrewdly conceived. The vital changes in the Federal Reserve were contained in Title II of the bill, which was flanked by two titles calculated to have strong appeal to the bankers who might attack Title II. The first liberalized the rate and nature of assessments for a permanent plan of federal deposit insurance, a major issue with bankers who felt that the provisions of the 1933 legislation had been burdensome, unsound, and discriminatory. The other title was more technical but, among other things, it extended the time in which officers who had borrowed from member banks could repay their loans without violating the Banking Act of 1933.[28]

The ABA executive committee took these matters under advisement at a meeting attended by both Aldrich and Eccles in Pas Christian, Mississippi, in early March 1935. The result was the appointment of a five-man ABA committee to act as liaison between the bankers and the administration leaders in the House and Senate. In addition to Aldrich, the bankers' committee consisted of Rudolph S. Hecht, the new ABA president; Robert V. Fleming of the Riggs National Bank in Washington, D.C.; Tom K. Smith of the Boatmen's National Bank of St. Louis; and Ronald Ransom of Atlanta, chairman of the ABA's committee on federal legislation. While the bill was before the House Banking and Currency Committee, the liaison group studied the measure thoroughly and discussed it with various congressmen and administration officials, as well as Eccles.[29] In these endeavors, Aldrich was as active as any of his colleagues, though bank affairs and his other obligations kept him in New York much of the time.

The report of the special liaison committee, endorsed by the ABA executive committee, was submitted to Chairman Steagall of the House Banking and Currency Committee on March 22, 1935. As Eccles had anticipated, the bankers offered no objection to Titles I and III. As he had also expected, they objected to Title II, though the tone of their criticism was moderate. In view of the fact that Title II had proposed to concentrate power in the Federal Reserve Board, the ABA group wanted changes "to insure, as far as possible, the absolute independence of the Board from partisan or political considerations." [30]

While Aldrich favored changes at the Fed, he did not want the results of change to make the System responsive to political pressures in Washington. The ABA special committee's report therefore reflected his position quite accurately, and his views were also formally relayed to the President, since Aldrich was serving concurrently as chairman of the Business Advisory Council's committee on the banking legislation.[31]

Among other things, the ABA committee called for reducing the Board from eight to five members and removal from the Board of the Secretary of the Treasury * and the Comptroller of the Currency, who served as ex officio representatives of the executive branch. In addition, the committee's report suggested that four governors of Federal Reserve Banks be given a vote in the Open Market Committee as a counterweight to the Washington orientation of that body.[32] In columnist Walter Lippmann's view, the report "defined the vital issues so clearly that no honest man can refuse to face them." [33] *The American Banker*, however, adopted a critical attitude toward the ABA committee's work and even

* Senator Glass had urged this step in 1933, based in part on his own experience as Secretary of the Treasury. The proposal was passed by the Senate in 1933 but was not acted on by the House at that time.

questioned the motives of its members in view of the fact that the RFC owned preferred stock in their banks.[34] Some bankers also shared the view that the ABA should move more slowly and that the enticements of Title I for quick action were not sufficient to warrant forfeiting a more extended study of the total banking problem.[35]

The House hearings on the banking legislation ended April 8, and the Glass subcommittee of the Senate Banking and Currency Committee opened its hearings on April 19. Eccles regarded the Senate hearings as the forum for a personal vendetta against him by Senator Glass, whose province Eccles was invading. Glass was certainly not pleased to hear from Aldrich that Eccles had received a copy of Aldrich's report to the President on behalf of the Business Advisory Council while the Virginia Senator had not.[36] Eccles later wrote that when he had discussed the pending legislation privately with Aldrich, he had believed the New York banker to be sympathetic. But, he wrote, he had difficulty in squaring this impression with what he heard Aldrich say before the Glass subcommittee.[37] The feeling was probably mutual.

Aldrich appeared before the subcommittee on May 15, 1935. In his effort to shape the legislation revising the Federal Reserve System he was following the example set by his father, to whom the Fed's creation owed so much. The banker opened his testimony by saying: "I regard this bill as one of the most important measures now before Congress. It is more than a banking bill: it is a credit and currency bill. As such it deserves the most careful consideration not only of bankers but of businessmen generally . . . it touches at vital points every person in the United States." Largely dismissing Titles I and III from his discussion, he set out to rebut the earlier testimony of Eccles that Title II was urgently needed and that its adoption would not seriously change the character of the Federal Reserve System. In Aldrich's view the proposals backed by Eccles were "not liberalizing the Federal Reserve System. It is making it over into an instrument of despotic authority." [38]

To anyone who had heard Winthrop Aldrich at the Senate hearings in 1933 on the causes of the national depression, or had read his Commonwealth Club address of December 1934, the principles that he enunciated in reviewing the proposed 1935 banking legislation would have been familiar. Freedom of enterprise and individual initiative were the keys to economic life, and the existing balance between central and local authority in the Federal Reserve System were in keeping with this concept.[39] In his view the pending bill "would make the administration of the 12 Federal Reserve banks directly subordinate to the central authority of the Federal Reserve Board." [40] What made this so objectionable, Aldrich said, was the possibility that it created for political manipulation of currency and credit,[41] since the Board was appointed by, and there was a possibility that members could be removed at the pleasure of, the President.* Accordingly, Aldrich supported the ABA recommendation that the Federal Reserve Board be given greater freedom from the President, that the Secretary of the Treasury and Comptroller of the Currency be eliminated as ex officio members, and that total Board membership be cut from eight to five members.[42]

* A case (*Rathbun v. U.S.*, 295 U.S. 602) was pending before the Supreme Court on the President's power to remove appointive officials from office. Aldrich feared the decision might affect the Federal Reserve Board's independence. The legislation before the Committee specified that the President could remove the Governor of the Board at his pleasure — a provision to insure a link between the executive branch and the Board. Aldrich did not object to such an arrangement if the ex officio representatives of the executive branch were removed from the Board, as he thought they should be. See also Eccles' testimony, 74 Cong. 1 Sess., House Committee on Banking and Currency, "Banking Act of 1935," *Hearings* (Washington, 1935), p. 191.

Aldrich's basic objections to Title II were based on the fear that it would, as written, facilitate experimentation with the currency and credit of the United States in pursuance of "one superficial, simple theory after another." [43] A case in point was open market operations. Eccles felt strongly that these operations, whereby the purchase or sale of government securities by the Federal Reserve raised or lowered bank reserves, were highly important in terms of controlling the country's supply of money. Under the existing arrangements, however, individual Federal Reserve banks could both initiate and decline to participate in these operations. In Eccles' view, this important activity was thus made subject to local or regional rather than national considerations. One important part of Title II, therefore, proposed to establish a powerful, centralized open market committee. [44]

Aldrich attacked the proposition that bank credit could be manipulated into business activity by open market operations, citing the experience of the past few years and the fact that idle member bank deposits with the Fed currently exceeded $2 billion. He was even more firmly opposed to financing Treasury deficits directly with central bank credit. [45] For the same reasons the New York banker attacked the proposal to transfer control of the rediscount rate from the district Federal Reserve Banks to the Federal Reserve Board. [46] And he likewise opposed the overliberalization of the definition of collateral on which Federal Reserve notes could be issued.* In his words: "It is practically the unbroken record of central banking that where there has been no restraint on the type of collateral against which notes can be issued, the currency has become debased." [47] In each instance he proposed modifica-

---

* The House bill made "any sound asset" eligible for discount at a Reserve Bank at the discretion of the Board. Eccles favored such a provision because he felt that unduly high eligibility requirements for discounts had contributed to the collapse of banks with good but illiquid assets.

tions to the pending legislation that would eliminate, in his judgment, the objection that he had raised.

Eccles was convinced that Glass, as a framer of the 1913 Federal Reserve Act, was determined to kill its revision as proposed in Title II and that the witnesses, including Aldrich, had been selected by the Senator with this particular end in view.[48] He saw in the frequent references to "political control" made by these witnesses an insubstantial invocation of unwarranted fears. During the Senate hearings, Senator Couzens had taken this line with Aldrich, suggesting that political considerations were always present no matter how a law was framed. Aldrich was forced to concur, but it was also clear that he genuinely feared a relationship between the administration in power and the Federal Reserve Board to control credit, with political ends in mind.[49] Once he had had his say, however, there was little he could do but await the outcome of legislative action.

The House bill, which incorporated many of Eccles' proposals, had been passed before Aldrich gave his Senate testimony, but the Senate hearings dragged on. Eccles became alarmed that the banking community would find some pretext or other to postpone final action until the following Congress, where he judged the chances of achieving his goals would be further diminished. The bankers seeking just this result proposed separation of the favorable Titles from the objectionable one. By appealing to Roosevelt, Eccles was able to circumvent this tactic. He was also able to win Congressional approval of additional time for consideration of the crucial Title II.[50]

On July 2, 1935, the Senate passed the version of the bank bill reported out by the Banking and Currency Committee, but the job of reconciling it with the House version that had passed in early May remained. With Eccles collaborating closely with Congressman Goldsborough on strategy in the conference committee, Glass was allowed to win a significant number of individual points while many of those that Eccles considered indispensable survived.[51] In the end, the results were surprisingly satisfactory to all concerned, including Aldrich.

The provisions of the 1935 act were quite close to what Aldrich and the ABA had advocated. The Federal Reserve Board, renamed the Board of Governors of the Federal Reserve System, was reduced from eight to seven members instead of the five that the ABA recommended. Glass was successful in eliminating both the Secretary of the Treasury and the Comptroller of the Currency from ex officio membership, a change endorsed by Aldrich. Board members were to hold office for 14 years unless removed sooner for cause by the President. In individual Federal Reserve Banks the posts of President and Vice President were created, and while they were named by the local boards they had to be confirmed by the Board of Governors. The Open Market Committee was reconstituted so that authority and responsibility were centralized in Washington, but there was consolation for Aldrich in the fact that representatives of five Federal Reserve Banks were also authorized to participate in the decisions, and district banks were no longer permitted to ignore them. Within limits, reserve requirements could be changed by the Governors without the declaration of an emergency by the President as had been the case in the past. The practical, though not the formal, definition of eligible paper on which Federal Reserve Banks could make loans was extended, but not to the extent feared by Aldrich. Admission to the System for state banks was simplified while the possibilities for real estate loans by national banks were expanded. Most important from Aldrich's standpoint, Eccles had failed to achieve his objective of rewriting the mandate of the Board in terms that specifically charged it with exercising monetary control for maintaining overall business stability and full employment.[52]

The work of the ABA's Special Committee of Five had been very satisfactory to the banking community, given the circumstances. A former president of the ABA wrote Aldrich on the occasion of the committee's March 1935 report: "I doubt if any ABA committee at any time has ever done a finer piece of work." [53] In August the current president of the ABA wrote: "While the legislation as finally passed is not in all respects to our liking, I think you will agree with me that it is on the whole a pretty satisfactory piece of legislation and far better than any of us believed possible a few months ago." He reported that bankers across the country shared this view and expressed his thanks for Aldrich's "fine support." [54] Aldrich, who was on vacation in Maine at the time, replied on September 5, "I read the Banking Bill as finally enacted while I was away and I agree with you that on the whole it is a very satisfactory piece of legislation." [55]

THE PUBLIC UTILITY HOLDING COMPANY ACT OF 1935

As far as Aldrich was concerned, much the same could be said of another piece of legislation passed in the same session of Congress, the Public Utility Holding Company Act of 1935. The pyramiding of holding companies in the public utility business during the 1920s had led to many financial abuses with disastrous results. The Chase National Bank was a major lender to many of these public utility holding companies, and in taking up its collateral on defaulted loans and in acting in a fiduciary capacity under trust indentures, the bank had by 1933 become virtually a public utility holding company itself.[56] Since deliverance from this unwelcome role depended on the slow-paced revival of a market for public utility securities, the process of extrication was a long one. As mentioned earlier, the Public Utility Department under Edward Love had been created at Aldrich's suggestion to handle all the bank's loans to, and investments in, public utility companies.

The introduction of the legislation that became the Public Utility Holding Company Act of 1935 posed a direct threat to the Chase, because the original provisions would have forced it to dump badly depreciated utility stocks on a depressed market. This threat led Love, Lawrence Bennett (the counsel to the Public Utility Department), and Aldrich to do what they could to temper the proposed law and after its passage to induce the Securities and Exchange Commission, charged with enforcing it, to take account of the special circumstances that obtained when a commercial bank found itself unavoidably and temporarily acting as a public utility holding company.[57] They were successful in these efforts. As a result, the Chase was enabled to proceed with the orderly liquidation of its public utility holdings.

ALDRICH'S APPRAISAL OF NEW DEAL LEGISLATION, 1935

Aldrich was afforded an opportunity to review both this legislation, the Banking Act, and the overall progress of the New Deal when he was invited to address the Houston, Texas, Chamber of Commerce on December 11, 1935.[58] Houston was the headquarters of Humble Oil & Refining Company, Jersey Standard's great Texas producing affiliate. During his tour a year earlier, Aldrich had met Robert L. Blaffer and Hines H. Baker, two of the leading members of Humble's top management, and they acted as hosts for Mr. and Mrs. Aldrich on the occasion of the 1935 visit.

As was generally the case with his speeches evaluating the national scene, Aldrich opened his address to the Houston Chamber on a positive note, followed by an analysis of selected problems. In this instance he reported that the upward movement of the economy from September 1934, which he had noted on his last Houston visit, had continued, with the most impressive display of economic strength and business confidence since the onset of the depression. He attributed these developments principally to the revision of the banking laws (for which he gave much credit to Senator Glass), the end of the National Industrial Recovery Act as the result of a Supreme Court decision, and the public's new confidence that Congress would no longer pass uncritically "all measures which have or are supposed to have the sanction of the Executive." In addition, both the Public Utility Holding Company Act of 1935 * and the current Tax Act,** while not all that he would have wished, were in his opinion considerably better in their final form than when introduced. Together, these developments, he thought, had relieved the fears of businessmen and of the public that government would control the economy, † and the resulting upsurge of confidence, combined with the pent-up demand for both producers' and consumers' goods as the result of the depression, augured well for continued recovery.

* As originally proposed, this measure would have limited a public utility holding company to one integrated system with not more than one subsidiary between the holding company and the operating company. The pressure against this requirement was so severe that the bill, as passed, allowed a holding company to control more than one system under specified conditions.

** The tax bill had been termed a "soak-the-rich" plan with a goal of "Share the Wealth." The legislation was, however, substantially revised prior to passage. For a contemporary evaluation, see Roy G. Blakey and Gladys C. Blakey, "The Revenue Act of 1935," *The American Economic Review*, vol. XXV (December 1935), pp. 673–690.

† Roosevelt in an exchange of letters with publisher Roy Howard, who stressed the extent of businessmen's discontent and fear, had promised a "breathing spell" in September 1935. By the following January, however, Roosevelt was in a more truculent mood and his annual message set the tone for the 1936 election campaign, among other things, attacking "entrenched greed" and "economic autocracy." (Moley, *After Seven Years*, pp. 317–318.)

On the other hand, he emphasized that what he regarded as very fundamental problems remained unsolved. Speaking in a cotton export center, he took advantage of the opportunity to stress that little progress had been made toward the revitalizing of foreign trade, while the administration's domestic program of paying farmers to take land out of production and subsidizing certain crops had merely "deferred" attacking a basic problem "through the vast outpouring of public money." Predictably, however, the areas where he saw the greatest danger were monetary and fiscal policy. He reiterated his now-familiar warnings against the "pump priming" concept and its attendant unbalanced budgets, and the dangers of inflation based on currency debasement and artificially supported prices. In his view the "inflationists have had their day"; their recommendations had been adopted, had failed to solve the problems to which they were addressed, and had created new ones.

Finally, and most specifically, he came down to the question of excess bank reserves, which he regarded as an invitation to speculation. He laid the responsibility for dealing with this threat at the door of the Federal Reserve System, and he proposed that the Federal Reserve Banks sell their government securities, thus drawing surplus funds from the liquid central money markets, and double the reserve requirement to eliminate what he regarded as a dangerously high level of excess reserves throughout the System. Acknowledging that such actions could not be taken lightly, especially in the matter of reserve requirements which affected all banks, Aldrich nevertheless maintained that the time to act had come.

In these recommendations he took specific issue with Marriner Eccles who, in a statement of November 22, had denied that there was an excessive expansion of bank credit or threat of inflation.[59] Aldrich agreed that the volume of excess reserves was not the product of Federal Reserve policy *per se* but rather was the byproduct of the inflow of gold to the United States since early 1934. This did not change the obligation of the Federal Reserve, as he saw it, to take corrective action. As to the fact that this might depress the price of government bonds and raise the cost of carrying the public debt, he argued that the Treasury would have to deal with this problem sooner or later and therefore it might as well face realities while the problem was still manageable.

The concluding paragraph of his Houston speech summed up his position concisely and forcefully:

> Gentlemen, I have come here to say old-fashioned things, things which a few years ago would have seemed so indisputable that my saying them would have sounded like recital of the alphabet or the multiplication table. I have come here to say that we should live within our means, that even this richest of all countries in the world cannot spend billions of dollars a year more than its income without disaster, that we should not delude ourselves with the notion that the expansion of bank credit can be endlessly a substitute for investors' savings, and that the Federal Reserve authorities should perform their obvious duty in the money market. And, finally, let me say that whatever the theory of the objectives of Federal Reserve policy, the Federal Reserve authorities should at least want to be in a position to control the volume of reserve money in the country. Even those who believe that bank credit has the magical power of controlling commodity prices and the volume of business still should not wish to have the throttle chained wide open and the air-brake system removed from the train.

Evidently he hit a responsive chord with many bankers and businessmen. They showered Aldrich with congratulations on the timeliness and appropriateness of his analysis. The Federal Reserve substantiated his view of excess reserves when the Board of Governors announced after its meeting on December

18, 1935, that the current volume was "far beyond the present or prospective requirements of credit for sound business expansion." [60] But the Board proposed no immediate action because it saw no overexpansion of business or credit.*

During 1934 and 1935, Aldrich had taken an active part in banking legislation. As a representative of the banking community he had been consulted by leading figures of the administration from the President on down, and in his public addresses he had attempted to shape public as well as banking and business opinion about the New Deal. Despite the constancy and consistency of his position, he had given an impression of being ambivalent. On the one hand he was clearly regarded by the administration as one of the more "enlightened" business and financial leaders and had certainly played this role in encouraging banks to accept RFC aid and in supporting bank reform. Furthermore, at every opportunity he had publicly stressed the amount of economic recovery that had taken place since mid-1934, a development which redounded to the administration's credit. On the other hand, he had just as consistently attacked the economic and social philosophy of the New Deal as incompatible with the American traditions of self-reliance and fiscal and financial responsibility. He seemed to be saying that most of the favorable developments since 1933 had come about despite the New Deal's experimentation but nevertheless that the New Deal itself was not "all bad."

This indeed appears to be where he stood. To the extent that statutory reforms would eliminate demonstrated abuses in

* S. Parker Gilbert of J. P. Morgan & Co. in a letter to the *New York Times* on the same day also opposed an increase in reserve requirements as risking a setback to recovery and the possible triggering of deflation. Unlike Aldrich he advocated use of open market operations and the discount rate if a check on credit expansion proved necessary. Both the Federal Reserve Board and Gilbert thought that recovery in Europe might reverse the gold flow that was swelling excess reserves.

the functioning of the private sector and within the context of a sound monetary system based in some measure on gold and responsive to market forces, he was an enthusiastic supporter of New Deal measures. To the extent that the administration attempted to manipulate money and markets, to substitute the administrative discretion of public officials for private business decision-making, and to centralize power over the economy in Washington, he was an outspoken critic of the New Deal. It was typical of Aldrich that he should have chosen to take such a stand, refusing to join the camp of those who opposed all change yet also refusing to endorse undiscriminatingly those who were attempting to engineer change wholesale.

DEVELOPMENTS AT THE CHASE

Aldrich's primary responsibility, of course, was to the Chase, and in his Washington activity during these two years, 1934–1935, he was serving his bank as well as the banking community. In matters of immediate and direct interest to the bank some substantial progress was being made toward liquidating problems inherited from the Wiggin era, though others remained as troublesome as ever. The most marked progress was in the Fox Film situation. Aldrich had overall responsibility for this problem, but Hermann G. Place bore the immediate responsibility. Their relationship made Place's job far easier than it might otherwise have been. As Place later recalled it, Aldrich "was a wonderful man to work for and work with because he had a keen mind and he had a lot of guts. . . . And if I talked to him — we've got to do this, we've got to do that — he'd listen and say, 'Okay, that's it.' And we went ahead and did it." [61]

Place was a financial expert with a keen strategic sense, so delegation of broad authority to him by the bank chairman carried little risk. For example, Place had discovered that one of the problems in the film industry was the failure to amortize films until they were shown. Thus the financial consequences of a "bad" film did not appear on the Profit and Loss statement on a regular basis. On his initiative, this procedure was soon changed so that Fox movie films were amortized on a regular basis regardless of when they were shown.[62]

In dealing with Fox Film, Place started from the premise that the company had important capital assets but that it lacked the knack of making financially successful pictures. The answer to this problem was found in the person of Darryl Zanuck, who had made a number of successful movies for a small company, Twentieth Century Pictures. In 1935 this company was merged with Fox to form Twentieth Century-Fox Film Corporation.[63] The new concern was successful from the start, and when the Skouras brothers — Charlie and Spyros — were brought into the picture via a very substantial personal service contract, the corner was definitely turned. When Place said Aldrich had "guts" he probably had in mind the fact that the Chase chairman had backed him on the Fox merger with Twentieth Century and on the Skouras contract despite serious misgivings among some influential officers and directors of the bank.[64]

The Chase also emerged with a direct 58 percent interest in the reorganized National Theatres Corporation, with the remainder being held by Twentieth Century-Fox Film Corporation.[65] At a later date the film corporation acquired the 58 percent interest in National Theatres from the Chase in exchange for stock. General Theatres Equipment, Inc., the holding company which Harley Clarke had promoted in his effort to gain a dominant position in the motion picture business, was successfully reorganized under court supervision and began a comeback.[66]*

* Place, backed by Aldrich, shortly performed a comparable operation

In contrast to these favorable developments, the Chase's loan for Cuban public works financing remained in default. Interest payments had been suspended by the Cuban government in 1933 and when the first sinking fund installment fell due in 1935, it was not paid.[67] All the bank could do was wait and hope. Meanwhile, the number of legal actions involving these and other matters, with Aldrich typically as one of the defendants because of his office, showed little sign of diminishing. The transition back to normalcy in the bank's affairs did not come easily or inexpensively.

ACTIVITIES OUTSIDE THE BANK

In addition to his work at the bank and in connection with legislative matters, Aldrich had added to his staggering load of outside commitments. He continued as a director of Westinghouse Electric, American Telephone and Telegraph, and the Discount Corporation of New York. He was elected president of the State Charities Aid Association in 1934, and continued as trustee of the Laura Spelman Fund, treasurer of the finance committee of Tuskegee Institute, and filled similar posts in half a dozen other organizations. In 1935 he was elected a trustee of the General Education Board and reelected chairman of the trustees' committee of the New York Community Trust. Amidst all these activities he was very active in Harvard affairs, becoming one of the Two Hundred and Fifty Associates of the Harvard Business School, member of the Board of Overseers to visit the Economics Department of the College, member of the Harvard Fund Council, and member of the committees on finance and appointments of the Harvard Club of New York.

---

in connection with International Paper Company, where the Chase had a major interest. Among other things, this financial support and reorganization enabled the ailing company's southern kraft subsidiary to build a new and efficient mill.

Under these varied and unremitting pressures it was imperative that Aldrich gain frequent respites from the frantic pace of his New York office, and he did not hesitate to take them. In the winter of 1935, for example, the Aldriches vacationed for several weeks in Florida; in the early spring they spent a few days at the Jekyll Island retreat that his father had so enjoyed; in May they stole a few days in Maine where they had recently bought a large cottage at Dark Harbor. The family returned there for the summer, and Aldrich made short visits until August when he divided his time between the Penobscot Bay retreat and the annual New York Yacht Club cruise. In September he went to Europe on a trip for the bank that included visits to Paris, London, and Berlin.

The varied activity of the busy year was almost perfectly symbolized by the entries in his appointment calendar for December 31, 1935: 10:00 a.m.–2:45 p.m., in court . . . with Mr. Embree; 3:00 p.m., Mr. Place and Senator Hastings; 6:00 p.m., tennis at Piping Rock. Winthrop Aldrich had settled into a challenging leadership role confidently and comfortably.

CHAPTER IX

The Transition Years, 1936-1939

IN THE years 1936–1939 the nation continued the slow transition from the depths of depression to renewed economic vitality, interrupted by a brief but sharp setback in 1937–1938. On the horizon loomed the growing threat of a world war, which was finally triggered in September 1939 by the outbreak of hostilities in Europe. Domestic problems then receded into the background as the nation confronted a new challenge to its existence.

For Aldrich these years involved the further liquidation of the bank's problems inherited from the Wiggin era, new advances for the Chase, and numerous opportunities to exercise his role as spokesman at home and abroad for an influential segment of the American business and banking community. The path to the future was far from clear, but in his assessment of it Aldrich steadfastly called for adherence to what he regarded as fundamentals of American life. His varied interests and activities, combined with a heavy load of civic and philanthropic responsibilities, imposed heavier burdens than even those of the hectic years 1933–1935.

CHANGES AT THE CHASE

In this new era the Chase made generally steady progress. Organizationally, the concept of specialized departments, inaugurated with the Public Utility Department soon after Aldrich came to the bank, was further developed. In 1936 it resulted in the creation of a Petroleum Department.

The Chase had always been close to the oil industry, and the Seaboard National Bank, which had entered the 1930 merger via the Equitable, was started as an "oil bank." In addition to oil loans, the Chase also held large amounts of oil company stock in its trust department. These companies represented every phase of the oil industry and included both large and small concerns. Aldrich therefore considered it essential that the bank organize to render expert and impartial service to the entire oil industry. He mentioned this idea to Walter Teagle, president of Standard Oil Company (New Jersey), and Teagle recommended that the bank hire an independent petroleum engineer to supervise its oil work.[1]

Teagle knew just the man, Joseph E. Pogue. Pogue was not seeking a new situation and had some reservations about sacrificing his independence by joining the Chase. However, on behalf of the bank, president Campbell made it clear that the Chase only wanted Pogue's independent judgment on its petroleum activities and would allow the engineer complete freedom in exercising it.[2] On this basis, Pogue agreed to head the new department, which over the next decade handled oil loans of more than $180 million.[3]

Another organizational development was the establishment of a Department of Financial and Business Research in 1939.[4] It was headed by the bank's new economist, Dr. B. Haggott Beckhart, Professor of Banking at Columbia University and Educational Supervisor, New York Chapter, American Institute of Banking. He had succeeded Dr. Anderson when

Anderson returned to teaching at UCLA. The new department represented a further step in institutionalizing the economists' role in the bank, for Anderson had reported only to Aldrich and Campbell.

Foreign Branches

The foreign activities of the bank continued to be a primary interest for Aldrich. His enthusiasm for them was not, however, shared by at least one former director who suggested in 1937 that serious consideration be given to abandoning all branches abroad except London. In reply Aldrich pointed out that there were practical reasons why this course of action was undesirable. In Paris, for example, the Chase owned the quarters of the Rue Cambon branch and had a long lease on the premises occupied by the Rue George V office. Closing these branches would not, therefore, eliminate all their expense. In Germany, the bank maintained only two rooms, and they were occupied by the bank's representative liquidating its German commitments. The Cuban branch had proved profitable for many years, and the only problems in that country revolved around the public works loan of the 1920s which had not yet been liquidated. The branches in the Far East, inherited from the Equitable, had been consistently profitable, though the Shanghai office was suffering from the current turmoil in that city.[5]

The foreign business was important to the Chase. In March 1938, for example, the bank had total commitments of $55 million in Great Britain, $26 million in Continental Europe, and $19 million distributed in the rest of the world, plus $151 million in foreign loans and discounts to Americans or secured by American collateral.[6] Considerable attention was being given to developing business in Latin America. During the year a new branch was established at Balboa in the Canal

Zone, and the settlement of the old Cuban public works loan was finally approved by the Cuban Congress.[7]

Settlement of Shareholders' Suits

Meanwhile, the shareholders' suits initiated after the Pecora hearings had been settled.* In the period since the initiation of the suits it had become apparent that the plaintiffs' estimates of losses to the bank had been exaggerated and that it would be difficult to sustain liability against individual directors, except possibly for Albert Wiggin. With only two exceptions, therefore, the individual suits were consolidated into a single action which finally came to trial early in April of 1937. Before it had gone very far, Mr. Wiggin and representatives of the estates of two deceased ex-directors offered to pay $2.5 million in settlement — $1.5 million to go to the Chase and $1 million to Amerex Holding Corporation, successor to Chase Securities.[8] Mr. Wiggin himself put up $2 million of this amount, denying the validity of the plaintiffs' charges and stipulating that all other officers and directors of the Chase and the former Chase Securities Corporation be discharged from any liability.[9]

The bank asked for the Court's guidance on accepting this settlement, and a referee was appointed to consider the matter. After examining several thousand pages of testimony and exhibits, the referee concluded that the offer was reasonable and adequate. On June 23, 1937, the Court accepted this recommendation and on the following day entered a judgment to that effect. Out of its $1.5 million, the bank had to pay the fees of the shareholders' counsel amounting to $375,000, and the remainder was transferred to the reserve for contingencies.[10] Thus ended another of Aldrich's problems inherited from the Wiggin days.

* See Chapter VIII.

The Troubles of William Randolph Hearst

The trial counsel for the Chase directors in the shareholders' suits was Judge Clarence J. Shearn, a close associate of William Randolph Hearst. The Chase had had minor dealings with Hearst, who found himself in major financial difficulties at this time. The famed publisher had been an equally famous spender, and the results had finally caught up with him. Threatened with bankruptcy, he turned control of his publishing empire over to Shearn, who called on the Chase for help.[11] This posed a major problem for Aldrich and his advisers. Loaning money to the sinking publishing empire did not look like a profitable undertaking relative to the risk. On the other hand, to let one of the great newspaper and magazine chains collapse when it might be rescued would be unthinkable.

This problem was dropped on the desk of Hermann Place, who had handled the Fox Film situation so deftly. He came up with a solution that would protect the Chase and make the necessary loans available. As a result, the bank at one time held all the Hearst magazines, such as *Good Housekeeping* and *Harper's Bazaar*, as collateral.[12] Place kept a close check on the progress of the Hearst group, whose affairs had been placed by Shearn in the hands of a "Conservation Committee," which included senior Hearst executives like Richard E. Berlin, head of the Hearst magazines. Place also found himself in friendly controversy with William Evarts of Aldrich's old law firm, which was handling the Hearst side of the problem.[13] In the end, the loans were repaid and the Hearst empire survived, though shorn of some of its properties.

ALDRICH APPRAISES DOMESTIC AND FOREIGN POLICIES

Although the recession of 1937–38 affected the Chase adversely, the bank in 1939 had the largest deposits in its history

— over $2.8 billions.[14] The Chase management team, partly inherited and partly selected by Aldrich, proved so capable that Aldrich was able to give a large part of his time to affairs outside the bank. He took advantage of this situation by speaking out with increasing frequency on the New Deal.

The editor of a respected business periodical summed up the results as far as the business community was concerned when he wrote Aldrich in November 1937: "Almost every person with whom I have talked agrees that your voice has been the most effective of any raised from the business or financial world." [15]

In assessing the domestic policies of the New Deal, Aldrich did not waver from the position that he had taken in February 1933 as to the basic principles — credit restraint, balanced budget, private initiative, and increased foreign trade — on which economic recovery should be based. Between April and August 1936 alone, he made four major speeches on current problems viewed in this framework.

Expansion of Credit

On April 2, 1936, he presided at the annual meeting of the Academy of Political Science at the Hotel Astor and delivered a short address entitled "The Control of Credit." The thrust of his message was substantially the same as the one contained in his speech to the Houston Chamber of Commerce the preceding December. The rapid growth of credit — stimulated by governmental spending and borrowing — called, Aldrich said, for prompt action by the Federal Reserve to bring it under control. He advocated an immediate increase in reserve requirements for member banks, with the possibility of the System's selling government securities as a second step,*

---

* An increase in reserve requirements directly alters deposit extension powers of member banks. There was disagreement over the practical effect of open-market sales of government securities on bank reserves.

depending on the success of the first. He again underlined the need for decentralized decision-making and responsibility on credit matters rather than dependence on government administrators.

For different reasons, Marriner Eccles and the Board of Governors of the Federal Reserve System had finally reached the same conclusion about the need to raise reserve requirements. But in view of the coming national elections — and not wishing to give the Republican National Convention in June a ready-made issue — Eccles delayed the action until late summer.[16]

Local Autonomy and Responsibility

Aldrich's views on individual responsibility provided the theme of his address to the Chamber of Commerce of the State of New York on the occasion of his acceptance of its presidency, May 7, 1936. Taking the 168-year-old charter of the Chamber with its emphasis on "local autonomy and responsibility" as his point of departure, the banker emphasized the dangers of deserting these fundamentals. As he saw it, there had been a distressing tendency since 1933 to enact hasty legislation causing the states and local communities to surrender their responsibilities to the federal government. He singled out the Social Security Act of 1935 as an example of a measure that was not fully understood and as one posing "a grave menace to the future security of the country as a whole and therefore to the security of the very people it was designed to assist." And he reiterated his belief, first publicly stated in his Commonwealth Club address in San Francisco in 1934, that the handling of relief by the federal government was inappropriate and dangerous. "The reversals of federal policy which have taken place in dealing with the relief problem have been disheartening to those of us who have studied and worked with the matter," he said.

Foreign Trade

Two weeks later, at a World Trade Luncheon in New York City, he was afforded an opportunity to state his views on foreign trade.[17] They clearly had not changed since he expressed them early in 1933 before the Senate subcommittee seeking to identify the causes of the depression. Freer trade would reduce the danger of war since "have-not" nations would not be forced to fight for what they needed; foreign trade would create employment both at home and abroad; and it would help to decrease the imbalance between the manufacturing and agricultural sectors, reducing the burden of government assistance to farmers. Restoration of foreign trade would also increase government revenues and thus help to balance the budget. But Aldrich warned against the policy of the 1920s which encouraged trade by the export of capital rather than by accepting goods and services in payment for American exports. In implementing a policy of freer trade he saw a national challenge, recognition of which had been obscured by what he termed the false issue of "nationalism versus internationalism." The real issue, he said, was one of "nationalism versus sectionalism."

National interests, Aldrich felt, should be controlling and they would be promoted by foreign trade. Secretary of State Cordell Hull had made this one of his primary concerns, encouraging the negotiation of reciprocal trade agreements whereby the participants would mutually reduce tariff duties and the United States would extend the same treatment to other countries that did not discriminate against American goods. Aldrich endorsed Hull's approach enthusiastically and urged public support for it.

The Social Security System

In July, Aldrich returned to his criticism of the federal Social Security System in a lengthy address to the Institute of

Public Affairs at the University of Virginia.[18] Both before and after its passage in 1935, the Social Security Act had met strong criticism in many quarters of the business community. To some business leaders the legislation seemed to invite individuals to ignore their personal responsibilities to work and save. To others it seemed that the financial structure of the program required the poor to finance the poor; to still others the program appeared open to manipulation on a large scale for partisan political ends. Criticism, in short, ran the gamut from attacking the concept of social security itself to challenging the financing and administration of the program.

The act covered a wide range of situations. Among the most important provisions were those seeking to cope with the problems of old age and unemployment. The legislation offered benefits to workers over 65 years of age in certain categories and under specified conditions. These benefits were financed by a tax on both employees and employers, and the taxes were turned over to the Treasury as "internal revenue collections." Funds paid out for old-age benefits were returned to the state plus an allowance for administration, and the federal government matched state funds up to 50 percent of total payments. Unemployment assistance was being administered by the states under a variety of programs, and the federal legislation recognized this fact. Employers paid a federal tax to the Treasury, but payments into state unemployment funds could be credited up to 90 percent of the federal tax.[19]

Aldrich had many reservations about these provisions. "I am deeply sympathetic toward the efforts to mitigate the chief economic hazards to which great masses of people are subject, particularly the hazards of unemployment and of poverty in old age," he said. "But I wish also to emphasize the side of the problem that is now being overlooked by many of us — the hazards of a hastily conceived program for accomplishing this."

He began by considering the unemployment insurance provisions. As Aldrich saw it, the tax on employers raised the costs of production and penalized firms providing employment. Even more objectionable to him, and probably unconstitutional in his opinion, was the requirement that the states pay unemployment taxes directly into the United States Treasury. He further pointed out that the federal grants back to states for administration of unemployment insurance were less than the 10 percent of the payroll taxes collected by the states and turned over to the federal government.

Aldrich was equally critical of the old-age insurance plan. He attacked the discriminatory basis on which contributions were collected from only certain classes of workers and the requirements imposed before benefits could be received. He was even more concerned with the financial aspects of the plan. He pointed out that government was not like a private company, where a reserve fund was essential. Government could handle insurance matters on a completely different basis: compelling participation, changing premiums, and making up deficiencies out of general tax funds. What troubled him most was that the old-age funds went into the government's general fund in exchange for government securities, which in his view amounted to transferring funds from one government pocket to another. Furthermore, there was no actuarial principle involved, he said, since after five years the fund would be taking in sixteen times as much as it was paying out.

Aldrich's solution was a current-cost plan that started paying benefits as soon as the taxes for them had been levied. He favored grants-in-aid to the states for unemployment assistance and would have similarly financed old-age benefits by substituting such grants for taxes on special classes of workers. There were many, even within the administration, who agreed with Aldrich's evaluation of the administration and coverage of Social Security, and changes were gradually made in them.

The banker's most important point, however, was that individual security could not be obtained within a system that undermined aggregate security. As he saw it, genuine security rested on the health of the economic system; yet the Social Security program as it was operating seemed to him so economically — and even morally — unsound that it endangered the economy.

This speech, reproduced in pamphlet form, was sent to over 135,000 recipients, and it received wide newspaper attention. The *Rocky Mountain News* of Denver, Colorado, made it the basis for editorial comment that was typical of many other papers. Suggesting that Aldrich was interpreting the 1936 Republican platform and disagreeing with practically every one of his points, the editorial nevertheless characterized his speech as "The most intelligent presentation of the conservative viewpoint on social security that has yet been made," and further credited the banker with "a social vision and conscience much more advanced than has been common among the big financiers of this country." [20]

The 1936 Election

Aldrich had certainly never wavered in his support of the Republican party and of course supported its presidential candidate Alfred M. Landon of Kansas in 1936. Landon was overwhelmingly defeated, but speaking to the stockholders of the Federal Reserve Bank of Boston on November 12, 1936, Aldrich declared "one very fine result of the election . . . [is that] the lunatic fringe has certainly been destroyed." [21] A week later at the annual banquet of the Chamber of Commerce of the State of New York he characterized the election as an "American reflection" of a worldwide movement in which individuals were giving up some of their freedom in return for security. [22]

RECOVERY AND RECESSION

In a speech to the Illinois Manufacturers' Association in Chicago early in December, Aldrich urged federal tax revision and the increase of bank reserve requirements to the full legal limit.[23] He addressed the Illinois manufacturers as accelerating recovery characterized the economy. The possibility that this development might turn into a run-away boom, fed by government expenditures and easy money, worried some analysts inside the administration and out.

Encouraged by the recovery, Roosevelt decided to cut government spending. The appropriateness of the decision seemed to be confirmed during the first half of 1937; personal income continued to rise as the net government contribution to income dropped sharply. Meanwhile, steps were taken to curb the inflationary possibilities represented by excess reserves in the banking system.*

In January 1937 the Federal Reserve announced that it would increase reserve requirements to the limit in a two-step process, effective March 1 and May 1. This decision had an adverse effect not only on Treasury refunding but on utilities and railroads, as well as on some industrial corporations. The increased reserve requirements, plus the tight money policy represented by sterilization of gold (i.e., the Treasury's accumulation of new gold in an inactive account) begun in December 1936, also lowered New York banks' reserves, inducing them to sell government securities and alarming investors.**

---

* Gold had continued to flow from abroad as the result of unsettling developments in Europe. Excess reserves in late 1936, if fully used, would have supported deposits of $15–$20 billion. Raising reserve requirements to their limit still left room for potential credit expansion of more than $5 billion. (Eccles, *Beckoning Frontiers*, pp. 290–291.)

** Eccles admits some short-run rise in interest rates and Treasury concern, but he denies they were significant or that they precipitated the recession. The banks' sale of government securities was anticipated, but the

The stock market began to slide downward in August. The industrial common stock index (1935–1939 = 100) fell from 130.6 for the week of August 11 to 113.1 for the week of September 8 and continued steadily downward. After peaking in June, personal income suffered a slight setback, recovered briefly, and then in September began a sustained downward slide. By mid-September the Federal Reserve and the Treasury had both sought to ease the money situation, but this was not enough to stop the downturn in the economy.[24]

The economic slump had major political implications. Roosevelt had already lost significant middle-class support as a result of his proposal to reorganize the Supreme Court. A major recession would add to the damage. As one response, Roosevelt began to look toward balancing the budget in fiscal 1938 and 1939, a new departure that pleased Treasury Secretary Morgenthau and Interior Secretary Ickes particularly.[25] Morgenthau, for example, was using his influence with the President against calling a special session of Congress to enact further reform legislation because the Secretary feared that Congress might take advantage of the opportunity to upset the progress toward a balanced budget.[26]

New York Fed mishandled its open market operations intially. (Eccles, *Beckoning Frontiers*, pp. 291–295). Aldrich agreed with Eccles that Federal Reserve policy had not caused the recession. However, a later analyst of the recession concluded, after a scholarly analysis, that "The action on reserves was unwise in view of the large-scale unemployment of resources." And further, "Had more attention been paid to the overall problem of the fuller utilization of resources than to the technical fact of excess reserves, it is less likely that the policy error of 1937 would have been made." (Kenneth D. Roose, *The Economics of Recession and Revisal: an Interpretation of 1937–1938* p. 252). The Board's action on reserves, combined with the New York Bank's failure to steady the government securities market, antagonized Treasury Secretary Morgenthau and led to the intervention of President Roosevelt. As a result, the Open Market Committee stepped up its activity before the May 1 increase in reserve requirements. See A. Jerome Clifford, *The Independence of the Federal Reserve System*, pp. 155–159.

Aldrich on the Stock Market Decline and the SEC

Early in September 1937 Aldrich received suggestions that he, together with large industrialists, see what could be done with key Washington officials to restore stability to the stock market. He discussed the matter in the Federal Advisory Council of the Federal Reserve on October 7 and decided to make the stock market the subject of a major address to the Rochester, New York, Chamber of Commerce a week later.[27] On this occasion Aldrich attributed the severity of the stock market decline to the "thin" market, which he felt exaggerated the effects of both limited buying and selling. More significant, however, he attributed the thinness of the market to the "cumulative effect of a variety of governmental policies." Among them he put taxes first on the list. High capital gains taxes, he said, discouraged men of substantial means from engaging in active trading. High income taxes also had an inhibiting effect on private investment.

Aldrich was equally concerned by the direction of the Securities and Exchange Commission's increasingly aggressive approach to its responsibilities.* He felt that SEC restrictions on stock market trading by "insiders," while worthy in their objectives, had definitely reduced the possibility of steadying markets. He further suggested that the SEC's "inquisitorial" interest in any large transaction had discouraged trading. Uncertainty about SEC rules on trading, plus the high margin

---

* The Chase, acting through Hermann G. Place, had recently completed a major rearrangement of the capital structure of International Paper Company based on resetting the claims of several classes of stockholders in the light of presumptive earnings and presumptive market value. The SEC had approved the plan, though apparently somewhat reluctantly. In August 1937 Commissioner Landis, who had some reservations on the reorganization, approved International Paper's exemption from the Public Utility Holding Company Act of 1935 for purposes of issuing securities. *The New York Times* (October 14, 1937) observed that under the SEC's new chairman, William O. Douglas, the exemption would probably have been denied.

requirements imposed by the Commission, were added deterrents to investment, he said.

Aldrich believed in a free market, properly policed. The New York Stock Market was to him "one of the most extraordinarily efficient mechanisms in the world." Viewed from this perspective, the debacle of 1929 had not been due to deficiencies in the market mechanism but to those who had been able to abuse it as a result of the easy money policies of the Federal Reserve. The current problem, as Aldrich saw it, was not one of hobbling the market but of restoring sound financial and fiscal policies and of opening the way for "informed speculation." In his words:

> To the extent that speculation is informed, to the extent that speculators trade within the limit of their ability to bear risks, to the extent that stock transactions are carried on by men of knowledge and experience and courage, the stock market is made safer, the whole body of investors is made safer, the collection of funds for industrial use from a wide body of people is made safer and easier, and our general economic life is served.

He also argued that the SEC misunderstood and therefore underestimated the importance of liquid assets. He maintained that, contrary to the SEC's position as he perceived it, there was a natural liquidity in securities as well as in commodities. In his view, the SEC had already gone far beyond Congress's primary interest in preventing manipulation of securities markets, and he urged that the Commission consider again the importance of marketability as an attribute of investment-grade securities. Excessive emphasis on a "quality" market, he maintained, could be just as unfortunate as ignoring abuses in a "quantity" market.

The Rochester speech received widespread attention and provoked a varied response. Roosevelt refused to comment when questioned about Aldrich's attack on SEC regulation.

Joseph P. Kennedy, former head of the SEC, agreed with the Chase chairman's evaluation of the adverse effects of the tax laws on business but sharply disagreed with the banker's comments about the SEC.[28] The most forthright attack on Aldrich came from Wiggin's old nemesis, Ferdinand Pecora. Apparently disregarding the distinctions carefully drawn by Aldrich in the Rochester speech, Pecora accused the banker of seeking a return to the "quantity" market of 1929 as opposed to the SEC's emphasis on a "quality" market.[29] *The New York Times*, however, criticized Pecora for misconstruing Aldrich's remarks and for failing to see that there was a middle ground between no regulation and the detailed regulations being imposed by the SEC.[30] In general, the business and financial communities applauded Aldrich's initiative in tackling the regulatory problem and endorsed the general thrust of his remarks.[31] As if to underscore the timeliness of Aldrich's analysis, the stock market took a nose dive a few days later.

The Rochester speech automatically involved Aldrich in both public and private investigations of the problems of the Stock Exchange. William O. Douglas, chairman of the SEC, was interested in Aldrich's criticisms of the Commission and the two men discussed them in Washington on December 3, 1937.[32] In January of 1938 Aldrich declined an invitation to write an article for *Fortune* on the SEC and the stock market. In doing so he made it clear that in this area he spoke simply as a commercial banker interested in a free market for securities, not as a spokesman for the Exchange and certainly not as one familiar with the details of its operation. He agreed with the *Fortune* writer that the Exchange should reorganize itself but stated that this was a matter for the Exchange itself and the SEC.[33] In December 1937, however, he had appeared before the Committee for the Study of the Organization and Administration of the New York Stock Exchange and reviewed his position on the need for remedial action.[34]

Aldrich's Analysis of the 1937 Recession

In his capacity as president of the Chamber of Commerce of the State of New York, Aldrich had been analyzing and reporting with some regularity his views on developments at the national level. In January 1937 he had been cautiously optimistic about the progress of the economy, but at the Chamber's annual dinner in November he deplored what he regarded as the administration's bias against big business.[35] In January 1938 he reported that his fears of a major setback had been confirmed. As he saw it, the recovery up to mid-1937 had been the product of "artificial" circumstances, and he saw the current problem as one of inadequate long-term capital for industrial use. This situation he related in turn to policies that drained off capital for government use, plus business and investor uncertainty about the soundness of the currency, government competition with private enterprise in public utility and other fields, and more general problems such as the Supreme Court reorganization plan.[36]

WASHINGTON TESTIMONY

On January 14, 1938, Aldrich was in Washington and had a morning appointment with Senator James Byrnes of South Carolina, chairman of the Senate Committee investigating unemployment and relief. Byrnes suggested that the banker testify on an impromptu basis before the Committee that afternoon,[37] and Aldrich accepted. In this appearance, he handled a variety of questions with ease and assurance. The burden of his testimony was familiar to anyone who had followed his recent speeches, but there were also some new ideas. Among them was the suggestion that commercial banks be allowed "to purchase from investment bankers securities of the type they are not allowed to invest in." This did not mean a return to the origination or distribution of securities, he was quick to point out, but the use of commercial bank credit to assist investment bankers in the flotation of securities.[38]

The Chase chairman emphasized again the need for cooperation between government, business, and labor — not merely token conferences but discussion followed by action. The problem of achieving such cooperation, he felt, was complicated by the tendency of some men in government to make inflammatory statements about business in general rather than pinpointing abuses and individuals. As he put it, "After all, government is a congregation of individuals and so is business, and if we all of us act with personal integrity and goodwill we can soon differentiate the people that have not got it." [39]

Aldrich made it very clear that he was not opposed to government regulation of stock exchanges or public utilities, but he did oppose excessive regulation of the former and government competition with the latter. Above all, he stressed the importance of balancing the budget. "I have expressed myself as being thoroughly in accord with Secretary Morgenthau in his efforts to bring about a balanced budget through saving and I do not think the importance of that can be overemphasized," Aldrich said.[40]

New Efforts to Stimulate the Economy

The economic downturn in late 1937 had given vitality to proponents of widely assorted remedies, ranging from anti-monopoly action to increased pump priming. Morgenthau had been urging Roosevelt to balance the budget in order to encourage private investors to pick up the current slack in the economy, but there was an influential element in the administration, including Roosevelt's confidant Harry Hopkins and economist Leon Henderson, who favored the resumption of large-scale spending along the lines suggested by the British economist John Maynard Keynes and endorsed by Federal Reserve Governor Eccles.[41] This group eventually won out, and on April 14, 1938, Roosevelt in a message to Congress and the nation asked for the resumption of government spending to stimulate the economy. In doing so he blamed the economy's current difficulties on overproduction and high prices. He pointed out that a year earlier the government had warned against both and that the Federal Reserve in cutting back bank credit and the Treasury in "sterilizing" gold had taken appropriate action under the circumstances. However, the President now urged a moderate reversal of both policies in an effort to make more bank resources available to the economy, plus new appropriations to increase employment and purchasing power. In arguing for adoption of this approach, Roosevelt declared that government alone could not do the job but that it must be a cooperative enterprise with business and labor.[42] Shortly after this message, the Federal Reserve lowered reserve requirements and the Treasury discontinued the gold sterilization program.[43]

The Committee of Sixteen

Aldrich was heartened by the President's emphasis on cooperation with business.* Therefore he responded favorably to the suggestion of John W. Hanes, a recently appointed SEC Commissioner, that the Chase chairman join other leading businessmen in promising Roosevelt this cooperation.[44] Together with 15 others, including Owen D. Young of General Electric and Frederick Ecker of Metropolitan Life, Aldrich signed a statement released to the press on April 26, 1938. In it the signatories declared: "It seems to us most

---

* By April 1938, however, Roosevelt had been won over sufficiently by the anti-monopolists to call for an investigation of the concentration of economic power, from which emerged the famed Temporary National Economic Committee.

important that we should all resolve to encourage the President in every effort he shall make to restore confidence and normal business conditions, and to support Congress in the position that its legislative program should be directed towards national recovery for employer and employee alike, rather than towards the enactment of legislation based upon untried social and economic theories." [45] The business leaders urged that government representatives remain in continuous consultation with the business community and encourage businessmen "to take the initiative to develop and stabilize their respective industries."

Hanes personally delivered this statement to the White House. Acknowledging it on April 27, Roosevelt indicated that he welcomed specific suggestions that would promote cooperation between business and government. [46] But the so-called "Committee of Sixteen" was not a committee in fact and therefore was not in a position to make any specific recommendations. Letters flowed into Aldrich's office suggesting positive action, and the "Committee" was even invited to participate in a round table discussion on the nationwide NBC Network. [47] However, the public statement had merely indicated a general attitude on the part of its signers, and they were not prepared to follow it up as a group.

In declining the invitation to participate in the radio broadcast, Aldrich declared: "It seems to me that the only way in which anything can be accomplished along the lines which we mentioned in the statement signed by this group is by direct contact with the President and I do not think that anything would be gained by discussion over the radio." [48] But the White House was no more ready to take the initiative than the Committee of Sixteen.

Aldrich Analyzes Roosevelt's Program

The annual dinner meeting of the American Section of the International Chamber of Commerce in Washington on May

2, 1938, gave Aldrich his first opportunity in a public forum to appraise Roosevelt's April message. He did so in a speech that ran to 21 printed pages. The title, "The Reciprocal Tariff Policy and the Proposed Government Spending Program," offered him scope to cover both domestic and foreign policies.

After renewing his endorsement of the administration's reciprocal trade agreements program, Aldrich launched into an extended analysis of the President's latest domestic proposals. First, he emphasized that they would involve a significant deficit, which could run from $3.5 to $5 billion by the close of the next fiscal year. In this possibility he saw a threat to government credit and to the currency, a matter which he felt should concern every citizen. He attacked both the President's theory that inadequate purchasing power was at the bottom of the current slump and the President's proposal to cure it by further government spending. Rather, Aldrich argued, purchasing power grew out of production. Thus, emphasis on the capital goods industries was more appropriate than on consumer spending,* and the adding of billions to the existing public debt was unjustified.

Aldrich was also highly critical of the new emphasis on desterilizing gold and lowering reserve requirements for Federal Reserve member banks. Both actions added to bank reserves, but Aldrich pointed out that, if anything, reserves had been excessive for some time. The raising of reserve requirements in May 1937 was said by some to have been the cause of the recession. Not so, said the Chase chairman. Bank loans and new securities issues had continued to increase while interest rates were going up.** A shortage of credit was not

* Government economists were heavily committed to the underconsumption theory; yet retrospective analysis of the data, except in the area of consumer installment credit, casts considerable doubt on the key importance of consumption factors in the recession. See Roose, *The Economics of Recession and Revival*, Ch. 10.

** The highest monthly level of new corporate capital issues since 1933 was in June 1937, but the decline thereafter was sharp.

responsible for the 1937 stock market slide and business troubles. Therefore, to push more reserves into the banks was only an invitation to inflation and trouble, not to sound economic activity.

Aldrich Offers Alternatives

His prescription was by now a familiar one. Reform had been needed but it had gone too far. Aldrich did not ask for wholesale retreat but for modifications of the reform measures in terms of actual experience and the needs of the time. For example, revisions in tax policy plus assurance of some stability in government policy would, he thought, generate private investment that would render great government expenditures unnecessary. What business most needed was a "breathing spell."

In this address Aldrich cited Karl Marx as the originator of the mass-consumption theory endorsed by Roosevelt. By making this connection he invited attack, and the New York *Daily News* singled out this portion of his speech, declaring in an editorial: "We never heard that Marx held this theory; but if he did, he was right, in our opinion. We don't KNOW any more economics than the bankers do — and they proved to the nation's satisfaction that they didn't KNOW much when banker-guided government led us into the 1929 smashup. But it seems to us that a person who never heard of economics could grasp the idea that mass-production goods cannot be sold to masses who have no money to buy them. In a profit system, that is." [49]

Secretary of Commerce Roper attacked Aldrich's appeal for a breathing spell. He maintained that what the country needed more was cooperation between business, government, and labor.[50] Aldrich, of course, had earlier advocated the same thing, as had Roosevelt, but the problem of who would call the tune for this cooperation remained unresolved.

Controversy over Causes of the Recession

Marriner Eccles of the Federal Reserve had also entered the debate. He held that monetary policy had not created the recession and could not cure it. He declared in December 1937: "In my opinion the extent of the present recession will depend upon how rapidly the more serious maladjustments between prices and buying power are corrected and increased national income is created by the activity of private business." Eccles felt that the decline of competition had led to monopolistic pricing, which he regarded as a key factor in the problem.[51]

Secretary of the Interior Ickes took a different approach. He charged in December 1937 that America's "60 families" appeared to be threatening a "sit-down strike" of capital unless they had things their own way.[52] This view gained support in important Washington quarters and with the President. Charges of this kind against the private sector contributed in 1938 to the creation of the Temporary National Economic Committee, charged with probing the problems of concentrated private economic power as they affected specific industries and the economy. Eventually, in 1940, Aldrich would testify before this body in connection with insurance company relations to commercial banks.[53]

Role of Chambers of Commerce

A few days after his Washington speech on the President's spending program, Aldrich made his farewell remarks as president of the Chamber of Commerce of the State of New York. In doing so he summed up his conception of the Chamber's role as one of approaching its problems "with complete objectivity, and so far as possible to avoid mere opposition to measures, governmental and administrative, which are proposed for adoption." He further stated that he believed the New York Chamber's resolutions during his term had had

a "very real effect" on the formulation of policies at both
state and national levels. "That is partly because of the resolutions themselves, partly because of the group that has adopted
them, and the method of their adoption, and partly because
of the fact that I think this Chamber has an outstanding
influence among the other chambers of commerce in the
country. . . ." [54]

ALDRICH AND INTERNATIONAL DEVELOPMENTS

During this period, Aldrich was turning his attention increasingly to problems of international economic relations,
viewing domestic issues in this larger framework. On July 6,
1938, for example, at a banquet for the Crown Prince and the
Crown Princess of Sweden, sponsored by the New Sweden
Tercentenary Committee of New York, he had an opportunity to compare the "planned economy" of the Scandinavian
country with contemporary developments in the United
States. Although by the nature of the occasion Aldrich was
constrained to put his major emphasis on the many contributions of the Swedes to America, he also stressed his view that
Sweden had achieved recovery by avoiding such panaceas as
economic nationalism, inflation, and curtailment of production. He noted that Sweden's experiments with deficit spending were limited in scope, her work week had been kept at
48 hours, and her tariffs maintained at a moderate level. Accordingly, as Aldrich saw it, "The basis of Sweden's prosperity has been international trade and ever-increasing national
productivity. That is the real lesson in economics taught by
the Swedish 'experiment.' " [55]

The International Chamber of Commerce, which Aldrich
had joined in 1931, gave him another sounding board against
which to test and expound his ideas on international financial
and commercial relations. War clouds were gathering over

Europe when he sailed in October 1938 to make his annual tour of European capitals and to attend a meeting of the International Chamber in Paris. Hitler had moved into the Sudetanland and Prime Minister Chamberlain of Great Britain had just returned from his famous encounter with the Führer at Munich where he secured an agreement that he mistakenly thought would insure peace. These developments gave urgency to any efforts, public or private, that might relieve the heightened tension of international relations, a matter very much on Aldrich's mind.

Views on International Trade

In assuming the chairmanship of the International Chamber's Committee on Monetary Policy and Credit, which had been established following the Chamber's Berlin Congress of 1937, Aldrich had an opportunity to review international trade relationships on a broad scale. Addressing the first meeting of the Committee in Paris, he made his basic propositions very explicit. "It is clear to me," he said, "that the general policies for which the International Chamber of Commerce stands, of sound currencies, sound public finance and the reduction of tariffs and the elimination of other impediments to the free interchange of goods amongst the nations, must be vigorously pressed if we are really to avoid the dangers of war." [56] The relationship between foreign trade and domestic policies was close and important, he pointed out. "We should press every opportunity to stabilize currencies. We should press every opportunity to reduce trade barriers. We should press every opportunity to improve the finances of the governments."

Aldrich urged that the Chamber take a definite position on "the fallacy that artificially cheap money is necessary for business activity and [the fallacy that] money markets must never again be called upon to stand the discipline of firm or tight money rates." His own position was crystal clear: A freely operating money market imposed a discipline and revealed the truth about how well a financial system was really operating.

Aldrich deplored the attempts at "autarchy" or economic self-sufficiency by countries like Germany and Italy. Such efforts were doomed to failure, he said, and could lead to war. It would be far better if national needs could be met in the context of free-flowing international trade. However, he recognized that countries low on gold and foreign exchange could not lower tariffs immediately upon negotiating a reciprocal trade agreement with a wealthier country. He therefore suggested a time-lag in such agreements: Creditor nations with adequate gold and foreign exchange could reduce their tariffs immediately; debtor countries would not lower their tariffs until six to nine months thereafter. He believed that this time-lag would give the debtor countries time to obtain bank credits in foreign countries, "especially for the financing of raw materials destined for manufacture into goods for export." If these arrangements worked out as he anticipated, the short-term foreign credits could be transformed into a revolving fund that bankers in creditor countries would be glad to maintain and increase.

International Finance and International Business

At the end of this address Aldrich made a frank statement of his own beliefs about monetary policy and credit. Admitting that they were "orthodox," he declared: "I believe in the gold standard; I believe in the discipline of the gold standard; I believe that Governments and central banks should keep their promises to pay gold even when it hurts. I believe that nothing is more important than the rebuilding of confidence throughout the world that Governments and central banks will keep their promises. I believe that our experience of recent years with currency depreciation as an instrument of policy has made it clear that no sound policy can be based upon it, because every debasement breeds a fear of further debasement, destroys credit and frightens investors and businessmen throughout the world. I believe that it is far more important to protect the quality of money and credit than it is to strive for an abundant quantity." Before the Paris meeting was over, the International Chamber of Commerce went on record as endorsing what Aldrich had urged.[57]

A concise summary of this address furnished the text for one that Aldrich made via trans-Atlantic telephone from Berlin to the 25th National Foreign Trade Convention meeting at the Commodore Hotel in New York City on October 31, 1938. Reporting on the program of the International Chamber, he pointed out that it was far easier to come to agreement on the goals of monetary and credit policy than it was to get governments to accept them. This problem he characterized as "the most important" one confronting businessmen. His answer to it, first advanced in connection with his endorsement of cooperation with the President the preceding April, was for government and business leaders to maintain continuing liaison and joint-study groups on major economic policy questions.[58]

Attack on Autarchy and Regimentation

Aldrich was afforded a further opportunity to review his impressions of the European economy and the work of the International Chamber when he addressed The Economic Club of New York extemporaneously on December 12, 1938. The Munich Pact of the preceding September had been regarded as a safeguard of lasting peace and accordingly the "political appeasement" that it represented was widely endorsed. In later years, of course, this term came to have a very unpleasant connotation, but in 1938 it appealed strongly to Aldrich and he talked of freer international trade as "economic appease-ment." Accordingly he prefaced his remarks to The Economic Club in these terms: "I believe that the most profound threat to individual liberty is the danger of internal regimentation. It seems to me that what we are faced with is not only the question of political appeasement in the world, not only the question of economic appeasement, but the question of accom-plishing this appeasement in time to save the institutions of the democracies." [59]

Although the bilateral trade treaties of the autarchy-seeking countries worried Aldrich, he saw in the corollary restraints on individual freedom within these countries an example of the far greater danger of "creeping collectivism." From efforts to control foreign trade, he suggested, came a whole series of internal restraints that eventually, as in Germany, could reach back to control of freedom of speech, thought, and action. He therefore urged his listeners to exercise their individual initiative and responsibility in foreign trade and to cooperate with one another and the government in dealing with these problems as a whole. "At the same time," he said, "I think we should all be extremely alert in watching our own internal situation to see that the terrible fate which has overtaken the autarchies does not overtake us."

By 1939 the main themes of Winthrop Aldrich's speeches on economic policy, both domestic and foreign, were well established — even the phraseology was frequently inter-changeable from one speech to another. Thus, while he adapted his presentations to specific occasions and audiences, his basic message never varied. A sound economy and society demanded that the individual exercise initiative and responsibility; gov-ernment's job was to protect this freedom, not to subvert it with handouts and make-work projects; the market mechanism was an efficient mechanism for allocating resources, but to work properly it had to be free of "artificial" manipulation of the money supply in the domestic sphere and the deadening hand of protective tariffs and exchange controls in international trade. In 1939 as in 1933, Aldrich maintained that governmental policies that encouraged foreign trade and private investment would best promote economic recovery and growth. He was convinced that no amount of deficit spending or other panaceas that attempted to circumvent the working of what he regarded as fundamental economic laws could be successful, except at great cost to the society.

Translated into political terms, these views became associated with his idea of a "democracy." The ideal of such a political and social entity would be a system where "we can use voluntary action more than compulsion, self-control more than law, a growth of public responsibility more than legislative enactment, education more than force." [60]

VIEWS ON CHARACTER, SCHOLARSHIP, AND EDUCATION

Using this framework of personal and social values, Aldrich addressed the Congress on Education for Democracy at the Waldorf-Astoria on August 16, 1939. He had been refining the definition of his credo in literally dozens of speeches and articles annually, and on this occasion the last sentence of his address summarized it succinctly: "If we can implant in our people the Christian virtues which we sum up in the word character, and, at the same time, give them a knowledge of the line which should be drawn between voluntary action and governmental compulsion in a democracy, and of what can be accomplished within the stern laws of economics, we will enable them to retain their freedom, and at the same time, make them worthy to be free." [61] There may have been those in the audience who questioned the assumptions or the conclusions of this statement, but to Aldrich the propositions were an expression of faith, principle, and conviction fortified by his experience.

Given this view of life and society, it is not surprising that Aldrich placed a high value on scholarship and the importance of education. In October 1938, just before departing for Europe, he had delivered an address stressing "The University as an Instrument of Social Progress" at the 40th Anniversary and Dedicatory Exercises at Northeastern University in Boston. On May 20, 1939, he spoke over radio station WOR on the "University Life" program, emphasizing that business needed university-trained men and women but, more important, education for leadership in a democracy should inculcate a sense of social responsibility and should seek a "scholarly understanding of the relations between government and economic life in a democracy." In his address to the Congress on Education for Democracy, he defined the aim of education in a democracy more precisely as one of teaching people to think "with discrimination and wisdom, to so instruct them that they are able not only to think but think things through, so that they can distinguish between the sound and the unsound, between propaganda and education, and between the false and the true." [62] This had also been the thrust of his address to the graduating class at Washington and Jefferson College the preceding June 3, entitled "The Incompatibility of Democracy and a 'Planned' Economy."

The Active Citizen

Aldrich not only talked about individual responsibility but he practiced it. His interests and activities outside the bank continued to grow. In the latter half of the 1930s he became a director of the Metropolitan Life Insurance Company, New York District Representative to the Federal Advisory Council, chairman of the banking policy committee of the New York Bankers' Association, and vice president of the National Institute of Social Sciences. He was also active in organizing the greater New York Fund and served as chairman of its Council.

In addition, he was a member of the New York World's Fair Corporation, spending more than a nominal amount of his time on its affairs during the several years of planning that preceded the opening of the Fair.

But even with all these activities in addition to his responsibilities at the bank, he still found time to be with his family and to take frequent, though often short, vacations. The increased tempo of his life, however, was reflected in the way he handled his favorite avocation — sailing and cruising. Instead of keeping his own yacht in commission he increasingly turned to chartering pleasure craft for limited periods in Maine or Florida waters as the season dictated.

During these years Aldrich fully exploited all the avenues open to a man in his position to influence public and business opinion and governmental policies on current problems. To a large extent he exerted his influence on government and public opinion through his activities in private organizations like the Chamber of Commerce of the State of New York, the International Chamber of Commerce, and the Business Advisory Council.* Although he still exchanged views on banking and currency with Senate leaders, his association was not in the context of the close liaison that had existed in the critical days of 1933–1935.

* This Council was organized on June 26, 1933, by Daniel C. Roper, who was then Secretary of Commerce, to advise him with regard to matters of interest to his Department. Secretary Roper and all succeeding Secretaries of Commerce continued to be ex-officio General Chairmen of the Council until the year 1961, when Secretary Luther H. Hodges requested that the name of the Council be changed to The Business Council and that the Secretary's name should no longer appear as ex-officio General Chairman. Accordingly from that date the Council has had no official connection with the Department of Commerce.

At the present time the membership of the Council is divided into three classes, depending on the age of the members, namely, Active, Graduate, and Honorary. Aldrich was appointed a member of the Council in 1934. He is, of course, classified today as an Honorary Member.

EVALUATION OF DOMESTIC AND FOREIGN TRADE POLICIES
OF THE NEW DEAL

In part, Aldrich's relative isolation from direct involvement in Washington activity sprang from a deepening conviction that the New Deal, as it was evolving, represented a sharp departure from the basic policies and principles which he saw as the cornerstones of America's past greatness. Unquestionably, also, Roosevelt had become increasingly alienated from the business and financial communities where Aldrich was recognized as a spokesman. Therefore, although the New York banker could still obtain access to the White House, there seemed to be little that could be accomplished thereby.

Aldrich frequently admonished Republican politicians that across-the-board opposition to the administration was ill-advised, but only in Hull's reciprocal trade agreements program did he find an administration policy that he could endorse enthusiastically. He summarized the problem concisely in an address to The Bond Club of New York on May 23, 1939: "We have in this country today, in the economic field, a radical conflict between our foreign policies and our domestic policies. On the one hand, we have the reciprocal tariff policy of our Government, which seeks to lower trade barriers and to increase the volume of imports, in order that we may increase the volume of our exports. On the other hand, we have a multitude of conflicting policies which have resulted in a variety of measures, the effect of which is to raise domestic prices, artificially to limit production, and, of necessity, to check exports." [63]

As Aldrich frankly admitted, his economic views were orthodox and, although he recognized that society bore new responsibilities to its unfortunate members in a complex industrial order, he felt that these responsibilities could not be discharged by adopting what he regarded as economic heresies.

It was here that the views of businessmen and financiers diverged sharply from those of politicians and humanitarians who were willing to experiment in relieving suffering or discontent without regard to orthodox economic wisdom or to the economic costs. In 1933–1935 Aldrich had been able to accept and even contribute to numerous New Deal reforms because he believed them to be improvements over existing economic and governmental institutions. In the latter half of the decade, however, the policies pursued by the administration increasingly seemed to him to pose a real threat to free markets and democratic institutions.

The New Deal in Perspective

A case could be made that the New Deal after 1935, despite large doses of antibusiness rhetoric, was just as dedicated to preserving the enterprise-capitalist system as Aldrich. One could cite, for example, the cuts in government spending preceding the 1937 recession. In this interpretation the economic difficulties experienced and the attacks on business would appear to result from frustration in the effective use of fiscal and monetary policy to stimulate private economic activity. The new round of government spending in 1938 could therefore be explained as a pragmatic response to the failure of these expectations to be vindicated rather than a calculated challenge to the private sector.

One must also take account of the fact that what were regarded by businessmen as extreme legislative measures when introduced, such as the Public Utility Holding Company Act, were appreciably modified prior to passage. Furthermore, their implementation was frequently not as stringent as had been feared. On the other hand, there is no question that many basic changes were taking place in the relationships of business and government, that many mistakes were made on both sides, and that the directions and implications for long-run change in the economy were far from clear to participants in the process of change.

The origins and basic consistency of Aldrich's position should be clear. It should also be clear that he did not oppose all change. Furthermore, Aldrich's prescriptions for recovery in 1933 seem in retrospect inadequate, he seems to have been more correct than the administration in diagnosing the problem of 1937.[*]

If on balance it appears that the New Deal was not basically dedicated to extreme change in the economic system, this was not true of all its members nor obvious from all the measures that gained the administration's support. As time went on, it appears that Roosevelt was less responsive to bankers and businessmen than he had been. This meant that there was less opportunity for men like Aldrich to engage in a meaningful dialogue with responsible government officials. In his case, the best opportunity had been created by the Committee of Sixteen in 1938, but none of that group was prepared to build on that opportunity, and Roosevelt did not actively encourage them to do so.

ASSESSING THE EUROPEAN SITUATION

Meanwhile, the need for improved communication and cooperation between government and business became even more pressing as the European situation deteriorated under the impact of Germany's expansionist moves. Aldrich's frequent trips abroad and interviews with political as well as business and financial leaders gave him firsthand knowledge

---

[*] For a thumbnail sketch of Roosevelt's position, see Rexford G. Tugwell, *FDR: Architect of an Era* (New York: Macmillan Co., 1967), pp. 170–174. Kenneth D. Roose in *The Economics of Recession and Revival* makes a very careful evaluation of the causes and character of the recession and concludes governmental policies resulted from "a narrow and inadequate appraisal of economic developments" (p. 253).

and even a minor role in some of these developments. The bank's good relations at high levels in Italy, for example, made him hopeful that something could be done to weaken that country's ties with Germany. In October 1938 he discussed this possibility with Georges Bonnet, French Minister of Foreign Affairs, who agreed that in the wake of Hitler's maneuvers over Czechoslovakia something might be accomplished.[64] Aldrich promised to sound out Italian officials during his forthcoming visit to Rome, but the results were disappointing.

Aldrich was also concerned about French reliance on Russian military support against Germany. When he saw Bonnet again in April 1939, he warned the Frenchman that American public opinion was suspicious of collectivist ideas and that too close a relationship of France with the USSR could be dangerous. He raised the question of whether the value of Russian military aid could, in fact, outweigh the threat of involving the USSR in the affairs of western Europe. Bonnet, however, took the position that if Poland and Rumania were attacked there would be little alternative to reliance on Russian assistance.[65] Judging from Aldrich's address to the Bond Club of New York upon his return from this trip, he did not think that this problem had yet reached an acute stage. Within a few months, however, it would, and his suspicions of the Russians would be confirmed when they moved into Poland in pursuit of their own interests rather than as a French ally.

THE END OF AN ERA

The attack of Germany on Poland in September 1939 marked the beginning of a new era of world history where problems of economic depression gave place to problems of survival for the western democracies. In a significant sense, though it was not fully appreciated at the time, this event also marked the end of a transition period in the internal affairs of the United States. The country had recovered from the worst of the depression, but many of the repercussions in terms of the unemployment of both men and capital were still clearly visible. The New Deal was still far from an unqualified success, and it had created a gulf of mistrust between the leadership of the business community and the country's political leadership.

Although Winthrop Aldrich had not been successful in his efforts to bridge this gap, he had at least contributed substantially to defining the issues between the administration and business. He explained his objective in a letter of December 1938. "Of course you realize," he wrote, "that everything I am trying to do, not only in connection with the foreign trade situation, but also in connection with our internal economy, is based upon the premise that private enterprise in the democracies must aggressively reassume the initiative. This is the only possible way of eventually avoiding worldwide regimentation." [66]

Within less than a year, even the remote possibility of achieving this objective peacefully and by private means had disappeared. For Aldrich, as for the country, the years of transition had come to an end.

CHAPTER X

The War Relief Years, 1939-1946

R ETURNING from Europe in April 1939, Aldrich had been optimistic about the possibilities of avoiding war in the near future, but the threat of hostilities grew steadily more menacing. In August the Soviet Union signed a nonaggression pact with Germany, deserting the French as Aldrich had anticipated. When war finally came in September with the invasion of Poland, Aldrich found an immediate humanitarian challenge in aiding the unfortunate civilian victims of the European conflict. He quickly undertook to organize private relief efforts. As an internationalist and advocate of private initiative and responsibility, he committed himself fully to this endeavor.

Although Aldrich took the lead in proposing to bring medical aid to British and French civilians, he was prevented from engaging in a fund-raising effort by the wording of the Neutrality Act of 1937. Its language was sufficiently comprehensive to make the raising of money for medical relief in belligerent countries a possible violation of the law. He called this problem to the attention of several Senators in early October 1939 and enlisted their help in obtaining an appropriate amendment to the Neutrality Act. On October 26

Senator Harry Byrd informed Aldrich that the desired change had been adopted.[1]

With the way thus cleared for fund raising, Aldrich was active in organizing and then heading the American Society for British Medical and Civilian Aid, Inc., and, at the suggestion of Ambassador William Bullitt, its counterpart for civilian relief in France. A New York committee was formed, and Aldrich drew leading financial figures like Thomas Lamont into the group.

British War Relief

The relief effort for Britain was implemented through the British and American Red Cross, while French relief was administered in conjunction with the American Relief Clearing House and the American Hospital of Paris. Fund raising for these activities in the United States was soon transferred to the newly organized Allied Relief Fund. In announcing the formation of a committee to support this work, the sponsors pointed out in January 1940 that it was a "rallying point for American friends of France and Great Britain in this hour of great need." [2]

During the winter of 1939–1940, the war was virtually at a standstill, but in the spring the German war machine moved into high gear. France was soon overrun and England, now standing alone, was subjected to intensive attack from the air and threatened with imminent invasion by sea. The "phoney" war had turned into a near-catastrophe for the Allies. This development, accompanied by mounting civilian as well as military casualties, gave new importance to the work of the Allied Relief Fund. The flood of refugees from the Continent to Britain, plus the relocation of British families, created a desperate need for clothing, mobile canteens, medical supplies, and many other items. Aldrich assumed major responsibility in the effort to meet this emergency.

In June 1940, as Hitler stepped up his efforts to break British morale by bombing, Aldrich helped to organize the British-American Ambulance Corps, Inc. Reporting the thanks of British officials for ambulances supplied under this project, Aldrich underlined in August 1940 the urgent need for increased support of Allied Relief and the maintenance of flexibility in the Fund's purposes.

He was being kept in close touch with the London situation by Bertram Cruger, who acted as a representative of the Relief Fund in addition to his duties in the Chase's London branch. By mid-September 1940, as the Battle of Britain reached its height, the Fund had raised $1 million, but the demands for aid far exceeded available resources. German air raids had left many British families homeless, and the situation was so acute that Cruger appealed by trans-Atlantic telephone for immediate assistance. Aldrich recommended a gift of $25,000 to cope with the immediate problem and announced that the Fund would seek additional contributions.[3]

Mrs. Aldrich joined the fund-raising effort by organizing a "Help England Ball" which opened the social season in New York and swelled the resources of the Allied Relief Fund. Later, in April 1941, she became chairman of the women's division of the New York campaign committee of the United Service Organizations (USO) for National Defense. But the most important of Mrs. Aldrich's contribution to the war effort was her service as Vice President of the Civilian Defense Volunteer Office of New York City for the five war years.

By the end of 1940 the Allied Relief Fund had been merged into the British War Relief Society, Inc., with Aldrich as its head. In announcing the Society's goal of raising $20 million by mid-1941, he summarized its predecessor's accomplishments. The Allied Relief Fund had supplied 546 mobile feeding kitchens to Britain, and 160 of them were in operation in bomb-stricken areas. One hundred ambulances had been provided, along with 21 portable x-ray units and a complete mobile unit for field hospital work. In addition, the Fund had sent 90,000 yards of bandages, 500,000 surgical dressings, 6,600 cots, 43,700 pairs of rubber boots, 11,000 cases of clothing and woolen goods, plus $1,000,000 in gifts to British relief agencies and more especially those caring for refugee children.[4]

Aldrich was a vital link in mobilizing these privately donated relief supplies, and British Foreign Minister Anthony Eden expressed his appreciation in a personal letter to the banker in late January 1941. "It is impossible to exaggerate the value to us of the generous help and sympathy which we are receiving from your organization and indeed from all your countrymen in these days," he wrote.[5]

Sustaining the relief program was a demanding task. Aldrich spent a large part of his time helping to organize support for Allied Relief not only in New York but in other cities. Increasingly, due to the lack of shipping space for relief supplies, he sought monetary contributions which could be cabled to Britain. In May 1941, Lord Marley, deputy speaker of the House of Lords, appeared with Aldrich before a luncheon for representatives of retail and wholesale grocery companies and reported that the "little people" of his country were "greatly encouraged" by the Americans' relief activities. Aldrich took advantage of the occasion to report that $400,000 had been cabled to London for relief work in bomb-devastated Plymouth.[6] Two months later he announced that since December 1939 the Society and its predecessors had received $10 million in cash and donations of clothing valued at $2 million.[7] This was evidence of the kind of resources that could be mobilized through voluntary, private efforts in which Aldrich believed so strongly and to which he had committed himself so fully.

Aside from the humanitarian aspects, Aldrich saw another

value in war relief work. There was no question in his mind that the United States would eventually become involved in the European conflict, but there was a real question of whether this involvement might not come too late to save Britain or to defeat the forces of regimentation and tyranny that the Axis powers had unleashed. One way of dramatizing this threat for the large segment of the American public that still clung to hopes of maintaining neutrality and isolation was to put on a drive for relief funds every time that Britain suffered a major air raid attack. Through the sympathy and commitment released in this way, Aldrich hoped and believed that public awareness of the United States' stake in the war could be heightened.

Mobilization for Defense

The impact of the war abroad was reflected in Aldrich's choice of topics for public addresses. Even in 1940 his speeches were beginning to shift away from criticism of the Roosevelt administration's domestic problems. Instead, he spoke out strongly in support of its defense policies. Thus on the eve of the first registration for the draft in October 1940, he went on radio over station WEAF to endorse the mobilization of the nation's manpower. As he put it, "The world will know tomorrow that we have another asset of strength to match our national resources and our industrial capacity. This asset is our mobilized manpower — a manpower of countless millions — a manpower made more potent still by the fact that it is inspired and strengthened by the spirit of a free people." [8]

In addressing the Boston Chamber of Commerce on December 12, 1940, he combined the defense theme with an economic and financial analysis of its effects. He set the background for his remarks with these words: "Historical experience should make us realize that we are a part of the whole complex of world forces, and that we must, in the future, try in a more active way, to shape those forces in the interests of world peace and in the preservation of man's freedom." He then advocated financial aid to England, either by a federal guarantee of British credit, by a loan from the Treasury, or by an outright grant. In this proposal he was anticipating the Lend-Lease Act of March 1941. His own convictions were clear: "We can no more afford to have England break down financially than we can contemplate her defeat in this war. In both cases our own interests are vitally involved." [9]

The financing of the defense effort especially concerned him, since he felt that the deficit spending program of the 1930s had left the country in a weakened financial position for prosecuting the defense build-up. Accordingly, he advocated a program of increased taxation and avoidance of easy money policies. He urged that the government borrow from savings banks, insurance companies, and individuals rather than sell government obligations to commercial banks. The latter course would only increase inflationary pressures and lead to detailed economic controls, he told the Boston Chamber of Commerce. The inflationary danger, he said, had been intensified by the 1938 decision to abandon the gold sterilization program,* plus the easy money policies that had added to member banks' excess reserves. To control the expansion of credit he advocated a return to gold coinage and gold redemption, resumption of the gold sterilization program, increased reserve requirements, return of monetary powers to the Federal Reserve, and vigorous pruning of nondefense spending. In his words, "Only by following conservative fiscal policies will the private citizen be protected, and will our industrial machine operate most efficiently to bring the defense program to a successful conclusion." [10]

* See Chapter IX.

As 1941 wore on, Aldrich saw that the administration was not likely to heed many of his suggestions. On the other hand, he did not feel that he could repeat his criticisms of its monetary and fiscal policies with the same freedom as in normal times. When he was asked in June 1941 to address the September meeting of the American Bankers Association, he declined. Writing to the program chairman, he said: "It seems to me very clear that such an appraisal would necessarily involve more or less severe criticism of the course of the Administration with regard to fiscal policy, methods of financing the defense program and other matters, and if by September we are actually involved in the war — which seems to me extremely likely — I do not believe that it would be wise at that moment to voice such criticism publicly." [11]

Aldrich had, however, pledged his full support to Roosevelt as Commander-in-Chief. In a letter of June 3, 1941, he commended the President for his radio address of May 27 proclaiming an unlimited national emergency and announcing that the United States would take any steps necessary to insure delivery of war materials and supplies to Britain and to protect the Western Hemisphere from Nazi aggression. "I want you to know that you have my unqualified support in the policy which you so inspiringly defined on Tuesday night," Aldrich wrote. In reply Roosevelt thanked the banker, whom he addressed as "Dear Winthrop," and said, "It strengthens my conviction that the American people will tolerate no compromise with totalitarianism or dictatorship." [12]

As the crisis deepened, Aldrich became increasingly involved in activities related to the defense effort. Consequently, the attack on Pearl Harbor, which launched the nation into the world war, only caused Aldrich to intensify and add to the defense-related activities in which he had been engaged for over two years. To aid the Army Air Corps, he had agreed to serve as treasurer of the Civilian Aviation Training Committee, a post he filled from July 1940 to December 1942. In 1941 Adolphus Andrews, whom he had known for many years, became head of the Third Naval District. Aldrich was associated with him as chairman of the Civilian Committee for Officer Procurement in the District, an office he held when he attended Army maneuvers in the Carolinas in the fall of 1941. In December of that year, at the request of Norman Davis, he became a member of the National Advisory Committee of the American Red Cross, and in January 1942, at the invitation of his college classmate and good friend Harold Vanderbilt, he agreed to serve on the Civilian Committee of the United States Coast Guard. At the request of John D. Rockefeller, Jr., he joined the National Sponsoring Committee for the 1941 USO Campaign, and he served on the executive board for the Army Emergency Relief Show in 1942.

Of course Aldrich aided war financing. He headed the group of New York bankers advising the Treasury through the Federal Reserve Bank of New York on this problem,[13] and beginning in 1942 he served on various committees spearheading war fund drives in the Second Reserve District. These efforts, which continued even into the postwar era, earned him a Treasury commemorative silver medal.[14]

WARTIME TRIP TO BRITAIN

As an outstanding leader in war relief work, Aldrich was invited in July 1942 by Brendan Bracken, the British Minister of Information, to visit that war-torn country. Without a thought to the hazards of such a wartime journey, Aldrich accepted. Entrusted with a message on a "second front" to Prime Minister Winston Churchill from Joseph Davies, former ambassador to Moscow, Aldrich left Baltimore airport in the early hours of July 25 and arrived at Poole, England, the next afternoon after an uneventful flight via Canada and Ireland.

On July 27 he had a long interview with American Ambassador Winant and then set out on a tour of bomb-blasted cities. He experienced air raids in London and Bath, saw two German planes shot out of the sky, and inspected bomb damage in places like Bristol, Birmingham, and Coventry. At Birmingham, which had been blitzed the evening before his arrival, he saw at first hand the ambulances at work and representatives of the British War Relief Society giving out clothing.[15]

Back in London on August 3, he settled down to a round of conferences on problems of war relief, the state of his bank's English business, and Anglo-American relations generally. With Edward Stettinius of the American Embassy he discussed the food problem. At Buckingham Palace he went over war relief matters with the King and Queen and ended that full day by having dinner with John Wallace, head of the Chase's London branch. In succeeding days he met with a number of London bankers and government officials, and their talk was usually about British as compared with American methods of financing the war.

In London Aldrich was entertained at numerous luncheons, one held by Brendan Bracken, another by Anthony and Mrs. Eden and still another by the Lord Mayor and Mayoress — the last followed by tea with Mrs. Churchill and Bracken. Aldrich reciprocated with a dinner at Claridge's, where Lord and Lady Mountbatten were guests, and Mountbatten explained how his Commandos planned and executed their operations. At yet another luncheon, held at W. Averell Harriman's apartment but hosted by Philip Reed in Harriman's absence in Moscow, Aldrich met leading figures in the wartime Cabinet. They included Eden; Sir Stafford Cripps; A. V. Alexander, the First Lord of the Admiralty; and Oliver Lyttleton, Minister of Supply. Each spoke briefly about the work of his Ministry. During his London stay, Aldrich also

met General Charles de Gaulle, whom he found "very disappointing" as a representative of the Free French movement
and almost indifferent to war relief problems.[16]

During the remainder of his visit in the British Isles, Aldrich
toured an RAF base, spent some time in Glasgow, and conferred with numerous representatives of the Red Cross, British
War Relief, and other relief agencies. Mrs. Roosevelt arrived
in London before he left, and Aldrich entertained her at lunch.

The return trip from Britain was one he would never forget.
On August 15, 1942, Aldrich and a small group left London
for Bristol on a special train that consisted of only a Pullman
car and a baggage car. After some delay the group, which
included such diverse traveling companions as an embassy
courier with an armed Marine guard and a former member of
the British Institute of Banking who had been torpedoed off
Nova Scotia in his last effort to reach the United States,
boarded a plane that had once been on the London-Paris run.
It had been stripped of its appointments and canvas covered
its windows. The two-hour flight to Limerick, Ireland, was
rough and noisy. The departure from there was delayed and
Aldrich spent the night with friends at Adare, the Dunraven
estate.

The plane carrying Aldrich back across the Atlantic left
Ireland at 7:30 p.m., August 16, but after 10 hours out it was
forced to turn back, arriving at Limerick in only 4½ hours
with the aid of a tail wind. He was again invited to stay at
Adare, and this afforded him an opportunity for an extended
conversation with Ambassador William Bullitt, also a guest,
who had just completed a long trip through the Near East
and Russia.

Finally, on August 18 the long air journey was resumed.
This time it went off uneventfully, though crossing the Bay
of Fundy the passengers saw what they believed to be three
German submarines and in Massachusetts Bay they sighted an

empty life raft, mute testimony to the effectiveness of German submarine warfare.[17]

On August 27, 1942, Aldrich reported on his trip to a luncheon meeting of the British War Relief Society at the Bankers Club in New York. Speaking extemporaneously, he gave the group his impressions of Britain under fire, emphasizing especially the high morale that he had found wherever he went. He described the work of the Society in aiding the homeless, the aged, and children. In conclusion he stressed "that this contribution through the British War Relief Society represents every part of our community. It represents men and women, and it represents labor, and it represents corporations, and in every case it comes from the heart. And I can tell you from personal knowledge that it is enormously appreciated, not only by the British Government, but by the British people, and by the man in the street." [18]

Gerard Swope of General Electric, chairman of the National Budget Committee for war relief agencies established by Community Chests and Councils, Inc., ended this meeting with an appraisal of Aldrich's own contributions. "Sir Robert [Appleby] spoke of Mr. Aldrich as a very good friend of Great Britain," Swope said. "I will go further than that. He has been a very good and constructive friend for all these war chest appeals. It was really through his energy and wisdom that this committee was formed, and this committee is working now in very close cooperation with the committee headed by Mr. Joe Davies and Mr. Keppel and Mr. Charles Taft in Washington. From these committees that have already started their war chest appeals, we hear very good results." [19]

THE EXPANDING WAR RELIEF EFFORT

Despite his primary identification with British war relief, Aldrich was instrumental in establishing war relief agencies for other countries. He was, for example, a director and member of the executive committee of the Greek War Relief Society, organized in 1940. From Twentieth Century-Fox he had recruited Spyros Skouras as president, and Harold Vanderbilt accepted the post of honorary national chairman. In fact, at the very time Aldrich was addressing the British War Relief Society in August 1942, its Greek counterpart had several shiploads of relief goods en route to the Mediterranean. As time passed, still other relief societies were established with Aldrich's backing. Eugene Black of the Chase, for example, headed Dutch War Relief and Myron Taylor, ambassador to the Vatican and former chairman of U.S. Steel, led the relief effort for Italy.

As the number of relief organizations multiplied, the need for controlling their numbers and coordinating their fund-raising efforts became urgent. By March 1941, for example, there were 41 voluntary societies working to aid Britain alone.[20] This kind of enthusiasm could clearly go too far, and the very rapid proliferation of relief organizations and their resulting competition became a source of concern both to Aldrich and to the administration in Washington. Aldrich reached the point in September 1942 where he felt compelled to decline even the request of his good friend Thomas J. Watson to join a new relief effort for Yugoslavia.[21]

NATIONAL WAR FUND

To bring some order out of the growing confusion, the President's War Relief Control Board was established by Executive Order on July 25, 1942, while Aldrich was in Britain. Joseph Davies, as chairman, and Charles P. Taft, son of the late President and Chief Justice, headed the new Board, aided by Frederick P. Keppel of the Carnegie Corporation and later by his successor Charles Warren. The Board asked

Chester Barnard of New Jersey Telephone on leave as executive head of the USO, Ralph Hayes of Coca-Cola and executive director of the New York Community Trust, and President Henry Wriston of Brown University to examine the war relief problem. This group recommended that a national agency be organized to coordinate the activities and fund-raising efforts of the various private war relief groups.[22] The result was incorporation in New York State of the National War Fund on January 12, 1943. Aldrich, Swope, Hayes, Wriston, and Barnard were the incorporators.

This step had been urged by Aldrich for some time. Addressing a meeting of the Community Chests and Councils at Cincinnati in June 1942, for example, he had suggested the organization of a United War Relief Corporation. The National War Fund was in effect only a slightly different version of such an organization.

Because of Aldrich's early and effective leadership in war relief efforts, he was a logical candidate to head the new National War Fund. President Roosevelt suggested the banker's name, and Taft sounded him out on this possibility in December 1942. Aldrich responded affirmatively. Roosevelt then extended a formal invitation, and on February 27, 1943, Aldrich accepted it.[23] It proved to be a major commitment and one of the most significant and satisfying ones in a long career of public service.

The initial members of the National War Fund were 16 organizations devoted to war relief or war-related functions in the various countries of the United Nations.* However,

---

* The member agencies of the National War Fund were:
1. USO
2. United Prisoners Aid
3. United Seamen's Service
4. United Nations Relief
    Belgian War Relief Society
    British War Relief Society (continued on page 266)

some of the member organizations were themselves federa-
tions. United China Relief, for example, consisted of eight
units and the United Service Organizations (USO) of six. To
further complicate the administrative problem, the distribution of relief goods had to be handled through a variety of
agencies in the recipient countries. It was in this context that
the National War Fund had to solve problems of liaison, of
finding shipping space, of getting packages to the right parties,
of avoiding inadvertent aid to enemies of the United States,*
and of meeting rapidly changing civilian needs as the war
progressed.

There were several reasons for the Roosevelt administration's interest in establishing the National War Fund. Most
important, the Fund was regarded as a convincing demonstration of the unity of the American people and of their
personal interest in the United Nations. In this connection the
fact that the Fund brought organized labor effectively into
the relief effort was important. From a practical standpoint,
the existence of the Fund also helped to systematize national
solicitation of private funds for a variety of purposes. Red
Cross fund drives could thus be scheduled in the spring, and

French War Relief Society
Greek War Relief Association
Norwegian Relief
Polish War Relief
Queen Wilhelmina Fund
Russian War Relief
United China Relief
United Czechoslovak Relief
United Yugoslav Relief Fund
5. Refugee Relief: Refugee Relief Trustees, United States Committee
   for the Care of European Children

* Aldrich stated the policy of distribution in July 18, 1943, as one of
utilizing in occupied or enemy countries "only those organizations which
are internationally recognized, or which are recognized by the government
involved, including that of the occupying power."

UN relief and other major drives in the fall, with war bond and other solicitations spread over the rest of the year.

The National Budget Committee that had been functioning under the Community Chests and Councils was brought under the National War Fund, and Gerard Swope remained its head. By combining fund raising and distributing efforts under one organization, it became possible to establish a consolidated budget. This in turn made it possible to allocate funds by function — food, clothing, medical supplies, and the like. Centralized budgeting also contributed to the flexibility that was essential in administering relief.

The heavy burden of allocating scarce funds among many worthy claimants fell primarily on Swope, though he was aided by a committee of which Aldrich was a member. The remaining War Fund officers in addition to president Aldrich were Robert O. Loosley and Harry P. Wareham (a veteran of Community Chest work), executive vice presidents; Ralph Hayes, secretary; Gordon S. Rentschler, treasurer; Henry M. Wriston, chairman of the publicity committee; and John F. Dulles, counsel. This was a distinguished group of citizens, and the millions of dollars that passed through the Fund's hands made their responsibility very great. Nothing could have been more disastrous to the relief effort than to have the Fund criticized for loose handling or allocation of its privately donated resources. This possibility was a matter of great concern to Aldrich, and one of his first actions as the Fund's president was to ask for monthly statements and semiannual audits.[24]

In many respects the organization and operation of the National War Fund, which drew on the example of united fund-raising efforts during World War I, embodied principles and a philosophy to which Aldrich had committed himself long before World War II. They were implicit and explicit in an address he made to Community Chest executives at the

Hotel Commodore in New York on March 7, 1943, outlining the origin, objectives and policies of the Fund. On that occasion he pointed out: "The National War Fund has been organized under singularly happy circumstances, for it is the result of the harmonious views of the general public on the one hand and the Government on the other." He then went on to stress that the Fund, although temporary, had more than wartime relief objectives: it was laying the foundation for the postwar world where voluntary cooperation would identify social needs on a unified basis but meet them on the basis of the local responsibility implied by decentralized administration. In his words, "The National War Fund expresses this ideal. It does not dictate programs to any of the agencies which cooperate. Beyond assurance that there is no duplication and overlapping, it has nothing to say and it wants nothing to say, about the shaping of their programs or their administration." [25] Guided by this concept, which Aldrich had first advanced in 1934 as the basis for administering unemployment relief, the Fund was organized. In December 1942 it had consisted of six men meeting in Aldrich's office; in a few months it had a budget of over $100 million and representatives in 43,000 communities.*

The progress of the Fund was reviewed by Aldrich at a meeting of the directors on October 9, 1944. Five new agencies had been admitted to membership,** but many more had been denied on the grounds that their purposes lay outside those of the Fund. To meet the need for broader representation of supporting groups, the number of directors had been increased from 150 to 175 and the executive committee from

* The history of the National War Fund is in Harold J. Seymour, *Design for Giving: The Story of the National War Fund, 1943–1947* (New York: Harper and Brothers, 1947).

** American Denmark Relief, American Relief for Italy, American Field Service, Phillipine War Relief, and United Lithuanian Relief Fund.

18 to 30. The current budget, Aldrich reported, was $115 million, the maximum that state and local war funds could be expected to raise in view of the Fund's inclusion in federated local campaigns with overall objectives of over $260 million. Aldrich was especially pleased to report that the Fund had achieved close cooperation with agencies of organized labor, such as the Labor League of Human Rights, A F of L, and the National CIO War Relief Committee, as well as the Railroad Brotherhoods and the United Mine Workers.[26]

The rapidity with which the nature of war relief demands changed and the number and size of requests for Fund assistance taxed even its $115 million budget. This pressure on scarce funds led to increased frequency of budget review, a step urged by the President's War Relief Control Board. As a result, the executive committee decided that annual commitments to member agencies should be limited to administrative expenses and long-term commitments; all other allocations were reviewed every three months.[27] Since the availability of funds did not always coincide with pressing needs for them, a group of New York banks and financial institutions arranged very sizable credits for the Fund.[28] Obviously Aldrich's connection with the organization was an important factor in obtaining this kind of assistance. His initiative also made it possible for commercial banks, including his own, to become active contributors to war relief.

Fortunately, National War Fund dollars went farther than the dollar budget alone might suggest. For example, American Relief for Italy received $200,000 from the Fund to finance a campaign to collect clothing, and the result of that drive was some 6 million pounds of clothing valued conservatively at $11 million.[29]

With the Allied invasion of Europe in June 1944 and the ensuing Allied advance toward the German heartland, Aldrich became concerned that the public's enthusiasm for giving to the National War Fund might lag. This could have been most unfortunate in view of the continuing needs of other war theatres and the increased demands of countries freed by the advancing Allies in Europe. Accordingly, late in the summer he made a public statement emphasizing the danger of letting down prematurely, and he reemphasized it at the November meeting of the Fund's directors. At their meeting in late April 1945, just before the final capitulation of Germany, he stressed once again the need for continuing the Fund's activities. For the first time, he pointed out, private relief could be brought directly to the peoples of liberated Europe. Newly repatriated prisoners and displaced persons desperately needed help. "Victory over Germany will tend to increase, rather than diminish, the need for help," he said.[30]

Aldrich identified three major problems confronting the National War Fund as the European war ended. The first involved its relations with various government and United Nations agencies, such as American Military Government, the Foreign Economic Administration, and UNRRA. Although he conceded that these relationships were currently so fluid as to defy a precise definition, he stated that the National War Fund should insist that such agencies clarify the scope of their relief operations and the extent to which they needed or welcomed private aid. The second problem was the budget for 1945–1946. Aldrich recognized that with the end of hostilities and all that this implied in terms of the domestic economy, there were sound arguments for reducing the Fund's budget. On the other hand, he was convinced that the need for Fund aid would not diminish in the near future. Therefore, it seemed best to await the outcome of current military operations before reaching a final decision on the budget.[31] The directors agreed, and later the budget was set at over $100 million.[32]

The budget problem was linked to the key question of

when the National War Fund, conceived as a temporary organization, should disband. It was Aldrich's view that this action probably could and should be accomplished by 1948, though a final decision necessarily required further investigation of member agency plans as well as the final outcome of military events.[33]

The passage of time of course helped to resolve some of these problems. With the Japanese surrender in August 1945, following the German capitulation in May, the war was over. The Fund's executive committee decided shortly after V-J Day to liquidate the operation by the end of 1946. Reporting this decision at a directors' meeting in February 1946, Aldrich declared: "The problems we face are the new problems involved in establishing a world of peace. The new problems call for new measures, new designs to fit the new circumstances."[34]

However, if the war had ended, peace had not been restored. Aldrich also made this point in addressing the Fund's directors. "We are in a period of transition," he said, "one of the greatest dangers in the present situation is that too many lack the perspective to see this truth." And he continued, "Let us recognize, therefore, that until peace is finally established we must keep sufficiently strong in a military sense to meet our world commitments; that this means substantial armed forces for some time to come, and that our obligation to help maintain the morale of those armed forces is with us until the task is done."[35]

The record of the Fund's wartime achievement in terms of private donations, personal commitment, and the outpouring of aid in the name of humanity was unsurpassed in American history. Over a period of three years, as part of a federated effort, the Fund had raised more than $250 million plus $100 million of gifts-in-kind from every part of the United States. Counting assistance to military personnel, merchant seamen, prisoners of war, refugees and other war victims, the Fund had aided more than 171 million men, women, and children in 126 countries on 6 continents. The Fund had distributed over 40 million pounds of food, nearly 100 million pounds of clothing and over 67 million pounds of medical and other supplies.[36] The entire operation was impressive testimony to what private efforts could accomplish under trying circumstances. It is an interesting commentary on the sources of support that the Fund's two largest individual benefactors were John D. Rockefeller, Jr., and Bob Hope, the latter through assignment of the royalties on his book, *I Never Left Home*.[37]

Although the President's War Relief Control Board was terminated by Executive Order on May 15, 1946, it proved impossible to wind up the affairs of such a complex and wide-ranging undertaking as the National War Fund without complications. One example of the problems involved was a project initially sponsored in 1943 by organized labor agencies affiliated with the Fund to provide relief to refugees in countries occupied by the Axis, and more especially Czechoslovakia. The arrangements, approved by United States government agencies, called for representatives of the Czech government-in-exile to administer the funds for the relief of their countrymen and to report through diplomatic channels to the U.S. Treasury Department. After the war it was discovered that a substantial amount of this money had not been expended and remained on deposit in London. However, recovery of the funds was complicated by the fact that the wartime Czechoslovak relief agencies had been reorganized and then disbanded, the principal trustee of the account was in Czechoslovakia, which had since come under Communist control, and the London depository was unwilling to give up the money without authorization from the group formally listed as trustees. A complicated and time-consuming series of legal and other maneuvers was necessary to solve this problem, which was not finally resolved until 1957.[38] In that year the National War Fund was finally liquidated, and its faithful administration of millions of dollars without irregularities was confirmed by court order.

Aldrich had provided outstanding leadership to the Fund during the war, but his task had been made lighter by the many able men and women who gave just as unstintingly as he of their time and abilities. The Fund represented the kind of cooperation between government, organized labor, and business that Aldrich had advocated for fighting the depression in the 1930s. This cooperation had proved far easier to achieve, of course, when the stimulus was war rather than economic distress.

The fruitful wartime experience gave hope that private postwar philanthropy would continue to reap the benefits. For one thing, the Fund's campaign had extended into cities and towns where such efforts had never been made before. If the Community Chests and Councils had proved indispensable to the Fund in organizing and channeling these efforts, the peacetime agencies in turn had been introduced to new opportunities through the wartime association.

THE CHASE UNDER ATTACK

In the light of Aldrich's many and varied contributions to the war effort, as well as those of his bank, it was especially ironical that the Chase should have been indicted for alleged violation of an executive order issued under the Trading with the Enemy Act. The indictment did considerable harm to the Chase's reputation at the time, and it severely tested Aldrich's courage before a court laid the charges to rest.

The case had a background in routine administration.[39] As the German army swept across France in May 1940, President Roosevelt had issued an order to block "substantial" accounts of nationals from German-occupied countries unless they were both resident and domiciled in the United States.* The purpose of the order was to protect such accounts from confiscation by the Nazis. For authority Roosevelt used the same World War I statute that he had employed in the 1933 bank crisis. The Presidential order required the Chase, like other banks, to examine all its accounts and to block those falling within the order. As a result of this examination, the Chase blocked some 12,000 out of 110,000 accounts, meaning that withdrawals from them had to have Washington's approval. Although apparently due care was exercised by bank officials in this procedure, the order was open to interpretation and, amidst the review of so many accounts, the possibility of an unintentional oversight was always present.

The fact that a problem of this kind existed was called to the attention of the bank by a Treasury agent in June 1941. It involved the firm of Anton Smit & Co. of New York and Elsantum, Inc. of Panama, both firms controlled by the same interests. It developed that through the British, the American government had learned that Smit was doing a brisk business with the Axis in industrial diamonds.

Smit was a Dutchman and his Belgian company had been introduced to the bank in late 1939. When Smit's New York firm was established, one of its accounts went to the Chase as did the allied Panama company's in December 1940. The Belgian account had been blocked routinely, but those of the New York and Panama corporations had not been. This gave rise to the charges against the bank, but there were, as defense counsel later brought out, extenuating circumstances.

Smit was resident and domiciled in this country and in no danger of falling into Nazi hands, a basic criterion of the

* This order extended one issued on April 7, 1940, in connection with the German invasion of Norway and Denmark.

executive order. The Chase also had a letter to show that the Smit concern was controlled by a parent company in the British Isles. Although the government knew that Smit's major accounts had been blocked in other banks, it did not inform the Chase of this fact. Even where Smit's accounts had been blocked, the government had licensed withdrawals. Moreover, after November 1941 the government had allowed foreigners physically in the United States as of June 1940 to operate their bank accounts freely.

That the Treasury Department should find cause for action against the Chase under these circumstances, particularly where the charge could only apply to a small account for a short period of time, seemed incredible to Aldrich; yet the government sought and obtained an indictment in 1944 from a federal grand jury. The indictment charged the Chase with conspiracy to release funds illegally to Belgian and Dutch nationals, the alleged co-conspirators. News of the charges received worldwide publicity and even led some American servicemen to write bitter letters to Aldrich, whom they pictured as presiding over a corrupt, unpatriotic institution.[40]

The timing of the indictment in an election year suggested to some of Aldrich's friends and colleagues that the action had a political motivation, but they had no evidence to support this view and he did not regard it as soundly based. However, his integrity and that of the bank, whose reputation was quite as dear to him as his own, had been challenged, and he was determined to exhaust fully every legal recourse.

The general preparation of the case was placed in the hands of the Milbank, Tweed firm, the bank's counsel and the successor to Aldrich's old law firm. William Evarts and Emmet Smith headed the group assigned to the case. John Cahill, previously United States Attorney for the Southern District of New York, was retained as trial counsel.

The work of preparing the case involved so many people

night and day that for a time it was necessary to hold dinner meetings to coordinate the various efforts. Government representatives as well as bank lawyers combed the bank's files, and one of the defense counsel's more inspired ideas was to have a female employee of the law firm supervise the proceedings while knitting away on garments for the Red Cross.[41] The fact that she did not know how to knit made her contribution to war relief presumably less valuable than the patriotic image conveyed to the government investigators.

The investigation by the Chase's counsel revealed that there had been technical violations of the Presidential order, but that they were equally clearly the result of administrative complexities. For example, it was discovered that only one bank officer had actually reviewed the Smit New York account; this officer was not in the Foreign Department, and he was looking at the Smit account solely from the standpoint of whether such a small, nonborrowing account should be encouraged. Cahill's strategy in the courtroom was to emphasize the difficulties and uncertainties of administering the blocking order, while challenging the validity of the prosecution's basic case that there had been a conspiracy.

On the eve of the trial, the government attorneys apparently recognized that proof of a conspiracy would be virtually impossible. In any event, the bank was offered the opportunity to plead guilty to one count and accept a token fine in return for the dropping of the conspiracy charge. Cahill recommended against accepting this offer, and Aldrich took the lawyer's advice though he thereby ran the risk that the result of a jury trial might be a disastrous blow to the bank.[42]

Aldrich had an unexpected opportunity to reverse his decision while the jury was considering the case. The judge had delivered his charge to the jury late in the afternoon and they then retired. As the hours of waiting for the jury's verdict wore on, Cahill decided that he could move a mistrial. In his words, "I called Aldrich about four [A.M.], and he had the control to be asleep and I said, 'You know I can move for a mistrial on the grounds that after these hours any verdict is coerced.' He said, 'No, I'll take the responsibility. See it through.' " [43] Aldrich's courage was rewarded, for the jury came in shortly thereafter with a verdict of innocent. Subsequently the banker felt justified in confronting Secretary of the Treasury Morgenthau with the charge that people in the Treasury Department, rather than at the Chase, had done the conspiring. [44]

Of course, the news that the Chase had been acquitted did not receive the same prominent and extensive coverage as the indictment. Both *The New York Times* and the *Herald Tribune*, however, took it on themselves to editorialize on the suit and the acquittal. The *Herald Tribune* pointed out that the suit was of minor importance since the Chase at worst could have been fined only $5,000. The editorial pointed out: "The banks have spent a vast amount of time and money — much of it in legal expenses — combing their records for some possible obscure evader of these complex regulations. Yet along comes the Justice Department to start an action which, even though unsuccessful, could seriously injure the reputation of a great financial institution." The editorial further stated that the Chase, next to the New York Stock Exchange, came closer to symbolizing the New York financial community than any other institution. This made the damage of the suit especially great since "in some parts of the country at least, people will believe things about a Wall Street bank that they would reject out of hand in the case of their own First National Bank." [45]

Aldrich had done what he could to minimize this damage by insisting that the suit be carried through on its legal merits, but the wide publicity given the initiation of the action constituted damage that neither he nor the acquittal could quickly repair. It was some satisfaction, however, to have the *Times* declare, "The vindication of the Chase National Bank is merely what those who knew its record and the sense of responsibility of its officers in such matters confidently expected." [46]

CHAPTER XI

Years of Preparation for the Postwar World, 1940-1946

W HILE Aldrich was deeply involved in the demanding effort to relieve the suffering of war victims, he was also looking ahead to the problems of the postwar world. His personal experience with the results of the World War I peace settlement made him keenly aware of the need to avoid repeating those mistakes. As a private citizen and as an international banker, he contributed effectively to the debate on postwar planning. Through his efforts the opportunities for bringing businessmen's insights and experience to bear on postwar problems were significantly enlarged.

The International Chamber of Commerce

During the war itself, Aldrich's most active contributions toward shaping postwar reconstruction were made as a leader in the International Chamber of Commerce.* A member of

* For a history of the International Chamber of Commerce, see George L. Ridgeway, *Merchants of Peace; The History of the International Chamber of Commerce* (Boston: Little, Brown and Company, 1959).

that group since the early 1930s, he became chairman of one of its monetary policy committees in 1937. Two years later he was elected American vice president. Accepting that post on May 7, 1940, as the German war machine rolled into France, Aldrich affirmed his confidence in the future and underlined the need to plan for it. "I think it is perhaps fair to say that my acceptance of the American vice presidency of the International Chamber of Commerce shows faith in some other things besides the International Chamber, because it shows faith that there will be a purpose in the future for such chambers of commerce," he declared.[1]

In his new post his proposals for action were forward looking. The Chamber should not only try to discover what went wrong in the years between the wars, he urged, but should also make its contributions to preparation for a durable peace. Such a peace would require a flow of world trade and access to a supply of raw materials adequate to permit countries to develop their full potentials. It would be necessary to reestablish a stable medium of international exchange and provide for the mobility of capital.

Aldrich felt that there was an immediate role for a private world organization like the International Chamber in studying many of the problems that would come with the end of hostilities, such as the transition from war to peace economies, reemployment of demobilized forces, and approaches to countering the threat of worldwide inflation. In his words: "If we could even begin to approach the solution of some of those problems, which in the last analysis will have to be solved by governments, and as to which we can only act in an advisory capacity to the governments, we would have performed the most enormous public service."[2] Thus he implicitly drew a distinction between the civilian war relief effort, where a private organization like the National War Fund could play a leading role, and the solution of postwar world economic problems, where governments necessarily would have to bear the prime responsibility. In both instances, however, by advocacy and example, he believed that private efforts were justified, important, and imperative.

VIEWS ON POSTWAR MONETARY AND FISCAL POLICY

Naturally, Aldrich's primary concern was with monetary and fiscal policies as they would set the economic climate for the postwar world. He said little publicly on these matters after 1940 until he addressed the Connecticut Bankers Association in January 1943 on "The Economic Implications of Internal Public Debts." Aldrich repeated the main points of his 1940 presentation to the Boston Chamber of Commerce,[3] but with particularly heavy emphasis on the importance of taxation in war financing and on the desirability of a wide distribution of the public debt among private investors, large and small, as well as commercial banks. The main thrust of his remarks, however, was directed to the postwar consequences of wartime financing. "The size of our domestic public debt and the manner in which it is financed will, to a considerable extent, determine the political and economic role of this country in the postwar world," he told his audience.[4]

In April 1943 he raised this question again in an address to the American Section of the International Chamber of Commerce. On that occasion he pointed out that: "One of the most difficult of all economic problems and one which will press for immediate solution is that of monetary stabilization."[5] This was so, he said, because only after such stabilization could businessmen make plans for future production, savings be encouraged, and international trade and capital exports resumed. Both the American and British governments had been giving attention to these problems, and groups of experts from each country had developed tentative plans for their solution. Aldrich, however, felt that neither the American nor British proposals was acceptable from an economic or political point of view. A basic defect in both, he said, was that international monetary stabilization had been approached independent of internal stabilization, which he strongly believed was a prerequisite to the effectiveness of any international plan.[6]

As was his custom, Aldrich did not criticize the proposals of others without offering an alternative one. Therefore in his address to the American Section of the ICC, he suggested establishing a "free dollar" in the postwar world. This step would, he said, check domestic inflationary pressures, permit the resumption of gold payments, and eliminate the need for foreign exchange controls. Combined with extension of the Reciprocal Trade Agreements program, the reintroduction of the gold standard would "make an important contribution to postwar economic recovery."[7] These ideas, clearly an extension of his prewar position, were to undergo continuing refinement in the coming months.

Meanwhile, Aldrich had been elected president of the Economic Club of New York. This position gave his pronouncements on postwar policies added significance, and he took full advantage of the fact. It was a policy of the club, composed of leading New York business and financial figures, to orient its annual programs around a central theme. For 1943–1944 it was "The Challenge of Tomorrow." Introducing the first speakers on this topic in November 1943, Aldrich stressed anew the importance of United States leadership in planning for the postwar period. In doing so, he said, "Responsibility for the course of peacetime economies will fall on the victors as a matter of course, hence the responsibility will be theirs whether postwar reconstruction is to be on sound principles or whether it is to be marked by a series of tragic and fateful mistakes." The United States, as one of the strong members of the world family, was under particular obligation "to contribute our vision and leadership and weight and strength to an organized and coordinated effort for the rebuilding of a good society on the earth." [8]

Stimulating Public Interest in Postwar Economic Problems

Given his own interest, it is not surprising that Aldrich associated himself with a variety of private efforts to promote these ideas and to stimulate action toward achieving the goals that they reflected. Representative of one such effort was the Committee on International Economic Policy established in 1944 under the auspices of a number of private organizations ranging from the Carnegie Endowment for International Peace to the Committee for Economic Development and the National Industrial Conference Board. At the request of Thomas J. Watson, Aldrich became vice chairman of this new Committee in January 1944; six months later he became its chairman. The basic purpose of the Committee, as he described it for *Printers' Ink*, was to take advantage of a "unique opportunity . . . to reduce trade barriers and to re-establish the system of multilateral trade." [9] To provide a basis for such action the Committee, among other things, sponsored a series of scholarly studies directed to postwar economic problems and prepared under the auspices of an advisory committee on economics headed by Professor James T. Shotwell of Columbia University.

While these efforts were aimed at influencing policymakers in both government and business, Aldrich also communicated his views directly to the American GI. Writing for the servicemen's paper at Camp Lee, Virginia, in October 1944, for example, he pointed out that what the postwar world would be like depended on the policies and attitudes of those who would live in it. "We must eschew the maintenance of artificially high prices and wages, or monopolistic practices on the part of business or labor. Special interests must not be advanced at the expense of the whole people," he told the servicemen.[10]

THE BRETTON WOODS CONFERENCE

By this time, the pace of postwar planning in the British and American capitals had accelerated. Monetary and development problems, viewed in the context of multilateral trade arrangements, were the subject of an international conference called by the United States, at Bretton Woods, New Hampshire, in July 1944. The proposals discussed there were the product of compromise between the so-called White Plan of the United States Treasury,* named for its author Harry Dexter White, and the Keynes Plan of Great Britain, named for John Maynard Keynes. The major proposals placed before the Conference were the establishment of an International Monetary Fund and an International Bank for Reconstruction and Development. A Morgenthau protegé, White had proposed a plan that would concentrate international financial power in Washington as compared to New York or London and also emphasized a continuing role for gold; Keynes had suggested an end to any pretense of an international gold standard.**

* The Treasury had commenced work on postwar monetary and financial problems in 1941, and proposals for an International Stabilization Fund had been discussed with representatives of numerous friendly countries prior to the Bretton Woods meeting. By mid-1943 a Bank for Reconstruction and Development was also under active discussion.

** For a detailed discussion of the Keynes and White plans see, Shigeo Horie, *The International Monetary Fund; Retrospect and Prospect* (New York: St. Martin's Press, Inc., 1964). Also see, Jacob Viner, "Two Plans for International Monetary Stabilization," *Yale Review*, vol. XXIII (Autumn, 1943), pp. 77–107.

Aldrich Opposes Bretton Woods Proposals

Aldrich became a leader in private groups opposing adoption of either of these Bretton Woods proposals. The Chase chairman made his position clear in an address to the Executives' Club of Chicago on September 15, 1944, entitled "Some Aspects of American Foreign Policy." Aldrich stated that he felt the Roosevelt administration's initiative in calling the Bretton Woods Conference had diverted attention from fundamental commercial and domestic problems by prematurely emphasizing currency stabilization and international loans. The basic economic problems of the postwar world could not be solved by currency manipulation, he told the Chicagoans. Only after the internal economic affairs of nations were put in order could the long-run stabilization of currencies and the international extension of loans be fitted properly into the pattern of economic reconstruction.

Aldrich attacked both the proposed International Monetary Fund and International Bank for Reconstruction and Development on the grounds that they could not accomplish, given their definition of objectives and specific organization, the laudable goals in whose name they were being put forward. The banker stated that the objectives of the Fund lacked "the focus essential to success." On the technical side he felt that the Fund as structured at Bretton Woods, would pull good currencies down to the level of poor ones and that its liberal provisions for altering exchange rates would encourage exchange instability rather than its avowed purpose of promoting stability. "Nations could employ exchange depreciation as a substitute for internal fiscal reform and for internal adjustments of costs and prices," he said.[11]

For somewhat different reasons he also opposed the proposal for an International Bank for Reconstruction and Development. He rejected the contention that use of this mechanism to promote large capital exports from the United States would benefit employment at home or aid the reconstruction and development of other countries.* The problem of foreign aid had to be approached in more specific terms, Aldrich maintained. For example, "If foreign funds are used when local capital is available, a needlessly heavy burden is placed on the debtor's balance of payments." It was even conceivable, he suggested, that projects made possible by a World Bank loan would have to be serviced by the debtor country's resort to the International Monetary Fund. The relationship of the proposed Bank to the existing Export-Import Bank as well as to the United States government also troubled him. He questioned whether there were real advantages in extending long-term foreign loans, presumably largely financed with United States funds, through a new international institution rather than through an established agency of this government.[12]

Proposal for Grant-in-Aid to England

Having rejected the White and Keynes plans, Aldrich offered an alternative approach.** The basis for this proposal was that the dollar-pound rate be stabilized as a prelude to further international action. As one important step to this end, he suggested that "the United States provide England with a grant-in-aid sufficiently large to establish stability be-

* Morgenthau told Detroit industrial leaders in February 1945 that adoption of the Bretton Woods agreements would create a large export market for cars. The CIO was led to believe that the Fund and Bank would create millions of jobs for American workers. (Richard Gardner, *Sterling-Dollar Diplomacy*, Oxford: Clarendon Press, 1956, p. 137.)

** Except for its heavy emphasis on expanding trade, the Aldrich plan had been anticipated in proposals made in November 1943 by Leon Fraser, president of the First National Bank of New York and a former governor of the Bank for International Settlements, and by Professor John Williams of Harvard, who was also a vice president of the Federal Reserve Bank of New York. (Gardner, *Sterling-Dollar Diplomacy*, p. 132.)

tween the dollar and the pround." * This action was to be taken in conjunction with a conference to remove trade barriers between the two countries. The grant would be contingent on the United States and England agreeing to shun "totalitarian tactics in international trade," and giving both countries full support "to the principles of economic liberalism." [13]

Assuming success in stabilizing the dollar-pound relationship, attention could then be given to the currencies of other nations. Under Aldrich's proposal the Export-Import Bank could provide funds for worthy projects in foreign countries that could not obtain private financing, and a bank for central banks could be formed to provide short-term stabilization loans to central banks, act as a clearing house for central banks, and perform similar functions. In addition, Aldrich urged that the slate should be wiped clean of intergovernmental war debts and that the United States should take appropriate action to establish a sound currency and to avoid postwar inflation.

Aldrich Under Political Attack

In some quarters Aldrich's speech was interpreted as a definition of the Republican party's position on international economic relations, advanced as part of its campaign to capture the Presidency later that fall. At least this was the light in which Democrat Senator Joseph F. Guffey of Pennsylvania saw it when he addressed the Senate a few days later. The Senator seemed bent on the discrediting of John Foster Dulles, rumored to be Thomas E. Dewey's candidate for Secretary of State if the Republican presidential candidate won in November, and of Winthrop Aldrich, reported by Guffey to be Dewey's choice for Secretary of the Treasury. In the

---

* For Leon Fraser's similar proposal, made nearly a year earlier, to grant credit to Britain, see New York *Herald Tribune*, November 21, 1943.

image-laden language of the politician, Guffey — invoking shades of William Jennings Bryan — asked rhetorically:

> In the offices of Wall Street's bankers and lawyers, what is cooking?
>
> Instead of a peace strangled by politics, are we going to have, this time, a peace crucified on a cross of gold?

He then used Aldrich as an example of the international bankers' selfish and self-interested point of view, though he characterized Aldrich as "at least forthright."

Guffey attacked Aldrich's views on gold, on balancing the federal budget, and on the need for a bank of central banks. The essence of his attack was contained in these words: "What this spokesman for Mr. Dewey was really asking was that we scrap the Bretton Woods proposals and abandon Government regulation of our money system and return it to the hands of the private bankers who led us into the orgy of speculation in the twenties and then were helpless to stem the disastrous depression of the early thirties." [14]

Senator Arthur Vandenberg, a Republican leader from Michigan, was not on the Senate floor at the time Guffey made his remarks but subsequently sought to set the record straight. Senator Vandenberg left no doubt that he respected Aldrich's credentials as "one of the distinguished and honored leaders in the financial life of America," who could be evaluated on his own merits. Vandenberg, who should have known if anyone did, denied that Aldrich had any authority to speak for Dewey. In any case, Vandenberg argued, Aldrich as a qualified person — in some respects better qualified than those who sat at Bretton Woods — should be applauded for giving the nation the benefit of his views. In the Michigan Senator's words: "The address made by Mr. Aldrich was a constructive discussion of a technical question concerning which he [Aldrich] knows more than the Senator from Pennsylvania or the Senator from Michigan will ever know in their lifetimes. I think his contribution is to be welcomed for whatever it may prove to be worth in the determination of this terrifically difficult problem." [15]

Aldrich and the Public

In many respects Aldrich's September 1944 speech to the Executives' Club in Chicago was comparable in importance to the one he had made at Rochester, New York, in October 1937.* Both were landmarks in his efforts as a private citizen to focus public attention on problems that he considered vital to the nation's welfare, yet, in his opinion, were being approached inadequately by those with formal responsibility for dealing with them. The shift in his emphasis from domestic to international issues between 1937 and 1944 was more reflection of events than of any change in Aldrich's own interests, which had always had an international cast.

In the Rochester speech he had spotlighted the difficulties of the stock market in terms of governmental policies that he thought had contributed significantly to the 1937 recession. His remarks had pinpointed an issue, stimulated controversy, investigation, and self-examination by both public and private agencies at that time. In addressing himself in September 1944 to the proposals for the International Monetary Fund and the International Bank for Reconstruction and Development, Aldrich had performed a similar service and launched himself into an area of continuing controversy.

The fact that Aldrich was an international banker led his critics, like Senator Guffey, to assume that this was the sole frame of reference in which he made his proposals. It would have been more accurate to say that Aldrich's perceptions of the problems confronting banking and the nation were the

* See Chapter IX.

product of deeply held personal beliefs in the efficacy of the market as opposed to centralized controls, whether the question was one of securities, foreign exchange, or the commodities of international trade. This conviction led him to advocate freer international trade and free internal markets, stressing the inseparability of the two.

His critics typically took the position that the questions to which Aldrich addressed himself had to be resolved either on the basis of government controlling the economy or of the private sector — in Aldrich's case "Wall Street banks" — controlling the government. They overlooked the fact that Aldrich did not deny the importance of governmental controls on markets to insure that they performed as they should; he had in fact taken the lead in imposing some of them on Wall Street banks. What he opposed so strenuously was the substitution of political or administrative decisions for market decisions. In this sense the choice for the nation was not simply between "Washington" or "Wall Street," as his critics liked to frame the issue, but rather recognition by the electorate that there was a broad spectrum of public and private responsibilities for the performance of the economy. While Aldrich placed primary emphasis on private rather than public decisions in the allocation of resources, his public speeches indicate that he recognized an appreciable overlap of the two in some areas and clear governmental primacy in still others.

The problem of winning popular acceptance of this message hinged on the fact that his predecessors had botched the job in exercising the freedom for which he asked. This was an irrefutable fact, and it was a fact that virtually every attack on Aldrich's proposals for national and foreign policy featured. It was, in short, a burden that the banker had to carry through no fault of his own. However heavy this burden, he refused to accept the mistakes of the past as sealing the verdict on the advantages of business and financial freedom. He would undoubtedly have held the same views even if he had not been a banker; he believed in their fundamental soundness because of his heritage, his training, and his experience.

Soviet Impressions of Aldrich

Soviet representatives who attended the Bretton Woods conference afterwards talked with Aldrich and others who opposed the proposals that emerged from it. The Chief of the Currency Administration of the People's Commissariat of Finance of the USSR reported his impressions in an article for *The War and the Working Class*, which appeared on October 15, 1944. His vignettes were incisive and to the point. The Soviet writer described Harry White as "very businesslike and sociable." The Russian visited White at his "two-storey" home outside Washington, and in this connection he wrote: "Generally speaking, America is a two-storey, and not a one-storey country, as it has sometimes been described." Of Lord Keynes, he said: "His speeches at the conference were often received with loud laughter. But his speeches, though humorous, usually contained very serious statements, in protection of the interests of his country."

After describing Marriner Eccles as being uninformed about the Soviet Union and American businessmen as being highly interested in what they could sell there after the war, the Soviet writer continued:

> After the conference the Soviet delegates met those repre-sentatives of American banking circles who were opposed to the conference and to the idea of settling postwar financial relations by agreements concluded between states, as recom-mended by Mr. Morgenthau and Mr. White. The most sig-nificant in this connection was the meeting with Mr. Aldrich, chairman of the Chase National Bank, who quite frankly and even bluntly explained to the Soviet delegates that he was in favor of direct contact, which he believed to be the best

means of bringing about mutual understanding in business questions.

The delegates visited Mr. Aldrich in his office on the 34th floor, a small and simply furnished room. He invited them to an ordinary, simple lunch — it is a common practice in America to conduct business talks over lunch.

Mr. Aldrich looked more like a professor or scientist than a businessman. He was Rockefeller's son-in-law, and thus a member of a family occupying the very top of the complex pyramid of American financial capital. . . .

Mr. Aldrich sharply criticized the conference. In a petulant moment he called Mr. White the "pale shadow of Keynes" and said that the American plan (accepted in the main at the conference) was practically based on Keynes' idea of a "managed currency." Aldrich and the group of bankers sharing his views regarded Mr. Morgenthau and Mr. White as representatives of a "different world" since they were in favor of the active intervention of the state in financial policy. Aldrich preferred to dispose of his own capital himself and to decide to whom he should lend money and on what terms, especially now, with a postwar scarcity of goods and credits already looming over Europe, and when there are as yet no signs of crises.[16]

Anyone who had followed Aldrich's recent speeches in any detail would have been forced to agree that the Soviet delegate had captured the essence of the banker's thinking, even though he incorrectly identified Aldrich's relationship to the Rockefellers.

WARTIME CONFERENCE OF WORLD BUSINESS LEADERS

Aldrich had an unusual opportunity to present his ideas on postwar planning to an international audience of key businessmen gathered for a conference at the Westchester Country Club in Rye, New York, in November 1944. The idea for the conference originated with Noel Sargent, secretary of the National Association of Manufacturers, who approached the other officers of that organization in April 1943 with a proposal to hold a wartime conference of world business leaders. Like Aldrich, Sargent and others in the NAM saw the approaching end of World War II as a challenge to sound economic planning and a new opportunity to shape the relationship of business and governments. When the idea was presented to Secretary of State Cordell Hull, he quickly recognized its potential and suggested that other American business organizations besides the NAM be included in the sponsorship. Acting on that suggestion, the NAM invited the Chamber of Commerce of the United States, the National Foreign Trade Council, and the American Section of the International Chamber of Commerce to participate in organizing the conference.[17]

The resulting undertaking was a large one that involved over a year of planning. Delegates, in some instances exiles from occupied countries, came from 52 nations and included observers from the Soviet Union. They assembled at Rye on November 10, 1944, for the first nongovernmental international conference of World War II. The topics to which they addressed themselves during the next week were as varied as cartels, raw materials and foodstuffs, industrialization in new areas, and currency relations among nations.

The purpose of the conference was well stated by Eliot Wadsworth of the American Section, ICC, at the opening session. "It will afford ample opportunity for a free and frank exchange of information among businessmen from all over the world," he said. "When the conference is over, these businessmen will have a general idea of what their counterparts in other countries will want when the war ends and international trade can move again. . . . They will return to their homes with a great fund of knowledge of business conditions to discuss with business colleagues. They will

be in a position to give advice and counsel to their governments. . . ." [18]

As far as foreign delegates were concerned, perhaps the
most startling development was the very obvious change in
American businessmen's thinking about world trade. The protectionist attitude had clearly lost ground. The American
delegates made it clear from the first that they recognized
international trade was multilateral and that postwar exports
of goods and capital would have to be repaid in goods and
services.[19]

The same note was struck in a telegram from President
Roosevelt to the conference. In it he said: "World business,
after the war, must be expanded on a basis of nondiscrimi-
nation and of freedom from excessive barriers and restraints.
The necessary expansion can be achieved only as nations and
their citizens work together cooperatively toward understanding each others' problems and taking effective and mutually
advantageous measures for solving those problems." [20] There
was no stronger advocate of this approach in the American
business community, or the Rye conference, than Winthrop
Aldrich.

At Rye, Aldrich was most active in the Section on Currency
Relations Among Nations, for which he had helped to do
much of the preliminary planning. He made two presentations
in the four sessions. One was entitled "The 'Key Nation'
Approach to the Problem of Currency Stabilization." This
idea, advanced by Professor John H. Williams of Harvard,[21]
found one of its strongest advocates and popularizers in
Aldrich. The "key nation" emphasis was important, the
banker pointed out to the Rye conference, because it required
a specific approach to the problem of currency stabilization
as opposed to the global approach adopted at Bretton Woods.
The time-phased plan that he proposed for implementing this
approach was the one he had advocated in Chicago two

months earlier: First, elimination of the war debt problem between the United States and the United Kingdom; next, reduction of trade barriers; and finally a grant-in-aid as a form of retroactive Lend-Lease.[22] Here was his blueprint for the future as well as his answer to those who urged that Britain be required to repay the United States for wartime assistance.

In a lengthier statement on "Currency Relations Among Nations: a Report," Aldrich spelled out these ideas in greater detail and related them to what business had been doing to help establish postwar monetary stability. "Despite the controversial nature of the subject, business opinion concerning solutions and remedies is remarkably uniform," Aldrich reported. "Such a [free enterprise] system implies free markets in which prices are permitted to exercise their economic function in influencing and directing production," he said. "It implies, too, the absence of international trade barriers in the form of high tariffs, quota restrictions, export subsidies, regional preferences, discriminatory import restrictions and foreign exchange controls." This was clearly his personal credo, and he reported to his international audience that businessmen in the United States generally shared it. More specifically, they had evidenced conviction that "the dollar-pound rate, the most important of all exchange rates, should be stabilized first." [23]

The formal report of the Section on Currency Relations Among Nations was largely a summary of the topics discussed. However, it did state explicitly that "a stable exchange relationship between the U. S. dollar and the pound sterling is an essential condition of international monetary stabilization," that domestic policies were intimately related to the achievement of stable international monetary and commercial relations, and that liberalized trade was essential.[24] Aldrich, of course, had been a leading American advocate of all three propositions.

The final tribute to Aldrich's work came with his election as the president of the International Chamber of Commerce. The chairmen of 12 delegations to the Rye conference and 90 of the delegates were members and officers of the ICC. Its outgoing president, J. Sigfrid Edstrom of Sweden, was able to enlist the support of five former presidents as well as a majority of the national delegations for the selection of Aldrich as his successor.[25]

Bankers' Review of Bretton Woods Proposals

In the same month that he received this new distinction, Aldrich joined yet another private effort to influence legislation that would help to shape the postwar world. In April 1943 he had been appointed to the American Bankers Association's Advisory Committee on Special Activities. As a representative of that group, he agreed in November 1944 to serve on a joint committee with the Reserve Bankers Association to study the Bretton Woods proposals. Anticipating the submission of these proposals to Congress by the President, the joint committee circulated a draft report of their conclusions early in January 1945. The report accepted the establishment of an International Bank as virtually a foregone conclusion but questioned the proposal for the Monetary Fund.

The document focused on alterations in the proposed operation of these institutions that would meet objections of the kind Aldrich had raised. The language of the report's concluding section could have come straight from one of his speeches, with insistence "that a primary foundation for the stabilization of currencies is the firm stabilization of the United States dollar in relation to gold." And further, ". . . any plan for general stabilization of currencies can endure only if it is based on sound internal economic policies of the nations and on sound international economic policies, including trade arrangements which make possible a continued two-way flow of trade." [26] In the transition from draft to publication, which took place February 1, 1945, the report came out even more strongly against establishment of the Monetary Fund, at least in the near future.[27]

Conflict Between the CED and the ABA on Bretton Woods

The Bretton Woods agreements were submitted to Congress while Roosevelt was taking part in the fateful Yalta Conference. They quickly became the subject of hot debate in Congress and generated a flood of literature from various private research organizations. When the Research Committee of the Committee for Economic Development published its report on the Bretton Woods Conference in March 1945, a clear conflict with the American Bankers Association stand was revealed. The CED group advocated approval of both the Fund and the International Bank. While conceding deficiencies in both, the CED took the position that the difficulties of renegotiating the agreements, particularly the one on the Monetary Fund, made it advisable to work with an imperfect mechanism rather than to start anew. Where the bankers had argued that stabilization loans could be handled through the International Bank in the immediate postwar period, thus putting off the need for the Fund until a later date, the CED recommended approval of both the Fund and the Bank on the grounds that their co-existence would clarify their respective functions — the Fund's short-term stabilization role and the Bank's long-run stabilization and general restoration loan function.[28]

Ralph Flanders, president of the Federal Reserve Bank of Boston, was chairman of the CED research committee, and Aldrich wrote him as soon as he saw the thrust of the CED committee's report. In this letter the New York banker pointed out that there was no time limit on credit extensions by the Fund and that it was therefore not restricted, as the CED seemed to be saying, to short-term operations. Indeed, there seemed to be a rather widespread expectation that the Fund would provide long-term credits. "It seems to me," Aldrich wrote, "that the result would be that two institutions instead of one would be active in the field, perhaps at cross purposes." [29]

Flanders was also concerned about this problem. Testifying before the House Committee on Currency and Banking on April 30, 1945, he pinpointed this issue specifically in terms of the need of some countries in the immediate postwar period to restock their reserves for currency issue and their need for working capital to reestablish their industries. He recommended that the International Bank's responsibility for this kind of assistance, as opposed to the Fund's, be clarified. However, he still took the position that "it would be better to accept an imperfect agreement rather than to fail of beginning joint action of the United Nations in this field." [30]

Dr. Benjamin Anderson, who had been the Chase National's economist during Aldrich's early years with the bank, and Dr. B. H. Beckhart, Anderson's successor, both testified before the Senate Committee considering the Bretton Woods proposals. Anderson, speaking as a professor of economics, rejected both the Fund and the Bank,* suggesting instead an American institution that would make stabilization loans, putting gold into the central banks of individual countries "on conditions of budget balancing and gold stabilization." [31] Beckhart, who made it clear that he appeared as an individual rather than a representative of the Chase or of Columbia University where he taught banking, endorsed the American

---

* A full exposition of Anderson's position is in his book, *The Postwar Stabilization of Foreign Exchange* (New York: Economists' National Committee on Monetary Policy, 1943).

Bankers Association plan, often employing language that suggested he had collaborated closely in the preparation of Aldrich's speeches.[32]*

Aldrich Suggests Alternatives to the Bretton Woods Proposals

Meanwhile, Aldrich had drafted a specific set of proposals for Congressional action, and he sent them to Herbert Brownell, Jr., of the Republican National Committee, with the request that they be distributed to the Republican leadership in Congress, and especially to Senator Vandenberg.[33] The Aldrich plan called for the pending House and Senate bills, proposing ratification of the Bretton Woods agreements, to be withdrawn and a new bill to be introduced authorizing United States participation in the International Bank, with the understanding that the Bank be specifically empowered to enter short-term stabilization arrangements. The remainder of Aldrich's proposal was close to what he had been advocating since the preceding September: Congressional endorsement of the need for international monetary cooperation but rejection of the proposed Fund as a means of achieving it, a declaration in support of freer international trade, and the calling of a world trade conference to promote it. Assuming the successful conclusion of such a conference, the final step would be consideration "of whether any further action were necessary to bring about international monetary stabilization — beyond the establishment of the International Bank for Reconstruction and Development." [34]

These suggestions did not get far. Although Roosevelt died in April 1945, his successor Harry S. Truman continued to

* Beckhart felt that the backers of a large International Monetary Fund and various provisions relating to exchange stabilization were trying to use the Fund as a way of aiding Britain and at the same time as a means of escaping the discipline of an international gold standard. See his article, "The Bretton Woods Proposal for an International Monetary Fund," *Political Science Quarterly*, vol. LIX (December, 1944), pp. 489–528.

rely on members of the Roosevelt administration who, like himself, were committed to the Bretton Woods proposals. Representatives of the executive branch had assured Congress that additional appropriations would not be needed to solve problems of postwar reconstruction.[35] The Treasury had also assembled strong support for the legislation and appealed to the prevalent feeling that timely action could avoid the mistakes that had followed World War I. This strategy insured Democratic support, and among the Republicans in Congress, Senator Robert Taft of Ohio became increasingly isolated in his opposition to the agreements.

In the idealism and optimism that accompanied the obviously imminent end of the war, the American Congress in mid-July 1945 accepted the Bretton Woods agreements, including both the Bank and the Fund.

Professor John Williams of Harvard, testifying earlier before the Senate Committee on Banking and Currency, had observed that adoption of the Bretton Woods plan might well give the United States the form of a solution to basic international economic problems without the substance.* He felt, for example, that the idea that there would be no need for postwar economic aid to Britain had gained unfortunate acceptance.[36]

This testimony supported Aldrich's analysis of the situation. The banker had stated unequivocally that the Fund and the Bank, as proposed, could not effectively meet the economic problems of transition from war to peace, especially where Britain was concerned. His concern about the future course of events was further intensified by Britain's refusal to ratify

* In several articles published before the Bretton Woods Conference, Williams had pointed to the need for stability in the currencies of the leading nations, the fact that this was only a part of a larger commercial and investment problem, and the need to differentiate between transitional and postwar stabilization periods.

the Bretton Woods agreements after the United States had done so, and by her return to a system of Imperial Preference rather than the multilateralism for which Aldrich had been pleading.*

With the British elections which unexpectedly returned a Labor Government to power, and the transition in the American Presidency from Roosevelt to Truman, the complexity of the two countries' relations was heightened. One fact, however, emerged with jolting clarity — Britain was virtually bankrupt. When the United States government abruptly terminated Lend-Lease on the grounds that it had been only for wartime assistance, the very situation that Aldrich had been working to avoid emerged as a full-blown crisis in Anglo-American relations.

The British Loan

In the fall of 1945 emissaries of Great Britain were hard at work trying to win financial aid from the United States. They had hopes of obtaining a grant-in-aid of the kind Aldrich had recommended a year before, but it soon became obvious that the American public was not contemplating this kind of assistance. The discussions therefore shifted to a loan, and this request became the subject of involved negotiations. In the process British adherence to multilateral trade became an issue. Although Anglo-American talks on the subject had been initiated as far back as 1943, Whitehall had managed to put off a decision on this matter. In the end, however, the British government yielded enough to obtain the promise of an interest-bearing loan of $3.75 billion from the United States [37] — an outcome that clearly owed a great deal to the efforts of men like Aldrich.

---

* Multilateralism had been defined in the Atlantic Charter (August 1941) and reaffirmed in the Mutual Aid Agreement (February 1942).

A MAN OF PUBLIC AFFAIRS

Aldrich, of course, was active throughout this period in attempting to shape business, public, and Congressional opinion on these important matters of national policy. As president of the International Chamber of Commerce, he had an unusually good opportunity to publicize his ideas about the postwar settlement before an influential, worldwide audience. In early June 1945, for example, he was in Toronto, where he was attempting — and, as it turned out, successfully — to promote the formation of a Canadian Section of the ICC. On that occasion he reiterated the plan that he had been so strongly advocating for many months. He remained firm on the need for reducing world trade barriers, followed by stabilization of the two key currencies, the United States dollar and the British pound. "I have been told," he said, "that this solution is politically impossible and it is certainly true that the suggestion has never received serious consideration by those in positions of political authority on either side of the Atlantic. This fact, however, does not alter the truth of the statement that the stabilization of the 'dollar-pound' rate must precede worldwide exchange stabilization." [38] Events were shortly to prove him correct.

International economic relations were only one aspect of the larger problem of building for peace, and earlier Aldrich had discussed these problems with General Dwight D. Eisenhower and members of his staff during their triumphal visit to New York City. The banker confirmed through these conversations that the military men felt it was up to civilians "to win the peace." This provided the theme for Aldrich's remarks at a luncheon for influential businessmen given by Thomas J. Watson at the Union Club in New York on June 26, 1945. Referring to the recently concluded meeting that created the United Nations, Aldrich said: "I have no doubt that these military men also believe that the work that has been done at San Francisco will have a profound effect in maintaining peace for many years to come; but I am afraid that neither they nor any of the rest of us have analyzed in detail what action must be taken in order to give vitality to the Charter of the new World Security Organization." [39] His own contribution was to emphasize the importance of cooperation between private and governmental world bodies.

The thrust of wartime agreements between Great Britain and the United States had been toward freer international trade and the importance of private enterprise in this trade. These were objectives endorsed by the International Chamber of Commerce. As president of that organization, Aldrich used his Union Club address to make an important proposal: That the International Chamber support a private organization to be affiliated with the Economic and Social Council of the UN.* "It is in [that] International Board of Trade," he said, "that the International Chamber of Commerce may have an opportunity . . . to do a very great public service." The possibilities of such an association between a world body representing governments and a private organization like the Chamber representing world business opened up "tremendous potentialities," as he saw it.[40] By these informal remarks at a private luncheon, he initiated a role for the Chamber that eventuated in its recognition by the UN on equal terms with such long-established bodies as the International Labor Office.

First Postwar Visit to Europe

With the European war at an end, Aldrich was most anxious to see its results for himself. He had been accustomed to semi-

* Both Mr. and Mrs. Aldrich were active on committees appointed by Mayor William O'Dwyer of New York City to insure a welcome for the first meeting of the UN Security Council and to assist in locating a permanent site for UN headquarters (*The New York Times*, March 24, April 10, 1946).

annual visits abroad before the war, but he had not crossed the Atlantic since his wartime journey to Britain in 1942. The calling of a Council Meeting of the International Chamber at London in August 1945 gave him a welcome opportunity to visit Britain at a critical time in Anglo-American relations. He took full advantage of this opportunity and extended his itinerary to include a tour of the Continent. He renewed old acquaintances, saw firsthand what destruction the war had wrought, and reviewed postwar problems of the bank and of European reconstruction with those directly involved.

Arriving in England by air on August 8, Aldrich quickly started his usual round of luncheons, dinners, and appointments. On the first day, for example, he met in the morning with a group from the ICC's Council to go over its agenda. This working session was followed by a visit with American Ambassador Winant and then a luncheon given by the American-British Commonwealth Association. That afternoon he met with Will Clayton of the United States' State Department and with Lord Keynes and Sir Wilfrid Eady at the British Treasury. In the evening he had dinner with Philip Reed of General Electric, who was also active in the International Chamber. Such a full schedule was typical of his entire visit, and it was an effective way of acquiring large amounts of information and a variety of insights in a short time.[41]

The purpose of the Council Meeting, which opened on August 13, 1945, was to plan for the next Congress of the International Chamber, but it also afforded the members an opportunity to review the objectives of the Chamber in the context of the postwar world. Representatives from 24 nations gathered to discuss these problems, and on August 20, Aldrich summed up the results of their deliberations in an address to the American Chamber of Commerce in London. The International Chamber had as its principal objective the expansion of world trade, he stated. To this end, "The International

Chamber is convinced that the private enterprise system is not only the best means, but the only means of establishing world trade on a multilateral basis and thereby of achieving the greatest possible volume." His organization was anxious and prepared to cooperate with the UN's Economic and Social Council, Aldrich reported. He again called for United States financial assistance to Britain in her transition from a war to peace economy, and he stressed once more the need for a world trade conference to speed the restoration of multilateral trade. In conclusion, he emphasized that the "International Chamber, serving as a world parliament of business, has a magnificent opportunity to promote those policies which will further peaceful trade and prosperity and raise the standards of life of all peoples. Peace, security and prosperity are indivisible." [42] These observations reached a far wider audience than the businessmen gathered to hear Aldrich, because his address was also broadcast by the B.B.C.

Aldrich was not overly optimistic about the possibilities of rapid progress toward freer trade so far as Britain was concerned. At a dinner hosted by Sir Clive Baillieu, Chairman of the Federation of British Industries, the New York banker had an opportunity for extended conversations with Sir Stafford Cripps, President of the Board of Trade, and Hugh Dalton, Chancellor of the Exchequer. Although both men assured Aldrich that the recent change of government would not mean a change in Britain's foreign policy, Aldrich came away convinced that the Labor government's domestic policy would require strict controls on foreign commerce and exchange. "It will take real statesmanship," he wrote a friend the next day, "to devise a formula which is satisfactory to both Great Britain and the United States in the field of foreign commercial and financial policy." [43]

Aldrich was widely known in England for his war relief work, and on Thursday, August 16, at Buckingham Palace he received the King's Medal for Service in the Cause of Freedom. He was the first recipient of this medal, and it was gratifying evidence that his wartime job had been done well and was now virtually finished. In another sense, however, it marked the beginning of yet another job — bringing private planning and initiative to bear on the reconstruction of war-devastated countries. To see for himself what was involved, Aldrich left London by air on August 21 for a visit to the Continent.

The first four days were spent in Paris. In the French capital he met with top government officials, including the Minister of Finance, René Pleven, and the Minister of Industrial Production, Robert Lacoste. He also conferred with Emmanuel Monick, Governor of the Bank of France, and other financial leaders. In Paris, as in London, he also talked at length with the managers of the Chase branches. In the process of discussing postwar problems with top figures in both countries Aldrich, of course, offered the services of his bank in any way they could be helpful.[44]

After Paris, the next stop was Germany. Aldrich's party, which consisted of Lt. Colonel Binns of the American forces and Shepard Morgan and Bertram Cruger of the Chase, flew to Frankfurt on August 25 and then to Berlin. They lunched with Ambassador Robert D. Murphy in Berlin, met with General Lucius Clay, Commander of the American occupation forces, and then toured the devastated city. For Aldrich, this opportunity to visit the German capital was, as he put it in a subsequent letter to Murphy, "in every way the high point of the trip." [45] It was clear to Aldrich that Berlin and Germany were in dire straits and that only policies made with a view to the long-run restoration of the country's economy could prevent Germany from dragging down the economies of neighboring countries. It was typical that Aldrich should see the problem in these terms while Treasury Secretary Morgenthau, with whom Aldrich and the Chase had so recently been in conflict, was advocating that the late enemy's countryside be reduced to an agricultural wasteland.*

The party next flew to Prague, Czechoslovakia. There Aldrich met with the American Ambassador, Laurence Steinhardt, and then with Prime Minister Jan Masaryk. The problem of the National War Fund's contributions for Czechoslovak relief "frozen" in London ** was one topic of conversation, as well as the overall relief and reconstruction picture.

The final visit was to Holland. Aldrich was very familiar with this small country as the result of having spent several summers there before the war with his family. As a yachtsman, he had been accustomed to chartering a boat to investigate the many fascinating waterways that crisscrossed the land. He therefore looked forward with special anticipation to seeing old friends and to assessing war damage in a territory he knew well from holiday jaunts in a more carefree era.

Aldrich's concern and fondness for the Netherlands insured that postwar relief and reconstruction there would have high priority in the National War Fund's program. To guarantee this kind of attention he had enlisted Eugene R. Black of the Chase bond department to head the effort. When the Aldrich party landed at The Hague on August 27, 1945, Black, who was also investigating the possibilities of a $200 million loan to the Netherlands by a group of New York banks, was already there. For Black this assignment marked the beginning of a new and distinguished career in international finance, eventually leading to his presidency of the World Bank.

In Holland Aldrich launched into a full schedule of activities. On the first day of his visit he lunched in Arnheim and had dinner in Utrecht, in each instance with leaders in those communities. The following day he toured the bomb-damaged

* See Henry Morgenthau, *Germany is our Problem* (New York: Harper & Brothers, 1945), pp. 76–78.
** See Chapter X.

harbor of Amsterdam, visited an exhibit of "Old Masters" returned to public view from their wartime hiding places, conferred with officials of the Netherlands Red Cross, and had a pleasant conference with Princess Juliana at the Royal Palace. As the visit continued, he added to his stock of information about the country's problems by talking with leaders in all walks of life.

Reporting the Aldrich visit, the Dutch newspaper *Het Parool* spared no superlatives. On August 30 it said:

> America is used to handle the matters, which are being taken up, in the right way and to push on thoroughly. That's why the man who is in charge of the greatest Bank in the world, the NATIONAL CHASE BANK, was called to the chair of the organisation mentioned above [the National War Fund], which has been established with the very exclusive purpose of rendering assistance and help to the allied countries hit by the war.
>
> This relief is not being limited to some thousand parcels of woollen socks and a bar of chocolate or a couple cycle tyres, no on the contrary, the goods so urgently wanted in Holland will be sent by ships loaded with full cargoes and we should not be surprised if in the near future complete hospitals and churches will arrive as royal gifts from the American nation to the allied Dutch people, for whom the Americans have still a soft and tender corner in their hearts.[46]

Such enthusiasm was embarrassing. Aldrich had in fact promised Princess Juliana that the National War Fund would contribute to an important new hospital,[47] but furnishing a complete church exceeded even his and the Fund's most generous impulses.

After a brief stay in England, this time largely concerned with bank business, Aldrich returned home on Thursday, September 6. On the following Sunday he flew to Washington, and on Monday he reported the findings from his trip to top administration officials, including President Truman. Their interest in what Aldrich had to say left no doubt that the Chase chairman was recognized by political Washington as perhaps the leading emissary of American business and finance in dealing with European countries.

Impressions of Europe, 1945

Although there is no record of Aldrich's report to Washington, the gist of it was unquestionably contained in his address to the Chamber of Commerce of the State of New York on October 4, 1945. Of his trip he said: "From what we were able to observe personally and from what we learned in the course of conversations with persons in a position to be informed, we were convinced that our allies in western Europe have made and are making substantial economic progress." On the other hand, he made it clear that the allies would continue to need assistance. "We must be prepared to devote our best efforts to help solve the tremendously difficult problems with which they are faced," he said.

His greatest concern was for Germany. Citing General Eisenhower's discouraging report about conditions in that country, and confirmed by his own personal observation, Aldrich pointed out: "The question which confronts us is not what to do with Germany, considered by itself, but what to do with Germany in relation to European economic requirements." In his opinion, Germany could not be allowed to remain an "economic slum" without affecting neighboring countries adversely. Constructive action, however, hinged on what could be done on a quadripartite basis to implement the decisions made at Potsdam earlier in the year, and the obstacles there seemed to Aldrich impressive.[48]

TESTIMONY ON BRITISH LOAN

During this period the proposed loan to Britain was in the

negotiating stage and eventuated in the December 1945 agreement mentioned earlier. The next step was to obtain Congressional approval, and this proved more difficult than anticipated.

On March 13, 1946, Aldrich appeared before the Senate Committee on Banking and Currency in support of the measure. He made it clear that when he had proposed a grant-in-aid in September 1944 it was with the thought that an outright grant would reduce the sum that had to be provided, would stimulate multilateral trade, and through the beneficial repercussions on world trade the United States would be repaid many times for her generosity. However, in view of what had happened since that time and the fact that the loan had already been negotiated, he was satisfied that the United States should proceed with the line-of-credit approach. He ruled out the International Monetary Fund or the International Bank as adequate sources of funds for Britain's immediate needs. The United States credit — subject to the restrictions that had accompanied its negotiation — would, he thought, be beneficial to multilateral trade, because the dollar was the "one currency which is available for multilateral transactions." It would, he predicted, increase United States exports to the United Kingdom and by stabilizing the key currencies break down nationalistic and bilateral trading practices.

In none of the objections to the loan that had been made did Aldrich find grounds for serious concern. Senator Robert Taft, however, pressed him rather closely on the question of whether the British loan would not add to inflationary pressures in the United States. Aldrich was willing to concede that it might have this effect, but he maintained that the degree to which this would be true hinged on the way in which the funds were raised and the general fiscal policies of the government. Using the same argument that he had advanced in connection with war financing, Aldrich argued that if bonds were sold to the public rather than banks, the inflationary impact would be reduced. Furthermore, since the proposed loan extended over a period of five years, the mere fact of the loan itself was not inflationary — its impact would only be felt as the money was spent.[49]

For the first time in many years Aldrich found himself siding enthusiastically with a Democratic administration. Like its leading members from President Truman down to Will Clayton, Assistant Secretary of State for Economic Affairs, Aldrich favored the loan because he thought it would speed up the removal of British controls on foreign trade and exchange long before the Bretton Woods agreements could make their effect felt. The administration's case for the loan had been made to Congress on these grounds, and in his testimony Aldrich presented similar arguments relating to the elimination of the sterling area as a result of the loan.

These expectations, it turned out, were sanguine, but in fact they were also largely irrelevant as far as the general public was concerned. According to surveys available to Clayton, the public was little concerned about multilateral trade as a factor in the loan and much more interested in it as a humanitarian gesture in which there might be political advantages to the United States.[50]

Congress still remained reluctant to approve the British loan. As the matter dragged through the Spring, Alben Barkley, President pro tem of the Senate, clamped down on his colleagues, refusing to permit their consideration of other legislation until action was taken on the loan. Even these tactics were not immediately productive of legislative action. In the end, the tide was not turned on the basis of economic arguments but on the basis of a growing fear that the Soviet Union and Communism posed a serious threat to western Europe. A loan to England as a stronghold of western democracy made the kind of sense that the American public and their repre-

sentatives in Washington could heartily endorse, and on these
grounds it was finally approved. On July 15, 1946, President
Truman signed the legislation authorizing the loan.

The travail that preceded this event had left a bitter taste
in England. *The Manchester Guardian* commented, for example, "The British public, it is only honest to say, has
watched the progress of the loan through Congress with
something like horror. Most people must often have felt they
would like to withdraw the whole thing rather than be under
obligation to a legislative body containing so many ignorant
and ill-natured members." [51] This was an overly harsh appraisal of a body that had shown unprecedented generosity in
wartime assistance and then cancelled all claims based on it,
but Britain's plight was so acute and the need for assistance
so obvious that extreme reactions to Congressional delay were
perhaps pardonable. Had Aldrich's proposal for a grant-in-aid
been adopted in 1944, the recriminations of 1946 might not
have arisen at all.

A Citizen's Contributions

With the adoption of the Bretton Woods agreements and
approval of the British loan, one phase of the transition from
wartime economies to those of peacetime had been completed.
However, the growing menace of the Soviet Union, which
helped the British loan through Congress, indicated that
"peace" was more likely to mean the absence of overt hostilities than a dedication to nonviolent solutions of world
problems. The actual course of events seemed to hinge largely
on policies of the Communist leadership and the heads of
governments whom Aldrich was certainly in no position to
affect. Nevertheless, an effective response to this menacing
challenge required close solidarity among the western allies
and a wide-ranging approach to the problems of reconstruc-

tion in western Europe. These were problems to which Aldrich had been addressing himself even before the United States became involved in the European conflict. His contribution had been to emphasize early and repeatedly that the private citizen and the private sector had a great stake in the way in which the postwar challenge was met and that the opportunities for constructive contributions were only limited by the extent of the initiative and determination brought to bear on the problem.

During the war he had put all his energies into this effort. As president of the National War Fund he had helped to mobilize private resources for war relief on an unprecedented scale, winning gratitude for American generosity in western Europe and providing the groundwork for postwar cooperation. As vice president and then president of the International Chamber of Commerce, he had used all his influence to promote postwar adoption of multilateral trade policies and to free this trade from the shackles of nationalistic, and even international, controls on commerce and exchange.

As usual, Aldrich analyzed these problems in concrete, specific terms, emphasizing that the transition from war to peace economies could not be made on the basis of grandiose, global approaches but required a sequential approach to interdependent problems. Even by 1946 the correctness of his analysis was beginning to be confirmed.

It was true that Aldrich was not the first to propose some of the policies for postwar stabilization that he ardently backed, nor was he the only prominent citizen to popularize them. It was equally true that his own program as spelled out for the first time in September 1944 did not win Congressional approval. However, it is equally clear that no American business or financial leader was more active than Aldrich in offering a constructive program of government-business cooperation to meet the problems of the postwar world or more dedicated to alerting not only this country but others to the pitfalls of shortsightedness and selfishness in laying the foundations for it. The esteem that these efforts had won for him were reflected in a letter from Francis Cardinal Spellman of New York to Count Enrico Galeazzi at Vatican City in July 1945, when a tentative visit to the Holy City was part of Aldrich's itinerary after the International Chamber meeting. "Mr. Winthrop W. Aldrich is one of our greatest Americans," the Cardinal wrote. "I shall appreciate every courtesy and honor possible for him to receive." [52]

CHAPTER XII

The Early Postwar Years, 1946-1948

THE MOST pressing international problem of the immediate postwar period was reconstruction of war-devastated economies; next came the longer run problems of
establishing a viable framework for the more normal conduct
of international trade. Private organizations, like the International Chamber of Commerce, interested in fostering this
trade had been looking to the end of hostilities as a time for
new beginnings. Aldrich, as an important member of several
of these groups, was a leading advocate of a role for private
enterprise aided by governmental action to stabilize currencies
and to remove trade barriers and controls. In the years immediately following World War II, he again demonstrated
that there was an important place for private initiative and
personal leadership in mobilizing resources to meet national
and international problems.

The war period had produced new government-backed
financial institutions that would implement any further plans,
public or private, developed to meet the problems of postwar
reconstruction. The International Bank for Reconstruction
and Development would presumably be a source of funds for

aiding underdeveloped and war-damaged nations; the International Monetary Fund would provide one mechanism for stabilizing exchange relationships; in the United States the Export-Import Bank offered a vehicle for extending credit to shippers in international commerce. The question that confronted all who, like Aldrich, were interested in these matters in 1946 was how these institutions would be related to one another and to the private sector, for it was obvious that the United States Government would be the chief supporter of all three.

PRESIDENT TRUMAN'S ADVISORY COMMITTEE FOR FINANCING FOREIGN TRADE

A National Advisory Council, composed of the Secretaries of Treasury, State, and Commerce, as well as heads of the Export-Import Bank and the Federal Reserve System, was established under the legislation approving the Bretton Woods agreements to give guidance on national policies with respect to foreign lending. The importance of the private sector in this connection led, in the spring of 1946, to President Harry S. Truman's appointment of a group of industrialists and bankers to consult with the National Advisory Council. On June 17, 1946, President Truman asked Winthrop Aldrich to serve on the Committee. The President wrote of his belief that: "The conduct and financing of our foreign trade should be handled by private industry with the cooperation and such assistance as is necessary from the proper Government agencies." [1] Of course, Aldrich shared these sentiments and welcomed the invitation to help in shaping national policy with respect to them.

The other members of the President's Advisory Committee for Financing Foreign Trade were in many instances friends and colleagues of Aldrich. They included A. W. Robertson, chairman of Westinghouse, where Aldrich was a board member; Tom K. Smith of the Boatman's National Bank of St. Louis, a long-time associate in the American Bankers Association; A. P. Giannini of the Bank of America, another friend of long standing and a substantial stockholder in the Chase; Gordon Rentschler, chairman of the National City Bank of New York, with whom Aldrich had worked in many causes including the National War Fund; and Aldrich's Harvard Law School classmate Irving S. Olds, chairman of the United States Steel Corporation.

In several cases the membership overlapped that of the Committee on International Economic Policy, of which Aldrich was the chairman. That privately sponsored committee, like the new governmentally sponsored one, was dedicated to "serious and competent consideration of the issues which confront all the free peoples of the world." [2] Its activities in research, publication, and education of the public on matters such as reciprocal trade agreements, begun in 1944, continued until September 1948.

In announcing the formation of the President's Committee, Truman stated on June 26, 1946, that private capital had an important role in postwar reconstruction. "I have appointed this committee of citizens of knowledge and experience," he said, "because our foreign trade, export and import, must in the long run be privately handled and privately financed if it is to serve well this country and world economy." [3] In the press release, however, the President failed to mention that Aldrich would serve as chairman,* though this appointment had been cleared prior to the publicity about the formation of the committee.[4]

* The President's invitation for Aldrich to head the committee was drafted by the banker's friend and Chase director, Arthur Page of American Telephone and Telegraph, and submitted for the President's approval through John W. Snyder, who had just succeeded Henry Morgenthau as Secretary of the Treasury.

Announcement of the new committee coming directly from the White House had reverberations in various parts of the Capital. For example, although the proposal had been cleared with Will Clayton in the State Department (also a member of the Committee on International Economic Policy), other higher echelons had apparently not been informed and the President's announcement brought worried calls from these officials. Those responsible for other business advisory committees were also worried that this latest one might be a supercommittee that would overshadow their own activities.[5] This kind of response made the public relations problem a delicate one, but it had been anticipated by those interested in the committee. These matters were competently handled by Fred Smith, a vice president of the American Broadcasting Company, who knew how to approach Truman, having served him well in connection with a Labor-Management Conference in the fall of 1945.

At the time of his appointment to the President's committee, Aldrich was in Europe in connection with the Council meeting of the International Chamber of Commerce. One of his first tasks upon returning to New York in early July was to get the President's committee organized and active.

At a press conference Aldrich outlined three major objectives in this effort. First, the committee would try to bring into an orderly common effort public and private finance in the foreign field. Second, it would attempt to foster the application of the United States' productive capacity to domestic consumption and foreign reconstruction. Third, it would seek to promote relations between American and foreign businesses that would develop and maintain a high and expanding level of foreign trade.[6] Aldrich promised, in accordance with the President's request, to put his committee to work on this agenda as soon as possible.

The first step in implementing the committee's assignment

was to appoint an informal working group. The ten members, who met for the first time in July 1946, included Eugene R. Black and Shepard Morgan of the Chase; John J. McCloy of Milbank, Tweed; Allen W. Dulles of Sullivan & Cromwell; Arthur Page; W. Randolph Burgess of the National City Bank; Charles J. Symington of Symington-Gould Corporation; Bradford Smith and George W. Wolf of U. S. Steel; and William F. Machold of Drexel & Company.[7] Shepard Morgan was chairman. This group framed the questions to be considered by the parent committee. One of the most important was whether the committee had a continuing role or could discharge its responsibility with a single report. At the first meeting of the full committee on September 25, 1946, it was decided that there was a need for its contributions that could only be satisfied by regular meetings for an indefinite period. On this basis the committee met frequently for the next two years and after a brief hiatus, resumed its activities until dissolved in July 1951.

Work of the President's Committee

The agenda for the committee's first meeting established a pattern for those that followed. In the case of the Export-Import Bank, for example, the committee considered the question of whether private investors or institutional purchasers could be authorized to purchase this bank's marketable items and thus help to increase its lending capacity without further resort to Congressional appropriations. The committee considered ways in which investment in International (World) Bank securities might be authorized for a broad spectrum of institutions. Ways of rating foreign securities, the desirability of equity investment overseas and its impact on the domestic economy, were other matters that engaged the committee's attention. At the conclusion of these deliberations the committee members visited the White House to report their progress to the President and then met with the National Advisory Council.[8]

Over the ensuing months and years proposals for the committee's consideration came from individual members of the committee, from interested businessmen, and from associations like the Investment Bankers Association and the San Francisco Chamber of Commerce, as well as from financial institutions like the Export-Import and World Banks. One of the most troublesome problems that occupied the committee's attention was how the risks of foreign investment and foreign commerce might be handled on a basis satisfactory to banks, industries, and federal agencies. The possibilities of special financial agencies and other arrangements were explored in these connections.

Contribution to Leadership of the World Bank

Perhaps the most important contribution made by Aldrich and his committee was to the leadership of the World Bank in the persons of Eugene R. Black and John J. McCloy. Black, son of a former governor of the Federal Reserve System, had been recruited by Aldrich into the Chase's bond department from the Harris Forbes organization in the early 1930s. Black had become increasingly interested in international finance in connection with the New York banks' loan to the Netherlands in 1946, described in the preceding chapter, and he had proved a valuable member of the President's Committee's working group. He was, in short, an experienced and able banker with a rapidly developing international orientation.

John J. McCloy, another member of the working group, had had a distinguished career in legal and governmental affairs. A top lawyer in the prestigious Cravath firm, he had joined Secretary of War Henry L. Stimson in 1940 first as a special assistant and then as Assistant Secretary of War. In this capacity McCloy had a hand in many matters of great importance to the military effort and to postwar planning. He had accompanied Roosevelt to the Cairo-Teheran Conference in 1943 and was with Truman at the Potsdam Conference in July 1945. His initiative, intelligence, and ability to work with and through people made a strong impression on both military and civilian colleagues. The Cravath firm felt his loss greatly when on January 1, 1946, he joined Aldrich's old law firm, which then became Milbank, Tweed, Hope, Hadley, and McCloy.

Although the World Bank had been formally organized in the spring of 1946, it had made very little progress by the end of the year. McCloy was acquainted with its problems because one of his former law partners, Chester McLain of the Cravath firm, was the Bank's counsel. Accordingly, McCloy was well aware of the difficulties he might face if he accepted the presidency of the World Bank when it was offered to him early in 1947. Eugene Meyer, the first president, had resigned and a number of prominent individuals, including Lewis Douglas (McCloy's brother-in-law), Averell Harriman, and Will Clayton, had reportedly declined to succeed him.

The World Bank was regarded in most financial circles as a risky enterprise. The American government's contribution had already been paid in, but it was obvious that the bank would have to seek additional capital in the public money market. The lack of enthusiasm for its securities, plus the restrictions on investing in them imposed by state requirements, was one concern of the President's Committee for Financing Foreign Trade. It was also a matter of importance to McCloy in making his decision on accepting the bank's presidency. He was a lawyer, not a banker, and his experience with war devastation during both World War I and II had made him very much aware that if the bank was to meet the challenge of postwar reconstruction, the raising of capital would be one of his prime responsibilities. Because he knew that Aldrich was one of the few leading bankers who supported the World Bank, McCloy turned to him for advice. Aldrich urged him to take the job, and this encouragement was important in McCloy's decision to do so.[9]

Recognizing the fact that the success or failure of the new institution hinged largely on the soundness of its financial practices, McCloy wanted an experienced banker of broad vision as a partner. He consulted Aldrich on this need, and the Chase chairman suggested several possibilities but did not include the name of Eugene Black, whom McCloy had already decided was the type of man he would like to have. McCloy's inquiries confirmed Black's reputation and ability and, with Aldrich's cooperation, he enlisted Black.

Although Aldrich was reluctant to lose such an able man from the Chase, he was proud of the team that he had helped to provide for the World Bank. During the succeeding years he helped McCloy gain acceptance of the bank's bonds as authorized institutional investments, and he held an annual dinner for the leading figures in the bank, flying them up to his Long Island home from Washington. When McCloy later became High Commissioner to Germany, Aldrich had the satisfaction of seeing Eugene Black succeed to the World Bank's presidency.[10]

TOURING SOUTH AMERICA IN VARIED ROLES

In the spring of 1947 Aldrich made one of the most arduous and extended trips of a life filled with travel. He undertook it primarily on behalf of the International Chamber of Commerce, which had now been recognized as a Class A nongovernmental consultative body to the United Nations Economic and Social Council. The trip took him and his party through the major countries of South America and afforded him an opportunity to encourage organization of new branches of the International Chamber, to brief United States representatives on the President's Advisory Committee for Financing Foreign Trade, and to determine the needs of Latin American countries for North American products and financing.[11] In addition, of course, he represented the Chase National Bank, which had important interests in these countries.

As was true of virtually all his trips, Mrs. Aldrich accompanied her husband. Barton Turnbull (a Chase director) and his wife, Charles Cain, and Louis Albarracin of the Chase Foreign Department completed the party. They departed La Guardia field in New York on a chartered Pan American airliner March 16, 1947, and did not arrive back there until April 30. In the interim they made major stops in Cuba, Brazil, Uruguay, Argentina, Chile, Peru, Venezuela, and the Panama Canal Zone.

At each place the routine was substantially the same. The Chase party would be greeted by local business and bank officials, the American Ambassador, representatives of American companies, and top officials of the host country's government. (In Chile, for example, Aldrich was an official guest of the Chilean government.) From then on, the whirlwind of social and business activities was unceasing. Cocktail parties, dinners, golf games and sightseeing supplemented the formal addresses, informal discussions, and business meetings that filled the party's crowded schedule.

This kind of activity required physical resiliency, mental agility, and great social poise, precisely the qualities that Aldrich possessed. Depending on the situation, he had to be prepared to give his formal address, to abandon it and talk extemporaneously, and to adjust his remarks to local problems. He had to be prepared to talk politics and American foreign policy with the heads of state, commercial and investment banking with the bankers, and organizational, financial, and other problems with potential supporters of the ICC. This type of effort was certainly not unfamiliar to other leading American bankers, businessmen, and government officials, but the difference in Aldrich's case was that he had to sustain the effort for six weeks in many different countries without the benefit of any let-up in the schedule. His time on the airplane was therefore largely spent in digesting the information about people and problems that would be encountered at the next stop. Obviously he could not have done the job without the most careful preparation and support from his wife and other members of the party.

Aldrich's method of operation amazed Charles Cain, who was on his first trip with the Chase chairman after having been promoted to head the Foreign Department of the Chase. "I was a new boy in the foreign business . . . so that was my first important trip," Cain recalled almost two decades later. "Well, this man was superb in both hats — as the chairman of the bank and as president of the International Chamber." The head of the Foreign Department recalled that he had been included in all of his chairman's business calls and many of his social engagements. "As a cub vice president, if I had made that trip alone I would not have seen the people that I saw with Mr. Aldrich. This even included Juan and Evita Peron," he said.[12]

Naturally, Cain was primarily interested in the trip from the standpoint of the bank's business and this was where Aldrich's access to high circles helped considerably. Aldrich's reputation as an internationalist had preceded him to Latin America, and his position at the Chase, as well as his relationship to Nelson Rockefeller, Coordinator of Inter-American Affairs, all helped to open doors that would otherwise have been closed to Cain. But, in Cain's opinion, it was Aldrich's "powerful personality" and obvious ability, demonstrated by his "manner of speech, his knowledge of the business, and his sympathy with international finance," that turned the new contacts into business for the bank. "I never knew him to be tired," Cain said. "This was a hard trip. 'Oh,' we'd say, 'this is hard . . .' But when the time came to operate, he operated. Even in the last place we went to, which was Venezuela. Then we flew over to Kingston, Jamaica, overnight, and then home. And he operated in Venezuela. Made several speeches; saw a lot of people." [13]

Mrs. Aldrich, of course, had a different perspective on the trip. She recorded her impressions of people and places in a series of lengthy letters that were sent to her children. She described Buenos Aires, for example, as "*very* sophisticated, beautiful, exciting, fascinating, just like Paris 1907–1914." But she was also well aware of the complicated and explosive political situation that centered around President and Mrs. Peron. The potential for trouble naturally worried Cain, and his investigations during the party's visit to Buenos Aires led to a reduction in Chase loans to Argentina, after consultation with Aldrich.

For Mrs. Aldrich the problem was how to fill her social role in a situation so fraught with tension. The test came at a luncheon given by American Ambassador and Mrs. Messersmith. After describing the controversial Evita Peron in detail for the benefit of her children, Mrs. Aldrich went on: "At lunch the President was on Mrs. Messersmith's right, then me, then Miranda [head of the central bank], while Daddy was on the other side of Mrs. Peron. Neither of them spoke English or French, so I asked Mrs. Messersmith right away to tell him that I had just started to learn Spanish but would try!" The conversation went surprisingly well. As Mrs. Aldrich reported to her children, "I got a big kick out of it myself, but I only wish I could have spoken just a little better." [14] Thereafter, she took advantage of every occasion during the trip to refine her skill with the language.

The South American trip was a success from all standpoints.

The Chase made important new contacts and Cain as well as Aldrich was afforded the opportunity to evaluate previous ones. Several new affiliates were added to the International Chamber of Commerce and several dormant ones were revived as a result of Aldrich's efforts. This was all the more impressive because it was accomplished in the face of competition from regional organizations seeking to improve their foothold in Latin America. The Chase chairman also came back with firsthand information about the economic needs of Latin America and the opportunities for private investment there. At the same time he had been able to brief key South American businessmen and governmental officials on the goals of the President's Advisory Committee for Financing Foreign Trade. In short, it was an exciting, arduous, but rewarding tour through a promising area both for the Chase and the private but quasi-official organizations that Aldrich headed.

Foreign Policy Decisions at Home

While the Chase party was in South America, important developments had been taking place in the formulation of postwar American foreign policy, especially in the field of economic affairs. In large measure they were a response to aggressive Russian policies. The hope of postwar cooperation with the Russians that Roosevelt had carried to the Yalta Conference in 1945 had been shattered by their subsequent failure to carry out their agreements. Even while the exhilaration of V-E and V-J Days still lingered, Communist penetration of any area of political or economic weakness was being revealed as the postwar policy of the Kremlin. By early 1947 it had precipitated a major crisis in the case of Greece and Turkey.

Although Aldrich had not been any more prescient about these developments than others, he had long and vigorously emphasized that European reconstruction involved far more than a grant to Britain. The Truman administration, however, had won Congressional approval of the British loan partially on the implied promise that further largesse from American resources would not be required or forthcoming. Nevertheless, in the two years after V-E Day the United States gave or loaned some $12 billion in an effort to revive and strengthen the war-torn economies of other countries.[15] Since the aid was extended and administered more on an ad hoc basis than in the framework of an overall plan, it proved inadequate.

The situation was revealed in stark clarity when the time for the British to withdraw from the eastern Mediterranean approached in March 1947. Greece was in turmoil as armed Communist bands defied the government's authority; Turkey lay in the path of a Russian effort to penetrate to the Mediterranean, and the burden of maintaining a defensive posture against such a move was more than the Turkish economy could stand. Four days before the Aldrich party commenced its South American tour, President Truman went before a joint session of Congress to seek aid for these two countries. "The free peoples of the world look to us for support in maintaining their freedoms," he said. "If we falter in our leadership, we may endanger the peace of the world — and we shall surely endanger the welfare of our own nation." He then asked for a total of $400 million in military and economic aid for Greece and Turkey.[16] Congress wanted to deliberate on this request, and it was not until the end of May that Truman's proposal was finally approved. In the interim a loan from the Reconstruction Finance Corporation got the aid program started.

The so-called Truman Doctrine made it clear that the United States would not remain passive in the face of the Communist threat; it was equally clear that economic weakness invited Communist aggression and that there was a pressing need for an articulated United States approach to this problem. The need was confirmed to the President by Undersecretary of State Will Clayton after a six-week fact-finding survey of the European economy. Truman therefore set the Policy Planning Staff of the State Department to work on the problem.

The first results became apparent when Undersecretary of State Dean Acheson, filling in for the President, addressed the Delta Agricultural Council at Cleveland, Mississippi, on May 8, 1947. He emphasized that in the war's aftermath, political and economic chaos, combined with adverse climatic conditions, had left European peoples with a "narrow economic margin" for survival. "It is one of the principal aims of our foreign policy today to use our economic and financial resources to widen these margins," he said. "It is necessary if we are to preserve our own freedoms and our own democratic institutions. . . . And it is our duty and privilege as human beings." [17]

The Marshall Plan

As it turned out, Acheson had outlined in tentative form the plan that Secretary of State George Marshall would announce to the world a month later at the Harvard commencement exercises.* The essence of his proposal was that the United States commit itself to the fight for economic recovery overseas, particularly in Europe, and make its effort one to treat underlying problems and not merely symptoms. Finally, the nations that would benefit from such aid would have to exercise the initiative and responsibility for their respective programs.

* The essence of the Marshall Plan was contained in a memorandum prepared by Will Clayton on the return flight from his fact-finding trip to Europe. (Ross J. Pritchard, "Will Clayton: a Study of Business Statesmanship in the Formation of United States Economic Foreign Policy." Unpublished thesis. Fletcher School of Law and Diplomacy, 1955, p. 289).

Aldrich on Postwar Reconstruction

These ideas were very much in accord with Aldrich's. During 1946 and early 1947 he had made frequent addresses on these topics and had discussed them at length in the Council Meetings of the International Chamber of Commerce at Paris in June and December 1946. In notes prepared for an informal address to the Alumni Luncheon at Columbia University June 4, 1946, he had differentiated between the pressing problems of survival in the transition period from war to reconstruction, and those of the longer run that were political as well as economic in character. In terms of the revival of world trade, Britain remained the key, he thought, but long-run recovery would require initiative on many different fronts, in many ways, and in many countries of western Europe.[18]

Within this complicated picture, Aldrich saw the activities of businessmen and their organizations, like the ICC, playing an important part. He was especially heartened by the possibilities of the ICC's cooperation with the United Nations through the Economic and Social Council. As he told the Boston Conference on Distribution, October 14, 1946, "Peace is dependent not alone upon political accord. It is dependent, too, upon the adoption of a constructive economic policy on the part of nations." [19] There was no question that his personal efforts and those of the organizations with which he was associated were directed to that end.

At the time of Marshall's Harvard speech, Aldrich was in Montreux, Switzerland, where he presided over the Eleventh Congress of the International Chamber and the first to be held since the war. Among other things, the Congress gave its support to the efforts being made to develop a World Trade Charter and voted to continue various committees concerned with the policies of the occupying powers in Germany and with Europe's general economic situation. Aldrich was there-

fore most pleased to learn of the Marshall proposals. In a
statement to the press he said:

> . . . I believe that it is proper to interpret his [Marshall's]
> words as meaning that if a workable plan for the reconstruc-
> tion of Europe can be devised through the efforts of Great
> Britain and the European nations themselves, the United
> States, to the extent that it is able to do so, will assist by finan-
> cial aid in making that plan effective.
>
> It is difficult to exaggerate the importance of the Harvard
> address. Europe has been given new hope, which a few weeks
> ago did not exist, of a successful outcome of its present
> difficulties. We must all most earnestly trust that there will
> now be forthcoming a plan which will be of such a character
> that the American people through Congress will support it
> financially to the full extent which will be necessary to make
> it successful. To do so will be of vital importance, not only
> for Europe, but for the United States itself and the rest of
> the world.[20]

The very magnitude of the proposed aid effort insured that
it would encounter domestic opposition from conservative
and isolationist elements, as well as from those who, while
they recognized Europe's need, feared the costs to the American economy of meeting it. President Truman had, of course,
evaluated the political difficulties in carrying through the program, and he worked shrewdly and effectively to build
support for it during the summer of 1947. In the last analysis,
however, much depended on educating public opinion, and
this was a matter for private efforts as well as political leadership.

Aldrich Urges Adoption of the Marshall Plan

Aldrich naturally enlisted in the cause. His first major
endorsement of the Marshall Plan came in an address to the
American Bankers Association on September 30, 1947, at

Atlantic City. In the interim since Marshall's Harvard address, 16 nations had convened in Paris and had drawn up a report of their needs and goals. The Soviet Union and its satellites had joined the conference briefly but at Stalin's direction abruptly withdrew, thus freeing the western European nations from the threat that the USSR would directly sabotage the plan or use it to their disadvantage. In the end the Paris conferees had agreed to ask the United States for $21.8 billion in aid over a four-year period.[21]

Addressing the bankers at Atlantic City, Aldrich gave his unqualified support to the Marshall Plan. He praised the Secretary's Harvard address as one embodying "the highest qualities of statesmanship," and he endorsed the concept of European cooperation and initiative that were integral parts of the approach. Aldrich estimated that the cost could be in the vicinity of $16 billion * as opposed to some $22 billion suggested by the European countries. "The cost of American aid can be held to a minimum," he suggested, "if the credits do not take the form of tied loans [i.e., if the borrowers were not required to spend the borrowed sums in the United States] and if the products shipped from this country do not have to be carried in American bottoms." [22]

On this occasion he also suggested a vehicle for administering foreign aid, which he felt should be dispensed by a body that was granted wide discretionary powers to deal with a complex and changing situation. To this end he proposed the organization of a government corporation that would be named the United States Corporation for Reconstruction. Its board would be composed of nonpartisan persons of "expert competency" appointed by the President and confirmed by the Senate. "Its operations should follow as closely as occasion allows the patterns of private enterprise. The Corporation

* The amount of the trading deficit of western European nations with the United States.

should give continuous review to the economic progress made in Western Europe in order to ascertain that assistance given is constructively used. It should be given the right and obligation to negotiate agreements concerning the measures which the beneficiary nations themselves will take to bring about reconstruction," he said.[23] Thus, while endorsing Secretary Marshall's overall proposal, especially for its emphasis that Europe's needs should be considered as a whole, Aldrich typically was concerned about the implementation.

This kind of endorsement for a massive foreign aid program coming from a leading New York banker was significant in light of the political situation. The 1948 presidential election was just over the horizon, and the Republicans in control of Congress for the first time in many years could have sought to make a record on the need for governmental economy which the Marshall Plan seemed to challenge. Senator Robert A. Taft, a Republican presidential hopeful, was in fact sounding out the country on the political promise of this approach.

President Truman therefore had good reason to consider carefully the political pros and cons of calling a special session of Congress in October to deal with the foreign aid problem, but in the end he decided to risk the possible repercussions of such a move. Congress proved willing to back the President, and in the special session voted $540 million * in stopgap aid to help meet the immediate emergency.[24]

The ECA

In December, Congress settled down to consideration of the comprehensive long-range aid program that the President submitted. In essence, the President's proposals involved authorization of $17 billion in foreign aid between April 1, 1948 and June 30, 1952; the immediate appropriation of $6.8 billion for the 15 months beginning April 1, 1948, and the creation of

* This amount included $18 million in aid to China.

an Economic Cooperation Administration, an independent agency answerable to the President, to administer the aid.[25] The latter proposal was obviously quite close to the government corporation that Aldrich had suggested in his Atlantic City address the preceding September. In the interim, the case for it had been strengthened by the so-called Harriman Committee, which reported to the President early in November, and by the report of a Congressional committee headed by Christian A. Herter of Massachusetts that further endorsed the need for aid after a fact-finding tour of Europe.[26]

Naturally, the proposed legislation became a subject of discussion in the President's Advisory Committee for Financing Foreign Trade, headed by Aldrich. Among the numerous questions considered by that group was the required amount of foreign aid. On this question the committee agreed that it should not support specific dollar figures such as the President had advanced. Another question was the composition and power of the Economic Cooperation Administration's leadership. The President's message had recommended broad powers for the Economic Cooperation Administrator; Aldrich approved of this centralization of responsibility but favored provision for a five-man advisory board of top caliber. The President had proposed that the ECA be subordinate to the State Department in aspects of the program that affected the conduct of foreign policy. Aldrich and other members of his committee, however, believed that ECA should be truly independent and therefore opposed this provision. The committee also felt that the bill should specify that the usual channels of commercial activity be employed wherever possible in extending foreign aid and that precautions should be taken that ECA not circumvent the functions and resources of such institutions as the World and Export-Import Banks.[27]

Aldrich was more inclined to see the need for governmental responsibility and a government corporation than some of his committee colleagues. Explaining his position to L. M. Giannini of the Bank of America, Aldrich wrote on January 27, 1948:

> We agree of course, on the part we should like private enterprise to play in carrying the plan through to a successful conclusion. There should be as much freedom of opportunity in that direction as possible; but we cannot overlook the fact that the financial credit of the United States is necessarily involved . . . So, at the beginning a considerable degree of government responsibility must be looked for.

He then went on to emphasize his view that the administration of the program was crucial to success. Accordingly, he put particular stress on the need for delegation of broad powers to the ECA administrator.[28]

The Aldrich Committee prepared and sent a revised draft of the European Recovery Program bill to Washington in early January 1948. Robert A. Lovett, Undersecretary of State, acknowledged it as "very useful to us and to those working on ERP." [29] Later in the month, Aldrich discussed his committee's position with the National Advisory Council.[30]

The recommendations made by Aldrich and the President's Advisory Committee for Financing Foreign Trade were only one of many private groups' contributions to the proposed legislation.* The administrative leadership problem in ECA, for example, was submitted to the Brookings Institution for study. But there was no question that Aldrich had anticipated

---

* Aldrich was also a member of the executive committee of the Citizens Committee for the Marshall Plan, which sought to inform the American people about the pending legislation and promote its passage. Henry L. Stimson was the national chairman and Robert P. Patterson was chairman of the executive committee, whose membership included labor leaders like David Dubinsky and industrialists like Philip Reed. (See Harry B. Price, *The Marshall Plan and its Meaning*, Ithaca: Cornell Unuiversity Press, 1955, pp. 55–56.)

the main points of the President's proposal and that he and his committee represented important support for the general concept that had been advanced for aiding European recovery, both with respect to the policy to be pursued and its implementation.

Continued evidence of Russian aggressiveness helped to firm support behind the aid bill. In February, Czechoslovakia was drawn behind the Iron Curtain and late in March the blockade of access to Berlin marked a further deterioration in the situation. Against this backdrop, the legislative progress of the aid bill was accelerated.

In an address at Washington on March 18, 1948, Aldrich again gave the aid program his public support, placing it in the context of a plea for the restoration of a free market economy throughout Western Europe and noting the need for financial and monetary stability and a determined attack on the problem of inflation that could otherwise result.[31]

The careful groundwork laid by the administration, the support of Republican leaders like Senator Vandenberg, and the endorsement of influential private groups and of individuals like Aldrich were rewarded. Both Houses of Congress passed the Foreign Assistance Act of 1948 on April 2, committing the United States to a foreign aid program of unprecedented dimensions and duration.

Aldrich on the Foreign Assistance Act of 1948

The new legislation embodied much that Aldrich had worked to include. These results were analyzed in his address to the Cleveland Chamber of Commerce and the Cleveland World Trade Association on May 19, 1948. Without reminding his audience of his own contributions, the Chase chairman showed the extent to which they had been reflected in the statute. For example, as he had urged, the legislation made the ECA Administrator the key figure in implementing the recovery program. The appointment of Paul G. Hoffman of Studebaker Motors (Aldrich's colleague on both the Committee on International Economic Policy and the President's Committee for Financing Foreign Trade) to this critical position fulfilled Aldrich's hope that the administrator's post would be occupied by a man of character and ability. The Act also directed the ECA Administrator to utilize private channels of trade as fully as possible — another recommendation of Aldrich's committee. The statute also provided for a Public Advisory Board, though instead of the five members that Aldrich had advocated, there could be up to twelve. In these and other respects, the Foreign Assistance Act met the tests for an effectively administered program as Aldrich and his colleagues had defined it.

As Aldrich reminded his Cleveland audience, however, the fact of the legislation was merely a prelude to a series of steps that would have to be taken if foreign aid was to produce the desired results. He enumerated these prerequisites as: adoption of monetary and fiscal reforms, the economic revival of Western Germany, and relaxation of European trade barriers and development of trade with the Western Hemisphere. In his words: "To list the prerequisites for success is to state the problem and to emphasize its difficulties. These difficulties are not insurmountable. With courage and determination, with wisdom and statesmanship, they can be overcome and the economic life of Europe given new vitality." [32]

Aldrich's work on behalf of the foreign aid bill, as in other causes, had been facilitated by the able Chase people he could call on both in New York and in Washington. Shepard Morgan in New York was an invaluable assistant in handling the many details of the President's Committee for Financing Foreign Trade. The Chase representative in Washington, Charles S. Dewey, provided useful liaison with the government. Soon after the passage of the ERP legislation, both these men left the Chase — Morgan to serve with the American military government in Germany and Dewey to serve as Agent-General of the Congressional Joint Committee on Foreign Economic Cooperation, created by the 1948 legislation.[33] Once again, as in the case of McCloy and Black in the World Bank, Aldrich's associates had moved from their cooperation with him in attempting to influence governmental policy to active participation in implementing it.

By July 1949 Aldrich was concerned about the pace of European revival, especially in Britain. "I am beginning to think that Western Europe, that is to say France, Italy, Belgium, and Holland will be able to stabilize their currencies in the near future," he wrote Ernest T. Weir of National Steel Corporation, "but that it is impossible to tell how soon Great Britain may be able to accomplish this. For this reason we may be forced to conclude that the wisest course for us to follow is to assist the Western European nations to stabilize their currencies leaving the problem of the stabilization of sterling until a later date." [34] In short, the course of postwar events had altered some of his basic priorities for stabilization. Nevertheless, no private American citizen had worked harder than Aldrich to identify and anticipate postwar problems of international reconstruction and development or to influence both private and public policies with respect to them.

Recognition of Aldrich's contributions in varied roles was reflected in a nationwide poll conducted by *Forbes Magazine*, which placed him among America's 50 foremost business leaders. Reporting on his career in January 1948, *Forbes* cited the Chase chairman as "A sturdy champion of the right of business to responsible self-determination as against excessive governmental controls. Internationally minded. An active participant in many worthy causes." [35] It was an accurate thumbnail sketch, attested to by yet another project in which Aldrich was involved simultaneously with his activities on behalf

of European economic recovery, the American Heritage
Foundation.

THE AMERICAN HERITAGE FOUNDATION

As problems of economic reconstruction abroad challenged
the nation's resources and ingenuity, an alarming wave of
cynicism, lawlessness, and seeming disregard for American traditions of fair play and individualism was unleashed at home.
Similarities with the post-World War I period were all too
obvious, but unlike the Attorney General of those days, Tom
Clark, Truman's Attorney General, proposed in the fall of
1946 to take constructive action to deal with the problem.
One of his assistants, Timothy A. McInerny, suggested that a
traveling exhibit of basic documents, like the Declaration of
Independence and the Constitution, relating to the founding
of the nation might reawaken interest in and dedication to the
fundamental principles that had governed the country's development.[36]

The problem of implementing this idea was formidable.
The Justice Department had no funds for such an enterprise,
and the National Archives, Library of Congress, and other
repositories of these invaluable documents could not be expected to entrust them to private hands. The solution to
this problem came out of another cooperative enterprise between government and the business community, with Aldrich
serving again as a vital link between the two.

Development of an Idea

Clark consulted a New York lawyer, Edwin L. Weisl, on
how to proceed with McInerny's idea. The Attorney General
offered for comment a modest proposal to attach a special
railroad car with a documents' exhibit to a regular train,
sidetracking the car for exhibition in major cities. Louis

Novins and Barney Balaban, president of Paramount Pictures, happened to be in the room with Weisl when he received Clark's call. Novins remembers the conversation. "After Clark had told him about his problem, Eddie said, 'Well, you've got the germ of a great idea.' Clark asked him to raise $25,000. Weisl told him that his was a very modest request — and Eddie suggested after talking to Barney — that the Attorney General send someone down with more details of what this was all about." After this more thorough briefing, it seemed to Novins and Balaban that such a promising idea should not be confined to a program of $25,000. In Novins' words: "A Special Train was required. The train had to be made a symbol, as well." [37]

Novins set to work developing a memorandum on the possibilities for a nationwide tour of a special train carrying an outstanding collection of original, basic American documents. He added the significant proposal that the train should also provide a springboard for a "broad program of public education." The idea was then tried out on a small group of representatives from the mass communications media, and it was well received. One member of this group, Thomas D'Arcy Brophy, an advertising agency head, had worked closely with Aldrich in both the wartime USO and the National War Fund, and he suggested that the Chase chairman be invited to head the new program. Though at the time the plans were in a completely tentative stage, Aldrich quickly saw their potential and agreed to help in any way that he could.

Aldrich's leadership role was valuable in countering any criticism that the project had been conceived by Clark as a vehicle to further the interests of the Democratic party. As Novins put it, Aldrich was eminently qualified as a Republican but was recognized as a broad-gauge, public-spirited individual rather than as an active, partisan Republican.[38] The first step was to incorporate the American Heritage Foundation and to provide an organizational framework. From then on, progress was very rapid — much faster, in fact, than the organizers had anticipated.

Aldrich's Role

In typical fashion, Aldrich quickly organized his many contacts with leading businessmen to provide support for the new project. On January 27, 1947, he gave a luncheon at the Union Club in New York for Tom Clark and potential donors to the project. They included such people as Spyros Skouras, president of 20th Century-Fox Film; Thomas J. Watson of IBM; Chester Barnard of New Jersey Bell Telephone; Charles E. Wilson, president of General Electric; Thomas Lamont of J. P. Morgan & Co.; and various bankers, corporate heads, and mass media representatives with whom Aldrich had worked in other causes. No one at that meeting knew even in rough terms what the proposed program would cost. This put Aldrich in a difficult position in raising funds, though he was sure that the budget would have to be much larger than what the original promoters had contemplated. Initially he had solicited $5,000 contributions from individuals and corporations, but after the Union Club luncheon he did not hesitate to ask corporate contributors to double this amount, even though the Foundation still had not been formally organized.[39]

The rapid rise in the size of the budget did not worry Aldrich. Novins recalled: "At one meeting . . . someone sitting there turned to Aldrich and said, 'Now, Winthrop, I remember that just a month or so ago I was here and the budget was about $200,000 less. Am I correct?' Mr. Aldrich turned to him and he said, 'I have never participated in anything that was operated on this kind of a financial basis. But I was never more confident that we would raise the funds to meet this expanding budget'."[40]

Since the flow of corporate contributions was initially slow and the individual amounts not large, Brophy and Aldrich had to work very aggressively at fund-raising. As in so many undertakings with which Aldrich had been associated, it was the broad-gauge vision of the early promoters and their initiative in seeking out "seed money" that made the critical difference between success and failure in this one.*

The selection of trustees for the American Heritage Foundation had to be handled carefully, with many criteria besides prospective financial donations in mind. For example, it was necessary to reflect the interest of Americans from all walks of life in the American heritage of freedom. Accordingly, while the roster of trustees included many businessmen, it also included representatives from labor, the intellectual community, and the distaff side. William Green of the AFL and Philip Murray of the CIO were vice chairmen of the Foundation. Aldrich was chairman and Brophy was president.

Developing a Program

By the end of April 1947 the complex job of bringing all the varied aspects of the program together was well under way. A skeleton staff had been assembled; the Pennsylvania Railroad was proceeding on its own initiative to recondition cars with appropriate security features to carry the exhibits; the Association of American Railroads had developed an itinerary that would carry the train through the 48 states; the Treasury Department was preparing a coordinated bond-selling campaign, and the Navy Department had approved assignment of a 40-man Marine detachment to accompany the documents. Meanwhile, the National Archives had selected the documents to be displayed. They were to be encased in fire-proof, water-proof, plastic envelopes and placed in metal frames, containing shatter-proof glass, bolted to the sides of

* John D. Rockefeller, Jr., became a major supporter. The unsolicited $25,000 that he contributed in September 1947 was worth many times that amount in attracting additional financial support.

the steel cars. The documents themselves would be in the custody of the Justice Department.[41]

While the train would be the focal point of public interest, it also was a means to an end — namely, public dedication to the proposition that "Freedom is *everybody's* job." * The arrival of the train itself in each city on its itinerary was planned as the climax to a "Week of Rededication." During this week, every conceivable type of effort was to be made to awaken interest in the American heritage. Thus, a typical week was to be inaugurated with a mass meeting, under municipal auspices, featuring national personalities as guests; each day of the week was to be dedicated to different groups and interests; school programs and religious services were to feature the sanctity of the individual, and so on. National attention was to be focused on the program through efforts of the Advertising Council and of periodical and newspaper publishers' associations. The motion picture industry was to provide special documentary films that would be shown in conjunction with the program. A "great idea" had clearly blossomed in less than six months into a major public affairs and public relations effort.

On May 10, 1947, President Truman wrote Aldrich endorsing and praising the Foundation program. "You are answering a need today for a dramatic reminder to our people of the American heritage which they enjoy," the President said. "It is my fervent hope that the rights and privileges endowed upon every American citizen under our system of Government may be shared by freedom loving people throughout the world." [42] Truman lent still further support to the undertaking on May 22 when he spoke on its behalf to a group of about 150 interested individuals at the White House.

---

* The initial slogan "Work at Democracy to Make Democracy Work" was dropped — presumably because of its possible political implications. (Brophy to WWA, July 3, 1947. Aldrich papers.)

At this point only $100,000 had been raised against a budget that had risen to $750,000. Accordingly, on the plane back to New York from the Washington meeting, Brophy and Aldrich composed a telegram that was sent to selected leaders in various industries, who were asked to seek contributions among their colleagues. Before the end of July, $200,000 had been raised in this manner.[43]

Criticism of the Program

Meanwhile, the program had come under attack from Representative Clare Hoffman of Michigan, chairman of the House Committee on Expenditures. Hoffman, a Republican, seemingly scented a Truman plot in the endeavor, and he called Attorney General Clark before his committee to explain what was happening. In the end, the Congressman was satisfied. *The New York Times* commented acidly on this episode:

> Representative Hoffman's attempt to find some political or subversive influence at work in the project to send on a country-wide tour some historic American documents, such as the Declaration of Independence and the Constitution, has been adequately frustrated, we hope, by the hearing before the House Expenditures Committee. Anyone conversant with the facts, which were available to the Michigan Republican, knows that the whole project was conceived on a nonpartisan basis with the sole intent of calling attention to our heritage of high moral and political principles.[44]

Brophy and other leaders of the Foundation watched editorial and newspaper reporting carefully. The Communist Party, for example, was reported to be trying to sabotage the Freedom Train as part of a "reactionary effort to destroy our constitutional liberties." [45] Brophy attributed much more importance to the position taken by Colonel McCormick's *Chicago Tribune*, since its position was thought to influence a wide segment of middle western opinion. Aldrich was asked to brief the Colonel personally on the sponsorship and motivation of the project, stressing that it was not a Democratic political device.[46] The general tone of the McCormick paper remained more critical than laudatory, however, until the train visited Chicago.

Opening of the Freedom Train

The opening of the Freedom Train was planned for Philadelphia on September 17, 1947, the 160th anniversary of the signing of the Constitution. On the preceding afternoon the train was delivered to the Foundation in the presence of Attorney General Clark, the trustees, and invited guests. A dinner, followed by ceremonies in Independence Hall, marked the formal launching of the American Heritage program.

Responding to Clark on this occasion, Aldrich made a few brief remarks on behalf of the Foundation. He pointed out, "We want all of the world to see and to understand that the magnificent declarations of liberty which constitute our sacred Heritage are living and honored by us and filled with meaning for the peoples of the world." [47]

Addressing the Mayor of Philadelphia the next morning as the train was opened to the public, Aldrich elaborated on this same theme. "Americans have been fed so much 'ideology' of recent years, and so many dry facts and statistics by economists," he said, "that we may forget our prime and overwhelming necessity — namely, that we should remain free men. From our freedom comes all our strength. It is the preservation of that freedom that counts. And it can only be preserved by *alert and active* citizenship — not on the part of a few, not on the part of any group or segment of the people, but on the part of all." [48]

Policy Problems

That the Foundation itself adhered strictly to the principles that it proclaimed was one of its greatest strengths. It would have been tempting, for example, to convert its activities into anti-Communist instead of pro-American ones, or to connect the campaign for rededication to freedom into a campaign for free enterprise. These temptations were strongly resisted, and the sincerity of the program and its leadership were indisputably critical in winning the enthusiastic response that came from the public.

A major test of Foundation policy came in connection with the train's visit to the South. Should the train, dedicated to the freedom and equality of men, stop in cities where visitors were segregated according to their color as a condition of gaining admission to the exhibits? The problem had been anticipated by the trustees of the Foundation long before they were confronted with a specific decision. In July 1947 they had resolved that "no segregation of any individuals or groups of any kind on the basis of race or religion be allowed at any exhibition of the Freedom Train held anywhere." On September 26, 1947, a statement to this effect, signed by Aldrich, was released to the press. In it, Aldrich said: "It is our firm determination that the American Heritage program shall be an instrumentality for strengthening the freedoms and liberties of all Americans regardless of race, creed, or color." [49]

The wisdom of this step was proved when columnist Walter Winchell on October 15 reported that major southern cities were planning segregated showings of the train. The American Heritage Foundation immediately sent a telegram to Winchell and emphatically repeated the position taken by the trustees that segregation would not be permitted under any circumstances. This position was reiterated to Mr. Walter White, Secretary of the National Association for the Advancement of Colored People, who expressed concern over the Winchell article in a telegram to Aldrich. In Aldrich's absence from New York, Louis Novins wrote White: "If any community insists upon designating certain days or hours for the exhibition of the Freedom Train for segregated racial groups, the Freedom Train will not be exhibited in that community." [50]

As it turned out, this decision had to be implemented in the case of Memphis, Tennessee, and Birmingham, Alabama. The Memphis situation, provoked by the Mayor's segregationist stand, led the San Francisco *Chronicle* to suggest that the train be scheduled into Memphis and opened to but one person, the Mayor, who seemed most in need of the lesson that it was intended to teach. [51]

The Freedom Train on Tour

The Freedom Train and rededication program quickly proved an overwhelming success, exceeding even the optimistic expectations of its promoters. In its first four months, the train visited almost 100 cities. Although nearly a million people saw the exhibits, thousands more had to be turned away. In Boston the line waiting to board the train extended, four abreast, over a mile.

Even more pleasing, and certainly more important, the program united disparate groups in pledges of common allegiance to American citizenship. Management joined with labor to take rededication pledges. In Lawrence, Massachusetts, for example, 12,000 employees in one mill and 7,000 in another held rededication ceremonies in which management also participated.

The programs arranged in conjunction with the train's visits touched literally millions of people who did not board the train itself. Between September 15, 1947, and January 4, 1948, 772 radio programs, including both commercially sponsored and sustaining ones, carried the American Heritage message; outdoor advertising agencies contributed billboard space, and publishers and motion-picture producers and distributors blanketed the country with the message. The contributions by mass media that made such widespread coverage possible were matched by Irving Berlin's assignment of royalties from his "Freedom Train Song," the donation of railroad equipment by the Pennsylvania Railroad, the Santa Fé, and the Pullman Company, and a year-long loan of a diesel locomotive, with fuel and crews, by the American Locomotive Company and General Electric.[52] The enthusiasm for the program, while carefully stimulated, was also self-reinforcing. Even the National War Fund, which involved a far more tangible appeal, had no greater success than this.

Problems of Success

But the very fact of success produced new problems. The program had originally been conceived to run not much over a year, but its widespread appeal led to requests that the train be scheduled into Mexico and Canada, that it be sent abroad, and that the American Heritage Foundation become allied with State Department efforts to combat Communist propaganda. A bill was even prepared and introduced in Congress authorizing the federal government to take over the train. These were all very seductive proposals, but acceding to them would have altered the purpose and the very characteristics of the program which had struck such a responsive chord in the American public.

No one was more conscious of the dangers of overplaying success than Aldrich. He therefore used his influence against extending the Freedom Train program beyond its original limits, and, having done his part to make it a success, he was even contemplating resignation as chairman in mid-1948.[53] In the end, it was decided to terminate the train as scheduled but to continue the Foundation's activities in other areas related to its original purpose.[54]

The American Heritage Foundation has continued in existence, and Aldrich maintained an active connection with it until the early 1950s. Its subsequent programs have been devised in accordance with its initial objectives but on a more limited scale. Among other things, they have included promoting patriotic observance of national holidays and successful efforts to encourage voter registration and exercise of the voting franchise, an indispensable ingredient of the kind of freedom to which the Freedom Train had been dedicated.

THE NATURE OF ALDRICH'S PUBLIC SERVICE

When the Freedom Train rolled to its final stop in Washington, D. C., early in January 1949, it had completed a journey that brought concrete examples of the American heritage to over 300 cities and to millions of citizens across the country. The whole project had been executed for a cash outlay of a little over a million dollars, contributed by private individuals and by business, labor, and other groups. As an undertaking that combined private initiative and financing with governmental cooperation, that was dedicated to a broad public purpose, and above all, as one that accomplished what it set out to do, the Freedom Train was typical of the causes with which Aldrich associated himself.

His activity in behalf of the American Heritage Foundation had its counterparts of course in the President's Advisory Committee for Financing Foreign Trade and the Committee on International Economic Policy, as well as others, in which Aldrich was active simultaneously. His contributions to these varied organizations clearly reflected his conception of individual responsibility as embracing a wide range of activities that transcended yet were intimately related to his responsibilities as a banker.

CHAPTER XIII

The Late Banking Years, 1941-1952

CHAIRMAN Aldrich of the Chase National Bank was able to devote himself to a wide range of activities outside the bank because there he had a smoothly operating organization. While he kept current on major aspects of the banking operation, his primary role was as an ambassador of the institution, as the selector of top-level personnel, and as overall strategist. This style of leadership fitted his personal proclivities and was just as vital to the bank's success as the more routine aspects of bank administration. His conception of his leadership role significantly affected the Chase's response to the challenge of change between 1941 and 1952.

PREPARING THE CHASE FOR A NEW ERA

H. Donald Campbell, as president of the Chase, had provided Aldrich's most direct link with day-to-day operations since 1934, but in 1946 Campbell moved up to Vice Chairman of the Board to be succeeded by Arthur W. McCain in the presidency. Further rotation in 1949 raised McCain to Vice Chairman, a position which Campbell had vacated after a year, and brought Percy Ebbott to the presidency.

During this period the Chase board of directors retained a

high degree of continuity,* although inevitably attrition made itself felt. Howard Bayne remained active throughout the period, as did a number of other long-time directors like Arthur Page, Thomas I. Parkinson, Henry Havemeyer, and Andrew Robertson. Bertram Cutler resigned in 1946 and Newcomb Carlton in 1947, but their loss was offset in terms of continuity by such newcomers to the board as Jeremiah Milbank, whose relationship to the Chase in a legal capacity went back many years, and Carl J. Schmidlapp, a senior officer of the bank. The deaths of Gordon Auchincloss (1943), John A. Brown (1944), Arthur Hoffman (1947), and Barton Turnbull (1948) were felt very personally by Aldrich, who regarded his directors as friends fully as much as advisers and colleagues in banking.

Personnel changes at the top operating level of the bank had helped to ready it for the postwar era, and the last of the Wiggin-era problems had also been cleared away before V-J Day. In 1943 the Chase sold its stock holdings in Twentieth Century-Fox Film Corporation, National Theatres Corporation, and General Precision Equipment Corporation (formerly Theatres Equipment Corporation). Aldrich himself found a buyer for the British film properties, Gaumont Pictures, in the J. Arthur Rank Organization.[1] These moves left the Chase with an insignificant amount of stock in corporate enterprises resulting from prewar defaults on loans from the bank.

During the war the Chase was very active in aiding both government and industry — particularly, in the latter case, aircraft and machinery manufacturers. In addition to contributing many of its personnel to the armed forces and several of its key officers to government and war industry posts, the bank, and Aldrich personally, were deeply involved in war bond sales. The bank had a War Loan Treasury account of

---

* Except for Laurance Rockefeller, all members of the board were more than 50 years old in 1950–1951.

TABLE XIII-1

CHART I

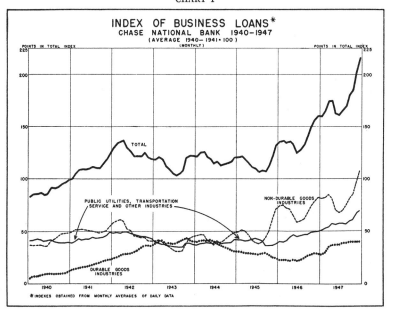

CHART II

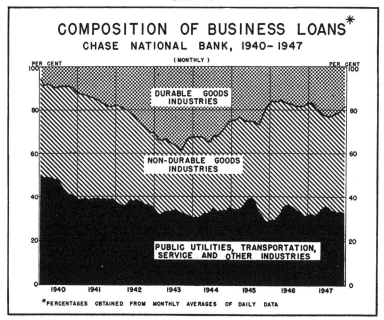

Source: Robert B. Rivel, "Industrial Composition of the Business Loans of the Chase National Bank, 1940–1947," *The Journal of Business*, Vol. XXII (The University of Chicago Press: January, 1949), p. 52.

over $1.25 billion at the very time it was under attack in the Anton Smit case previously described.[2] The Chase's premier position may be judged from the fact that it was the New York City correspondent of more than half the American banks with representation in that financial center.

The challenge of preparing the Chase for postwar domestic operations had been recognized long before V-J Day, and some basic policies changed as the result of an emerging new strategy. Before the war, the bank had engaged in both wholesale and retail banking, but its basic orientation had been toward service to large corporations. During the war, however, a slow but perceptible shift toward a new emphasis on consumer credit and service to small business occurred. The Chase, for example, was a leader in the organization of the Bank Credit Group of New York in 1944, which established a pool of bank credit for use by small and medium-sized business.[3] In 1945 the Chase was offering household electric and gas appliance financing plans and promoting loans to veterans outside the provisions of the GI bill.[4] Special checking accounts for the small depositor were soon added, and the importance of these new activities was reflected in the creation of a Consumer Credit Department in January 1946.[5] A new type of retail banking was supplementing, not supplanting, the traditional emphasis on large accounts.

As a result of this planned expansion, the Chase had more depositors and borrowers in 1946 than in any year since it was founded. It handled 160 million checks representing $111 billion; commercial loans rose steeply; and loans against securities dropped from 43 percent of the total to 13 percent. Although loans increased in all industrial categories, the Chase was particularly active in lending to public utilities for plant and equipment expenditures deferred by the war, and to retail stores for financing inventories and installment credit sales. To aid industrial financing the Chase entered into stand-by arrangements which committed it for a specified length of time to make loans whenever needed. Other flexible arrangements for repaying loans were designed to encourage yet stabilize industrial bank borrowing. In addition to seeking new opportunities, the Foreign Department returned to one of its prewar mainstays: the financing of staple commodities like cotton and grain in overseas trade. The Trust Department alone had 24,000 customers.[6]

During the last six years that Aldrich was chairman the Chase continued to grow, but it lost its number one position in terms of total resources to the Bank of America and was slightly behind the National City, its old rival. These three institutions, however, remained far ahead of other American banks in terms of both deposits and total resources.*

ALDRICH AND OTHER BANKING ACTIVITIES

During these years Aldrich continued to serve on bodies that established the general environment of banking. In July 1946, at the request of Allan Sproul of the New York Federal Reserve Bank, he became chairman of the General Committee of the New York Money Market. In November of the same year he was elected a director of the New York Federal Reserve Bank for a three-year term, beginning January 1, 1947. In this capacity he served as a member and then chairman of the Committee on Foreign Relations and the Committee on Supervision of Member Banks. He also remained active in the American Bankers Association.

In view of his position on the Bretton Woods agreements it was an interesting coincidence that he should have been invited to address the New York State Bankers Association at the New Hampshire resort in June 1948. But it was no

* See the *American Banker's* annual surveys, published each January, of the 300 largest banks based on deposits.

coincidence that he took advantage of that opportunity to call for the creation of a monetary and credit commission to review and make recommendations to Congress on the numerous problems and inter-relationships in these fields. Like his father early in the century, Aldrich felt that the time had come for a thorough review of the nation's monetary system. In the course of his remarks at Bretton Woods, he suggested that "The Federal Reserve Act itself is in need of thorough reexamination from the point of view of its administrative framework, the relation of the Federal Reserve System to other banking supervisory agencies, reserve requirements, discount and open-market powers and the issuance of Federal Reserve notes." [7] Eventually such a commission was established,[8] but Aldrich had anticipated the event considerably.

International Banking

International banking remained one of Aldrich's major interests. Prior to 1939, his primary concern had of necessity been the restoration of the Chase's image and position in domestic banking to its pre-1933 standing. Nevertheless, he had made a special point of encouraging the bank's overseas operations by giving them his personal attention and support. Influenced by the stern lesson of post-World War I overcommitment to foreign loans, he had moved cautiously but effectively in expanding this kind of lending. As a result, the Foreign Department as a whole, as well as the overseas branches, proved consistently profitable.[9] Using the yardstick that the Chase should have foreign deposits in percentage terms equal to its share of deposits in the New York Clearing House,* performance had been more than satisfactory.[10]

World War II, of course, dealt a severe blow to the Chase branches in Paris and in the Far East. The Paris Office was

---

* In 1945 the Chase was the New York correspondent of more than 1,000 foreign banks.

taken over by the Germans, but a nucleus of Chase people kept an operation going in the territory controlled by the Vichy government. The Far Eastern branches, originally established by the Equitable Trust Company, were completely cut off from communication with the home office as the result of the Japanese advance. Some officials in these branches were interned temporarily and others were held as prisoners of war for the duration of hostilities. To some extent offsetting the wartime loss of these branches, the Chase opened new ones to accommodate the American expeditionary forces in North Africa and Europe.[11] By virtue of his high-level government contacts in various other connections, Aldrich was in an especially good position to offer the services of his bank to American authorities, who were also anxious for these facilities to be made available.[12]

The Foreign Department

By the end of the war, the Chase was confronted with the problem of replacing the seasoned leadership in its Foreign Department. The co-heads of that department, Siegfried Stern, who had come into the Chase from the Equitable, and Joseph Rovensky, who had had charge of the department under Wiggin, both wanted to retire. Selection of a successor to this able pair was a matter of especially great concern to Aldrich in view of the importance he attached to the Foreign Department. It was therefore a surprise to some of the directors when he recommended for this job a vice president from the department, Charles Cain, Jr., who had been chiefly concerned with domestic customers with foreign operations. No one was more surprised than Cain himself, who pointed out to the Chairman that he lacked foreign travel or direct experience with foreign credit. But Aldrich was as adept at identifying potential as he was in evaluating experience. He was so confident of his judgment in this instance that he recommended Cain to the board on his personal responsibility and promised to teach Cain what he ought to know.[13] One of the first major steps in this process, as previously recounted, was to include the new head of the Foreign Department in the 1947 South American tour. Cain took hold as Aldrich had expected, and under his direction the department grew steadily.

Even before the Allied invasion of Europe in 1944, the Foreign Department had begun to develop its postwar strategy with a view to pinpointing where it wanted to lead, where it would not want to lead, where cooperation with other banks and with the Export-Import Bank seemed to be indicated, and so on.[14] There was no question that its foreign activity would be expanded. Thus, on the very heels of the American invasion troops, the Chase reestablished its Paris branch and soon after V-J Day was back in operation at Shanghai, Hong Kong, and Tientsin. By the end of 1947, in addition to these branches, the Chase had added new ones in Frankfurt/Main and Stuttgart, Germany, and in Tokyo, Japan, along with representatives' offices in Mexico, Egypt, India, and Italy.[15] By the end of the following year the bank had a total of 17 overseas branches and 5 nonbanking offices. The number of branches was not, however, a true measure of the full extent of the Chase's foreign business. Unlike some other New York banks, it preferred wherever possible to work with foreign institutions rather than to compete with them through branch offices on foreign soil.[16]

Latin American Operations

With some of its important prewar overseas branches in enemy hands, as well as with heightened recognition of the potential business to the South, the Chase during the war years had begun careful study of the market for its services in other countries in this hemisphere. Although the Chase had done business in Latin America for many years, it was not the leader among New York banks in this field.* Aldrich's 1947 South American trip to seek support for the International Chamber of Commerce therefore fitted very well with his bank's interest in strengthening its position in this promising area.

The strategy of expanding the bank's Latin American operations and Aldrich's method of operation as chairman were exemplified in the matter of extending a line of credit to the Central Bank of Brazil shortly before his South American trip. The Chase had made loans in that country but had not developed a long-run policy with respect to them. Both Percy J. Ebbott, at that time a senior loan officer, and Charles Cain of the Foreign Department retained vivid memories of Aldrich's decision to commit the Chase in Brazil in a major way. Ebbott recalled: "I'll never forget one day . . . the Central Bank of Brazil needed an emergency loan. Charlie Cain came to see me about it, and I said, 'Well let's go in and talk with the Chairman; it'd do him good to get in on one of these credit jobs.'" [17] Several banks were involved, and a decision at the Chase had to be made quickly. When Cain and Ebbott went into Aldrich's office, Cain pointed out that the Chase lacked a firm policy with respect to Brazil, and he recommended that the bank extend a line of credit and stay with it. Recalling the conversation many years later, he still remembered the dialogue with Aldrich:

> "I think a bank of our importance has got to be there in a big way if we're going to be an international bank." He looked at me and he said, "What do you recommend?" I said, "Ten million dollars." He said, "What do you think of the Brazilians?" I said, "They're unpredictable. But the country

* The National City Bank had entered the region prior to World War I and had 25 branches in Central and South America in 1945. (See National City Bank, *Annual Report*, 1945.)

is still there, and if we get frozen, some day we'll get unfrozen. But in the middle, I don't want you or the directors worrying. I want it fixed." And he said, "All right." And that line was never reduced or frozen.[18]

This was the kind of decision making for which Aldrich was noted. Under normal conditions he relied on his officers to make their own decisions. When he became involved as the ultimate resort, he relied on their formulation of the issues. His capacity to digest quickly large amounts of information, to separate the important from the unimportant, and to arrive at a decision without equivocation or hesitation made him a respected arbitrator. But it is apparent that such decisions were not sought lightly or often from the chairman.

Growth of Foreign Business

Outside the western hemisphere the Chase continued to build steadily in the postwar years on its already powerful position in the international field. For example, it became the principal banking connection for the National Bank of Yugoslavia beginning in 1948,[19] and for the Central Bank of the Philippines organized in 1949.[20] The following year, among other transactions, it made a credit of $62.5 million available to the Spanish Government,[21] and participated in a $225 million loan to France.[22] In 1951, through its Edge Act subsidiary, the Chase cooperated with the International Basic Economy Corporation and 14 leading commercial banks in Brazil[23] to provide a variety of investment banking services in that country.* Ties with banking and industry in countries like Italy and Japan, where the Chase established branches, were strengthened by Aldrich's activity in the America-Italy Society and the Japan Society respectively.

* The story of this effort to demonstrate an investment pattern that could be followed in other developing countries, and the difficulties encountered, is told in Wayne G. Broehl, Jr., *The International Basic Economy Corporation* (The National Planning Association, 1968), pp. 161–166.

Value to the Chase of Aldrich's Outside Activities

The range of Aldrich's interests outside the bank was importantly related to his responsibilities within in. His part in promoting the European Recovery Program is a case in point. Though his commitment to ERP grew out of personal conviction, the Chase also benefited from the business created by adoption of this program. (See Table XIII-2.) As the bank's *Annual Report* for 1949 pointed out, the Chase was a leader in financing under the Economic Cooperation Administration's letters of commitment, accounting for about one-sixth of the whole. This was one measure of the Chase's important position in the foreign field. In addition to being in close contact with the American program for European rehabilitation, the bank was also active in the creation of overseas markets for American products and the fostering of general international trade — matters to which Aldrich devoted considerable personal attention.

Aldrich's service in the International Chamber of Commerce and on various committees concerned with postwar international trade and finance, brought him into intimate contact with bankers, industrialists and government officials who were potential customers of the Chase. He did not accept heavy outside responsibilities solely in the interests of the bank, but they unquestionably provided a helpful base for developing new business when the occasion arose. Officers of the bank recognized the asset their chairman's personality and his manifold activities represented. On their initiative, as well as his own, he was constantly entertaining visiting foreign dignitaries, and "lunch at the Chase" became almost as much a part of a New York welcome as a visit to City Hall. When Aldrich visited overseas, Chase representatives would typically arrange for him to meet important bankers, members of the stock exchange and insurance companies, lawyers, and leading

TABLE XIII-2

ECA AND MSA LETTERS OF COMMITMENT ISSUED TO LEADING BANKS BETWEEN NOVEMBER 29, 1951, AND MARCH 20, 1952, INCLUSIVE

(in Thousands of Dollars)

	Chase	City	Bankers	Guaranty	Bank of America	Morgan	Irving	Mfrs.	French Amer.	Man-hattan	Hanover	Chemical
Austria	2,638	1,651	1,880	8,000	188	—	4,072	340	—	341	72	2,188
Denmark	26	461	87	—	—	—	48	65	—	—	—	29
France	17,578	5,018	11,487	—	2,400	15,654	1,254	1,433	174	1,803	189	500
Germany	128	562	—	3,830	10	—	319	296	—	561	2,576	314
Greece	649	—	490	—	—	—	313	—	—	—	—	—
Italy	890	4,773	748	80	4,206	1,040	50	143	—	23	117	1,055
Netherlands	497	690	—	—	—	—	1,022	—	—	—	694	1,326
Norway	74	187	—	—	—	—	—	—	—	—	—	—
Portugal	410	450	6	—	—	—	9	67	—	—	—	—
Trieste	70	—	—	—	—	—	—	20	—	128	143	11
Turkey	364	24	51	498	—	—	349	200	—	—	—	1,410
Yugoslavia	18,988	—	—	—	—	—	—	—	—	—	—	—
All Countries Including Above	41,610	20,561	16,646	15,737	7,581	14,614	8,156	3,446	4,665	2,197	3,561	5,001

NOTE: Figures underscored denote decreases.
SOURCE: Chase National Bank, Foreign Department memorandum, Charles Cain, Jr., to Winthrop W. Aldrich, April 10, 1952. Aldrich papers.

businessmen in social as well as business settings. They enjoyed the experience, and he thrived on it.

Trip to the Middle East

The range of the bank's international interests and the duality of Aldrich's roles were reflected in a trip that he made in 1950 to Europe and the Middle East. In one sense it was a fact-finding tour for the benefit of the President's Advisory Committee for Financing Foreign Trade, since Aldrich planned to investigate the practical problems of foreign investment by American corporations. In another sense it was a good will tour on behalf of the Chase, which had important existing or potential business contacts in the countries visited. It was, for example, clearly not accidental that Aldrich spent time in France and Spain, where the Chase shortly extended major credits to the government of those countries, or that he visited the oil fields of the Middle East where major Chase oil-company customers had extensive operations. In each instance, he was in touch with top-level business, financial, and governmental leaders, exchanging impressions and information on a variety of topics, including problems with which the bank or he personally could be of some assistance.[24]

Included in the party that left New York on April 14, 1950, were Mrs. Aldrich, the Aldriches' daughter Mrs. David W. Devens and her husband, and Thomas H. McKittrick, Senior Vice President of the Bank,* and his wife. After a brief stop in Paris, the party moved on to Italy, visiting Milan and Rome. During their visit to the Eternal City, Aldrich and McKittrick were accorded a private audience with Pope Pius XII, as well as meeting with bank and government officials.

* McKittrick had served as president of the Bank for International Settlements before joining the Chase in 1946. Previously, he had had extended experience overseas, chiefly as a partner of Higginson and Co., London.

The Aldrich party's reception in Greece illustrated the manner in which Aldrich's manifold activities and contacts tied into one another. The way had been paved by letters from Spyros Skouras of Twentieth Century-Fox to the Greek King and Queen. The Chase had rescued the film company from the debacle of 1933 and brought the Skourases into it; Aldrich in turn had helped Skouras organize Greek War Relief and had been responsible for bringing Harold Vanderbilt into that effort with all that this implied for attracting financial support. Skouras had also been very helpful to the American Heritage Foundation. Of Aldrich he wrote to the Greek monarchs, "In my estimation, no other person has rendered a greater service to the people of Greece. . . ." [25] With this kind of introduction, which was only one of many provided by influential American friends, the Aldriches of course had access to the highest circles in Athens and elsewhere in the country. The story was the same throughout their trip.

From Greece the party moved on to Egypt, where the Chase had recently established a branch. There Aldrich met with the Minister of Finance, had an audience with King Farouk, and lunched with representatives of leading American companies in Egypt as well as with various Arab businessmen. Farouk made special arrangements to meet with Aldrich and in the course of their interview informed the banker of his intention to abdicate.[26]

From Cairo the Aldrich party flew on to Jeddah, Saudi Arabia, in an Arabian-American Oil Company plane, viewing from the air the site of the Aswan Dam, which a few years later would take on considerable personal significance for Aldrich as Ambassador to the Court of St. James's at the time of the Suez Crisis. Dharahan, Kuwait, and Abadan were other stops as the party moved toward Teheran, Iran, where the familiar round of business and social activity was climaxed by an audience with the Shah.

Returning to Western Europe, the Aldrich party stopped in Lebanon and Turkey. The itinerary then took them to Brussels, Amsterdam, Paris, and on June 4 to Madrid. By this time Charles Cain and Alfred Barth of the Foreign Department had joined the group.

The Chase had been among the first foreign banks to extend credit to the Franco regime, and the relationship had been carefully cultivated for many years by the bank's Foreign Department. The party's reception in Madrid reflected this groundwork, and the visit culminated with Aldrich seeing General Franco alone for an interview that lasted over an hour and a quarter. The same cordial welcome was extended in Portugal, where Aldrich and Prime Minister Salazar discussed possible joint American-Portuguese investment in Portugese colonies.[27]

The trip ended in London, where the Aldriches felt so much at home and where the recent Conservative victory had brought Aldrich's old friends, Churchill and Eden, back to power. After a short but busy visit, the party sailed for the United States on June 16.

Like the 1947 South American tour, the 1950 Middle East trip provided Aldrich with important new contacts and firsthand knowledge of political, social, and economic problems in an important group of countries. As already indicated, his visits contributed to the leading role of the Chase in making loans to the French and Spanish governments as well as to international oil companies caught in a delicate sterling-dollar problem. In addition, Aldrich was able to furnish valuable information to Washington officials interested in private investment abroad and broader political problems.

THE CHASE IN A CHANGING ENVIRONMENT

The outbreak of Korean hostilities in 1950 put new demands on the Chase.* Again, as in World War II, its financing of aircraft and machinery manufacturers increased rapidly. Loans and unused credits to aircraft manufacturers, for example, rose from about $25 million to $133 million during the course of 1951. The Real Estate and Mortgage Loan Departments also found new business in the defense and military housing fields.[28]

By this time the wisdom of the bank's comparatively recent emphasis on small as well as large business accounts had been amply validated and impressively so in the case of the telephone industry. Although one or more representatives of the giant American Telephone and Telegraph Company, of which Aldrich was a long-time director, served on the Chase board, the bank aggressively sought business with small, independent telephone companies. This program, begun in 1949, was so successful that the bank reported for 1951 that it had made loans to about 50 independent telephone companies in 23 states and had sponsored a successful conference at which their problems were discussed with bank and insurance company representatives.[29]

The Chase's total resources now exceeded $5 billion, or two-and-a-half times what they had been when Aldrich entered the bank's service 20 years before. Employees numbered about 7,500 clerical personnel in New York and some 1,200 overseas.

During Aldrich's chairmanship, efforts to develop and maintain a satisfied and efficient work force had produced increasingly systematic personnel administration and expanded fringe benefits and improved salaries. The importance of this area was acknowledged in 1950 with the appointment of a

---

* The Communist take-over in China in 1949 led to the closing of the Chase branches on the Chinese mainland. In 1951 the Hong Kong branch was also closed to avoid any unintentional dealings with the Chinese Communists.

vice president to head the Personnel Department. Although personnel and administrative matters were one of Aldrich's concerns, he left direct supervision of them to President Ebbott and to the other responsible officers.

Strategy for Growth

As chairman, Aldrich's basic responsibility involved development of a long-run strategy for the bank's continued growth. By 1950 he was giving increased attention to the bank's retail banking position in New York City and environs. The Chase had maintained its commanding position in commercial loans, where it was consistently the nation's leader. However, despite the new postwar emphasis on the small customer, it had suffered relative to the Bank of America and the National City Bank in its overall position. An important contributing factor was the spread of liquid wealth in the hands of the general public and the fact that this public had been growing at a faster rate in the West than in the East.

President Percy Ebbott underscored these developments to a stockholder in November 1951, when he wrote, "Naturally banks with large branch systems have benefited more from this diffusion of liquid wealth in the hands of many people than have those banks which have fewer branches and whose business in the past was predominantly of a 'big business' and 'central reserve' character." [30] This situation demanded action by the Chase if it was to continue in its leadership position.

Under the laws of New York State, the Chase was not permitted to have branches outside the city, and in 1951 it had only 27 branches in Greater New York, or five less than it had had in 1938. The National City Bank, by comparison, had 67. Many other New York banks, while lacking the size and variety of the Chase's other activities, had expanded the number and size of their branches significantly. To match their progress, the Chase would either have to begin aggressive and expensive expansion of its own branches or acquire established ones through a merger with another bank.

Frustrated Plans for a Merger

The bank of which Aldrich was chairman was itself the product of many mergers during the period of Wiggin's presidency, climaxed by the merger with the Equitable Trust Company which had brought Aldrich into a banking career. In subsequent years, and especially in the post-World War II period, the possibility of yet another merger was occasionally considered. Although various possibilities were brought to Aldrich's attention from time to time, no progress was made toward a serious move in this direction. Several New York banks of the Chase type like the First National Bank and J. P. Morgan & Co. had likewise made no major moves toward increasing their retail business by expanding branch operations. Members of the Chase board, virtually all of them representatives of very large enterprises, were apparently not enthusiastic about aggressively expanding retail banking operations.[31] In 1951, however, the old and respected Bank of the Manhattan Company, which had extensive branches in the New York City area, appeared a particularly likely prospect for merger. Impressed by this possibility, Aldrich entered into serious talks with the other bank's chairman.[32]

The Chase chairman had gradually altered his own ideas about the importance of branch banking over the years. The federal government, going back to New Deal days, had sought in various ways to put credit at the disposal of the small businessman. Aldrich had always opposed governmental competition in banking, and he served for many years on ABA Committees concerned with meeting small business credit problems. He had become convinced that for the Chase the answer to this challenge posed by government interest in this area, as well as competition from other banks, lay in increasing the number of the Chase's branches. In 1966 he said: "If you have a branch every three or four blocks, which is the situation now, you are bound to do business with a lot of small businessmen. . . . I don't think the government has any real justification for organizing corporations to make loans to small business — the idea is on the theory that banks don't make loans to small business, which of course they do if they have the branches in the locality. . . . As time went on I became more and more convinced that the answer to many problems was to have branches wherever they could be of service to the local community. That if you didn't do that, you would inevitably lose ground to your competitors." [33]

In the summer of 1951 Aldrich completed what both he, and apparently his opposite number in the Bank of the Manhattan Company, J. Stewart Baker, regarded as an agreement to merge their respective banks on terms that were mutually satisfactory. If executed, it would have added 58 New York City branches to those of the Chase and would have given it more deposits than the National City Bank, though not more than the Bank of America.

But this was not to be — at least during Aldrich's tenure. The formal obstacle was legal. The Bank of the Manhattan Company had been chartered in New York State in 1799 and in order for it to be merged into the Chase, the Manhattan Company's counsel insisted that the charter required 100 percent stockholder approval of the move.* This, of course, was an impossible requirement to satisfy, and very much to Aldrich's personal disappointment, the negotiation was terminated.[34]

The desirability of such a merger as he had planned was

---

* There was speculation at the time that the Manhattan Company really wanted to sell its assets but not its name and charter, thus opening up the possibility for a new departure in its activities with the cash received from sale of its branches.

obvious. Under Aldrich's successor it was achieved by approaching the problem from a new angle. This time the Chase was merged into the Bank of the Manhattan Company, though at the cost of surrendering — temporarily — the Chase's national charter.

ALDRICH'S RETIREMENT FROM THE CHASE

On November 2, 1952, Aldrich celebrated his 67th birthday. He had been associated with the Chase for 23 years, 5 as president and 18 as chairman. He recognized that it was time to step down. The specific impetus to make this move came when President-elect Dwight D. Eisenhower offered Aldrich the post of Ambassador to the Court of St. James's immediately after the 1952 national elections.

One of Aldrich's biggest problems in deciding to accept this post was finding a successor to whom he could entrust the continued development of the institution to which he had devoted so much of his life. By coincidence a man of the type that he instinctively favored was then available. John J. McCloy, whom Aldrich had encouraged some years before to take the World Bank's presidency, had gone from there to United States High Commissioner in Germany and had just relinquished that post. Like Aldrich he was a lawyer, and he had been engaged in large affairs domestically and overseas. Aldrich's own experience suggested that lack of training as a commercial banker did not negate such qualifications as McCloy's when it came to the Chase chairman's job.

McCloy naturally had many job opportunities, and he was on the verge of taking one of them when Aldrich asked him one evening to ride uptown. On that ride he asked McCloy to take the chairmanship of the Chase. The idea was intriguing to McCloy, because, in his words, "It was an institution with broad interests, wide interests, it involved of course matters of finance, trade, commerce. And in view of the work I'd been involved in as a lawyer — which in large part had been involved in so-called financial law — together with my experience in the World Bank, it seemed to fit." [35] Nevertheless, he still wanted to explore the possible problems in some detail before making a final decision.

Aldrich assured McCloy that he would find an able and experienced banker in Chase president Percy Ebbott, who had 40 years of commercial banking experience. As for the problems that came across the chairman's desk, experience in the law was as good preparation as any.

There were, Aldrich said, only two major problems confronting the institution as he left it. First, the expansion of retail banking and the acquisition of branches had to have a high priority. Second, there was the question of a new bank building. Chase operations were spread through nine downtown buildings and this situation could not be allowed to continue much longer. The question that would confront McCloy, Aldrich pointed out, would be whether to move the bank's headquarters uptown or remain in the downtown Wall Street area. In virtually all other respects the Chase seemed to Aldrich to be in very good shape.

After some further investigation, McCloy decided to accept the challenge. At a special meeting of the board on December 23, 1952, the change was announced. The retirement of Aldrich and the election of McCloy as his successor were confirmed at the bank's annual meeting in January 1953. An eventful era in the history of The Chase National Bank of New York City thus came to an end, but the immediate goals set by the retiring chairman were met by his successor in a framework that Aldrich, aided by many able men like Campbell, Cain, Ebbott, Love, Morgan, and Pogue had erected solidly in the two decades since the near-disaster of 1933.

The directors' resolution on the occasion of Aldrich's retirement summarized his contributions to the bank succinctly and accurately. In it they said:

> He had the statesmanship and courage to advocate the divorce of investment banking from commercial banking. He had the courage of the Chase tradition to support its banking and commercial customers who were in difficulties through the long years of their recovery. He had the imagination to set up specialized departments of great technical skill for service to particular industries. And all during this period his was a potent voice advocating policies to lead the country out of the financial wilderness. He had a conception of the Chase Bank as a great and responsible financial citizen of the Republic, that should accept the risks and responsibilities of working for sound policies under which banks could best serve a free and energetic economy in the country.
>
> He leaves the Bank stronger in personnel and resources, and in better position than it has ever been to serve the country's great industries that are its customers and the great number of banks for which it acts as correspondent.[36]

Aldrich appreciated these words of commendation, but he was already busy preparing for a new role as his country's Ambassador to Great Britain.

CHAPTER XIV

The Ambassadorial Years: 1952-1955

$\mathbf{A}$ LDRICH'S appointment as Ambassador to the Court of St. James's was appropriate both in terms of the post's requirements and his qualifications. It was an important position in the capital of the United States' closest ally, and Aldrich was well versed in international affairs and very favorably known in Great Britain. No private American citizen had done more than he to strengthen ties of Anglo-American friendship and understanding — first in British war relief and then in postwar economic aid. For the Aldriches, in fact, London was like a second home.

Aldrich's immediate predecessor at the London Embassy was Walter S. Gifford, retired chairman of American Telephone and Telegraph Company, on whose board Aldrich had served for many years. Like Gifford, Aldrich had the personal resources to meet the many expenses over and above the Ambassador's salary and allowances, but before he left the post he had also done much to convert it into one that a career diplomat could afford to hold. In the interim he performed his ambassadorial role enthusiastically and effectively, making a major contribution during the difficult days of the 1956 Suez Crisis.

Political Background of Appointment as Ambassador

The Ambassador's job was of course a political appointment, and in this sense it could be regarded as Aldrich's reward for long and faithful service to the Republican party and more especially for his efforts in the 1952 campaign that elevated General Dwight D. Eisenhower to the Presidency.

A lifelong commitment to the Republican party came as naturally to Aldrich as did acceptance of an obligation to work actively on its behalf. As the son of an influential Senator, he had been raised in an environment of which politics and politicians were an integral part. Unlike his father, he had never had a desire to seek public office himself although it had been suggested to him on more than one occasion. He preferred instead to make a different kind of contribution to the party's success from the ward level on up to the national tickets. He was a faithful financial contributor to campaigns, attended national conventions, and served on numerous Republican committees. In these activities he put his money-raising talents to full use and, as in his civic and philanthropic efforts, he could generally count on sympathetic consideration from the Rockefeller family, which frequently set an example for other contributors to the causes that Aldrich aided.

Aldrich's service on various Republican committees went back to the early 1920s when both he and Mrs. Aldrich were Republican ward leaders in New York City. In 1930 he was appointed to the Advisory Committee of the Republican party in New York County. He became a life member of the National Republican Club and in the early 1940s was appointed to its National Affairs Committee and elected Treasurer of the United Republican Finance Committee for Metropolitan New York. When he became a director of the New York Federal Reserve Bank in 1946, he resigned this political affiliation but resumed it after his three-year term with the Bank.

Aldrich had enthusiastically supported Thomas E. Dewey, the crusading young District Attorney of New York County, who was elected Governor of New York State in 1942. He had helped to raise money and other support for Dewey's unsuccessful wartime bid to displace President Roosevelt in the 1944 election, and in 1946 Aldrich was an active member of the Citizens Committee for the Reelection of Governor Dewey.[1]

In view of the fact that a Republican Congress had been elected in 1946 and that Harry Truman had succeeded to the Presidency by virtue of Roosevelt's death rather than by election in his own right, the Republicans were confident that Dewey could win that high office in 1948. Aldrich shared this conviction, and London papers rumored that in the event of Dewey's election he would appoint Aldrich ambassador. In the United States there was speculation that Aldrich might be made Secretary of the Treasury. Of course as it turned out, much to the surprise not only of Republicans but of many political analysts, Dewey was defeated. Once more he returned to Albany.

The New York gubernatorial contest two years later brought Aldrich's name into newspaper headlines in a political context for the first time. Republican Lieutenant Governor J. R. Hanley had announced his candidacy to succeed Dewey, who seemingly had decided not to run again. As interpreted by the press, this situation had some bearing on Republican chances in the 1952 presidential election, because Hanley's chief support came from upstate New York which might prove unresponsive to cooperation with internationalist New York City Republicans in the choice of a presidential candidate. In any event, Herbert Brownell of the Republican National Committee became increasingly alarmed about the situation. Aldrich cut short a Maine vacation late in August to return to New York for a strategy conference on drafting Dewey and inducing Hanley to withdraw from the gubernatorial contest.

New York State Republican leaders gathered in Aldrich's office at the Chase on August 28.[2] At that meeting publisher Frank Gannett, who was a leading Hanley supporter, declined to withdraw his support from the Lieutenant Governor, despite warnings that Hanley could not count on aid from the Republican organization in Metropolitan New York.[3] Dewey himself had remained silent, but the strategy conference produced the desired results. Hanley stepped aside a few days later.[4]

The publicity that accompanied these developments annoyed Aldrich because it exaggerated and distorted his aims and role. Drew Pearson, for example, reported in his column that Aldrich and the Rockefeller family were behind a movement to draft Dewey for Governor and yet another try at the Presidency.[5] Replying to a correspondent who called this item to his attention, Aldrich wrote: "While I have felt very strongly that Governor Dewey should run again for Governor of New York, I believe that it is premature to discuss at this time the question of Republican candidates for the Presidency in 1952, and if Mr. Drew Pearson has made a statement that I have been behind a move to draft Dewey for 'another try at the Presidency' he is in error."[6]

The published reports of the conference of Republican leaders at the Chase were also exaggerated, judging from Aldrich's correspondence. Writing to Frank Gannett, he pointed out: "It is quite apparent that the information which 'leaked' to the press concerning my private luncheon, which I don't have to remind you was not held in the Board Room of the Bank, has been and will be used by the Democrats as a campaign ammunition. I have no particular regret with regard to the publicity which was given to the holding of the luncheon but what I do think is unfortunate is that the story was so distorted and exaggerated. However, this is water over the dam." [7]

As Aldrich had anticipated, the chairman of the State Democratic Convention was soon charging that Dewey was not being drafted by rank-and-file Republicans but by Wall Street interests. Aldrich's name was brought into the developing political controversy with increasing frequency. Walter A. Lynch, the Democrats' candidate for governor, charged that Aldrich was Dewey's "boss." The furore continued with Lynch derisively calling his opponent "Tom (Chase Bank) Dewey." Other candidates chimed in with similar charges.[8]

In the end, Dewey was reelected. It was thus confirmed that the New York delegation to the 1952 Republican Convention would be in the hands of the downstate group. And Dewey, whom this group had endorsed for Governor, supported General Dwight D. Eisenhower as the next Republican presidential candidate.

The 1952 Republican presidential nomination developed into a contest between the General and Senator Robert Taft of Ohio. Eisenhower was a war hero with no clear political ties or ambitions even in 1950. Taft was an able, experienced, but austere and dry politician whose conservatism on American commitments in international affairs had little appeal for Republicans like Aldrich, though he and the Ohio Senator were old friends. Their fathers, President Taft and Senator Aldrich, had been staunch political allies and the two families had maintained close ties for many years. But for Winthrop Aldrich and other Republicans of his persuasion, Eisenhower's great personal popularity and broad experience in dealing with America's allies seemed to offer a winning combination that more than offset the General's lack of political expertise compared with Taft's. The problem was to get Eisenhower to commit himself to the contest.

Aldrich had met Eisenhower for the first time in 1945 when the General had made a triumphal visit to New York City. Subsequently, they were in touch occasionally on such non-political matters as the National War Fund and the American Heritage Foundation. When Eisenhower became president of Columbia University, his contacts with the Chase chairman increased. In April 1949, for example, he invited Aldrich to serve as trustee for the National Fund for Medical Education,[9] and in early 1950 he was inviting Aldrich to various affairs held at Columbia. Later that year Eisenhower returned to military service as Supreme Commander of NATO military forces. Characteristically, soon after this appointment, Aldrich wrote him offering the full facilities of the Chase's Paris Branch.[10]

As the result of the publicity about Aldrich's role in the draft-Dewey movement in the late summer of 1950, he received letters from a number of citizens expressing the hope that he was not also advocating Dewey's nomination as the 1952 Republican presidential candidate. As he had done in connection with the Pearson column, Aldrich replied that it was too early to make any such choice. In some letters sent to Aldrich, Eisenhower was mentioned as the only man who could win the Presidency for the Republicans. Answering one such communication, Aldrich wrote in September 1950: "If the election were to be held tomorrow, I am inclined to agree with the conclusions expressed in your letter." [11]

By 1951 some Republican leaders saw a potential President in the military hero, and various of them began visiting Eisenhower's headquarters to urge him to undertake the campaign. On a visit to Paris Aldrich also sounded him out, but the General remained noncommittal. In fact, his assessment of the shifting political scene continued for almost another year. By

January 1952, however, he had announced that he was a Republican and by June, after a strong showing in presidential primaries, Eisenhower committed himself to the race and returned home. In the interim Aldrich had written the General, whom he addressed as "Dear Ike," on several occasions — once, following a trip to Texas, reporting that the General's prospects in the Lone Star State were improving, and on another occasion pointing up the inflation issue.[12]

Aldrich worked hard to raise funds for the 1952 Republican campaign. A colleague in many Republican fund-raising efforts in Greater New York testifies as to the effectiveness of the banker's work: "Extremely good. Extremely good. He was so engaged with other matters it was often very hard to get him to go to work, but when he went to work he was most effective." The same individual, when asked whether he thought Aldrich's motivation was appointment to some such job as Secretary of the Treasury, replied: "No, I never felt that he was doing it with any idea of getting a job in the political world for himself." [13]

The Chase chairman attended the Republican Convention in Chicago, where a major fight developed between Taft and Eisenhower supporters. Despite his friendship with Taft, Aldrich was firmly committed to the General. It was subsequently charged in the press that Aldrich "went all out to land the nomination for Eisenhower, applying financial pressure on industrial enterprises throughout the nation to this end." [14] Aldrich denied this charge. His position on such matters was put forth explicitly in reply to a stockholder who had suggested earlier that the Chase organize itself for effective political action. At that time Aldrich wrote:

> Personally, I happen to be a Republican. As a private citizen I believe that I am free to speak and vote on political questions and political candidates as I may think best. On the other hand, I feel that my trust as chairman of the board of

this bank requires me to exert every effort to guard the bank
as a corporate entity, having a franchise from the United
States Government solely to engage in the business of banking, and having some 84,000 stockholders and possibly twice
as many customers (presumably of all shades of political
opinion), from taking part in any activities that could fairly
be characterized as political.[15]

Appointment as Ambassador

With Eisenhower's victory in November, the question of
specific appointments arose. As had happened when Dewey
was running for President, it was again rumored that Aldrich
would be appointed Secretary of the Treasury. Aldrich himself did not put any credence in such rumors, because appointment of a New York banker to this post would have been
politically an unwise move. In the Eisenhower group of
advisors it was considered desirable to put an early end to
speculation about Aldrich's appointment. Less than a week
after the election, therefore, the President-elect offered Aldrich the post of Ambassador to the Court of St. James's.[16]

At the time, Aldrich was attending a meeting of the Business
Advisory Council at Sea Island, Georgia. Although he felt the
London appointment was one that he would find congenial
and one where he might be of real use to the nation and the
administration, he wanted to think over the implications of
the move both from the standpoint of his personal affairs and
from the standpoint of the Chase National Bank's best interest.
He therefore asked and was granted a few days in which to
arrive at his decision.

On other occasions when confronted with a particularly
momentous decision, Aldrich had sought the counsel of his
brother-in-law, John D. Rockefeller, Jr. He did so on this
occasion, flying to Williamsburg where the Rockefellers were
staying. Perhaps interpreting the delay in receiving a reply
from Aldrich as an indication that London was not the banker's

first choice for ambassadorship, Eisenhower offered him the choice of Paris where he knew Mrs. Aldrich and her sisters maintained a house. But Aldrich was not delaying because he preferred some other Embassy to London's, but because acceptance would mean retirement from the bank, the need to insure adequate succession there, plus the termination of his part in innumerable civic and philanthropic activities with which he had long been associated. With John D. Rockefeller, Jr.'s, encouragement, however, he decided to take these steps and so informed the President-elect. In the process he recalls imposing only two conditions — first, that he be permitted to object to anyone assigned to him in London by the State Department and second, in cases where he felt it essential, that he be permitted to contact the President directly rather than communicate through the Secretary of State.[17]

Aldrich had assumed that the cabinet post would go to Tom Dewey, with whom he knew he could work effectively. It was therefore with some surprise that he learned John Foster Dulles was being named Secretary of State. Dulles had had long experience in foreign affairs, going back to The Hague Peace Conference of 1907. As a Wall Street lawyer in the firm of Sullivan & Cromwell, his path and Aldrich's had crossed many times. In the 1920's Aldrich had endorsed him for membership in Nisi Prius, a lawyers' club, and Dulles had served the National War Fund as counsel. In these and other connections the two men had had common interests over many years, but no bonds of close personal friendship had ever developed between them. Based on his acquaintance with Dulles, Aldrich thought it very likely that the Secretary-designate would conduct American foreign affairs from the Secretary's office, not through his ambassadors. Subsequent experience amply substantiated this expectation.

For all the prestige connected with the post in London, the ambassadorship involved a new and unfamiliar role for Al-

drich. For three decades he had been accustomed to running
his own show, first as a lawyer and then as a banker. As Ambassador, it would be one thing to act as spokesman for the
United States reporting directly to the President of the United
States; it would be something else again to act as an errand-boy
for Foster Dulles, about whose qualifications for the office of
Secretary of State Aldrich had some reservations. As mentioned earlier, Aldrich made at least some of his doubts known
to Eisenhower and accepted the Ambassadorship under the
impression that he could contact the White House directly if
he thought it necessary.

News of Aldrich's selection as American Ambassador met
a very favorable reception in England. The *Daily Press*, for
example, headlined its report "Ike picks a friend of Britain"
and noted that Aldrich was the first holder of the King's
Medal for Service in the Cause of Freedom, as well as an
honorary Knight Grand Cross, Order of the British Empire.[18]
The Statist on December 6 pointed out with approval that:
"Mr. Aldrich was the only prominent American public figure
to advocate, in three important speeches, a proposal much
canvassed at the time in Britain, namely, *retroactive* lend-
lease." Owing to the fact that a Republican administration
was to guide United States foreign affairs for the first time in
20 years, Eisenhower's appointment of Aldrich obviously
helped to quiet any British fears that the United States might
adopt a new course toward the United Kingdom.

For Aldrich the two months preceding his departure for London were hectic — winding up affairs at the bank, resigning
from outside activities, and preparing for the new assignment.
Although 67 years old, he seemed as vigorous as a man much
younger. But even his constitution rebelled at the pace. Shortly before Christmas he went home ill, and after the holiday
he spent a few days recuperating in Bermuda.

In January he resumed his active schedule. On his first day

back from Bermuda, he conferred with Dulles, and the following evening met with the incoming Secretary of State and Winston Churchill at the home of Bernard Baruch. In mid-month he went to Washington for briefings at the State and Defense Departments, the inauguration, and interrogation by the Foreign Relations Committee prior to Senate action on his appointment.[19]

Senators Wayne Morse and William Langer of the Foreign Relations Committee made it clear that they disapproved of appointing the banker to the London post. Among other things, they wanted to know why Aldrich had not taken action against the newspapers that charged he had used undue influence in behalf of Eisenhower's nomination. Aldrich replied that he had not done so because he did not think anyone would believe the charges.[20] Venerable Theodore Greene, the senior Senator from Rhode Island, came to Aldrich's defense, pointing out that he had known Aldrich since the nominee was a youth and that he was honorable and trustworthy. This endorsement helped to insure approval by the committee, but Senator Langer cast a negative vote and expressed a desire to address the Senate on the matter. At Senator Morse's request, the approval of Aldrich's appointment was deferred until it could be put to a floor test in the Senate.

On February 2, 1953, this test came. Senator Morse declared that the nomination was "most unfortunate," because in his opinion the banker personified "the dollar sign and dollar diplomacy" to many Britons. Senators Irving Ives and Herbert Lehman of New York came to Aldrich's support, however, and praised his integrity and dedication to public service. In the end, the appointment was approved easily by voice vote.[21] Two days later Aldrich took the oath of office at the State Department in the presence of various officials, family, and friends. The lawyer-banker was beginning a new career, this time as a diplomat.

THE AMBASSADOR'S LIFE

After appointments with the President and the new Secretary of State, Aldrich saw Mrs. Aldrich off on the S.S. *America* on February 10 and that evening he boarded a TWA plane for London. As the airliner sped smoothly through the night over the Atlantic which Aldrich had crossed so many times, his thoughts surely went back to the dangerous wartime crossing that he made more than a decade before to inspect the progress of war relief. His endeavors of that era in a private capacity had a direct, if not causal, relationship to the official mission on which he was now embarking. On landing in Britain the next morning he told reporters: "It is with feelings of real emotion that I return as my country's official representative to a land I have known long and loved and to a people for whom I have the warmest feelings of friendship and admiration." [22]

The next few days were occupied with the details of getting acquainted with his staff and the various facilities of the Embassy. Julius C. Holmes, Minister-Counsellor of the Embassy in charge of the Chancery at 1 Grosvenor Square, was especially helpful in this orientation. Aldrich also found Lincoln Gordon, head of the Foreign Operations Mission, U.K., and Embassy Minister of Economic Affairs, a most congenial and able associate. The new Ambassador was of course introduced to the Embassy's full complement of specialists in economic, military, naval, air, and other matters, as well as those concerned with political affairs. He found that the Embassy had its own Security Officer as well as a detachment of Marines to provide physical security. The new Ambassador had brought with him his own secretary and had asked John Ames of the Boston Ameses to serve as his private secretary, or "special assistant."

The Ambassador's residence was at 14 Prince's Gate in a

house that had been presented to the United States government by J. P. Morgan and had been occupied by Andrew Mellon when he was Ambassador. The furnishings were magnificent, and the large panelled rooms formed a perfect backdrop for the entertaining expected of the Ambassador. However, as Aldrich noted when he lunched there for the first time on the Sunday following his arrival, Prince's Gate, despite its many attractive features, was seriously deficient as far as security was concerned. It shared a party wall with the house next door, and there was nothing to prevent an unfriendly power from moving there at any time.

On February 17 he met Mrs. Aldrich at the dock in Southampton, and three days later he presented his credentials to the Queen. It had been eight years since he had last visited Buckingham Palace to receive from King George VI the first King's Medal for Service in the Cause of Freedom. Despite the significance of that occasion, it had been relatively informal compared to this one. This time he arrived by horse-drawn carriage and was wearing formal attire. He enjoyed the ritual and Mrs. Aldrich, standing on the sidelines, enjoyed capturing it with a camera as the carriage swept by.[23] With the formalities out of the way, Aldrich settled down to the new routine of an ambassador.

On the occasion of Ambassador Gifford's departure, Anthony Eden, Secretary of State for Foreign Affairs, had defined an ambassador's duties as embracing three functions: To report how the country to which he was accredited was "getting on"; To be a representative "who is respected, popular amongst those with whom he works and very well liked"; and "To promote good relations between the two countries."[24] He might well have added that an ambassador was also expected to be host, guide, and counsellor to a steady stream of fellow countrymen seeking information, business, or pleasure in the country to which he was assigned.

Aldrich took these responsibilities seriously. He already had many friends in high places in the British government and in the social and business worlds. Over the years many of his activities had both directly and indirectly paved the way for his warm reception and acceptance in these circles. He was known to British yachtsmen for his campaign in British waters in 1921 and of course for his part in the America's Cup defense in 1930. He had been in constant touch with leading English bankers since the early 1930's. His work for British war relief and his trip in 1942 to inspect war damage and to hasten aid had won him special esteem. His postwar role as the leading advocate of financial assistance to Britain had further confirmed the respect in which he was held by Englishmen.

As Ambassador, Aldrich was welcomed with unusual enthusiasm, which was reflected, among other things, in invitations to join the most prestigious clubs, receipt of honorary degrees and even initiation into an honored place in British legal circles as a Bencher of the Middle Temple.[25] His relations with the Bench were such that he was even invited to sit with them in Westminster Abbey at the opening of Hilary Term.* With the aid of Mrs. Aldrich, the Ambassador cultivated and added to these many pleasant relationships in a seemingly endless whirl of lunches, dinners, and parties of one sort or another.

At that time Senator Joseph McCarthy was creating an ill-substantiated furor over Communists in the State Department. His famous investigating team of G. David Schine and Roy Marcus Cohn paid a fleeting call on the London Embassy in April 1953. Based on a few hours' briefing and observation, and much to Aldrich's amusement, they reported that "for a

---

* Hilary Term refers to one of the four sessions or sittings of the High Court of Justice at Westminster. By an Act of Victoria in 1875 the term begins on January 11 and ends on the Wednesday before Easter.

man who has been here only two months he seems to have grasped the problems very well." [26]

There were, in fact, no problems of unusual importance between the two countries. Therefore, Aldrich's task was to strengthen the firm ties and solid foundations of understanding that already existed. In his public appearances he emphasized three main themes, which he had been accustomed to propound as a private citizen. First, he stressed the importance of liberalized trade between the United States and the United Kingdom. In fact, he had been in London less than a month when he joined a British party headed by Anthony Eden and Chancellor of the Exchequer R. A. Butler on a trip to the United States for a conference on stimulating world trade.[27] Second, he interpreted movements of the American economy to the British in a positive vein, emphasizing the dynamic elements for continued economic growth. And, third, he took every opportunity to underscore the importance of the partnership between the United Kingdom and the United States, stressing the similarity of their goals whatever differences might arise over the means for attaining them.

The tone of Aldrich's ambassadorship was set in his March 19, 1953, address to the Pilgrims Society, customarily the first organization to honor new American Ambassadors. Arrangements for his appearance had been made long before he left the United States, and the importance of the occasion was emphasized by the distinction of the audience gathered to do him honor. Aldrich subsequently wrote Viscount Simon that he did "not remember ever seeing a more distinguished gathering." [28]

Following the Pilgrims' address, which reached a wide audience via radio, complimentary letters flowed into the Embassy. One of the most appreciated came indirectly from John D. Rockefeller, Jr., who had read a copy of the speech and reported his reactions to Sir Campbell Stuart who had presided at the dinner. Terming the occasion a highly significant one, Rockefeller wrote:

> That my brother-in-law, Mr. Aldrich, whom I have known from his early youth, and with whom I have been closely associated in many ways ever since, has been appointed to this most important post, which he is so eminently fitted to fill, has given me the highest satisfaction. He will represent his country with distinction and ability. He is wise in counsel, sound in judgment and, withal, a delightful person to work with. That through him, the ties between Great Britain and the United States will only become closer, is my confident belief.[29]

Shortly after the Pilgrims' dinner, Aldrich was asked to address the English Speaking Union. In keeping with personal belief, and the policy of the current and past administrations in Washington, Aldrich as a matter of course stressed the importance of the partnership between his country and the United Kingdom. In the process he made it clear that he considered the United States to have been slow to realize the moral implications of the two world wars of this century while Britain had had to bear the military burden until America awakened to the danger.[30] Colonel McCormick's *Chicago Tribune* was quick to react to this statement. In an editorial on April 4, 1953, the paper stated flatly, "This is the gospel according to Roosevelt and Wall Street and it is vicious nonsense." According to the editorial, it was actually Britain's lack of moral courage that produced the Second World War while America's entrance into the first one had only produced disaster for all concerned. Aldrich was not disturbed by such reactions on the part of the Chicago paper. He believed in speaking frankly whether he was appearing as Ambassador or private citizen.

A major item on the Aldriches' schedule that first spring in London was the coronation of Queen Elizabeth II. Making the arrangements for the flood of distinguished American visitors and entertaining them was expensive in terms of time, money, and attention to detail. But the pageantry of the event itself on June 2 was just as thrilling an occasion for the Ambassador and the distinguished Special Representatives of the United States * with the front-row seats, as for the Britishers and the American tourists crowded behind police lines along the line of march to Westminster Abbey.

The Aldriches had little time after the Coronation to prepare for a visit to the United States, where Ambassador Aldrich received an honorary Doctor of Laws degree from Harvard University and spoke at the opening of Aldrich and Kresge Halls on the Harvard Business School campus. The new Aldrich classroom building had been given by John D. Rockefeller, Jr., in memory of his father-in-law, Winthrop's father, and was especially designed to facilitate case discussion, the method of instruction for which the Harvard Business School was famous. The new buildings also represented the first major additions to the Business School campus since 1927 when Owen D. Young had made a dedicatory address remembered as a landmark in the history of business. For these reasons, then, Aldrich was challenged to deliver a significant address.

Inevitably, owing to the nature of the occasion, his major theme was set in terms of his father's contributions to American life and the developments since the turn of the century that had produced the responsibilities with which the United States was faced in the 1950's. Reviewing Senator Aldrich's well-known support for protective tariffs, for example, his son put them in the perspective of American economic

* General of the Army George Catlett Marshall, Special Representative; Honorable Earl Warren, Governor of California, Assistant Representative; Mrs. Gardner Cowles, Assistant Representative; General of the Army Omar Nelson Bradley, Sole Military Representative. (Materials on the Coronation, 1953. Aldrich Papers.)

growth, noting also that his father at various times had favored reciprocity tariffs. He went on to state: "I am convinced that if my father were alive today he would approve of these reductions and would favor even lower rates than now prevail. He would be among the first to recognize the changed international position of the United States, brought about by two world wars as well as by natural developments. And, in consequence, he would recognize that protectionism belonged to an earlier period, when we were an international debtor and not a creditor nation. He would want us to assume the obligations and responsibilities of the world's foremost creditor. It is my strong belief that we shall meet the challenge." [31]

Aldrich was in good form, and his remarks were well received. Among others, the Dean of the Harvard Law School subsequently congratulated the Ambassador on an outstandingly clear and effective statement of the change and development in United States affairs, but understandably the Law School Dean chided him gently for not noting that he had graduated from the Harvard Law School where case-method instruction had its origins.[32]

After conferring with Secretary Dulles and President Eisenhower in Washington, Aldrich returned to his London post on June 16, 1953, and that afternoon met with the Prime Minister. One major topic of these conversations appears to have been international trade relations. Aldrich had preached for many years that the imbalance between the American dollar and British sterling, as well as other currencies, could not be manipulated out of existence by governments. Eisenhower had appointed one of Aldrich's predecessors in London, Lewis Douglas, to direct studies of American foreign economic policy, and Douglas was also inclined to believe that trade, not manipulation of foreign exchange, would have to correct the maladjustments. He and Aldrich were in close touch on these questions in the spring and summer of 1953 as Douglas prepared his report for the President.

Aldrich had the opportunity to express his views on such matters at a dinner of the British National Committee of the International Chamber of Commerce on June 23. As former vice president of the American section of the ICC and as past president of the world organization, Aldrich was particularly pleased to be able to accept the invitation to address the British group.

In his address the new American Ambassador stressed trade relations. Although there were vocal protectionist groups in both Congress and American industry, he said, the publicity accorded their views should not obscure his country's basic dedication to reducing trade barriers and thereby stimulating international trade. Citing trade statistics involving Britain and the United States, he went on: "I think the record shows clearly that American receptivity to imports in general and British goods in particular is greater than ever and still expanding." [33] Although he did not refer to his Senate testimony of February 1933 on the causes of the depression, his statement that "there is a growing realization in the general community that higher levels of international trade will provide a greater export market for American goods and thereby create greater employment generally" was a logical corollary to that presentation of long ago.*

Aldrich also had a prescription for the British as well as the Americans seeking increased international business. After declaring that the United States would have to adapt her policies to those of a creditor nation and buy more abroad, he told his audience of British businessmen: "Your task here is to demonstrate the urgent necessity for an increase in productivity, which would make your costs competitive with those of other exporting nations, and for energetic salesmanship,

* See Chapter VII.

which would sell the necessary volume of exports you must have to survive." And, as he generally did, he closed on a note of encouragement, pointing out that a "strong Britain is essential for the safety and welfare of the whole free world." [34]

ALDRICH AND THE BRITISH PUBLIC

Aldrich did not believe in confining his movements and his public utterances solely to the world inhabited by the higher echelons of British business and society; rather he took every opportunity to put himself in touch with every level of British life. When he accepted an invitation to visit Manchester on July 24–25, 1953, for example, it was the first time in four years that an American Ambassador had set foot in that industrial city. The specific occasion was the opening of the "U.S.A. Today" exhibition. This visit gave him an opportunity to see and talk with residents of the city, where he had also visited during his 1942 war relief inspection tour.

In his address at Manchester on the evening of July 24,[35] instead of discussing trade, as he took occasion to do later at the opening of the exhibition, Aldrich reported on his recent trip to Washington in conjunction with the Foreign Ministers Conference held there.

The recent death of Premier Stalin of Russia plus the uprising of workers in East Berlin had created a rapidly changing international situation. Although it had originally been planned that a conference to consider these developments would be between heads of state, Winston Churchill's illness had made it necessary to defer such a meeting. Instead, the Foreign Ministers of Britain, France and the United States had met to assess common strategy and to prepare for a later meeting between their superiors.

Aldrich's account of this conference held the close attention of his Manchester audience. The local American Consul reported to London that the outstanding reaction was "one of pleasant surprise and gratification that he [Aldrich] chose in Manchester to give frank and timely comment on top level international developments and to bring to a work-a-day world a sense of firsthand participation in world affairs." But it was equally typical of Aldrich that when he and Mrs. Aldrich departed by plane that Saturday afternoon, they were bound for a weekend with the Governor General of Northern Ireland and Lady Wakehurst.

The Social and Diplomatic Routine

The remainder of 1953 passed quickly. The appointment calendar in London was crowded full. There were visiting Congressmen to entertain, Fulbright scholars to greet, officials of the State Department to brief, high-ranking military and naval officers and members of the Cabinet to become acquainted with, plus the usual ceremonial duties: unveiling a plaque at John Paul Jones' birthplace, awarding prizes at the Edinburgh film festival, and the like. There were few days in the average week on which the Aldriches did not entertain one or more groups at 14 Prince's Gate, and when they were not so engaged they were in all likelihood being entertained elsewhere in the city or the country. For Aldrich there were frequent meetings with Foreign Office officials, ambassadors from other countries, and numerous visits with the Prime Minister. In fact, one of the Ambassador's friends reported jokingly that he had heard from a reliable source that Churchill frequently opened Cabinet meetings with: "Winthrop says. . . ." [36]

Aldrich, who marked his 68th birthday in November, was accustomed to unrelenting activity of this type, but he reported to friends that it exceeded even the pace to which he had become accustomed in the troubled Chase National Bank

of the early 1930s. In December, therefore, the Aldriches returned home for the Christmas holidays. The Ambassador's
initiation had been arduous but rewarding. He had clearly
succeeded in communicating as an official representative of
the United States his personal enthusiasm for the partnership
of the two countries.

During his visit in the United States, Aldrich combined
business and pleasure. In addition to a round of activity in
New York, he spent some time in Washington early in January 1954, conferring at the White House, at the State Department, and with various members of the Senate Foreign
Relations Committee. He sandwiched in a flying visit to California before spending a few more days in New York,
whence he departed for London on January 23.

In February he visited Cardiff, Wales, where he addressed
a businessmen's group. It was the first time in a decade that
an American Ambassador had set foot in Wales, which in
Aldrich's private opinion was most unfortunate. The theme
of his public remarks, however, was that there was a need for
the Welsh businessmen to get to know Americans better, a
matter of considerable importance in view of the number of
American troops stationed in the British Isles. Aware of the
criticism that had been directed to this situation in some quarters, Aldrich stressed that the American forces were in Britain
for collective security purposes under NATO, that they were
there at the invitation of the British Government, and that
tolerance and understanding were needed. To this end he
urged further development of exchange programs between
American and British business and professional men and students like those already functioning for Fulbright scholars,
for students under the Smith-Mundt plan, and for British
productivity teams introduced to the latest industrial practice
in the United States under the auspices of agencies of both
governments.[37]

THE MIDDLE EAST SITUATION

During this period the American Ambassador was meeting informally and frequently with Foreign Secretary Eden and Prime Minister Churchill. On April 10 and 11, 1954, Aldrich dined with both British leaders on the occasion of Secretary Dulles' visit to London. The specific topic of their dinner conversation is not on record, but it undoubtedly included the Middle East policies of both countries, which would become a nightmare for all concerned before Aldrich ended his ambassadorship.

Dulles had framed American policy toward the Middle East following a fact-finding tour in the area a year before. In the course of that trip he had presented General Naguib of Egypt with a silver-plated Colt revolver as a gift from President Eisenhower.[38] Unfortunately, Dulles did not know what the gift was to be when he presented it to Naguib in front of photographers. After he had opened the box and learned its contents, it was too late to do anything but sit smiling beside Naguib while the latter pointed the revolver directly at the cameras. The publication of this picture in Great Britain created the impression that Dulles was encouraging Naguib to maintain a firm military stance against the western powers in the Middle East.

Dulles had returned from his 1953 trip apparently convinced that the United States must disassociate itself from the colonialist policies of France and Britain in the Middle East.[39] However, he also felt it necessary to avoid alienating these two key allies of the United States in NATO, whose virtues Ambassador Aldrich was conscientiously pointing up in so many of his public appearances. The reconciling of the two positions was not to prove easy.

In February 1954 Naguib had been succeeded by Colonel Gamal Abdel Nasser, with whom Eden would later in the year sign the Anglo-Egyptian Agreement that called for British withdrawal from the Suez Canal Zone. Undoubtedly this shift in the Middle East picture was at least one of the topics covered in Dulles' conversations with Eden, Churchill, and Aldrich when the American Secretary of State visited London the following April.

Major Addresses, 1954–1955

Upon returning to Britain from his 1953 Christmas visit at home, Aldrich found numerous invitations to visit and speak in various British cities. Among those that he chose to accept was one from the British government to attend the British Industries Fair being held in Birmingham, England's second largest city, in May. This invitation was accompanied by another to attend a civic reception by the Lord Mayor and a request to address the Birmingham Chamber of Commerce. The usual detailed preparations were made for this trip, including travel by Embassy plane to Birmingham. As a result of careful planning, the Ambassador's schedule was full and carefully paced to bring him into contact with the maximum number of people short of personal inconvenience.

In his remarks before the Birmingham Chamber, Aldrich showed more than the usual amount of humor in his public addresses. But even here he used it to make a serious point. Noting that street names in the city reflected its long history, he said: "There is undoubtedly some lesson to be learned, though I am not sure what, from your preservation these many years of 'Needless Alley.' And I take it that this has long been a city with a sense of humor, for only a man with his tongue in his cheek would dare suggest that in this hard-working community one could reach 'Paradise Street' just by sauntering along 'Easy Row'." Later he gave point to the story by declaring that British industry had to improve its efficiency as well as quality: "For, despite some local indications to the contrary, there is *no* Easy Row to Paradise Street." [40]

Changing to a more encouraging theme, the American Ambassador cited the vast increase since prewar days in the number of motorcycles, bicycles, and motor cars that Britain — and Birmingham in particular — exported to the United States. Noting the American effort to reduce automobile accidents through a campaign against drunken drivers, Aldrich added another note of humor based on Britain's large export of whiskey. "Let me hasten to assure you that this is no part of an American protectionist campaign directed against British exports! The U.S. market is large enough to absorb both these British products without necessarily mixing them or affecting our road safety efforts." [41]

He also took this occasion to discuss the work of the Randall Commission in which he had been much interested. President Eisenhower had asked Clarence Randall of Inland Steel to head a commission to review American foreign economic policy and make recommendations with respect to it. The majority report had favored further tariff reductions, trade liberalization, relaxation of "Buy American" legislation, and had urged the administration to use the International Monetary Fund and the Federal Reserve System to assist in bolstering currency convertibility between countries.[42] Eisenhower had already acted to implement these recommendations. "The direction of events and of Governmental thinking is obviously toward greater trade liberalization and the promotion of higher levels of world commerce," the Ambassador assured his Birmingham audience.[43] He also told them that the current recession in his country, whose economic reverses in the past had been mirrored and magnified in Britain, was minor and that its effects would not be severe in the British Isles. As usual, he concluded by stressing the importance to the free world of continued solidarity between British and American people.

The basic themes of his Birmingham address — the importance of liberalized trade agreements, the economic strength of the United States, and her dedication to the partnership with Britain in the preservation of world peace — were reflected in virtually all of Aldrich's addresses in 1954 and 1955. Of course he adapted them to his specific audience. At Leeds on November 11, 1954, for example, he spoke on the occasion of International Night and the celebration of the centenary of the YMCA, which had been founded at Leeds. After reviewing the major facets of American foreign policy, he related them to the worldwide efforts of the YMCA in the continuing search for peace and brotherhood. In January 1955 during a visit to Liverpool to dedicate a new library,[44] Aldrich reverted to the trade and tariff theme. A summary of his remarks was broadcast over the B.B.C., and the local response was excellent.[45]

The following March Aldrich made his second appearance before the Imperial Defence College, where he reviewed American foreign policy once again. As usual, his straightforward lawyer's style, rational, unadorned, but pointed, proved effective. As one of his listeners, a high-ranking British air officer, put it, the Ambassador's talk was a "clear exposition of the policy and position of the United States in World Affairs. . . ."[46] There was an equally favorable response to his analysis of Russia and China presented to the Political Council of the Junior Carlton Club on March 22.[47] This organization sponsored talks by leading members of the Cabinet and equally distinguished speakers. Accordingly the good reception of Aldrich's off-the-record remarks was particularly gratifying.

One secret of the Ambassador's success as a public speaker was his willingness to admit lack of expertise when in fact this was the case. Thus, for example, in a question-and-answer session following an address to the British Empire Club, he readily admitted lack of knowledge on some of the detailed questions addressed to him. On matters of general American foreign policy, however, he was emphatic. Replying to a question about the extent of isolationist spirit in the United States, he declared that there had been a complete reversal of the attitudes of the public toward international affairs during the period he had just described, and one of the things that had become most apparent was that "these new commitments represented the beliefs and purposes of the vast majority of the American people." [48] For the most part, of course, Aldrich was interpreting American policy to the British, but he could speak with special conviction on the internationalism, especially in the economic area, of the Eisenhower administration.

CEREMONIAL DUTIES

Aldrich's appearances in a ceremonial capacity continued to be numerous and varied. On June 2, 1955, for example, he opened the Atoms for Peace Exhibition in London. Sponsored by the United States Information Service, the trailerized exhibits were commencing an extended tour of the British Isles in support of President Eisenhower's efforts to promote the peaceful uses of atomic energy. The following September the Ambassador opened Washington Old Hall at Durham, which had been deeded to the United States. The ancestral home of George Washington's family, the dwelling had been restored by contributions from Britain and the United States. The affair had all the colorful ceremony associated with a memorable event, including the review of a troop of Washington Greys, music by the Royal Tanks Corps band, and a luncheon in the Great Hall of Durham Castle for some 160

guests. Aldrich's assignment was to open the door of Washington Old Hall with a silver gilt key and appropriate remarks. Although he was presented with the key, Aldrich later
thoughtfully returned it after having a duplicate made as a
memento of the occasion.[49] Such activities, though perhaps
minor in the larger scale of Anglo-American relations, nevertheless made their incremental contributions to Aldrich's primary mission: the maintenance and reinforcement of good
relations between British and Americans at all levels.

A New Ambassador's Residence

Since his arrival in London, Aldrich had been concerned
about the physical security of 14 Prince's Gate. Early in his
ambassadorship, therefore, he began to explore possibilities for
relocating the Embassy residence.[50] Winfield House, a magnificent building presented by Barbara Hutton to the United
States government some years before, soon aroused his interest. The property was situated on the inner circle of
Regent's Park in the midst of its own beautifully landscaped
grounds and was in both accommodations and location perfectly suited to be the home of the American Ambassador.

There were many reasons why Winfield House did not
seem to be available when Aldrich looked into the matter.
Two ambassadors had already refused to move there in the
belief that it would involve too heavy an expense to maintain
the building and keep up its grounds and gardens. During
World War II, the house had been turned over to the United
States Air Force as a club and was still occupied and used for
that purpose. The entrance hall had been remodeled, and the
house generally had been allowed to deteriorate. Most of the
former beautiful furnishings had been in storage for years.
To bring the building back to the condition suitable for the
residence of the Ambassador would require the expenditure

of a considerable sum of money. Moreover, the lease from the Commissioners of Crown Lands, which was the only title Barbara Hutton could give to the United States government, had very few years left to run. Under the provisions of an English law passed after Miss Hutton's gift of the property to the United States government, no further lease and no extension or renewal of a lease of Crown Lands within the confines of a public park could be granted by the Commissioners without the specific approval of the British Cabinet.

Since for these reasons Winfield House did not appear to be available, Aldrich made every effort for more than a year to find another building that would be suitable as a residence. He could find nothing which compared with Winfield House in beauty, or more important, in the security offered by the wide expanse of grounds in Regent's Park. And no available building sites seemed as promising.

Convinced that there was no satisfactory alternative to Winfield House, Aldrich decided to discuss the matter with Winston Churchill. The Prime Minister quickly concurred that Winfield House would make an excellent Ambassador's residence, but he wanted absolute assurance that it would be used for no other purpose. Aldrich was seeking a 99-year lease, which was an unusually long one in view of past practice, and he took immediate advantage of Churchill's insistence that the house be used only as the Ambassador's residence. This being the case, Aldrich pointed out, the commercial value of the property was nil. Accordingly, he proposed that the rental be a token £5 per year. In return, Aldrich promised Churchill to use his best efforts to get the United States government to agree not to use the premises for any purpose other than the Ambassador's residence without the written consent of the British government, and to covenant to restore the residence and maintain it and the grounds in fitting style for the duration of the lease. A corollary benefit to such an agreement from the Ambassador's point of view would be that his successors would be relieved of some significant household expenses if this arrangement were confirmed.

The British Cabinet approved the arrangement presented to Churchill. The Commissioners of Crown Lands at first did not wish to make so long a lease, but in the end they also gave their consent. Thereafter, the proper Congressional authority was obtained and Aldrich surrendered what remained of the Hutton lease in return for one that was to run 99 years on the terms that he had proposed.

Gaining a long-term lease on Winfield House was only the first step in creating a suitable new Ambassador's residence. As an Air Force club, the building had been subjected to unusually hard wear and tear, and its interior had been rudely altered to make it suitable for the entertainment of large groups of military personnel. Aldrich's next step, then, was to get the Air Force to reimburse the State Department for restoring the building to an acceptable state for a private residence. In this, too, he was successful. The sale of the Prince's Gate residence provided additional funds for refurnishing Winfield House, and the furniture was moved from the old residence to Regent's Park. Mrs. Aldrich and a decorating consultant from the State Department selected the color schemes and materials that completed the transformation of Winfield House, a process which took about a year.

The resulting facilities offered great flexibility and could easily be adapted to entertaining on a small or large scale as the Ambassador might choose, or the occasion might require. The only unusually large room was the entrance hall, where Mrs. Aldrich met regularly with the Embassy wives. Otherwise the reception rooms were of moderate size and so arranged that one or more could be kept closed if entertaining was to be confined to small groups. The same was true of the dining rooms. The smaller one could accommodate an intimate group of 14, but adjoining it was a room that could seat some 70 people comfortably. The Ambassador was, therefore, no longer the prisoner of a large establishment whose physical facilities left him no choice but to entertain on a large scale or otherwise to appear antisocial or penny-pinching, or both. Finally, and perhaps most important, some 12 acres of grounds maintained at government expense, gave the residence the privacy and security that had been impossible at Prince's Gate.

In order to celebrate the happy occasion of the opening of the new Embassy residence, Aldrich decided to invite the Queen and Prince Philip to a dinner-dance at Winfield House.[51] Of course, the date of the party had to be arranged at the Queen's pleasure through her private secretary. Much to Aldrich's delight, the Queen not only accepted his invitation but suggested herself that the party should be held on Washington's Birthday, which she felt would be a most appropriate date.

The party was a great success because the Queen wished it to be as informal as possible. She directed that protocol be ignored so that American and British guests could be intermingled at dinner, and she also asked that American guests be given every opportunity to be presented and to dance with her.[52]

For the Aldriches, this visit by the young British Queen to their official residence and her graciousness and charm on that occasion was never to be forgotten. Every detail was etched indelibly on their memories. At their Maine house in the summer of 1967, they talked about the Washington's Birthday party in London as though it had been only the night before.

A NEW PRIME MINISTER

While pleasant social and civic occasions made up the bulk

of the Ambassador's routine, Aldrich kept in close touch with the changing picture in British politics and the British economy. These developments were far from reassuring. In April 1955 the grand old war-horse of the Conservative Party, Winston Churchill, resigned and was succeeded by Anthony Eden. Eden had long experience in foreign affairs, but was really untested as a leader in his own right. Indecisiveness in this new role could be fateful, and there was perhaps a suggestion of it in his failure to make a clean sweep of the Cabinet when he entered office.

A few months later there was a Summit meeting of Britain, France, the United States, and Russia at Geneva. Although the Western powers had hoped for some progress toward the reunification of Germany, these hopes were disappointed. In fact, little of a significant nature came out of the meeting except Eden's invitation to the Russian leaders to visit Britain.* Aldrich had no occasion to attend the Geneva conference, but shortly afterward when he was interviewed upon his return to the United States, he told the press that the meeting had strengthened this country's image and the President's as being dedicated to avoidance of war. As for United States-British relations, they were "absolutely the top." [53]

By this time, however, the deterioration of Britain's economic position had become alarming. Since arriving in London, Aldrich had been urging British businessmen to make themselves more competitive and to improve their market opportunities overseas; on the American side he had supported trade liberalization. But Britain seemed caught in a downward economic spiral, a fact reflected in the fall of 1955 by the introduction of a supplemental government budget, increased

---

* That visit, which took place in April 1956, had unfortunate repercussions when it was discovered that a British frogman had disappeared while apparently inspecting the visiting Russian ships without the authority or permission of the Eden government.

taxes, rationed credit, reduced subsidies to housing, and diminished overseas investment. R. A. Butler, who had held Britain's Treasury post for four years, had good reason to seek a less demanding office. Eden therefore appointed Harold Macmillan to the Treasury while Selwyn Lloyd took over the Foreign Office. Macmillan was forced to continue and expand the stringent financial measures that were scarcely calculated to heighten the government's popularity. Newspaper criticism of the Eden government became more vocal, with heaviest emphasis on the Prime Minister's alleged indecisiveness.[54] Aldrich watched these developments closely and kept current on them by frequent meetings with Macmillan and occasional ones with Eden.

Before leaving the United States after his 1955 summer vacation in Maine, he discussed the London situation with Washington officials and flew to Denver to confer with President Eisenhower, who was recuperating from a heart attack. Back in Britain, he resumed his busy schedule and during the fall he met with Dulles in Paris and in Vienna, as the Secretary of State made his flying visits to European capitals. In December Aldrich was back in Washington again for further conferences and the Christmas holidays.

The ambassadorial years had thus far gone quickly, smoothly, and pleasantly. But, though Aldrich could not have anticipated it, he was about to be plunged once more into another of the world crises that had marked turning points in his career and had repeatedly tested his capacity for leadership.

CHAPTER XV

The Ambassadorial Years: The Suez Crisis, 1956

ALDRICH returned to London on January 22, 1956, but he scarcely had time to clear his desk before he boarded the *Queen Elizabeth* to accompany Prime Minister Eden and his party to a Washington conference with President Eisenhower. The main purpose of the meeting was to reach some agreement on an Anglo-American policy with respect to the worsening situation in the Middle East. Eden was concerned over the growing tension between Egypt and Israel, where border incidents were occurring almost daily, and he went to Washington to urge joint action under the Tripartite Declaration of 1950 to prevent violation of the Arab-Israel frontiers.[1] Although Eden professed to be generally satisfied with the outcome of his visit, neither Dulles nor President Eisenhower committed himself to use force to give effect to the Tripartite Declaration.[2]

Aldrich stayed in close touch with these high-level proceedings. He rode in the President's plane with the British party from New York to Washington, attended the meetings at the White House and the dinner parties tendered by Dulles to Eden and by Eden to Dulles. On February 5, he was back again in London.[3]

The remainder of that winter and spring went as usual, with routine appointments, receptions, cocktail parties, visits in the country, dedications and speeches. Aldrich met the visiting Soviet leaders Marshall Bulganin and Nikita Khrushchev at a reception held in their honor by the Russian ambassador on April 24; received an honorary LL.D. from the University of Liverpool on May 14; and escorted former President Truman and Mrs. Truman during their visit to England that June.

On the last occasion, Aldrich saw Eden for the first time since April. Although the American Ambassador had met with the Prime Minister five times between the end of February and mid-April,[4] thereafter his chief contacts with the British government, according to his appointment book,* seem to have been through visits to the Foreign Office.

THE MIDDLE EAST SITUATION

During this period Britain had been experiencing some major reverses in the Middle East. On March 1, for example, General John Glubb, who had commanded the British-financed Arab Legion, had been dismissed by the young Jordanian King. This challenge to British power in the Middle East went unanswered, and Aldrich conferred about it with Eden on March 6. When Eden addressed the House of Commons on the following day, he made it clear that he was not then prepared to take strong action. This announcement was received with roars of disapproval, and from that date Randolph Churchill in his biography of Eden marks the beginning of Eden's downfall.[5] The acid test of British policy in the Middle East, however, came in July when President Nasser

---

* Aldrich's dispatches to the State Department were not made available to the author despite Aldrich's personal request to the Secretary of State.

of Egypt seized the Suez Canal and confronted the major maritime powers with a serious crisis and Eden, in particular, with a test that broke him.

American policy toward Egypt had helped to provoke the crisis. In December 1955 the American Government, the British Government and the World Bank * (contingent on the action of the first two) offered to contribute in loans to Egypt a total of some $271 million of the $700 million that it would take to build the Aswan Dam, a giant power and irrigation project on the Nile. By the following June, Eisenhower and his Secretary of the Treasury, George Humphrey, were becoming convinced that Nasser was using the American offer to bargain for better terms from the Soviet Union.[6] On July 19, 1956, Dulles — under pressure from economy-minded Congressmen and cotton lobbyists, and disturbed by the Egyptians' rapprochement with the USSR — informed the Egyptian Ambassador that the American offer was withdrawn.[7] Britain followed suit the next day.

A week later, on July 26, President Nasser retaliated by announcing seizure of the Suez Canal. Eden had long made it clear that he regarded that waterway as vital to Britain, and Nasser's action seemed to the British Prime Minister to call for a prompt and forceful response.

As luck would have it, Aldrich was in the air bound for New York when news of Nasser's action reached London. Not knowing of the American Ambassador's departure, Eden had invited him to attend a meeting of the British Cabinet that was being called immediately. In Aldrich's absence, the American Chargé d'Affaires, Mr. Andrew Foster, received the

* Eden had earlier discussed the problem of Britain's role in this loan with Aldrich, who suggested the course of action that led to the December 1955 agreement. The World Bank, of course, was still headed by Aldrich's old colleague and friend, Eugene Black. (Aldrich speech at McCloy dinner, April 23, 1957. Aldrich papers.)

news from Eden and attended the Cabinet meeting in Aldrich's stead.[8] He reported to President Eisenhower that the British took a very grave view of the situation and already had alerted their military commanders in the Mediterranean.[9]

Eden cabled Eisenhower on July 27 that firm action was necessary, that the British were prepared to use force but that the first step should be an exchange of views between France, Britain, and the United States on "how we can best bring the maximum pressure to bear on the Egyptian government."[10] Eisenhower was quite unwilling to commit the United States to any use of force, and in Dulles' absence in South America, he dispatched Deputy Under Secretary of State Robert Murphy to London to analyze and report as to the facts.[11]

As soon as he learned of Nasser's move, Aldrich flew directly to Washington where he met with Dulles (who had just returned home) and the Secretary's staff.[12] It was obvious that face-to-face discussion with Eden was essential, and arrangements were quickly made for Dulles to confer with the Prime Minister in London.

Aldrich arrived back in England at 9 a.m., Wednesday, August 1. On the same day, Dulles and a small staff also arrived. At 1:30 that afternoon Aldrich and Dulles had lunch with Eden, and in the evening they dined with French Ambassador Chauvel. Murphy, having completed his assignment, returned to Washington.[13]

As Eisenhower subsequently explained United States policy in his autobiography, it was based on the belief that Britain and France had dubious legal grounds for any use of force against Egypt. The main issue, as the President saw it, was whether Nasser could keep the Canal open to traffic of all nations in accordance with the Convention of 1888.[14] Since only time would provide the test of this capability, the American policy emerged as one of "wait and see."

While not ruling out completely the use of force against Nasser, the President and his advisers feared, among other things, that the United Nations at that stage of affairs might be weakened or destroyed by any such move.[15] Eden, for his part, felt that the American position as relayed by Murphy was strictly a legalistic one, at least partially influenced by considerations of the United States' position with respect to the Panama Canal. Although the Convention of 1888 guaranteed the Suez Canal as an international waterway, Eden believed that it gave a poor legal basis for any action against Nasser since Russia, which had to be counted on Egypt's side, had signed the Convention and the United States had not.[16]

In London, Dulles explained the American position in much the same terms as Murphy, but with new arguments. Nevertheless, he conveyed the impression to Eden that the United States might in the last eventuality use force and that for this reason the legal underpinning of any such action should be made unimpeachable.[17]

Before leaving Washington, Dulles had informed Eisenhower that intelligence from London indicated the British Cabinet had already reached a firm decision to "break Nasser." Accordingly, in a personal letter to Eden transmitted through Dulles, Eisenhower warned against the use of force. Still, the phraseology did not seem to rule it out as a last resort.[18] When Dulles on August 1 added to this communication his statement that a way had to be found to "make Nasser disgorge," Eden interpreted it as a sign that the United States was not as opposed to forceful action as it had seemed.[19] Eden was further encouraged in this belief by Dulles' emphatic view that the Canal should not be permitted to remain under the domination of a single country without any international control.[20]

Dulles' visit to London at least won time to work toward

negotiation. It was agreed that a conference of canal-using nations should assemble in the British capital. France and Britain asked for an immediate meeting; Dulles wanted several weeks to prepare for it, and his view prevailed.[21]

Dulles and his party, accompanied by Aldrich, returned to Washington to plan for the London conference, which was scheduled for August 16. For most of the next two weeks Aldrich remained in Washington as the American position was defined and refined.[22] The objective of these discussions was to find some way out of the Suez problem short of the use of force. The Secretary of State kept his options open,* and the President, while obviously opposed to the use of force, does not seem as of that time to have ruled it out completely under some circumstances.** In view of the national elections scheduled for November 6, an important factor in any decision on this question was the probable reaction of American public opinion.

Aldrich and Dulles returned to London on August 15. After conferring at the Embassy, Aldrich lunched with Eden while Dulles dined with the British and French Foreign Ministers.[23]

THE LONDON CONFERENCE

The next morning Dulles held a staff meeting † at Winfield

* Dulles in a television appearance with the President stated that the United States had given no commitments as to what it would do if the London conference failed. But he also stressed that "moral forces" would prevail. Finer, *Dulles over Suez*, pp. 105–106.

** Eisenhower states in his autobiography that if the fate of Europe had to be placed at the whim of a dictator, "it was conceivable that the use of force under *extreme* circumstances was conceivable." Eisenhower, *Waging Peace*, p. 43.

† This group included, in addition to Aldrich, Charles Bohlen, Ambassador to the Soviet Union; C. Douglas Dillon, Ambassador to France; Herman Phleger, Legal Adviser to the State Department; Gordon Gray, Assistant Secretary of Defense; Robert Bowie of the State Department's

House prior to the opening of the conference, which took place at 11 a.m. at Lancaster House. The conference included 22 nations. Although Egypt was not represented, an "observer" for President Nasser kept close track of events from the Egyptian Embassy.[24]

The London sessions continued until August 23. The final result was that 18 nations subscribed to an Anglo-American-French declaration that asserted the principle of international control of the waterway, recognized the sovereign rights of Egypt, guaranteed her a fair return on use of the canal, and proposed a new convention under which operation of the canal would be supervised by a board composed of representatives of countries using the waterway.[25]

During this period, according to his appointment book, Aldrich entertained the Edens, the Harold Macmillans, and Foreign Minister Selwyn Lloyd at the Ambassador's residence, and he attended the reception for the Dulles party given at 10 Downing Street on August 20. On that occasion, Eden reportedly asked that Dulles lead a delegation to Egypt to explain the proposals emanating from the conference, but Dulles declined.[26]

The next evening, Eden and Lloyd joined Dulles and Aldrich at Winfield House to discuss the Egyptian mission. They agreed that Prime Minister Robert G. Menzies of Australia should be approached. As Dulles argued it, "he knows how to put a case." [27] Because he was a close personal friend of the Australian leader, Aldrich was delegated to call Menzies to the meeting at the American Ambassador's residence. It was then 2 a.m., and this was an assignment that would have trespassed on the bonds of even the closest friendship except

---

Policy Planning Staff; William Rountree, Deputy Assistant Secretary of State for Near Eastern, South Asian and African Affairs; Walworth Barbour, Deputy Chief of Mission, London Embassy; and Carl McCardle, Assistant Secretary of State for Public Affairs.

for the urgency of the occasion. Menzies, without knowing the reason for Aldrich's call, accepted it as an emergency, and arrived at Winfield House at 2:30 a.m. by Embassy car. A period of discussion followed, but the Australian would not accept a place on the committee until he had cleared his continued absence from Australia with his Deputy Prime Minister.[28] In the end this was arranged and Menzies led a five-man delegation to Cairo.* With this matter settled, Aldrich resumed his interrupted vacation, flying to the United States on August 24.

In a lengthy cable to Eisenhower, Eden professed himself pleased with the results of the London conference.[29] The American President, however, was becoming concerned as to whether Eden really cared about the results of the Menzies mission, a suspicion generated by information that the British and French were ordering evacuation of their nationals from Arab countries and that French troops were being stationed on Cyprus.[30]

According to Anthony Nutting, at that time the British Minister of State at the Foreign Office, the French and Israelis were, in fact, "planning a method of recapturing the Canal," and Nutting was warning Eden of the danger of associating Britain with this adventure. Nutting urged an approach via the United Nations, a course that had little appeal for Eden but was supported by Selwyn Lloyd as a desirable preliminary for whatever further action might be taken.[31] The British government finally decided that it would take the matter to the UN in the event the Menzies mission failed.[32]

Suez Canal Users Association

Meanwhile, Dulles had proposed a new approach to the

---

* The delegation consisted of Menzies, Loy Henderson (USA), Dr. Ardalau (Iran), Ato Aklilou Hapte-wold (Ethiopia), and Osten Enden (Sweden). Menzies, *Afternoon Light*, pp. 160–161.

whole problem involving the formation of a Suez Canal Users Association (SCUA) that would operate the Canal and collect the dues pending a longer term settlement. The British feared that pilotage required such skills that a pilots' walkout would close down the Canal. The SCUA plan therefore proposed to provide the technical know-how in such an eventuality, as well as to unite the maritime powers using the waterway. Eden immediately assumed that this plan had been devised by Dulles for the purpose of justifying the use of force if Egypt would not cooperate; [33] Dulles, on the other hand, viewed it solely as an honest collective endeavor to solve a difficult problem. [34]

Eden on September 12 jubilantly presented his interpretation of SCUA to the House of Commons. Although Aldrich did everything he could to warn Eden that this interpretation of Dulles' motives was erroneous, [35] the American Ambassador was unsuccessful. As it turned out, Eden's misunderstanding of Dulles' purposes in SCUA was crucial in the train of events that followed the making of that proposal.

Earlier, on September 3, Eisenhower had told Eden that American public opinion rejected the use of force in the settlement of the Canal question, [36] but this warning from the American President had failed to destroy Eden's key assumptions, or self-deceptions, about the American position. In an extended message to Eisenhower on September 6, the British Prime Minister made it clear that he regarded Nasser as comparable to Hitler and that, if necessary, Britain would not shrink from the use of force to deal with him. "We have many times led Europe in the fight for freedom," the Prime Minister said, "It would be an ignoble end to our long history if we elected to perish by degrees." [37]

Eden pointed out on this occasion that the two Western leaders had made very different assessments of the threat posed by Nasser. However, Eisenhower later wrote that while he agreed with much that Eden had said, he differed on the conclusion that the alternatives lay solely between immediate use of force or demise.[38] Delay therefore became even more firmly entrenched as a basic American strategy in the hope that time would help to clarify the situation.

Aldrich returned to London on September 11 and met that afternoon with Prime Minister Menzies, who had just returned from his unsuccessful mission to Cairo. Menzies had reported to Eden that Nasser interpreted Eisenhower's public statements to mean that Britain could not count on American support for the use of force. This interpretation of the American President's position had encouraged the Egyptian leader in rejecting SCUA and rebuffing Menzies.[39] The Australian Prime Minister discussed with the American Ambassador every phase of his talks with Nasser.[40]

The walkout of Canal pilots occurred on September 14, but the British fears that this would force the closing of the Canal proved baseless. Hastily recruited pilots, including even some Americans, kept the traffic moving in better fashion than before.[41] This, in Eisenhower's opinion, rendered the basic assumption of the SCUA plan meaningless. And, as he later put it, the "thought of using force, under these circumstances, was almost ridiculous."[42] Nevertheless, the consequences of the walkout in terms of Canal navigation were still unclear when a conference to discuss implementation of the SCUA plan convened on September 19.

Eden has written that he, and some of his Ministers, had grave doubts about going ahead with Dulles' plan. However, after much soul-searching he decided that since the Americans had taken the initiative and since he desired to maintain as united a front as possible, he would take responsibility for moving into an exploration of SCUA, meanwhile deferring an appeal to the United Nations.[43] Contributing to this decision was the fact that Britain was intent on preventing Nasser from collecting any Canal tolls. Although the Americans had professed themselves unable to prevent these payments by private American companies, Eden hoped that SCUA would provide the answer to this problem.[44] As it turned out, however, this was not to be the case.

The SCUA Conference adjourned after two days, and Nasser refused to have anything to do with the plan. (Eden thought that Dulles' statement to the effect that there were "no teeth" in the Users' Plan encouraged Nasser's unrelenting stand.[45]) Nevertheless, the ambassadors of the SCUA nations in London were instructed to go ahead with organizing the Association. Aldrich, who was of course involved, thought this move would not accomplish anything.[46] Dulles apparently still believed that Britain would not attack Egypt because British opinion was divided.[47]

THE UNITED NATIONS

The British and French now decided it was time to go to the United Nations. Egypt did likewise, and the United States endorsed putting both petitions on the calendar. However, Washington was undecided whether the British and French were merely seeking window dressing for an impending military effort, or were genuinely interested in seeking peace. Neither country had bothered to keep Dulles currently informed of their intended UN action, though the possibility had been outlined in general terms some time before the actual move was made.[48]

On September 26 Eden and Lloyd flew to Paris to confer with their French opposite members. Without revealing a maturing French-Israeli plan for an attack on Egypt, the French leaders reportedly informed Eden that there would soon be an occasion to use force but that moves in the UN and SCUA were necessary preliminaries.[49]

At the UN Security Council meeting in New York the Egyptian Foreign Minister gave some indication that his country might cooperate with SCUA,[50] but the French and British ended any possibility of negotiation to this end by insisting on a vote that Russia felt compelled to veto. As Anthony Nutting of the British Foreign Office saw it, the French government had by this maneuver achieved its aim of showing the world that a stalemate existed between Egypt and Russia on the one hand and Britain and France on the other.[51]

THE FRENCH PLAN FOR AN ATTACK ON EGYPT

According to Nutting, the French took the initiative to pressure Israel into agreeing to attack Egypt and thus to provide a pretext for France and Britain to move in, seize, and occupy the Canal. It was not until October 13–14, however, that French emissaries outlined this plan to Eden and Nutting (Lloyd was still in New York). Eden did not give immediate assent to British participation, but Nutting, who was designated to deliver the British answer to Paris in 48 hours, believes Eden had already decided to cooperate with the French.[52]

Lloyd hurried home from the UN and advised against any such involvement. Before making a final decision, Eden decided that he and Lloyd should go to Paris instead of Nutting. Nutting shortly informed Lloyd that he would resign if Britain went through with the French plan.[53]

On October 22 Lloyd met with Israel's Ben Gurion at Sèvres outside Paris. The Israeli leader had major misgivings about the French plan and discussed them with Lloyd.[54] Eden, however, had apparently made his decision, and on October 23 he assured French Foreign Minister Pineau that Britain would support Israel.[55] Two days later Israel agreed finally to the plan and the British Cabinet resolved to go ahead. Lloyd informed Nutting: "Israel will attack through Sinai that evening [October 29] and the following morning we and the French will issue an ultimatum to her and Egypt to clear the Canal Zone for us to move our troops in. Egypt will, presumably, refuse and directly she does so we shall start bombing Egyptian airfields." Nutting decided that he would have to resign rather than defend these actions as a member of the Cabinet.[56]

During this period there was an ominous silence from the usual sources of American information that could have helped in devising a strategy to cope with the situation. While Lloyd was still in New York, Dulles had cabled several of his ambassadors, including Aldrich, asking for any information they might have on what Israel was planning to do in view of her mobilization and the growing uncertainty about her intentions. Aldrich replied that he had a dinner date with Lloyd for October 28 and would query him. On that occasion, Walworth Barbour, Aldrich's deputy, and Harold Beeley, the Foreign Office expert on the Middle East, were also present.[57] The British Cabinet, of course, had already agreed to the French plan and knew exactly what Israel's role in it was to be. Furthermore, it had already been agreed that as a "cover story," Britain would officially warn Israel that if her mobilization were directed against Jordan, Britain would have to fulfill her treaty obligations to the latter country.

This was the story given Aldrich by Lloyd on October 28, and he persisted in it under pointed questioning by the American Ambassador. Aldrich seemed magnanimous when he later wrote that: "Since no ambassador can admit that he does not credit the statements of the Foreign Secretary of the country to which he is accredited, I have always taken the position, in spite of later evidence to the contrary, Mr. Lloyd did not deliberately mislead me." [58] Nevertheless, from that time on,

Aldrich made it a practice to draft all telegrams to Washington jointly with Walworth Barbour and to have him present during all conversations with the British.[59]

The following day, as planned, Israel launched her attack on Egypt. What happened next as far as the American Ambassador to London was concerned is best told in his own words:

The next day, October 29, on hearing the news of the Israeli attack on Egypt, I asked at once for an appointment with Mr. Lloyd. At 10 a.m. the day following, he and Mr. Beeley met with me and Mr. Barbour in the Foreign Office. I asked Mr. Lloyd what the British Government intended to do in view of Israel's action. He replied that he thought Her Majesty's Government would immediately cite Israel before the Security Council of the United Nations as an aggressor against Egypt. Surprising as it may be in retrospect, that was his exact statement. He added that the French Prime Minister and Foreign Secretary were on their way to London and that the British Government would want to discuss the situation with them before taking action, as they wished to act in concert with the French. Moreover, he said, the British had shipping and cargo of great value in the Canal and it would be necessary to take this into consideration. Mr. Lloyd concluded by saying that he could not tell me definitely what action the British would take until after the meeting which was to be held at once, but that he would inform me of the decision immediately after luncheon. I reported Mr. Lloyd's statements to Washington by cable and arranged to keep a telephone line open to Washington for further communications.

At 1:30 p.m. Mr. Lloyd's private secretary called James Moffett, my private secretary, and said that Mr. Lloyd would have to go directly to the House of Commons after luncheon, so he could not see me at the time arranged. However, Sir Ivone Kirkpatrick, Permanent Under Secretary of the Foreign Office, would see me at 4:45 and tell me exactly what had been decided. When I saw Sir Ivone at the appointed hour, he started the interview by handing me two sheets of foolscap paper. When I asked what they were he replied, "They are ultimatums, one addressed to Israel and the other to Egypt." I then read the documents and asked whether the demand that Egypt withdraw all armed forces to a point ten miles from the Canal meant that these forces must withdraw to a point ten miles west of the Canal. He replied, "To points ten miles away from the Canal on both sides." After reading these ultimatums, I expressed the opinion that Egypt could not possibly accept the conditions addressed to her. At this, Sir Ivone simply shrugged his shoulders. I then asked whether they had been already served and he replied, "Yes. The ultimatum to Egypt was served at 3:20 p.m. and that to Israel at 3:30 p.m., in each case on their Ambassadors in London."

I asked if the ultimatums had been made public and he answered, "Yes. The Prime Minister is making the announcement in the House at the present moment."

"In that case," I said, "the only thing I can do is telephone the contents of these documents to Washington immediately, but of course the President and the Secretary of State will have already learned of this action taken by Her Majesty's Government on the news services."

It is worth noting that the ultimatum stated that the British and French intended to go in and occupy Port Said, Ismailia and Suez whether or not the Egyptians and Israelis complied with the demand that they withdraw their forces from the vicinity of the Canal. When Mr. Barbour and I telephoned the news to Washington we were, as expected, met by the statement that it had already appeared on the news tickers. The only thing we could contribute was to read the actual text of the ultimatums to the State Department.*[60]

*At the time these events took place, Aldrich had no idea that collusion between the French and British had been involved. Even a decade later when he wrote the article from which the extended quotation above was

Eisenhower, who had a full campaign speaking schedule at this critical time, was returning to Washington each evening to keep abreast of events. On the evening of October 29 the White House announced that the United States was taking the Israeli attack to the UN Security Council in the morning and stood ready to honor its pledge under the Tripartite Declaration of 1950.[61]

Meanwhile, the British Cabinet worked through the night on the next British steps, and Eden sent off a message to Eisenhower, embodying the Cabinet's invitation for general American support.[62] This message crossed one from Eisenhower stating his dismay that the British would not join the United States before the United Nations in condemning the Israeli attack. Further messages passed back and forth in what Eisenhower later termed "a sort of transatlantic essay contest."[63] The two countries were at loggerheads on the situation even before word of the Anglo-French ultimatums had been received in Washington. When this news came by public wire, Eisenhower was furious. Dulles was described by an observer as "close to apoplexy."[64]

WAR AND PEACE MOVES

In the United Nations the United States had already introduced a resolution calling for an Israeli-Egyptian cease-fire, for Israel to withdraw its forces behind armistice lines, and for all members of the UN to refrain from the use of force in the area or any other assistance to Israel until she complied with the resolution. Russia voted with the United States for this resolution, while Britain and France voted against it. A Russian resolution to the same ends was similarly vetoed.[65]

---

taken, there was no documentation of it. The subsequent appearance of Nutting's book, however, confirmed the fact of collusion from the personal experience of a top member of the British Foreign Office.

The Anglo-American alliance in whose behalf Aldrich had worked all his adult life had seemingly collapsed.

For Aldrich, the job of Ambassador now became the difficult one of interpreting Eisenhower's, Dulles's, and UN Ambassador Henry Cabot Lodge's moves to the British government. As Eden's relations with Dulles and Eisenhower reached their nadir, it was Aldrich who managed to keep the top-level lines of communication between the two governments open. In addition, he was active in the various efforts to evacuate Americans from Egypt, to unblock the Suez Canal, and to establish an emergency oil supply route to Europe.[66]

On November 1 the French and British ultimatums expired, and the two allies began their attack on Egypt. The next day the UN General Assembly accepted a softened version of the cease-fire resolution defeated in the Security Council on October 30. France and Britain, however, declined a cease-fire unless the UN would guarantee it and also "satisfactory arrangements" concerning the Suez Canal.[67]

On November 4 the UN General Assembly adopted a Canadian resolution asking the Secretary General to submit a plan for an emergency UN force to obtain and supervise a Middle East cease-fire. Next, the Afro-Asian countries sponsored a resolution renewing the cease-fire directive and calling for compliance within 12 hours. Three days later a cease-fire went into effect in the Canal zone. A UN Emergency Force landed in Egypt on November 15 and was ordered to take up truce supervision positions in the Port Said area November 20.[68]

Israeli, French, and British forces were still in Egypt, and the Russians were making the most of the situation. On November 23 the Russian Foreign Minister called for immediate and unconditional withdrawal of the invading forces and demanded that the "aggressors" pay the costs of maintaining the UN force and of clearing the Canal. On the same day the Afro-Asian countries' resolution requiring withdrawal of the invading forces "forthwith" came up for a vote. In this connection, Aldrich felt that the United States' UN representative, Ambassador Lodge, did more to damage Anglo-American relations than anything that had happened thus far.[69]

The requirement for withdrawal "forthwith" was equivalent to almost "instantaneously," and the language had been placed in the resolution with this intent.[70] Paul-Henri Spaak of Belgium, however, had introduced an amendment that would have eliminated the preemptory wording.

At this time, Aldrich was visiting Lord Salisbury at the Conservative Party leader's country place. He recalls that he was contacted by Robert Murphy, who informed him over the telephone that the State Department was instructing Ambassador Lodge to vote for the Belgian Amendment and, if it should fail, not to vote for the Afro-Asian resolution. Aldrich considered this information so important that it should be heard firsthand not only by Lord Salisbury but also by Harold Macmillan and R. A. Butler. Accordingly the necessary telephone connections were arranged, and the British Cabinet members listened as Murphy again outlined the United States' position on the impending vote. As Aldrich later put it, "With the news that the United States would support this [Belgian] amendment, I went to bed in a happier frame of mind than at any time since the crisis started."[71]

Unfortunately, the optimism engendered by this trans-Atlantic telephone call was undercut in the General Assembly the next day. Ambassador Lodge refrained from voting on the Belgian Amendment, which would have permitted French and British withdrawal in an orderly fashion and without humiliation. Instead, he voted for the Afro-Asian resolution with its demand for withdrawal "forthwith."[72] Aldrich did not believe that the State Department could have reversed itself after making such an explicit statement of position to him and members of the British Cabinet. On the other hand, he never learned by what authority Lodge voted as he did.[73]

Deterioration of Anglo-American Relations

The Suez Crisis created the severest strain that Anglo-American relations had experienced in many decades. Many observers felt that the unfortunate course of events had been significantly influenced by the poor health of the leaders on both sides of the Atlantic. Dulles was hospitalized during this critical period and Eisenhower had taken over the management of relations with the various parties to the Crisis. Eden was also ill. On November 23 he left England for a recuperative visit to Jamaica, turning his responsibilities over to a caretaker group headed by Butler and Macmillan.

By this time the lines of communication between Washington and London at the highest level had virtually broken down. Eden had sought a conference with Eisenhower for himself and French Prime Minister Mollett on November 7. At first the American President had agreed, but, apparently on the advice of the State Department, he had then reversed himself.[74] This snub to the United States' NATO partners added to the unexpectedly strong anti-American sentiment developing in Britain.

After the UN's adoption of the Afro-Asian resolution on withdrawal of British troops, over a third of the Conservative Party's members of Parliament met to draft a resolution condemning American policy and protesting the party leadership's yielding to it.[75] In view of these developments, it was fortunate for the United States that Aldrich was on excellent personal terms with both Butler and Macmillan, as well as Lord Salisbury. As a result, he was in as good a situation as any American Ambassador could have been in trying to repair the damaged relations between the two countries.

Official Washington, however, remained unrelenting. Pressure on the British pound had mounted steadily in the immediate wake of the Suez attack, and it had been an important factor in the British decision to agree to a cease-fire.[76] The monetary pressure continued to be acute, and American Secretary of the Treasury George Humphrey saw it as a lever to encourage British withdrawal from Egypt.[77] This tactic, combined with the oil shortage in Western Europe that resulted from the closing of the Canal and the fact that American companies were in the best position to relieve it, added to the pressure on the British government to terminate its Egyptian adventure.

There were also counter forces at work. The impending NATO meeting, scheduled for December 10, made it desirable for the United States to offer prompt concessions on financial aid if Britain would close out her Suez involvement. Washington had also begun to fear that under mounting pressure, the Conservative government might collapse with unpredictable consequences.[78] Therefore, despite the strained relations that existed between the two NATO partners, there were compelling reasons on both sides for resolving their differences — and quickly. On December 3 Lloyd announced in the House of Commons that a phased withdrawal of troops from Egypt was being initiated.[79] The way was thus cleared for American financial aid, and the first step had been taken toward restoring the alliance.

ALDRICH ENDS HIS AMBASSADORSHIP

During Prime Minister Eden's absence from England, Aldrich had kept in close touch with both Macmillan and Butler. By the time Eden returned to London on December 14, the worst of the crisis in Anglo-American relations was over and Aldrich was ready to end his ambassadorship.

When he had undertaken the London mission, Aldrich had not expected to remain there for an extended period. As a matter of course, the reelected President had the Ambassador's resignation, but as badly as Aldrich wanted to return to the United States, he did not propose to do so until the Suez difficulty had been resolved. And, for the reasons outlined above, it was highly unlikely that his resignation would have been accepted before that time. By December this obstacle had been removed, and Eisenhower accepted Aldrich's request to be relieved.

Immediately after Christmas, John Hay Whitney was announced as Aldrich's successor.[80] While awaiting Whitney's arrival in London, the outgoing American Ambassador continued to work actively to heal the wounds resulting from the Suez Crisis. On January 7, 1957, for example, he called on Selwyn Lloyd to explain the recent Eisenhower statement to Congress on Middle East policy that asked authority for economic and military aid to countries in that troubled area seeking to maintain their independence. Lloyd avoided giving any official reactions, reportedly stating that American policy did not address itself to the current issues in the Middle East as he saw them.[81] One reason for Lloyd's caution was illuminated the next day when Eden submitted his resignation to the Queen. Within 48 hours she had summoned Harold Macmillan to form a new Cabinet.

Aldrich and the new Prime Minister had developed a warm personal friendship that brought them together on many more occasions than performance of their official duties required. Evidence of their cordial relationship was the fact that the retiring Ambassador lunched with the Macmillans once and called on the Prime Minister three times within a fortnight during January 1957.[82]

Aldrich's departure for home had now been set for February 1. The preceding days were filled with official and social farewell visits, climaxed by luncheon with the Queen on January 31 and the traditional Pilgrims' dinner to the retiring American Ambassador that evening.

The dinner was held at the Savoy, with the Earl of Halifax, a former British Ambassador to the United States, presiding, and Prime Minister Macmillan among the distinguished guests gathered to honor Aldrich. The after-dinner toasts and speeches were prefaced by the reading of a message from President Eisenhower, who took advantage of the occasion not only to congratulate and thank his Ambassador but also to stress that he regarded the Anglo-American partnership as unshaken by recent events. In Eisenhower's words: "As Ambassador Aldrich has sought to strengthen the traditional Anglo-American alliance, it is fitting he be honoured by a group which has contributed so much to that cause. The presence of Prime Minister Macmillan is further evidence of the abiding strength of the partnership between our two countries. To our public servants on both sides of the Atlantic who bravely hold the vision of a working peace among nations, I offer my congratulations and deepest thanks." [83]

This message set the theme for the remarks made by Halifax, by Prime Minister Macmillan, and by Aldrich. The first in proposing his toast declared that Aldrich had performed his duties well under some trying circumstances. Most important to the relationship between the two countries, Halifax said, was the fact that the retiring Ambassador had been constantly concerned "without fear, favour, or prejudice, to maintain the true two-way traffic of interpretation, interpreting the United States to the United Kingdom and the United Kingdom to the United States." [84]

When the Prime Minister rose to pay "my personal tribute to a very dear friend," Macmillan further documented the role that Aldrich had played. Referring to the strains and tensions of the preceding few months, the Prime Minister said:

> Faced with this situation, Ambassador Aldrich had a unique opportunity and he took it. To my personal knowledge I can tell you that he has played a remarkable and indeed an historic role during these anxious weeks. We owe him a debt which we cannot easily repay, and I like to think that his countrymen will feel that they should be equally grateful for what he has done. This is not the time to reveal the whole of this story, but I would say this. At such a time an Ambassador has to be completely loyal to the policies and purposes of his own Government. Yet he has the task of interpreting with sympathy and knowledge the views of the Government to which he is accredited. This task our guest performed with conspicuous success. And it is largely because of what he did during this period that I look forward with such confidence to the complete and successful re-establishment of our relations upon the old level.[85]

On this pleasant occasion Aldrich could easily have chosen to avoid the subject of the late difficulties between the two countries. Instead, he made this delicate question the central focus of his response to the Prime Minister and Halifax. He did so in a context that he introduced in these words: "I trust that you will permit me to speak in a very personal manner about my own views and feelings concerning the relations of our two countries. I am assuming this privilege on the ground that I have been an outstanding advocate of a strong and active Anglo-American partnership all my life. My appointment as Ambassador to this country came as the culmination and, I might say, crowning of hopes and views which I have held for many, many years." He then proceeded to emphasize his belief, which he felt was shared by the great majority of Americans, that the "alliance" with Britain was a cornerstone of United States foreign policy and essential to protection of his country's own interests and its position in the world. In fact, the degree to which this had been true on both sides of the Atlantic had, he suggested, contributed to the misunderstanding over Suez. "We had each fallen so completely into the habit of thinking in terms of the multitude of things that bind us together that we had lost our sensitivity to other compelling interests and obligations of each of us which could have the effect of forcing us apart." [86]

As he saw it, the difficulty over Suez had not been one of respective national goals but of means. The actions of Britain had been understood in the United States and there was no resentment as a result of it. He did not believe the same was true in Britain. "It is our act which has been misunderstood here," he bluntly told his British audience. Each country, however, had to reappraise its relations with the other. "I think that we must start by recognising that there were faults on both sides. Honest self-criticism by both of us can help to clear the air. We must also give our most earnest thought to appraising the realities of our own and others' situations, to gain a better understanding of the influence which *must* determine our policy decisions," Aldrich said.[87]

It was clear from the forthright language and the directness with which Aldrich addressed the problem of Anglo-American relations that he was speaking from deep personal conviction. It was equally clear that his remarks were motivated by a deep-seated respect, indeed admiration, for the British and confidence in the fruitfulness of their partnership with the United States in world affairs. "I do not envisage Anglo-American policies as merely an endeavor to hold some kind of line, but as a concerted effort to break new ground and to bring into being a new and greater measure of well being, security and opportunity for ourselves and for others," he said. There was no doubt in his mind that the alliance would continue. "The need for it is imperative, and our every instinct and tradition impels us in that direction. But we cannot afford to take our co-operation for granted. We must work together to create the conditions in which we can function most effectively." [88]

On this positive and optimistic note, Aldrich ended the exposition of his views on the meaning of the partnership to which he had devoted so many years of his life in both private and public capacities. The next morning he boarded the liner *United States* bound for home and the retirement that his service as ambassador had postponed more than four years. The *New York Times* took editorial note of the event a few days later and, complimenting Aldrich on the effectiveness of his ambassadorship, quoted from his Pilgrims' speech his prescription for the continuance of the Anglo-American friendship: "Let us seek to construct a working partnership that cannot again be betrayed by the shock of events. The test of our partnership should not be an unreal perfectionism that accepts no deviation whatsoever, but the healthy capacity to accept with mutual respect the occasional divergencies which must arise between us." [89] The editorial might well have added that these words summarized Aldrich's personal philosophy as well as his prescription for the conduct of international affairs.

CHAPTER XVI

The Vital Link

IN RETIREMENT Winthrop Aldrich has maintained his zest for life and his interest in the many causes to which he devoted so much time during his working career. He has continued active behind the scenes in many areas of civic and philanthropic importance. The trips abroad have continued but for social rather than for business purposes, and the changing seasons find the Aldriches in their accustomed locations and beloved retreats: Dark Harbor in the summer; Providence in the spring and fall; Nassau in the winter; with longer or shorter interludes at their New York apartment. In his eighties, Aldrich remains mentally alert and physically active. He and Mrs. Aldrich enjoy chartering a yacht and cruising the Maine coast or the Caribbean. Like most parents and grandparents, they take great interest in the activities of their childen and joy in their grandchildren. If one were designing a lifetime existence full of rewarding experiences, one could do much worse than choose the Aldriches for a model. More important, in terms of his career as a lawyer, banker, and diplomat, Aldrich has demonstrated in a variety of contexts how a single individual can act as a vital link between groups, causes, and even governments.

Winthrop Aldrich is unquestionably a man of unusual ability and a person who has put his talents to effective and significant use. He was endowed with the physical stamina, the intellectual curiosity and ability, and a drive and determination that have enabled him to perform many varied and demanding roles with an unstudied grace and calm effectiveness that many gifted and able people have envied. The common denominator of comments by all Aldrich's colleagues interviewed for this biography was that he had courage. This seemed to be the most distinctive and also the most necessary attribute for the Chase National Bank's chairmanship. The examples already cited are numerous, but perhaps of all those reviewed the action that took the most moral courage — given Aldrich's position in banking — was to call for the separation of commercial and investment banking in 1933. Perhaps the most dramatic example of his physical courage was flying the Atlantic in wartime to inspect British war relief activities.

Aldrich's native intellectual abilities were sharply honed by his training and experience as a lawyer. He reasons quickly, logically, and incisively, and he has an unusual memory for facts, dates, places, people, and events. His rational powers, coupled with the creative spark reflected in his painting and in his innovative approach to legal and business problems, make a most formidable combination. Although these characteristics might be overpowering even in a peer group, they are relieved by a sense of humor and by an interest in people as individuals.

Mr. Aldrich was outstandingly successful in his leadership at the Chase. He picked up the reins of power at a crucial time in the bank's affairs. While financial solvency was never an issue, the legacy of serious problems and the tarnished image of the world's largest commercial bank were matters of major importance. The personal abilities that he brought to that difficult situation fitted its requirements uniquely. His leadership at the Chase in the 1930s would alone have established his reputation as a banker, but in the succeeding years he continued to build solidly on those early accomplishments. In the process he served the entire commercial banking community by his leadership in various groups that influenced the environment of banking, legislatively and otherwise. He always preferred this use of his influence to the direct participation in politics that had appealed to his father.

In his position on New Deal policies Aldrich was explicit, consistent, and constant. There are few who would maintain that the New Deal had either a monopoly of the "right" answers to the depression or was an unqualified success in reviving the economy. Aldrich must be credited with an unflinching dedication to the proposition that the ultimate answer lay in personal initiative and the exercise of personal responsibility. And, he lived by what he preached.

In his internationalism Aldrich was very much in tune with the Roosevelt administration and its successors, and in this respect he was a leader among American bankers. His emphasis, long before the end of World War II, on the need for postwar financial aid to Britain and later his support for the Marshall Plan were soundly based and forward looking, as was his leadership in the International Chamber of Commerce. His early, sustained, and successful effort to organize relief for the victims of global war was an impressive demonstration of how to mobilize large private resources for the relief of human suffering. His internationalism, and more particularly his long-standing attachment to Britain and the British, helped him to win his appointment as Ambassador to the Court of St. James's, where for these very reasons he was an effective representative of the United States.

Aldrich was also active in domestic movements of broad social consequence. His connection with the Tuskegee Nor-

mal and Industrial Institute is a case in point. In this instance,
as in many others, like the American Heritage Foundation, he
was able through his own example and initiative to develop
interest and support for an important undertaking by acting
as a vital link between private individuals and groups.

Founded in 1881, the Institute was the creation of Booker
T. Washington, the outstanding Negro leader who perceived
the importance of education to the future progress of his
race. During the mid-1920s, Chellis Austin, at that time president of the Seaboard National Bank, was asked to help in
fund-raising for the Institute. He accepted this request and
did his usual competent job, in the process developing an
interest that led to his continued association with the Institute as a trustee and as chairman of its Finance Committee.[1]
Upon Austin's untimely death, Aldrich succeeded him in
the presidency of the Equitable Trust Company, as described
earlier, and in April 1930 he was also elected to Austin's place
on the Tuskegee Board and Finance Committee.[2] In this way,
as was so often the case, a seemingly unrelated series of events
came to a focus and presented Aldrich with a new opportunity
and challenge. In this particular instance it led to an association that has continued down to the present and resulted in
Aldrich's being awarded an honorary degree by Tuskegee
in 1967.

As befitted his special expertise, Aldrich's most direct contributions to Tuskegee have been in the management of its
financial affairs. When the Equitable Trust was merged into
the Chase National, the Chase took over the job of guiding the
Institute's investments. George Warren of the Chase Trust
Department developed a special interest in this activity and,
at Aldrich's suggestion, also was elected a trustee.[3] At Aldrich's invitation, the trustees and officers of the Institute
held their annual meetings at the Chase and lunched in its
private dining room. Although it would not cause any com-

ment today, Aldrich knew he was setting a precedent and risked criticism in 1931 when he invited Negroes to be his guests on occasions of this kind.[4]

As Tuskegee enlarged its activities and added to its programs, which came to include graduate training, Aldrich was afforded additional opportunities to serve as a vital link with other business leaders in fund-raising. In the midst of World War II, when so much of Aldrich's time and energy was being devoted to the National War Fund, Dr. F. D. Patterson, head of Tuskegee, urged him to accept the post of Treasurer of the United Negro College Fund Drive.[5] Despite the many demands on him at this particularly difficult time, this was the kind of appeal Aldrich could not ignore. The service begun in 1943 lasted until he resigned from all such activities upon his appointment as Ambassador, but it was resumed upon his return to the United States from Britain.

As in most of Aldrich's activities, friends and colleagues from other areas of his interest were also involved in this one. They included John D. Rockefeller, Jr., who was chairman of the Fund Drive's national advisory committee at the time Aldrich joined it; Jesse Jones, head of the Reconstruction Finance Corporation, a friend with whom Aldrich had cooperated in the depths of the 1933 banking crisis; Walter Gifford of American Telephone and Telegraph on whose board Aldrich served; Thomas D'A. Brophy with whom he was associated in the National War Fund; Jeremiah Milbank, counsel and director of the Chase; and numerous other business leaders with similar kinds of connections.

In the fall of 1952 Aldrich took the initiative in acquainting a number of prominent businessmen with the programs and financial needs of southern Negro colleges at first hand. To this end he conceived the idea of a tour that would visit Atlanta University and Tuskegee. The tour was a complete success. Aldrich reported that it had been "tremendously

inspiring," and the director of the organization mobilizing
resources for Negro colleges stated that the experience had
been a reciprocal one as far as the institutions were concerned.[6]

The public furor over problems of Negro education and
integration erupted shortly after this trip and has continued
with varying degrees of intensity. In the course of public
debate and federal legislation on the problem, private efforts
of long standing have either been forgotten or derided. Nevertheless, the fact that they existed and were supported by men
like Aldrich is evidence that the cutting edge of public responsibility was anticipated by business leaders with a sense
of private responsibility for an underprivileged element of
society. In this respect Aldrich's association with Negro education illustrates the range of his interests; at the same time
the ways in which he became involved in this endeavor illus-
trate the varied processes through which his activities prolif-
erated.

The significance of Aldrich's career, viewed by a contemporary biographer, lies most clearly in its example of the
role of individual responsibility and leadership in a changing
world — a world characterized by increasing interdependence
of nations, of great technological achievement, yet one plagued
by crises, confusion and uncertainty about the appropriate
goals of personal and national life and the paths that must be
followed to achieve them. In the midst of convulsive change,
Aldrich proved himself a capable leader in his chosen field,
law; in his adopted field, banking; not to mention his favorite
sport, yachting; and in major philanthropic, relief, and civic
projects. Comparable opportunities for leadership were denied him as Ambassador, but in a moment of major crisis in
Anglo-American relations he stepped into the breach to act
as a vital link between the two governments during a brief but
critical period. And in all these capacities he never lacked

certainty about the relevant goals or the appropriate strategy. As a result, he never had difficulty in making even the most important decisions.

In conclusion, it appears that Aldrich possesses leadership qualities that are not unique except as he has employed them in relation to time, place, and opportunity. What is most unusual is the expanse of the arena in which he has applied them, and the broad purposes to which he has put them. The ultimate value of this biography, then, rests in the challenge that it poses to present and potential business leaders — and to those who must seek out and develop such men — to perceive their responsibilities, as Aldrich has, in terms of forging the vital links between and within the private and public sectors of the nation and between the past and the future.

APPENDIX

BIBLIOGRAPHY

NOTES

INDEX

APPENDIX

Articles, Public Statements, and Speeches of Winthrop W. Aldrich, 1933–1959

1933

February 22	"The Causes of the Present Depression and Possible Remedies," Testimony before the Finance Committee, U.S. Senate, Washington, D.C.
March 8	Statement re Divorcement of Security Affiliates.
November 29	"Suggestions for Improving the Banking System," Testimony before the Sub-Committee of the U.S. Senate Committee on Banking and Currency, Washington, D.C.
December 5–6	"Current Banking Questions," Testimony before the U.S. Senate Committee on Banking and Currency, Washington, D.C.

1934

November-December	Informal address during western tour.
December 3	"The Financing of Unemployment Relief," Address before The Commonwealth Club of San Francisco, California.

1935

May 15	"Proposed Banking Act of 1935," Testimony before the Sub-Committee of the U.S. Senate Committee on Banking and Currency, Washington, D.C.
December 11	"Business Revival and Government Policy," Address before the Chamber of Commerce, Houston, Texas.

1936

April 2   "The Control of Credit," Address before the Academy of Political Science, New York.

May 7   Speech on Election as President of the Chamber of Commerce of the State of New York, New York City.

May 22   "Foreign Trade and Our National Interests," Address at World Trade Luncheon under the auspices of the Merchants Association of New York City, Astor Hotel, New York City.

July 10   "An Appraisal of the Federal Social Security Act," Address before the Institute of Public Affairs, University of Virginia, Charlottesville, Virginia.

October 22   Remarks at Trustees' Meeting of the United Hospital Campaign, Chamber of Commerce Building, New York City.

November 12   "The Responsibilities of Business Leadership," Address before the 168th Annual Banquet of the Chamber of Commerce of the State of New York, Waldorf-Astoria Hotel, New York City.

December 8   "Business Recovery and Government Policy — National and International," Address before the 39th Annual Dinner of the Illinois Manufacturers' Association, Chicago, Illinois.

December 11   Remarks at Essay Contest at the New York State Chamber of Commerce.

1937

January 4   "Aldrich Urges Steps to Safeguard Recovery," Statement for release by the New York State Chamber of Commerce.

January 21   "Government Intervention in the Field of Credit," Address before the Rhode Island Bankers Association, Providence, R.I.

March 4   "The Constitution and the Supreme Court," Address at the monthly meeting of the Chamber of Commerce of the State of New York.

March 24	Address at the 30th Anniversary Dinner of the Economic Club, New York City.
May 25	Statement re the Death of Mr. John D. Rockefeller, Press release of the Chamber of Commerce of the State of New York.
October 14	"The Stock Market from the Viewpoint of a Commercial Banker," Address before the Rochester Chamber of Commerce, Rochester, New York.
November 18	"Causes of the Present Business Depression," Address before the 169th Banquet, New York State Chamber of Commerce, Waldorf-Astoria Hotel, New York City. Reprinted in the Chamber of Commerce of the State of New York *Monthly Bulletin*, XXIX (November, 1937).

1938

January 3	"Aldrich Analyzes Business Recession in Relation to Government Policy," Press release of the New York State Chamber of Commerce.
February 14	"Banks now in Strong Position," Article published in the *Daily Telegraph and Morning Post*, London, England.
February 27	"America's Interest in Foreign Trade," Radio Address under joint sponsorship of Economic Policy Committee and N.B.C. over WJZ, New York City.
March 30	"Research — Its Importance to Bankers," Address before the Association of Reserve City Bankers, Belleair, Florida.
April 26	Statement to the Press by sixteen business leaders re cooperation with the President.
May 2	"The Reciprocal Tariff Policy and the Proposed Government Spending Programme," Address before the Annual Dinner Meeting of the American Section of the International Chamber of Commerce, Mayflower Hotel, Washington, D.C.
May 5	Remarks upon retiring from the Presidency of the New York State Chamber of Commerce. Reprinted

in the Chamber of Commerce of the State of New York *Monthly Bulletin*, XXX (May, 1938).

July 6   "Sweden and the United States," Address at Banquet for the Crown Prince and Princess of Sweden, Waldorf-Astoria Hotel, New York City.

October   Remarks at the first meeting of the Committee on Finance of the International Chamber of Commerce, Paris, France.

October 3   "The University as an Instrument of Social Progress," Address at the 40th Anniversary and Dedicatory Exercises of Northeastern University, Boston, Mass.

October 31   Address transmitted by trans-Atlantic telephone from Berlin, Germany, to the Luncheon of the 25th National Foreign Trade Convention.

November 18   Radio Address over WJZ, New York City.

November 22   Remarks at Dedicatory Ceremonies of the National Advisory Committees Building at the New York World's Fair.

December 12   Address to the New York Economic Club, New York City.

1939

January   *The Consensus*, XXIII (January, 1939). Aldrich speech recorded.

February 13   "The Banking Outlook for 1939," Article published in the Financial Supplement of the *Daily Telegraph and Morning Post*, London, England.

April   "Currency and Trade Campaigning for a World Monetary Order," *World Trade* (April, 1939), pp. 13–23.

April 10   Statement issued for use at opening dinner of the Campaign for Citizens' Committee for Planned Parenthood.

May 11   Address at a dinner in honor of the Honorable Sir Ronald Lindsay, British Ambassador and the Right Honorable Robert S. Hudson, M.P.

May 20	Radio Address on "University Life" over station WOR, New York City
May 23	Address at luncheon meeting of the Bond Club of New York, New York City.
May 27	"The Effect of Easy Money Policies on Savings, Savings Institutions, Insurance Companies, Endowed Institutions, and Commercial Banks," Address before the Annual Convention Dinner of the Field Managers of the Metropolitan Life Insurance Co., Waldorf-Astoria Hotel, New York City.
June 3	"The Incompatibility of Democracy and a Planned Economy," Address at the 138th Commencement Exercises of Washington and Jefferson College, Washington, Pennsylvania.
Summer	"World Trade and the Fair," *Think* (Summer, 1939), pp. 26, 56.
July 21	"French Exhibit at New York World's Fair will Mark Traditional Friendship of France and the United States," *Le Temps* (July 21, 1939), p. 30.
August	*The Coupon*, LX (August, 1939), published by the Bond Club of New York. Aldrich speech recorded.
August 16	"Voluntary Action and Government Compulsion in Democracy," Address before the Congress on Education for Democracy, Waldorf-Astoria Hotel, New York City.
October 19	Address before the Advisory Conference on Financial Research, National Bureau of Economic Research, New York City.

1940

January–February	"Correct Evils of Old Methods of Education, Aldrich Says," *Ideas*, a publication of the Nassau County Tuberculosis and Health Association, X (January–February, 1940), pp. 1, 7.
March 10	Statement for the Salvation Army's special issue booklet, "Diamond Jubilee."

April 5	"An Appraisal of the Salvation Army," Address before the final report luncheon of the Diamond Jubilee Drive, The Bankers' Club, New York City.
April 29	Address before the International Chamber of Commerce, Mayflower Hotel, Washington, D.C.
May 1	"Report on Research Program," Address before the Association of Reserve City Bankers, Hot Springs, Virginia.
	"The Present Day Gold Problem," *Chapter Notes*, a publication of the New York Chapter of the American Institute of Banking, XXX (May, 1940), pp. 182–185. Reprinted in *The Chicago Banker* (May 4, 1940), and *The Boston Banker* (June, 1940).
September 28	Statement for use in special issue, *Editor and Publisher*.
October 10	Remarks at presentation of the Goodrich Award for Distinguished Service, Goodrich Arena, New York World's Fair Grounds.
October 15	Radio Address re the Selective Service Bill, over WEAF, New York City.
December 6	Extemporaneous address at dinner of the St. Nicholas Society, Plaza Hotel, New York City.
December 12	"The Public Debt and the Private Citizen," Address before the Boston Chamber of Commerce, Boston, Mass.

1941

January 14	Supplementary Statement made at the Annual Meeting of the Chase National Bank, New York City.
March 7	Extemporaneous address at the British War Relief Society Banquet, Dallas, Texas.
May 5	"Report on the Research Program of the Banking Research Fund," Address before the Association of Reserve City Bankers, Hershey, Pennsylvania.

May 26	Remarks on behalf of the Campaign for United Service Organizations, New York State Chamber of Commerce.
September 25	Remarks at exercises to commemorate the signing of the Bill of Rights, Sub-Treasury Building, New York City.
October 7	Introductory Remarks as Toastmaster, World Trade Dinner of National Foreign Trade Council, Hotel Pennsylvania, New York City.
October 30	Extemporaneous remarks at luncheon for British War Relief Society, Columbia Club, Indianapolis, Indiana.

1942

February 7	Extemporaneous remarks on receipt of the New York Chapter of the American Institute of Banking Annual Award, Hotel Astor, New York City.
April	Statement for use in the United Service Organizations Campaign Drive.
April 27	"Report on Research Program of the Banking Research Fund," Address before the Association of Reserve City Bankers, Hershey, Pennsylvania.
May 4	Extemporaneous remarks, 70th Anniversary Luncheon, State Charities Aid Association, Commodore Hotel, New York City.
May 18	Remarks on the 150th Anniversary of the New York Stock Exchange, Sub-Treasury Building, New York City.
June 6	Extemporaneous remarks re British War Relief Society and Community Chests, luncheon meeting, Cincinnati, Ohio.
June 15	Remarks at United Service Organizations Rally, sponsored by the New York Chamber of Commerce, Sub-Treasury Building, New York City.
August 27	Extemporaneous remarks re trip to England at British War Relief Society luncheon, Bankers Club, New York City.

September 2	Remarks on Trip to England at Dinner in his honor given by Mr. Thomas I. Parkinson, Metropolitan Club, New York City.
September 9	Remarks on Trip to England at dinner for officers of the Chase National Bank, Hotel Pennsylvania, New York City.
September 23	Remarks on Trip to England at Open Forum in the office of Calvin Bullock, 1 Wall Street, New York City.
September 24	Remarks on Trip to England at British Luncheon Club, 53 Broadway, New York City.
November 9	Remarks at Piccadilly Arcade, 6 East 57th St., New York City.
November 24	Remarks at British War Relief Society, Labor Committee dinner, Hotel Astor, New York City.
November 27	Radio Interview in connection with exhibit on The History of Counterfeit Money in cooperation with the United States Secret Service.
December 1	Address before the Women's Luncheon, British War Relief Society, Biltmore Hotel, New York City.
December 17	Remarks at Economic Club Dinner, Astor Hotel, New York City.

1943

January 21	"The Economic Implications of Internal Public Debts," Address before the Annual Midwinter Banquet, Connecticut Bankers Association, New Haven, Connecticut.
February 25	Remarks at Economic Club Dinner, Astor Hotel, New York City.
March 3	Remarks before French Chamber of Commerce and French Institute Dinner, Waldorf-Astoria Hotel, New York City.
March 7	Statement on the origin and objectives of the National War Fund, Inc., before a group of Community Chest executives, Hotel Commodore, New York City.

April 1   Remarks at Economic Club Dinner, Astor Hotel, New York City.

April 29   "The Problem of Postwar Monetary Stabilization," Address before the American Section of the International Chamber of Commerce, Waldorf-Astoria Hotel, New York City.

May 6   "Savings and War Finance," Address at the Annual Business Meeting of the National Association of Mutual Savings Banks, Waldorf-Astoria Hotel, New York City.

May 21   Radio talk on the National War Fund for the National Maritime Day Program, N.B.C., New York City.

June 2   Commencement Address, Foxcroft School, Middleburg, Virginia.

June 8   Remarks at Economic Club Dinner, Hotel Astor, New York City.

June 22   Address at Russian War Relief Rally, Chicago Stadium, Chicago, Illinois.

June 24   Remarks at National War Fund Luncheon, Radison Hotel, Minneapolis, Minnesota.

June 25   Address at Russian War Relief Rally, Randall Island Stadium, New York City.

June 30   Remarks at Founders' Meeting of the New York Committee of the National War Fund, Council Chamber, City Hall, New York City.

July 14   Remarks at Meeting of War Activities Committee of the Motion Picture Industry, Waldorf-Astoria Hotel, New York City.

October 5   Remarks at the "Tribute to Gallantry," Dinner of the National War Fund, Waldorf-Astoria Hotel, New York City.

October 7   Remarks at Queen's County National War Fund Committee Dinner, Forest Hills Inn, Forest Hills, Long Island, New York.

October 16   Remarks at Nassau County National War Fund Commitee Dinner, Piping Rock Club, Locust Valley, Long Island, New York.

November 12	Radio Address re National War Fund, station WOR, New York City.
November 23	Remarks at Economic Club Dinner, Hotel Astor, New York City.
December 6	Remarks to Women's Committee, National War Fund, St. Regis Hotel, New York City.
December 17	Remarks at National War Fund Final Report Luncheon, Hotel Pennsylvania, New York City.

1944

February 7	Remarks Welcoming State Leaders of National War Fund, Waldorf-Astoria Hotel, New York City.
February 10	First Annual Report by the President of the National War Fund, Board of Directors Meeting, Waldorf-Astoria Hotel, New York City.
March 8	Remarks at Economic Club Dinner, Hotel Astor, New York City.
April 2	Extemporaneous remarks at the launching of the *S.S. Nelson W. Aldrich*, Providence, Rhode Island.
May 9	Remarks at Economic Club Dinner, Hotel Astor, New York City.
July 2	Remarks before the Postwar Small Business Credit Commission, Waldorf-Astoria Hotel, New York City.
September 15	"Some Aspects of American Foreign Economic Policy," Address before the Executive Club, Chicago, Illinois.
September 20	Remarks at the opening Dinner of the New York War Fund Drive, Waldorf-Astoria Hotel, New York City.
September 26	Remarks at Luncheon of the Community and War Fund of Chicago, Hotel Sherman, Chicago, Illinois.
October	"The Problem of the Postwar World," *The Lee Traveler* (Camp Lee, Virginia), October, 1944.
October 9	Annual Report by the President of the National

	War Fund, Board of Directors Meeting, Waldorf-Astoria Hotel, New York City.
October 9–11	"World Trade and Currency Stabilization," *The Journal of Commerce*, Special issue for the National Foreign Trade Convention, October 9–11, 1944.
October 11	Extemporaneous remarks, National Foreign Trade Convention Luncheon, Hotel Pennsylvania, New York City.
October 15	"For Our Own and for Our Allies," *New York Times Magazine* (October 15, 1944), p. 13.
October 20	"Importance of Liberal Trading Policies," *Printers' Ink*, CLX (October 20, 1944), p. 32.
November 13	"The 'Key Nation' Approach to the Problem of Currency Stabilization," "Currency Relations Among Nations, a Report," Addresses before the International Business Conference, Rye, New York.
December 27	Remarks at National War Fund Dinner, Waldorf-Astoria Hotel, New York City.

1945

January	"Women's Postwar Future in Banking," *Magazine of the New York State Federation of Business and Professional Women's Clubs* (January, 1945).
February 13	"Aldrich Outlines World Chamber's Future Program," *Journal of Commerce*, annual Shipping and Foreign Trade Number, February 13, 1945.
February 20	Remarks at New York War Fund Annual Report Luncheon, Commodore Hotel, New York City.
March 29	Press release re "New Charter for Labor and Management."
April 12	Statement to the Press on the Death of President Franklin D. Roosevelt.
April 13	Radio Address on behalf of United National Clothing Collection, Station WMCA, New York City.

April 18	Extemporaneous remarks at opening meeting of the campaign committee of the United Negro College Fund, Rockefeller Center, New York City.
April 30	Annual Report by the President of the National War Fund, Board of Directors Meeting, Waldorf-Astoria Hotel, New York City.
May 8	Press statement re V–E Day.
June 6	"The Bases for World Trade," Address before the Canadian Manufacturers Association, Toronto, Canada; Remarks to a group of businessmen, Royal York Hotel, Toronto, Canada.
June 14	"The Work of the International Chamber of Commerce," Address before the American Section of the International Chamber of Commerce, Waldorf-Astoria Hotel, New York City. Repeated in Radio Address, Station WEAF, New York City.
June 16	Remarks on receipt of Honorary Degree, Lafayette College, Easton, Pennsylvania.
June 26	Remarks at a luncheon in his honor given by Thomas J. Watson, Union Club, New York City.
August	"The American Conscience in Action," *Facts* (August, 1945). "A Question of Our Own Capacity for Leadership," *Think* (August, 1945), pp. 12–13.
August 16	Address of Welcome delivered at the Council meeting of the International Chamber of Commerce, London.
August 20	Radio Address re International Chamber of Commerce, B.B.C., London, England.
	"The Objectives of the International Chamber of Commerce," Address before the American Chamber of Commerce, London, England.
September 27	Remarks re European trip to Board of Directors of the Federal Reserve Bank, New York City.
	Remarks at National War Fund Agencies Dinner, Waldorf-Astoria, New York City.

October 4	"The Future Program of the International Chamber of Commerce," Address before the Chamber of Commerce of the State of New York, New York City. Radio Address, Station WJZ, New York City.
October 5	Address at the opening of the 1945 Campaign of the New York National War Fund, Hunter College, New York City.
December 7	"The Problem of British Credits," Address before the International Session of the Fiftieth Annual Congress of American Industry, New York City.

1946

February 4	Annual Report by the President of the National War Fund, Board of Directors Meeting, Waldorf-Astoria Hotel, New York City.
March 13	"Proposed Credit to the United Kingdom," Testimony before the Senate Committee on Banking and Currency, Washington, D.C.
May 2	"The Control of Inflation," Address before the Annual Convention Dinner of the Illinois Bankers Association, Jefferson Hotel, St. Louis, Missouri.
May 14	"The International Chamber of Commerce," Address before the U.S. Associates of the International Chamber of Commerce, Waldorf-Astoria Hotel, New York City.
May 17	"The Anglo-American Financial Agreement," Address before the Annual Luncheon Meeting of the Boston Chamber of Commerce, Boston, Mass.
June 4	"The Problem of European Reconstruction," Address before the Alumni Luncheon, Columbia University, New York City.
June 20	Address before the 64th Meeting of the Council of the International Chamber of Commerce, Paris, France.
October 14	"International Economic Policy and the Future of Business," Address before a luncheon session

of the Boston Conference on Distribution, Boston, Mass.

November 11 Address before the luncheon session of the National Foreign Trade Convention, Waldorf-Astoria Hotel, New York City.

November 14 "World Business will give active help to United Nations Work, Says Aldrich," Press release, U.S. Associates of the International Chamber of Commerce.

December 3 Address before the meeting of the Council of the International Chamber of Commerce, Paris, France.

December 22 "See no Likelihood that Next Recession will Resemble the 1930–1933 Depression," Press release, U.S. Associates of the International Chamber of Commerce.

December 24 "The Economic Basis for Peace," *The Daily Telegraph and Morning Post* (December 24, 1946), p. 4.

1947

January 2 "Comprehensive Employment Program Outlined as Means to Moderate the Business Cycle," Press release, U.S. Associates of the International Chamber of Commerce.

January 8 "The International Chamber of Commerce and the Economic and Social Council," Article sent to the Instituto di Economia Internazionale, Genoa, Italy.

March 15 Statement for inclusion in *World Trade* (March 15, 1947).

March 17 "The International Chamber of Commerce and Expanding World Trade," Address at Havana, Cuba.

March 26 Luncheon address at a meeeting of the American Chamber of Commerce for Brazil, Rio de Janeiro.

March 31 "The International Chamber of Commerce and Expanding World Trade," Rio de Janeiro, Brazil.

The same speech was given also on the following date at the places shown:

April 7	Montevideo, Uruguay.
April 11	Buenos Aires, Argentina.
April 18	Santiago, Chile.
April 23	Lima, Peru.
April 28	Caracas, Venezuela.
May 2	"International Chamber Says State Trading Nations Should Show How They Can Fit into World Trade Body," Press release, U.S. Associates of the International Chamber of Commerce.
May 5	"International Chamber urges Policy Changes to make Germany Self-Supporting," Press release, U.S. Associates of the International Chamber of Commerce.
May 6	"The International Chamber of Commerce and the Economic and Social Council of the United Nations," Address before the annual Dinner Meeting of the U.S. Associates of the International Chamber of Commerce, Waldorf-Astoria Hotel, New York City.
June 2	"Freedom and Economic Progress," Address before the Eleventh Congress of the International Chamber of Commerce, Montreux, Switzerland.
June 30	Statement to the Press on return from Europe.
July 11	Statement re Senate Resolution 111, restricting travel, submitted to the Senate Committee on International and Foreign Commerce.
September 5	Remarks at the christening of the "Freedom Train" engine, Schenectady, New York.
September 16–17	Remarks at "Freedom Train" ceremonies, Philadelphia, Pennsylvania.
September 24	Remarks at "Freedom Train" ceremonies, Grand Central Terminal, New York City.
September 30	"American Interest in European Reconstruction," Address before the 73rd Annual Convention of

the American Bankers Association, Atlantic City, New Jersey.

Remarks at dinner of the New York University–Bellevue Medical Center, Waldorf-Astoria Hotel, New York City.

October 6 Radio Address re significance of the Freedom Train, station WRUL, World Wide Broadcasting Co.

November "The American Heritage Program," *The Public Relations Journal*, III (November, 1947), pp. 9–12.

1948

March 4 Press release re Death of Gordon Rentschler.

March 8 "The Importance of Thrift," Press release for publicity in connection with Savings Bond Drive.

March 18 "Inflation in Europe," Address in support of the Treasury Department's Savings Bond Drive, Washington, D.C.

April 26 Remarks before the Greater New York Fund Dinner, Astor Hotel, Washington, D.C.

May 19 Press statement re Community Chest, Cleveland, Ohio.

"The Foreign Assistance Act of 1948," Address before a luncheon meeting of the Cleveland Chamber of Commerce and Cleveland World Trade Association.

May 20 Remarks on the Freedom Train before the Society of Mayflower Descendants, 122 East 58th St., New York City.

June 14 "Economic Significance of Postwar Changes in Commercial Bank Portfolios," Address before the 52nd Annual Convention of the New York State Bankers Association, Bretton Woods, New Hampshire.

October 13 Address before the Pilgrims of the United States Dinner, Waldorf-Astoria Hotel, New York City.

November 3 Remarks at the Annual Dinner of the Chamber of

Commerce of the State of New York, Waldorf-Astoria Hotel, New York City.

November 22   "Capital Formation and the Equity Market," Address before a dinner meeting of the Association of Stock Exchange Firms, Hotel Commodore, New York City.

December 28   "The Management of the Public Debt," Address before a joint session of the American Finance Association and the American Economic Association, Hotel Cleveland, Cleveland, Ohio.

1949

January   "A Message to the Bankers of America," *Banking* (January, 1949).

February 16   "The Electric Utility Industry and the National Economy," Address before a dinner sponsored by the Westinghouse Electric Corporation, Pittsburgh, Pennsylvania.

April 26   Extemporaneous remarks before the American Chamber of Commerce, Excelsior Hotel, Rome, Italy.

May 23   "Economic Problems of Western Europe," Address at a luncheon of The Pilgrims, Savoy Hotel, London, England. Reprinted in the *Sunday Times* under the title, "Beyond the Marshall Plan."

August 9   Testimony re Point IV Program, Senate Committee on Banking and Currency, Washington, D.C.

1950

September 20   Remarks at dinner of the America-Italy Society in honor of Count Sforza, Waldorf-Astoria Hotel, New York City.

1951

February 13   Radio Address re Philharmonic Membership Drive, C.B.S., New York City.

July 30	Statement for use in the Defense Bonds Program, Savings Bond Division, U.S. Treasury.
September 17	Remarks at dinner in honor of The Lord Mayor and Lady Mayoress of London, Union Club, New York City.
November 15	"Inflation — Everyman's Responsibility," Address before a luncheon meeting of the Austin Chamber of Commerce, Austin, Texas.

1952

September 26	Short talk re American Heritage Register and Vote Campaign, recorded at N.B.C., New York City.
November 19	"The Basis for a New Foreign Economic Policy," Address before the World Trade Dinner of the 39th National Foreign Trade Convention, Waldorf-Astoria Hotel, New York City.
November 30	Press statement re announcement of appointment as Ambassador to the Court of St. James's.

1953

February 11	Press statement on arrival in London as Ambassador.
March 19	Address before The Pilgrims, Savoy Hotel, London.
April 1	Address before the English-Speaking Union, Dorchester Hotel, London.
April 21	Address before the Canada Club, Savoy Hotel, London.
May 7	Address at Newspaper Press Fund Dinner, Grosvenor House, London.
June 12	Address at Dedication of Kresge-Aldrich Halls, Graduate School of Business Administration, Harvard University, Boston, Mass.
June 23	Address before the British National Committee of

	the International Chamber of Commerce, Dorchester Hotel, London.
July 3	Remarks at the presentation of a portrait of Edward Winslow to Lord Bailliue, at the English-Speaking Union, London.
	Address before the American Society Independence Day Dinner, Dorchester Hotel, London.
July 24	Address before Civic Dinner, Manchester, England.
July 25	Address at the opening of "U.S.A. Today," Manchester, England.
July 30	Address at the unveiling of John Paul Jones Tablet at Kirkbean, Kircudbrightshire, Scotland.
August 27	Address at luncheon of the English-Speaking Union, Edinburgh, Scotland.
August 30	Remarks at award of First Golden Laurel Trophy to Sir Alexander Korda, Edinburgh, Scotland.
September 17	Remarks at Forfeit Feast, Sheffield, England.
September 29	Remarks at American Chamber of Commerce Luncheon, Grosvenor House, London.
November 4	Off-the-Record Talk to Harvard Club, English-Speaking Union, London.
November 9	Statement before the U.S. Commission on Foreign Economic Policy, Paris, France.
November 26	Thanksgiving Day Remarks before the American Society of London.
December 3	Off-the-Record Talk to the British-American Forces Dining Club, London.
December 5	Response to Toast at King's College, Cambridge, England.
December 8	Address at the Annual Dinner of the Farmers' Club of London.

1954

| February 4 | Address to students of the Imperial Defence College, London. |

February 15	Address at Cardiff, Wales.
February 19	Remarks at the Royal Society of Painter-Etchers and Engravers, London.
March 1	Address before the Insurance Institute of London.
March 26	Address before the Chamber of Commerce, East Anglia.
April 28	Address before the Association of American Correspondents, London.
May 10	Address before the Chamber of Commerce, Birmingham, England.
May 25	Address before a luncheon of the City Livery Club, London.
June 9	Remarks at the Opening of the Antique Dealers' Fair, London.
June 10	Remarks at Westminster Abbey.
July 5	Address before the American Society Dinner, Dorchester Hotel, London.
July 24	Address at Ye Fyshinge Feaste, Plymouth, England.
July 26	Remarks at The Middle Temple, London.
October 5	Remarks at Reception for Marshall Scholars, Lancaster House, London.
October 14	Address before the Board of Trade, New York City.
November 11	Address at International Night of the City of Leeds.

1955

January 27	Address at the opening ceremony of the Commercial and Local Government Reference Library, Derby House, Liverpool.
February 2	Off-the-Record Remarks at the Constitutional Club, London.
February 18	Address before the Chamber of Commerce, Glasgow, Scotland.

March 1	Address at the Imperial Defence College, London.
March 9	Toast at the Livery Dinner of the Worshipful Company of Fishmongers, London.
March 21	Toast at the Annual Dinner of the Worshipful Company of Coachmakers and Coach Harness Makers, Mansion House, London.
March 22	Off-the-Record Remarks at the Junior Carlton Club, Pall Mall, London.
March 24	Address before the Royal Empire Society, London.
March 25	Remarks at a Dinner of the Reserve Officers Association, London.
April 18	Address before the Rotary International, London.
June 2	Remarks at the Opening of the "Atoms for Peace" Exhibition, London.
June 3	Remarks at Harvard Dinner, Emmanuel College, Cambridge, England.
June 9	Toast at Dinner in Honor of Mayor Wagner, Fishmongers Hall, London.
June 22	Remarks at opening of Currier and Ives Exhibition, London.
July 4	Grace given at the American Society Dinner, London.
July 6	Remarks at City Hall Luncheon, Belfast, Ireland. Address at Vice Chancellor's Dinner, The Queen's University, Belfast, Ireland.
September 26	Remarks at presentation of a plaque from American War Correspondents to the B.B.C., London.
September 28	Remarks at the opening of Washington Old Hall, Durham.
September 30	Remarks introducing the Minister of Defence, Reserve Officers Association Dinner, London.
October 12	Address before Traders House Dinner, Glasgow, Scotland.
November 30	Toast at the Royal Society of London.
December 9	Toast of the Dockland Settlements, Mansion House, London.

1956

April 19	Address before the Warwickshire Rotary Clubs, Coventry, England.
May 11	Remarks at Fulbright Reception, London.
May 14	Remarks at Graduation Ceremony, University of Liverpool.
May 17	Remarks at 11 Downing Street, London.
May 23	Remarks at National War College, London.
May 24	Address at College of Arms, London.
May 31	Remarks at Kodak House, London.
July 11	Remarks before American Center, P.E.N., Guildhall, London.
July 16	Remarks at dedication of the American Military Cemetery, Cambridge, England.
September 25	Remarks at inauguration of the Transatlantic Telephone Cable Service, Lancaster House, London.
October 5	Remarks at the opening of the Pilgrim Fathers' Memorial Church, London.
October 31	Toast at the Annual Dinner of the Royal Society of St. George, London.
November 3	Address before the Inaugural meeting, Geynedd Branch, English-Speaking Union, Bangor, Wales.
November 22	Toast at American Society Thanksgiving Dinner, London.
December 20	Remarks at Virginia 350th Anniversary Ceremonies, English-Speaking Union, Blackwall, London.

1957

January 7	Remarks at the opening of President Eisenhower's "Open Skies for Peace," Exhibit, London.
January 31	Address before The Pilgrims, Savoy Hotel, London.
February 1	Remarks in press interview, Southampton, England.

March 28	Address on Suez Crisis at a dinner in his honor given by Mr. Sunderland, Union Club, New York City. Repeated at dinners in his honor on the following dates:
April 13	Governors' Dinner, Knickerbocker Club, New York City.
April 25	James Bruce's Dinner, The Brook Club, New York City.
April 26	Harvard Class of 1907 Dinner, Harvard Club, New York City.
June 8	Address at Commencement Exercises, Stevens Institute of Technology, Hoboken, New Jersey.

1959

October 21	Address at Convocation, Brown University, Providence, Rhode Island.

BIBLIOGRAPHY

Books

Allen, Frederick L. *The Lords of Creation*. New York: Harper & Brothers, 1935.

Anderson, Benjamin. *Economics and the Public Welfare*. New York: Van Nostrand, 1949.

Anderson, Benjamin. *The Postwar Stabilization of Foreign Exchange*. New York: Economists' National Committee on Monetary Policy, 1943.

Anderson, Clay. *A Half-Century of Federal Reserve Policymaking, 1914–1964*. Philadelphia: Federal Reserve Bank of Philadelphia, 1965.

Austin, Edna P. *A Gallant Gentleman: The Life of Chellis A. Austin*. New York: The John Day Co., 1932.

Batsell, Walter R. *The Debt Settlements and the Future*. Paris: Lecram Press, 1927.

Bayne, Samuel G. *Derricks of Destiny: An Autobiography*. New York: Brentano's, 1924.

Beal, John R. *John Foster Dulles, A Biography*. New York: Harper & Brothers, 1957.

Beckhart, Benjamin H. *The New York Money Market*. 4 Vols. New York: Columbia University Press, 1931–1932.

Bendix, Ludwig. *The Aldrich Plan in Light of Modern Banking*. New York: Robert R. Johnston, 1912.

Blum, John Morton. *From the Morgenthau Diaries: Years of Crisis, 1928–1938*. Vol. I. New York: Houghton Mifflin, 1959.

Bolton, Reginald P. *From Sheep Pasture to Skyscraper.* New York: The Equitable Trust Co., 1926.

Books in the Library of Nelson W. Aldrich, Warwick, Rhode Island. 2 parts. Boston: The Merrymount Press, 1914–1916.

Brigham, Herbert O. and Mary H. *Ancestry of Nelson Wilmarth Aldrich and his wife Abby Pearce Truman Chapman.* Providence, 1938.

Broehl, Wayne G., Jr. *The International Basic Economy Corporation.* The National Planning Association, 1968.

Buley, R. Carlyle. *The Equitable Life Assurance Society of the United States, 1859–1964.* 2 Vols. New York: Appleton-Century-Crofts, 1967.

Burgess, W. Randolph. *The Reserve Banks and the New York Money Market.* Rev. Ed. New York: Harper & Brothers, 1936.

Burr, Anna Robeson. *The Portrait of a Banker.* New York: Duffield and Co., 1927.

The Centennial History of the Harvard Law School, 1817–1917. Cambridge: Harvard Law School Association, 1918.

Chandler, Lester V. *Benjamin Strong, Central Banker.* Washington: Brookings Institute, 1958.

Chapman, John M. *Concentration of Banking: the Changing Structure and Control of Banking in the United States.* New York: Columbia University Press, 1934.

Churchill, Randolph. *The Rise and Fall of Sir Anthony Eden.* London: MacGibbon & Kee, 1959.

Clark, Lawrence. *Central Banking under the Federal Reserve System; with Special Consideration of the Federal Reserve Bank of New York.* New York: The Macmillan Co., 1935.

Clifford, A. Jerome. *The Independence of the Federal Reserve System.* Philadelphia: University of Pennsylvania Press, 1965.

Coolidge, Harold J. and Robert H. Lord. *Archibald Carey Coolidge: Life and Letters.* New York: Houghton Mifflin Co., 1932.

Crafts, Prescott, Jr. *A Management Re-Examination of Expansion Overseas by American Banks.* New Jersey: Graduate School of Banking, Rutgers University, 1957.

Dana, Julian. *A. P. Giannini, Giant in the West — A Biography*. New York: Prentice-Hall, 1947.

David, Paul T., Malcolm Moor, Ralph Goldman. *Presidential Nominating Politics in 1952, The National Story*. Baltimore: The Johns Hopkins Press, 1954.

Davies, Wallace. *The New Deal and Business Recovery*. New York: Holt, Rinehart and Winston, Inc., 1960.

Drummond, Roscoe. *Duel at the Brink, John Foster Dulles' Command of American Power*. New York: Doubleday, 1960.

Dulles, Eleanor L. *The Bank for International Settlements at Work*. New York: The Macmillan Co., 1932.

Eccles, Marriner. *Beckoning Frontiers, Public and Personal Recollections*. New York: Alfred A. Knopf, 1951.

Eden, Anthony. *Full Circle*. Boston: Houghton Mifflin Co., 1960.
———. *The Reckoning*. Boston: Houghton Mifflin Co., 1965.

Eisenhower, Dwight D. *Mandate for Change, 1953–1956*. New York: Doubleday and Co., Inc., 1963.
———. *Waging Peace, 1956–1961*. New York: Doubleday and Co., Inc., 1965.

Eliot, Charles W. *Harvard Memories*. Cambridge: Harvard University Press, 1923.

Epstein, Leon. *British Politics in the Suez Crisis*. Urbana, Illinois: University of Illinois Press, 1964.

Fainsod, Merle and Lincoln Gordon. *Government and the American Economy*. New York: W. W. Norton & Co., Inc., 1941.

Farley, T. *The Edge Act and United States International Banking and Finance*. New Jersey: Rutgers University, 1962.

Feis, Herbert. *1933: Characters in Crisis*. Boston: Little, Brown and Company, 1966.

Finer, Herman. *Dulles over Suez: The Theory and Practice of His Diplomacy*. Chicago: Quadrangle Books, 1964.

Fish, Harvey. *The Inter-Ally Debts*. New York: Bankers Trust Co., 1924.

Fosdick, Raymond B. *John D. Rockefeller, Jr., a Portrait*. New York: Harper and Brothers, 1956.

Frederick, J. George. *A Primer of "New Deal" Economics*. New York: The Business Bourse, 1933.

Friedman, Milton, and Anna J. Schwartz. *A Monetary History of the U.S., 1867–1960.* Princeton: Princeton University Press, 1963.

Fusfeld, Daniel R. *The Economic Thought of Franklin D. Roosevelt and the Origins of the New Deal.* New York: Columbia University Press, 1956.

Gardner, Richard N. *Sterling-Dollar Diplomacy.* Oxford: Clarendon Press, 1956.

Garrison, Colonel Elisha. *Roosevelt, Wilson and the Federal Reserve Law.* Boston: The Christopher Publishing House, 1931.

Garwood, Ellen Clayton. *Will Clayton, A Short Biography.* Austin, Texas: University of Texas Press, 1958.

Giddens, Paul H. *Standard Oil Company (Indiana): Oil Pioneer of the Middle West.* New York: Appleton-Century-Crofts, 1955.

Glass, Carter. *An Adventure in Constructive Finance.* New York: Doubleday, Page & Co., 1927.

Gleisser, Marcus. *The World of Cyrus Eaton.* New York: A. S. Barnes and Co., Inc., 1965.

Godwin, George. *The Middle Temple: The Society and Fellowship.* London: Staples Press, Ltd., 1954.

Goldsmith (Goldschmidt), R. W. *The Changing Structure of American Banking.* London: George Routledge and Sons, Ltd., 1933.

Goold-Adams, Richard. *John Foster Dulles, a Reappraisal.* New York: Appleton-Century-Crofts, 1962.

Groseclose, Elgin. *Fifty Years of Managed Money: the Story of the Federal Reserve, 1913–1963.* London: Macmillan & Co., Ltd., 1965.

Hansen, Alvin. *America's Role in the World Economy.* New York: W. W. Norton & Co., Inc., 1945.

Harris, Seymour E. *Twenty Years of Federal Reserve Policy.* 2 Vols. Cambridge, Mass.: Harvard University Press, 1933.

Hawley, Ellis W. *The New Deal and the Problem of Monopoly; A Study in Economic Ambivalence.* Princeton, N.J.: Princeton University Press, 1966.

Heilperin, Michael. *International Monetary Reconstruction: The*

Bretton Woods Agreements. New York: American Enterprise Association, Inc., 1945.

Hepburn, A. B. *A History of Currency in the United States.* New York: The Macmillan Co., 1915.

Hiebert, Ray E. *Courtier to the Crowd: the Story of Ivy Lee and the Development of Public Relations.* Ames, Iowa: Iowa State University Press, 1966.

Horie, Shigeo. *The International Monetary Fund: Retrospect and Prospect.* New York: St. Martin's Press, Inc., 1964.

Hughes, Emrys. *Macmillan Portrait of a Politician.* London: George Allen and Unwin Ltd., 1962.

Hunt, Pearson. *Portfolio Policies of Commercial Banks in the United States, 1920–1939.* Cambridge, Mass.: Bureau of Business Research, 1940.

Hurd, Charles. *When the New Deal was Young and Gay.* New York: Hawthorn Books, Inc., 1965.

Ickes, Harold L. *The Secret Diary of Harold L. Ickes.* 2 Vols. New York: Simon & Schuster, 1953, 1954.

Jenks, Leland. *Our Cuban Policy: A Study in Sugar.* New York: Vangard Press, 1928.

Johnson, Allen, ed. *Dictionary of American Biography.* Vol. I. New York: Charles Scribner's Sons, 1928.

Jones, Jesse. *Fifty Billion Dollars.* New York: Macmillan Co., 1951.

Keller, Morton. *The Life Insurance Enterprise, 1885–1910.* Cambridge, Mass.: Harvard University Press, 1963.

Kimmel, Lewis H. *The Availability of Bank Credit, 1933–1938.* New York: National Industrial Conference Board, Inc., 1939.

Koenig, Louis W. *The Truman Administration, Its Principles and Practice.* New York: New York University Press, 1956.

Lamont, Thomas W. *Henry P. Davison.* New York: Harper and Brothers, 1933.

Laurence, J. S. *Banking Concentration in the United States: a Critical Analysis.* New York: Bankers Publishing Co., 1930.

Leffingwell, Russell. *Leffingwell's Papers, 1920–1950.*

Lewis, Oscar. *The Big Four.* New York: Alfred A. Knopf, 1938.

Loth, David. *The City Within a City: The Romance of Rockefeller Center*. New York: William Morrow and Co., 1966.

McCormick, Edward T. *Understanding the Securities Act and the S.E.C.* New York: American Book Co., 1948.

McDonald, Forrest. *Insull*. Chicago: University of Chicago Press, 1962.

McNaughton, Frank and Walter Heymeyer. *Harry Truman, President*. New York: McGraw Hill Book Co., Inc., 1948.

Menzies, Robert Gordon. *Afternoon Light: Some Memories of Men and Events*. London: Cassell & Co., Ltd., 1967.

————. *Speech is of Time*. London: Cassell & Co., Ltd., 1958.

Mintz, Ilse. *Deterioration in the Quality of Foreign Bonds Insured in the United States, 1920–1930*. New York: National Bureau of Economic Research, 1951.

Moley, Raymond. *After Seven Years*. New York: Harper & Brothers, 1939.

————. *The First New Deal*. New York: Harcourt, Brace, & World, 1966.

Morgenthau, Henry. *Germany is our Problem*. New York: Harper Brothers, 1945.

Morison, Samuel E. *The Development of Harvard University, 1869–1929*. Cambridge: Harvard University Press, 1930.

————. *Three Centuries of Harvard, 1636–1936*. Cambridge: Harvard University Press, 1936.

Muhleman, Maurice. *Monetary and Banking Systems*. New York: Monetary Publishing Co., 1908.

Murray, George W. *Random Jottings from a Long Memory*. Part I, Murray, Aldrich, and Webb. Privately Printed, March 8, 1937.

Nadler, Marcus and Jules I. Bogen. *The Banking Crisis: the End of an Epoch*. New York: Dodd, Mead and Co., 1933.

Nevins, Allan. *John D. Rockefeller; the Heroic Age of American Enterprise*. New York: Charles Scribner's Sons, 1940.

The New Monetary System of the United States. New York: National Industrial Conference Board, Inc., 1934.

Noyes, Alexander. *Forty Years of American Finance*. New York: G. P. Putnam's Sons, 1909.

Nutting, Anthony, *No End of a Lesson: The Story of Suez*. London: Constable and Co., Ltd., 1967.

Paris, J. D. *Monetary Policies of the United States, 1932–1938*. New York: Columbia University Press, 1938.

Payne, Robert. *The Marshall Story, a Biography of General George C. Marshall*. New York: Prentice Hall, 1951.

Peach, William Nelson. *The Security Affiliates of National Banks*. Baltimore: John Hopkins Press, 1941.

Pecora, Ferdinand. *Wall Street Under Oath*. New York: Simon and Schuster, 1939.

Perine, Edward T. *The Story of the Trust Companies*. New York: G. P. Putnam and Sons, 1916.

Pfeiffer, Timothy and George W. Jacques. *Law Practice in a Turbulent World*. New York: Charles P. Young Co., 1965.

Phillips, Cabell. *The Truman Presidency*. New York: The Macmillan Co., 1966.

Prescott, Marjorie Wiggin. *New England Son*. New York: Dodd, Mead & Co., 1949.

Price, Harry B. *The Marshall Plan and its Meaning*. Ithaca: Cornell University Press, 1955.

Randall, Clarence. *A Foreign Economic Policy for the United States*. Chicago: University of Chicago Press, 1954.

Redlich, Fritz. *The Molding of American Banking*. 2 Vols. New York: Hafner, 1951.

Rees-Mogg, William. *Sir Anthony Eden*. London: Rockcliff, 1956.

Ridgeway, George L. *Merchants of Peace: The History of the International Chamber of Commerce*. Boston: Little, Brown and Co., 1959.

Robertson, John Henry. *The Most Important Country: the True Story of the Suez Crisis and the Events Leading to It*. London: Cassell and Co., Ltd., 1957.

Robertson, Terrence. *Crisis: the Inside Story of the Suez Conspiracy*. New York: Atheneum, 1965.

Rochester, Anna. *Rulers of America: a Study of Finance Capital*. New York: International Publishers Co., Inc., 1936.

Rockefeller Center, Inc. *The Last Rivet*. New York: Columbia University Press, 1940.

Rodgers, Cleveland. *The Roosevelt Program*. New York: G. P. Putnam's Sons, 1933.

Roosevelt, Elliot. *F.D.R., His Personal Letters, 1928–1945*. 2 Vols. New York: Duell, Sloan, and Pearce, 1950.

Roosevelt, Franklin D. *On Our Way*. New York: The John Day Company, 1934.

Romasco, Albert. *The Poverty of Abundance: Hoover, the Nation, the Depression*. New York: Oxford University Press, 1965.

Roose, Kenneth D. *The Economics of Recession and Revival, An Interpretation of 1937–1938*. New Haven: Yale University Press, 1954.

Rothbard, Murray Newton. *America's Great Depression*. New Jersey: D. Van Nostrand Co., 1963.

Rovere, Richard. *The Eisenhower Years*. New York: Farrar, Straus, and Cudhay, 1956.

Satterlee, Herbert L. *J. Pierpont Morgan, an Intimate Portrait*. New York: Macmillan and Co., 1939.

Schlesinger, Arthur M., Jr. *The Coming of the New Deal*. Boston, Mass.: Houghton Mifflin Co., 1959.

Seymour, Harold J. *Design for Giving: The Story of the National War Fund, 1943–1947*. New York: Harper Brothers, 1947.

Sinclair, Upton. *Upton Sinclair Presents William Fox*. California: Upton Sinclair, 1933.

Smith, James G. *The Development of Trust Companies in the United States*. New York: Henry Holt, 1928.

Smith, Rixey and Norman Beasley. *Carter Glass*. New York: Longman's Green and Co., 1939.

Sprague, O. M. W. *History of Crisis under the National Banking System*. Washington: Government Printing Office, 1910.

Stephenson, Nathaniel. *Nelson W. Aldrich: a Leader in American Politics*. New York: Charles Scribners' Sons, 1930.

Studenski, Paul and Herman E. Krooss. *The Financial History of the United States*. New York: McGraw-Hill Book Co., 1963.

Swaine, Robert T. *The Cravath Firm and Its Predecessors, 1819–*

1948. Vol. II, *The Cravath Firm since 1906*. New York: Ad Press, Ltd., 1948.

Taft, Robert A. *A Foreign Policy for Americans*. New York: Doubleday and Co., Inc., 1951.

Thomas, Hugh. *Suez*. New York: Harper & Row, 1966.

Timberlake, Richard H., Jr. *Money, Banking, and Central Banking*. New York: Harper & Row, 1965.

Timmons, Bascom N. *Jesse H. Jones, The Man and the Statesman*. New York: Henry Holt & Co., 1956.

Tugwell, Rexford. *F.D.R.: Architect of an Era*. New York: The Macmillan Co., 1967.

U.S. Commission on Money and Credit. *A Progress Report, February, 1960*. New York: Committee on Money and Credit, 1960.

———. *Money and Credit: Their Influence on Jobs, Prices, and Growth*. New Jersey: Prentice-Hall, Inc., 1961.

Vanderbilt, Harold S. *Enterprise: The Story of the Defense of the America's Cup in 1930*. New York: Scribners' Sons, 1931.

Walker, Stanley. *Dewey; An American of this Century*. New York: McGraw-Hill Book Co., Inc., 1944.

Warburg, Paul M. *The Federal Reserve System, Its Origin and Growth*. 2 Vols. New York: The Macmillan Co., 1930.

Weissmar, Rudolph L. *The New Federal Reserve System: The Board Assumes Control*. New York: Harper & Brothers, 1936.

White, William S. *The Taft Story*. New York: Harper and Brothers, 1954.

Whittlesey, Charles R. *Banking and the New Deal*. Chicago: University of Chicago Press, 1935.

Wicker, Elmus. *Federal Reserve Monetary Policy, 1917–1933*. New York: Random House, 1966.

Wilbur, Ray L. and Arthur M. Hyde. *The Hoover Policies*. New York: Scribners' Sons, 1937.

Williams, John H. *Postwar Monetary Plans and Other Essays*. Oxford: Basil Blackwell, 1949.

Willis, Henry Parker and John M. Chapman. *The Banking Situation*. New York: Columbia University Press, 1934.

Willis, H. P. *The Federal Reserve System: Legislation, Organization and Operation.* New York: The Ronald Press Co., 1923.

Winkler, John K. *The First Billion.* New York: Vanguard Press, 1934.

Young, Harold H. *Forty Years of Public Utility Finance.* Charlottesville, Virginia: University Press of Virginia, 1965.

United States Government Publications

Commission on Foreign Economic Policy. *Report to the President and the Congress.* Washington: Government Printing Office, 1954.

———. *Staff Papers.* Washington: Government Printing Office, 1954.

Comptroller of the Currency. *Annual Report of the U.S. Comptroller of the Currency.* Washington: Government Printing Office, 1920–1935.

Department of State. *The Suez Canal Problem, July 26–September 22, 1956; a documentary publication.* Washington: Government Printing Office, 1956.

Department of the Treasury. *Documents and Statements Pertaining to the Banking Emergency.* 2 parts. Washington: Government Printing Office, 1933.

Economic Cooperation Administration. *A Report on Recovery Progress and U.S. Aid, 1949.* Washington: Government Printing Office, 1949.

Library of Congress (Legislative Reference Service). *Point Four, Background and Program.* Washington: Government Printing Office, 1949.

National Monetary Commission. *Publications of the National Monetary Commission.* 23 Vols. Washington: Government Printing Office, 1912.

Select Committee on Small Business. *Staff Report of the Board of Governors of the Federal Reserve System on Concentration of Banking in the United States.* Washington: Government Printing Office, 1952.

Temporary National Economic Committee. *Final Report and Recommendations.* Washington: Government Printing Office, 1941.

United States Statutes.

Federal Social Security Act, 49 Stat. 620 (1935).

Public Utility Holding Company Act, 49 Stat. 803 (1935).

Congressional Documents.

Congressional Record. Washington: Government Printing Office, September 21, 1944, February 2, 1953.

60 Cong., 2 Sess. House Committee on Banking and Currency. "Proposed Currency Legislation." *Hearings and Arguments.* Washington: Government Printing Office, 1908; *Hearings and Arguments on Senate Bill, No. 3023, An Act to Amend the National Banking Laws.* Washington: Government Printing Office, 1908.

63 Cong., 1 Sess. House Committee on Banking and Currency. "Changes in the Banking and Currency System of the United States." *Report.* Washington: Government Printing Office, 1913.

71 Cong., 3 Sess. Senate Committee on Banking and Currency. "Operation of the National and Federal Reserve Banking Systems." *Hearings.* Washington: Government Printing Office, 1931.

72 Cong., 1 Sess. Senate Committee on Banking and Currency. "Operation of the National and Federal Reserve Banking Systems." *Hearings.* Washington: Government Printing Office, 1932.

72 Cong., 1 Sess. Senate Committee on Finance. "Sale of Foreign Bonds and Securities in the United States." *Hearings.* 4 parts. Washington: Government Printing Office, 1932.

72 Cong., 2 Sess. House Committee on Interstate and Foreign Commerce. "Relation of Holding Companies to Operating Companies in Power and Gas Affecting Control." *Report*. Part I. Washington: Government Printing Office, 1933.

72 Cong., 2 Sess. Senate Committee on Finance. "Investigation of Economic Problems." *Hearings*. Washington: Government Printing Office, 1933.

73 Cong., 1 Sess. Senate Committee on Banking and Currency. "Securities Act." *Hearings*. Washington: Government Printing Office, 1933.

73 Cong., 1 Sess. Senate Committee on Banking and Currency. "Stock Exchange Practices." *Hearings*. 8 parts. Washington: Government Printing Office, 1933.

73 Cong., 2 Sess. Senate Committee on Banking and Currency. "Gold Reserve Act of 1934." *Hearings*. Washington: Government Printing Office, 1934.

74 Cong., 1 Sess. House Committee on Banking and Currency. "Banking Act of 1935." *Hearings*. Washington: Government Printing Office, 1935.

74 Cong., 1 Sess. Senate Committee on Banking and Currency. "Banking Act of 1935." *Hearings*. Washington: Government Printing Office, 1935.

74 Cong., 1 Sess. Senate Committee on Interstate Commerce. "Public Utility Holding Company Act of 1935." *Hearings*. Washington: Government Printing Office, 1935.

75 Cong., 3 Sess. Senate Special Committee to Investigate Unemployment and Relief. "Unemployment and Relief." *Hearings*. Washington: Government Printing Office, 1938.

76 Cong., 3 Sess. Senate. Temporary National Economic Committee. "Investigation of Concentration of Economic Power." *Hearings*. 37 Vols. Washington: Government Printing Office, 1939–1941.

79 Cong., 1 Sess. House Committee on Banking and Currency. "Bretton Woods Agreements Act." *Hearings*. Washington: Government Printing Office, 1945.

79 Cong., 1 Sess. Senate Committee on Banking and Currency.

"Bretton Woods Agreements Act." *Hearings*. Washington: Government Printing Office, 1945.

79 Cong., 1 Sess. Senate Committee on Banking and Currency. "Participation of the United States in the International Monetary Fund and the International Bank for Reconstruction and Development." *Report*. Washington: Government Printing Office, 1945.

79 Cong., 2 Sess. House Committee on Banking and Currency. "Anglo-American Financial Agreement." *Hearings*. Washington: Government Printing Office, 1946.

79 Cong., 2 Sess. Senate Committee on Banking and Currency. "Anglo-American Financial Agreement." *Hearings*. Washington: Government Printing Office, 1946.

80 Cong., 2 Sess. Senate Committee on Foreign Relations. "European Recovery Program." *Hearings*. Washington: Government Printing Office, 1948.

81 Cong., 1 Sess. Senate Committee on Banking and Currency. "Foreign Investment Guarantees." *Hearings*. Washington: Government Printing Office, 1949.

Periodicals

American Banker. 1930–1952.

American Economic Review. E. M. Bernstein, "A Practical International Monetary Policy," Vol. XXXIV (December 1944), pp. 771–784.

———. Ray G. Blakey and Gladys C. Blakey, "The Revenue Act of 1935," Vol. XXV (December 1935).

———. Frederick A. Bradford, "The Banking Act of 1935," Vol. XXV (December 1935), pp. 661–672.

———. Henry Bruere, "Constructive vs. Dollar Diplomacy," Vol. XIII (March 1923), pp. 68–76.

Bankers Magazine. 1911–1935.

Business History Review. Thomas V. DiBaco, "American Business and Foreign Aid: The Eisenhower Years," Vol. XLI (Spring 1967), pp. 21–35.

Business Week. "Wiggin is the Chase Bank and the Chase is Wiggin" (April 30, 1930), pp. 22–24.

———. "World's Biggest Bank Becomes World's Biggest Bond House" (August 13, 1930), p. 14.

———. "Deposit Insurance" (April 12, 1933), p. 3.

———. "Next, Morgan & Co." (April 12, 1933), p. 12.

———. "Bank Reform by Bankers" (April 26, 1933), pp. 6–8.

Federal Reserve Bulletin. 1930–1950.

Forbes. Winthrop W. Aldrich, "Proposed Banking Changes Would Hurt All," Vol. XXV (June 15, 1935), pp. 12–13.

———. Carter Glass, "Shall Bank Deposits be Pawns of Politics?" Vol. XXV (June 15, 1935), pp. 10, 31.

———. William H. Hillyer, "Men of Achievement — Winthrop Aldrich," Vol. LXI (January 15, 1948), pp. 18–19, 40.

Foreign Affairs. Winthrop W. Aldrich, "The Suez Crisis," Vol. XLV (April 1967), pp. 541–552.

———. Henry Morgenthau, Jr., "Bretton Woods and International Cooperation" (January 1945), pp. 128–194.

———. John H. Williams, "Currency Stabilization: American and British Attitudes" (January 1944).

———. John H. Williams. "Currency Stabilization: The Keynes and White Plans" (July 1943).

———. John H. Williams. "International Monetary Plans: After Bretton Woods" (October 1944), pp. 38–56.

———. H. D. White, "The Monetary Fund: Some Criticisms Examined" (January 1945), pp. 195–210.

Fortune. Fred Rodell, "Douglas over the Stock Exchange," Vol. XVII (February 1938), pp. 64–65, 116–126.

———. Russell C. Leffingwell, "How to Control Inflation," Vol. XXXVIII (October 1948), pp. 90–91, 135–137.

———. Tugwell, Rexford G., "Grass Did Not Grow," Vol. XIV (October 1936), pp. 115–117, 202–208.

———. Arthur H. Vandenberg, "The Republican Indictment," Vol. XIV (October 1936), pp. 110–113, 178–184.

————. Ernest T. Weir, "I Am What Mr. Roosevelt Calls an Economic Royalist," Vol. XIV (October 1936), pp. 118–122, 198.

————. "Biggest Banker, Portrait of Wiggin of the Chase," Vol. I (June 1930), p. 91.

————. "For Example: The Chase National Bank," Vol. XIII (January 1936), pp. 55–60, 124–138.

————. "In the New Wall Street," Vol. XII (October 1935), pp. 78–83, 114–120.

————. "The Bankers," Vol. XXXVIII (November 1948), pp. 114–120, 230–235.

————. "The Case of William Fox," Vol. I (May 1930), pp. 48–49, 108–118.

————. "The New Deal, Second Time Around," Vol. XVII (February 1938), pp. 59–61, 150–152.

————. "The Rockefellers: a Financial Power and a Family," Vol. IV (December 1931), pp. 51–53, 128–132.

————. "Twentieth Century Fox," Vol. XII (December 1935), pp. 85–93, 130–138.

Journal of Business. Anatol Murad, "The Reichsbank in the Financial Crisis of 1931," Vol. V (April 1932), pp. 175–191.

————. Robert B. Rivel, "Industrial Composition of the Business Loans of the Chase National Bank, 1940–1947," Vol. XXII (January 1949), pp. 50–59.

Journal of Political Economy. Ray Westerfield, "The Banking Act of 1933," Vol. XLI (December 1933), pp. 721–749.

Nation's Business. Francis H. Sisson, "Men, not Laws, Make Sound Bankers," Vol. XXI (January 1933), pp. 13–16, 62.

Political Science Quarterly. B. H. Beckhart, "The Bretton Woods Proposal for an International Monetary Fund," Vol. LIX (December 1944), pp. 489–528.

The Quarterly Journal of Economics. A. D. Gayer, "The Banking Act of 1935," Vol. L (November 1935), pp. 97–116.

Trust Companies Magazine. 1911–1931.

U. S. Department of State Bulletin. John Foster Dulles, "Report on the Near East," Vol. XXVIII (June 15, 1953), pp. 831–835.

Yale Review. Jacob Viner, "Two Plans for International Monetary Stabilization," Vol. XXIII (Autumn 1943), pp. 77–107.

Pamphlets

American Bankers Association. *Practical International Financial Organization through Amendments to Bretton Woods Proposals.* February 1, 1945.
———. *Proceedings of the Thirty-Seventh Annual Meeting.* November 21, 1911.
Anderson, Benjamin. *International Currency — Gold Versus Bancos or Unitas.* Address before the Chamber of Commerce of the State of New York, February 3, 1944.
Bond & Goodwin, Inc. *The Chase National Bank of the City of New York.* November 1930.
The Chase National Bank of the City of New York, 1877–1922. New York: Chase National Bank Publication, 1922.
Christy, Francis T. *Memorandum on the Legal Career of Winthrop W. Aldrich.* March 10, 1966.
First National Corporation of Boston. *Report on the Chase National Bank,* January 8, 1929. Boston: 1929.
Harvard Law School. *Class of 1910. Fiftieth Reunion Report.* Cambridge: 1960.
International Business Conference, Final Reports. Rye, New York: 1944.
Leffingwell, Russell. *The Gold Problem and Revaluation.* Address before the Academy of Political Science, March 21, 1934.
National Board of Trade. *Proceedings of the Forty-First Annual Meeting, January, 1911.* Philadelphia: J. R. McFetridge & Sons, 1911.
Research Committee of the Committee for Economic Development. *The Bretton Woods Proposals.* March 1945.
Talbert, Joseph. *Progress in Banking.* Address to the New York

State Bankers Association, June 22, 1911.

The Trust Companies of the United States. New York: United States Mortgage and Trust Co., 1908–1912.

Untermyer, Samuel. *Who is Entitled to the Credit for the Federal Reserve Act? An Answer to Carter Glass.* June 18, 1927.

Warburg, Paul M. *A Plan for a Modified Central Bank.* November 12, 1907.

Financial Guides

Moody's Manual of Investments. New York: Moody's Investors Services, 1920–1930, 1934, 1935, 1936.

Poor's Financial Records. Government and Municipal Section. New York: Poor's Publishing Co., 1920–1930.

Annual Reports

Bank of America. *Annual Reports.* 1940–1952.

Bank of Manhattan Co. *Annual Reports.* 1940–1952.

Bankers Trust Co. *Annual Reports.* 1940–1952.

Chase National Bank. *Annual Reports.* 1915–1953.

Chemical Bank and Trust Co. *Annual Reports.* 1940–1952.

Continental Illinois Bank and Trust Co. *Annual Reports.* 1940–1952.

Guaranty Trust Company. *Annual Reports.* 1940–1952.

Manufacturers Trust Co. *Annual Reports.* 1940–1952.

National City Bank. *Annual Reports.* 1940–1952.

Newspapers

Commercial and Financial Chronicle (New York), 1911–1952.
Daily Press (London, England), 1952.
The Harvard Crimson (Cambridge, Mass.), 1903–1910.
Herald-Tribune (New York), 1933, 1946.
Daily News (New York), 1938.
Morning News (Dallas, Texas), 1934.
New York Times, 1913–1957.
Press-Scimitar (Memphis, Tennessee), 1947.
Rocky Mountain News (Denver, Colorado), 1936.
The Statist (London, England), 1952.
Times-Herald (Washington, D.C.), 1952.
Times-Picayune (New Orleans, La.), 1935.
Tribune (San Diego, Calif.), 1933.
Tribune (Chicago, Illinois), 1929, 1947.
Washington Post (Washington, D.C.), 1935, 1950.
Wall Street Journal, 1927–1947.
World-Telegram (New York), 1933.

Court Cases

Banque De France *v.* Equitable Trust Co. of New York, 33 F 2d 202 (1929).
Banque De France *v.* Chase National Bank of City of New York, 60 F 2d 703 (1932).
Bookbinder *et al. v.* Chase National Bank of New York City *et al.*, amended complaint. Supreme Court of the State of New York, April 28, 1934. Aldrich Papers.

Equitable Trust Co. of New York *v.* Green Star Steamship Corp., *et al.*, 291 Fed. 650 (1922).

Equitable Trust Co. of New York *v.* Green Star Steamship Corp., *et al.*, 297 Fed. 1008 (1924).

Equitable Trust Co. *v.* Prentice, 250 N.Y. 1 (1928).

Gould *v.* Gould, 197 N.Y.S. 515 (1922).

Gould *v.* Gould, 203 N.Y.S. 399 (1923).

Gould *v.* Gould, 124 M. 240; 207 N.Y.S.137 (1924).

Gould *v.* Gould, 209 App. Div. 155; 204 N.Y.S.123 (1924).

Gould *v.* Gould, 213 N.Y.S. 286 (1925).

Habirshaw Electric Cable Co. *v.* Habirshaw Electric Cable Co., Inc., *et al.*, 296 F 875 (1924).

Rathbun *v.* U.S., 295 U.S. 602 (1935).

Rockefeller Foundation *v.* State, 258 N.Y.S. 812 (1932).

U.S. *v.* Sisal Sales Corporation, 274 U.S. 268 (1927).

United States of America *v.* Leonard J. A. Smit, Anton Smit and Co., Inc., Elsantum, Inc., and the Chase National Bank. United States District Court, Southern District of New York, April 16–May 2, 1945 [stenographer's Minutes]. 4 Volumes.

Interviews

A. M. Johnson with Winthrop W. Aldrich, December 9, 1965, New York City; December 10, 1965, New York City; December 18, 1965, Providence, Rhode Island; April 14, 1966, New York City; May 26, 1966, New York City; August 8, 1966, Dark Harbor, Maine; October 18, 1966, New York City; February 14, 1967, New York City; July-August, 1967, Dark Harbor, Maine.

A. M. Johnson with Sam Ballin. May 25, 1966, New York City.

A. M. Johnson with Laurence Bennett. June 10, 1966, New York City; October 19, 1966, New York City.

A. M. Johnson with John B. Bridgewood. April 22, 1966, New York City.

A. M. Johnson with Thomas Brophy. May 25, 1966, New York City.

A. M. Johnson with John T. Cahill. April 21, 1966, New York City.

A. M. Johnson with Charles Cain, Jr., May 25, 1966, New York City.

A. M. Johnson with H. Donald Campbell. April 22, 1966, New York City.

A. M. Johnson with George Champion. May 2, 1966, New York City.

A. M. Johnson with Kenneth Chorley. October 18, 1966, New York City.

A. M. Johnson with Percy J. Ebbott. February 1, 1966, New York City.

A. M. Johnson with Harold Helm. October 16, 1966, New York City.

A. M. Johnson with Edward Love. June 10, 1966, New York City; October 19, 1966, New York City.

A. M. Johnson with John J. McCloy. April 22, 1966, New York City.

A. M. Johnson with Louis Novins. May 26, 1966, New York City.

A. M. Johnson with Hermann G. Place. April 14, 1966, New York City.

A. M. Johnson with David Rockefeller. May 4, 1966, New York City.

A. M. Johnson with John C. Traphagen. June 10, 1966, New York City.

A. M. Johnson with Harrison Tweed. February 1, 1966, New York City; February 14, 1967, New York City.

A. M. Johnson with George E. Warren. February 2, 1966, New York City.

A. M. Johnson with Crawford Wheeler. February 2, 1966, New York City.

A. M. Johnson with Robert G. Zeeler. April 21, 1966, New York City.

Personal Papers

The Aldrich Papers, currently on deposit at the Baker Library, Harvard Graduate School of Business Administration, are comprised of the following materials:

I. Personal correspondence of Winthrop W. Aldrich, 1918–1950, arranged chronologically and relating mainly to his cars, clubs, insurance, homes, yachts, and family.

II. Personal correspondence of Winthrop W. Aldrich, 1929–1953, arranged alphabetically by subject and chronologically within each subject. These papers include correspondence pertaining to each organization with which Mr. Aldrich was affiliated; activities of and matters related to the Chase National Bank, including several folders of memoranda from various departments of the bank; correspondence related to his speeches and a complete file of the speeches themselves; correspondence from friends, colleagues, and individuals across the country arranged by date; and trip itineraries.

III. Personal correspondence of Winthrop W. Aldrich, 1953–1959, arranged by year and then alphabetically. Includes information on invitations, receptions, addresses, toasts, memberships, and visitors during his term as Ambassador to Great Britain. Also correspondence and activities during his retirement years, 1957–1959.

IV. Speeches of Winthrop W. Aldrich, a complete set, 1933–1959.

V. Oral History — a series of interviews conducted by Mr. Crawford Wheeler with Mr. Winthrop W. Aldrich, covering his years at the Chase National Bank. Recorded at several sessions, 1960–1962.

VI. Clippings books — two scrapbooks of newspaper clippings covering major banking events, 1933–1945, as well as the activities and interests of Mr. Aldrich and members of his family.

VII. Photographs — several albums of photographs of Mr. Aldrich on various occasions, plus portraits at significant stages of his life.

VIII. New York World's Fair materials including minutes of both the Executive Committee and the Board of Directors meetings, 1935–1939, plus notebooks concerning charter members and the activities of the Finance Committee.

IX. Appointment Books — Daily calendars of Mr. Aldrich's activities, 1929–1959.

X. Recording of remarks made by Mr. Aldrich when he became Ambassador to Great Britain, February, 1953.

XI. Books and pamphlets related to banking, international finance, and government policy.

NOTES

CHAPTER I: The Formative Years

1. See Nathaniel W. Stephenson, *Nelson W. Aldrich: a Leader in American Politics* (New York: Charles Scribners' Sons, 1930), and Herbert O. Brigham and Mary H. Brigham, *Ancestry of Nelson Wilmarth Aldrich and his wife Abby Pearce Truman Chapman* (Providence, 1938).
2. *Ibid.*
3. Data on the Aldrich Family (mimeographed). Aldrich Papers.
4. Winthrop W. Aldrich to Abby Aldrich, Aldrich Papers.
5. *Ibid.*
6. Stephenson, *Nelson Aldrich*, p. 61.
7. *Ibid.*, p. 62.
8. *Ibid.*, p. 60.
9. *Ibid.*, p. 98.
10. *Ibid.*, p. 439, n. 12.
11. Interview, A. M. Johnson with Winthrop W. Aldrich, Providence, Rhode Island, December 18, 1965.
12. *Ibid.*
13. *Books in the Library of Nelson W. Aldrich, Warwick, Rhode Island.* 2 parts (Boston: The Merrymount Press, 1914–1916).
14. Interview, A. M. Johnson with Winthrop W. Aldrich, New York City, December 9, 1965.
15. *Ibid.*
16. *Ibid.*
17. *Harvard University Catalogue, 1903–1904* (Cambridge: Harvard University, 1903), and Samuel E. Morison, *Three Centuries of Harvard, 1636–1936* (Cambridge: Harvard University Press, 1936), p. 419.

18. Interview, A. M. Johnson with Winthrop W. Aldrich, Providence, Rhode Island, December 18, 1965.
19. *The Harvard Crimson*, March 18, 1907.
20. Harold Jefferson Coolidge and Robert H. Lord, *Archibald Carey Coolidge: Life and Letters* (New York: Houghton Mifflin Co., 1932), pp. 40–52.
21. Interview, A. M. Johnson with Winthrop W. Aldrich, New York City, October 18, 1966.
22. Winthrop Aldrich, "Diary of European Trip, 1905," 110 Benevolent Street, Providence, Rhode Island.
23. *The Harvard Crimson.*
24. *Ibid.*
25. Interview, A. M. Johnson with Winthrop W. Aldrich, New York City, October 18, 1966.
26. *Ibid.*

CHAPTER II: The Seasoning Years

1. *The Centennial History of the Harvard Law School, 1817–1917* (Cambridge: Harvard Law School Association, 1918), p. 209.
2. Harvard Law School, *Class of 1910. Fiftieth Reunion Report*, 1960 [pamphlet].
3. The Lincoln's Inn, incorporation papers and other historical material (Lincoln's Inn, Cambridge, Mass.).
4. Interview, A. M. Johnson with Harrison Tweed, New York City, February 1, 1966.
5. For a general account of the bankers' activities in the Panic of 1907, see Anna Robeson Burr, *The Portrait of a Banker* (New York: Duffield and Co., 1927), pp. 223–238; Thomas W. Lamont, *Henry P. Davison* (New York: Harper and Brothers, 1933), pp. 72–87; and Herbert L. Satterlee, *J. Pierpont Morgan, an Intimate Portrait* (New York: Macmillan and Co., 1939), pp. 459–492.
6. Elgin Groseclose, *Fifty Years of Managed Money: the Story of the Federal Reserve, 1913–1963* (London: Macmillan and Company, Ltd., 1965), p. 41.

7. Stephenson, *Nelson Aldrich*, pp. 322–323.
8. *Ibid.*, p. 333.
9. "Defects and Needs of our Banking System," *The New York Times Annual Financial Review*, January 6, 1907.
10. Paul M. Warburg, *The Federal Reserve System, Its Origin and Growth* (2 vols.; New York: The Macmillan Co., 1930), Vol. I, p. 19.
11. *Ibid.*, Vol. I, pp. 19–20.
12. Paul M. Warburg, *A Plan for a Modified Central Bank*, November 12, 1907 [pamphlet].
13. Warburg, *The Federal Reserve System*, Vol. I, p. 31.
14. Quoted in Stephenson, *Nelson Aldrich*, p. 334.
15. Paul M. Warburg to Nelson Aldrich, December 31, 1907, quoted in Warburg, *The Federal Reserve System*, Vol. I, pp. 555–557.
16. Stephenson, *Nelson Aldrich*, p. 328; *Congressional Record* (March 27, 1908), p. 4,025.
17. Groseclose, *Fifty Years of Managed Money*, pp. 46–48; *Congressional Record* (May 30, 1908), p. 7,260.
18. Lamont, *Henry P. Davison*, p. 92.
19. U.S. National Monetary Commission, *Publications of the National Monetary Commission* (23 vols.; Washington: Government Printing Office, 1912).
20. Memorandum by G. M. Reynolds, quoted in Stephenson, *Nelson Aldrich*, p. 339.
21. Lamont, *Henry P. Davison*, p. 98.
22. Warburg, *The Federal Reserve System*, Vol. I, p. 59.
23. National Board of Trade, *Proceedings of the Forty-First Annual Meeting, January 1911* (Philadelphia: J. R. McFetridge and Sons, 1911), pp. 184–187.
24. *Suggested Plan for Monetary Legislation. Submitted to the National Monetary Commission by Honorable Nelson W. Aldrich* [61 Cong. 3 Sess. Sen. Doc. 784].
25. *Ibid.*
26. Warburg, *The Federal Reserve System*, Vol. II, pp. 11–12.
27. American Bankers Association, *Proceedings of the Thirty-Seventh Annual Meeting, November 21, 1911* (New York: Wynkoap, Hallenbeck, Crawford Co., 1911), pp. 60, 92. See also address by Nelson W. Aldrich, pp. 68–85.
28. U.S. National Monetary Commission, "A Bill to incorporate the National Reserve Association of the United States, and for other

purposes." *Publications of the National Monetary Commission* (Washington: January 1912), Vol. I, p. 49.

29. A. Jerome Clifford, *The Independence of the Federal Reserve System* (Philadelphia: University of Pennsylvania Press, 1965), pp. 55–57.

30. Carter Glass, *An Adventure in Constructive Finance* (New York: Doubleday, Page and Co., 1927), p. 248.

31. H. P. Willis, *The Federal Reserve System: Legislation, Organization and Operation* (New York: The Ronald Press Co., 1923), pp. 85, 523.

32. Warburg, *The Federal Reserve System*, Vol. I, p. 408.

33. U.S. Congress. House Committee on Banking and Currency, *Money Trust Investigation* (3 vols.; Washington: Government Printing Office, 1913).

34. Interview, A. M. Johnson with Winthrop W. Aldrich, New York City, October 18, 1966.

35. Interview, A. M. Johnson with Harrison Tweed, New York City, February 1, 1966.

36. Interview, A. M. Johnson with Winthrop W. Aldrich, New York City, October 18, 1966.

37. *Ibid.*

38. Interview, A. M. Johnson with Lawrence Bennett, New York City, June 10, 1966.

39. Interview, A. M. Johnson with Harrison Tweed, New York City, February 1, 1966.

40. Interview, A. M. Johnson with Winthrop W. Aldrich, New York City, December 9, 1965.

41. *New York Times*, September 2, 1916.

42. Aldrich family records, 110 Benevolent Street, Providence, Rhode Island.

43. For a brief account of Charles Crocker's career, see Oscar Lewis, *The Big Four* (New York: Alfred A. Knopf, 1938) pp. 49–123.

44. Interview, A. M. Johnson with Mrs. Winthrop W. Aldrich, Providence, Rhode Island, December 18, 1965.

45. Winthrop W. Aldrich to John J. Hylan, U.S.N., September 27, 1920. Personal correspondence. Aldrich Papers.

46. Interview, A. M. Johnson with Winthrop W. Aldrich, New York City, December 9, 1965.

47. *Ibid.*

CHAPTER III: The Later Law Years, 1919–1929

1. Winthrop W. Aldrich to Gordon Auchincloss, American Commission to Negotiate Peace (Paris, France), February 13, 1919. Aldrich Papers.
2. Timothy N. Pfeiffer and George W. Jacques, *Law Practice in a Turbulent World* (New York: Charles P. Young Co., 1965), p. 2.
3. *Ibid.*
4. *Ibid.*, pp. 18–19.
5. Mr. Francis T. Christy, Memoranda on the legal career of Winthrop W. Aldrich, March 10, 1966 [typescript]. Aldrich Papers.
6. Gould *v.* Gould, 197 N.Y.S. 515 (1922); *New York Times*, May 12, 1922.
7. Pfeiffer and Jacques, *Law Practice in a Turbulent World*, p. 41.
8. *New York Times*, April 2, 1929.
9. Christy, Memoranda on the legal career of Winthrop W. Aldrich, March 10, 1966.
10. Interview, A. M. Johnson with Sam Ballin, of Milbank, Tweed, Hadley and McCloy, New York City, May 25, 1966.
11. Equitable Trust Co. *v.* Prentice, 250 N.Y. 1 (1928).
12. Pfeiffer and Jacques, *Law Practice in a Turbulent World*, pp. 24–25.
13. Christy, Memoranda on the legal career of Winthrop W. Aldrich, March 10, 1966. See also, Robert T. Swaine, *The Cravath Firm and Its Predecessors, 1819–1948* (New York: Ad Press, Ltd., 1948), p. 312.
14. Christy, Memoranda on the legal career of Winthrop W. Aldrich, March 10, 1966.
15. U.S. *v.* Sisal Sales Corporation, 274 U.S. 268 (1927); Interview, A. M. Johnson with Winthrop W. Aldrich, New York City, December 10, 1965.
16. Equitable Trust Co. of New York *v.* Green Star Steamship Corp., *et al.*, 291 Fed 650 (1922); Equitable Trust Co. of New York *v.* Green Star Steamship Corp., *et al.*, 297 F 1008 (1924).
17. Habirshaw Electric Cable Co. *v.* Habirshaw Electric Cable Co., Inc., *et al.*, 296 F 875 (1924)

18. Christy, Memoranda on the legal career of Winthrop W. Aldrich, March 10, 1966.

19. *Ibid.*

20. Pfeiffer and Jacques, *Law Practice in a Turbulent World*, p. 42.

21. *New York Times*, June 1, 1923.

22. Raymond B. Fosdick, *John D. Rockefeller, Jr., a Portrait* (New York: Harper and Brothers, 1956), p. 410; Christy, Memoranda on the legal career of Winthrop W. Aldrich, March 10, 1966.

23. Fosdick, *John D. Rockefeller, Jr., a Portrait*, pp. 272–282.

24. Christy, Memoranda on the legal career of Winthrop W. Aldrich, March 10, 1966; interview, A. M. Johnson with Kenneth Chorley, New York City, October 18, 1966.

25. Christy, Memoranda on the legal career of Winthrop W. Aldrich, March 10, 1966.

26. Interview, A. M. Johnson with Kenneth Chorley, New York City, October 18, 1966.

27. *New York Times*, December 6, 1929.

28. David Loth, *The City within a City: The Romance of Rockefeller Center* (New York: William Morrow and Company, 1966), p. 42.

29. Christy, Memoranda on the legal career of Winthrop W. Aldrich, March 10, 1966. Approval of consolidation cited in *New York Times*, January 4, 1929.

30. Rockefeller Foundation *v.* State, 258 N.Y.S. 812 (1932).

31. Paul H. Giddens, *Standard Oil Company (Indiana): Oil Pioneer of the Middle West* (New York: Appleton-Century-Crofts, 1955), pp. 361–367.

32. *Ibid.*, p. 366.

33. *Ibid.*, p. 365.

34. *New York Times*, March 2, 1928. For Rockefeller's testimony see U.S. Congress. Senate Committee on Public Lands and Surveys, *Leases Upon Naval Oil Reserves* (Washington, 1929), pp. 311–323.

35. Giddens, *Standard Oil Company (Indiana)*, pp. 380–381. See also statement by Thomas Debevoise, *New York Times*, March 3, 1928.

36. *New York Times*, April 28, 1928.

37. *Ibid.*, May 10, 1928.

38. Giddens, *Standard Oil Company (Indiana)*, pp. 387–388.

39. *Ibid.*, p. 388.

40. *New York Times*, January 15, 1929.

41. *The Chicago Tribune,* January 16, 1929.
42. Interview, A. M. Johnson with Sam Ballin, of Milbank, Tweed, Hadley and McCloy, New York City, May 25, 1966.
43. Giddens, *Standard Oil Company (Indiana),* p. 413.
44. *Ibid.,* pp. 420–422.
45. *New York Times,* February 8, 1929.
46. *Ibid.,* March 8, 1929; Giddens, *Standard Oil Company (Indiana),* pp. 427–432.
47. Interview, A. M. Johnson with Sam Ballin, of Milbank, Tweed, Hadley and McCloy, New York City, May 25, 1966.
48. *Ibid.*

CHAPTER IV: Family and Yachting Years

1. *New York Times,* January 13, 1931.
2. Interview, A. M. Johnson with Winthrop W. Aldrich, November 5, 1966.
3. *Ibid.*
4. Raymond B. Fosdick, *John D. Rockefeller, Jr.: a Portrait* (New York: Harper & Bros., 1956), pp. 207–210.
5. Winthrop W. Aldrich to R. G. Goodman, March 19, 1923. Aldrich Papers.
6. The history of the campaign of 1930 for the America's Cup is told in detail in Harold S. Vanderbilt, *Enterprise: The Story of the Defense of the America's Cup in 1930* (New York: Scribners' Sons, 1931).
7. *New York Times,* January 13, 1931.

CHAPTER V: The Fateful Year, 1929–1930

1. Edward T. Perine, *The Story of the Trust Companies* (New York: G. P. Putnam and Sons, 1916), pp. 217–219.
2. Morton Keller, *The Life Insurance Enterprise, 1885–1910* (Cambridge, Mass.: Harvard University Press, 1963), p. 281.

3. *Trust Companies Magazine*, Vol. XII (April 1911), p. 295; R. Carlyle Buley, *The Equitable Life Assurance Society of the United States, 1859–1964* (New York: Appleton-Century-Crofts, 1967), Vol. II, p. 837.

4. *Bankers Magazine*, Vol. LXXXII (June 1911), p. 823.

5. *The Trust Companies of the United States* (New York: United States Mortgage and Trust Co., 1908–1912).

6. *Trust Companies Magazine*, Vol. XXXI (August 1920), p. 162.

7. *Ibid.*, Vol. XXXVI (June 1923), pp. 736, 819.

8. *Ibid.*, Vol. XLV (August 1927), p. 236.

9. *Ibid.*, Vol. XLVI (January 1928), p. 130.

10. *Trust Companies Magazine*, Vol. XLV (September 1927), p. 363. Also see *Wall Street Journal*, August 22, 1927; *New York Times*, November 15, 1927.

11. Interview, Crawford Wheeler with Winthrop W. Aldrich, May 26, 1960. On file at Baker Library, Harvard Graduate School of Business Administration.

12. *Ibid.*

13. *Trust Companies Magazine*, Vol. XLVIII (May 1929), p. 759.

14. Samuel G. Bayne, *Derricks of Destiny: an Autobiography* (New York: Brentano's, 1924), pp. 148–153.

15. Edna Page Austin, *A Gallant Gentleman: The Life of Chellis A. Austin* (New York: The John Day Company, 1932), p. 58.

16. *Ibid.*, p. 26.

17. *Ibid.*, p. 55.

18. *Ibid.*, p. 64.

19. Interview, A. M. Johnson with H. Donald Campbell, New York City, April 22, 1966.

20. *Ibid.*

21. *Ibid.*

22. Quoted in Austin, *A Gallant Gentleman*, p. 94.

23. *Trust Companies Magazine*, Vol. XLVIII (May 1929), p. 760; *ibid.*, Vol. XXXIV (February 1922), p. 205.

24. *Ibid.*, pp. 89, 129.

25. *Ibid.*, p. 135.

26. From letter of Chellis Austin, quoted in Austin, *A Gallant Gentleman*, pp. 187–188.

27. *Ibid.*, pp. 188–189.

28. *Ibid.*, p. 266.

29. Timothy N. Pfeiffer and George W. Jaques, *Law Practice in a*

Turbulent World (New York: Charles P. Young Company, 1965), p. 74.

30. Notes from interviews, A. M. Johnson with Winthrop W. Aldrich, New York City, December 10, 1965; Providence, Rhode Island, December 19, 1965.

31. Interview, A. M. Johnson with Percy J. Ebbott, New York City, February 1, 1966.

32. Bernard M. Baruch to Winthrop W. Aldrich, December 19, 1929. Aldrich Papers.

33. Fred I. Kent to Winthrop W. Aldrich, December 18, 1929. Aldrich Papers.

34. Albert H. Wiggin to Winthrop W. Aldrich, December 18, 1929. Aldrich Papers.

35. *Ibid.*

36. Winthrop W. Aldrich to Manley O. Hudson, December 23, 1929. Aldrich Papers.

37. Winthrop W. Aldrich to Thomas W. Lamont, December 23, 1929. Aldrich Papers.

38. Winthrop W. Aldrich to Lewis H. Brown, December 19, 1929. Aldrich Papers.

39. *Moody's Manual of Investments, 1930* (New York: Moody's Investors Service, 1930), pp. 1,451–1,452.

40. Interview, A. M. Johnson with Edward Love, New York City, June 10, 1966.

41. *Ibid.*

42. *Ibid.*

43. Chellis Austin to Shepard Morgan, May 28, 1929. Aldrich Papers.

44. Chellis Austin to Shepard Morgan, June 17, 1928. Aldrich Papers.

45. Chellis Austin to Shepard Morgan, September 27, 1929. Aldrich Papers.

46. Winthrop W. Aldrich to Shephard Morgan, December 17, 1929. Aldrich Papers.

47. Interview, A. M. Johnson with Winthrop W. Aldrich, New York City, December 10, 1965.

48. Interview, A. M. Johnson with H. Donald Campbell, New York City, April 22, 1966.

49. *Ibid.*

50. Interview, A. M. Johnson with Winthrop W. Aldrich, New York City, December 10, 1965.

51. For the life of Albert H. Wiggin, see Marjorie Wiggin Prescott, *New England Son* (New York: Dodd Mead & Company, 1949).
52. *The Chase National Bank of the City of New York, 1877–1922* (New York: Chase National Bank Publication, 1922), pp. 4–5.
53. *Ibid.*, p. 6.
54. Prescott, *New England Son*, p. 93.
55. First National Corporation of Boston, *Report on the Chase National Bank*, January 8, 1929, p. 2 [pamphlet]. Aldrich Papers.
56. Chase National Bank, *Annual Report*, January 14, 1930.
57. *The American Banker*, Vol. XCV (January 21, 1930), p. 7.
58. Interview, A. M. Johnson with H. Donald Campbell, New York City, April 22, 1966.
59. Pfeiffer and Jaques, *Law Practice in a Turbulent World*, p. 76.
60. Albert G. Milbank to Winthrop W. Aldrich, March 7, 1930. Aldrich Papers.
61. *Trust Companies Magazine*, Vol. XLIX (July 1929), p. 82.
62. Interview, A. M. Johnson with Percy J. Ebbott, New York City, February 1, 1966.
63. Memo, April 11, 1930. Aldrich Papers.
64. Interview, A. M. Johnson with Winthrop W. Aldrich, New York City, December 10, 1965.
65. Chase National Bank, *Annual Report*, January 13, 1931, p. 20; and *Trust Companies Magazine*, Vol. L (June 1930), p. 932.
66. Interview, A. M. Johnson with H. Donald Campbell, New York City, April 22, 1966.
67. Interview, Crawford Wheeler with Winthrop W. Aldrich, May 26, 1960.
68. *New York Times*, March 7, 1930.
69. *Trust Companies Magazine*, Vol. L (April 1930), p. 643.
70. *Ibid.*

Chapter VI: The Years of Revelation, 1930–1932

1. Winthrop W. Aldrich to John C. White, March 20, 1930. Aldrich Papers.
2. Interview, A. M. Johnson with John C. Traphagen, New York City, June 10, 1966.

3. Presidents of the Chase National Bank, 1920–1929:
    1920 — Eugene V. R. Thayer
    1921–1925 — Albert H. Wiggin
    1926–1927 — John McHugh
    1928 — Robert L. Clarkson
    1929 — Charles S. McCain

4. Interview, A. M. Johnson with Percy J. Ebbott, New York City, February 1, 1966.

5. Marjorie Wiggin Prescott, *New England Son* (New York: Dodd, Mead & Co., 1949), pp. 154–155.

6. Meeting of New Business Committee of Directors, June 25, 1930 [typescript]. Aldrich Papers.

7. *Ibid.*, December 10, 1930 [typescript]. Aldrich Papers.

8. *New York Times*, August 2, 1930.

9. *Trust Companies Magazine*, Vol. LI (August 1930), p. 258.

10. *Wall Street Journal*, August 1, 1930.

11. *Ibid.*

12. *Trust Companies Magazine*, Vol. LI (August 1930), p. 258.

13. *Ibid.*, Vol. LIII (July 1931), p. 110.

14. Interview, A. M. Johnson with George E. Warren, New York City, February 2, 1966.

15. Chase National Bank, *Annual Report*, January 13, 1931, pp. 14–15.

16. *Fortune*, Vol. XIII (January 1936), p. 124.

17. Memorandum, December 9, 1929. Paris office, 1929–1930. Aldrich Papers. Aldrich appeared in the New York District Court on March 21, 1929; see Banque De France *v.* Equitable Trust Co. of New York, 33 F (2d) 202 (1929). Also see memoranda re: Bank of France claims, William D. Embree to Winthrop W. Aldrich, various dates, January–September, 1931; Milbank, Tweed, Hope and Webb, 1931. Aldrich Papers.

18. Banque De France *v.* Chase National Bank of City of New York; Banque De France *v.* Equitable Trust Co. of New York, 60 F (2d) 703 (1932).

19. Winthrop W. Aldrich to John C. White, December 3, 1930. Aldrich Papers.

20. John M. Wallace to Winthrop W. Aldrich, November 28, 1930. [Memo on meeting held November 22, 1930]. Aldrich Papers.

21. Bond and Goodwin, Inc., *The Chase National Bank of the City of New York*, November 1930 [pamphlet]. Aldrich Papers.

22. Chase National Bank, *Annual Report*, January 13, 1931, p. 7.

23. Memorandum, Lee Higginson and Co. to Winthrop W. Aldrich, June 29, 1932. Aldrich Papers.

24. Memorandum, German Commitments as of February 29, 1932. Aldrich Papers.

25. Memorandum, Dr. B. M. Anderson and Mr. Shepard Morgan to Winthrop W. Aldrich, June 19, 1931. Aldrich Papers.

26. *Ibid.*

27. Cablegram, A. H. Wiggin to W. W. Aldrich, August 17, 1931. Aldrich Papers.

28. Memorandum, John McHugh, December 11, 1931.

29. Chase National Bank, *Annual Report*, January 12, 1932, p. 11.

30. *Wall Street Journal*, November 26, 1931.

31. Memoranda, June 4–10, 1931, American Express Company (June–December 1931), Aldrich Papers.

32. Winthrop W. Aldrich to Albert H. Wiggin, August 10, 1931. Aldrich Papers.

33. 73 Cong., 1 Sess., Senate Committee on Banking and Currency, "Stock Exchange Practices," *Hearings*, 2417.

34. *Ibid.*, 2423.

35. *Ibid.*, 2431–2432.

36. Winthrop W. Aldrich to Albert H. Wiggin, August 10, 1931. Aldrich Papers.

37. Cablegram, A. H. Wiggin to W. W. Aldrich, September 14, 1931; cablegram, W. W. Aldrich to A. H. Wiggin, September 15, 1931. Aldrich Papers.

38. Winthrop W. Aldrich to C. D. Buck, President, Equitable Trust Co. (Wilmington, Delaware), July 6, 1931. Aldrich Papers.

39. Interview, A. M. Johnson with Winthrop W. Aldrich, Boston, Mass., September 26, 1966.

40. Marcus Gleisser, *The World of Cyrus Eaton* (New York: A. S. Barnes and Co., Inc., 1965), pp. 64–66.

41. Winthrop W. Aldrich, Memoranda Re: Continental Shares, September 9, 1931; Winthrop W. Aldrich to E. N. Wood, June 28, 1933. Aldrich Papers.

42. 73 Cong., 1 Sess., Senate Committee on Banking and Currency, "Stock Exchange Practices," *Hearings*, 3690–3691.

43. *Ibid.*, 3558.

44. *Ibid.*, 3586.

45. *Ibid.*, 3442.

46. *Ibid.*, 4018.

47. *Ibid.*, 3806.
48. *Ibid.*, 2918.
49. *New York Times*, November 12, 1933.
50. *Ibid.*
51. *Ibid.*, May 10, 1931.
52. Interview, A. M. Johnson with Edward Love, New York City, June 10, 1966.
53. Interview, A. M. Johnson with Percy J. Ebbott, New York City, February 1, 1966; and interview, A. M. Johnson with H. Donald Campbell, New York City, April 22, 1966.
54. *Investor's Guide Stock Reports*, Vol. VI, April 13, 1939, Sec. 10.
55. Ralph W. Wells to Charles S. McCain, April 18, 1931. Aldrich Papers.
56. 72 Cong., 1 Sess., "Sale of Foreign Bonds or Securities in the United States," *Hearings before the Committee on Finance, United States Senate* (Washington, 1932), pp. 406–407.
57. *Ibid.*, p. 401.
58. *Ibid.*
59. *Ibid.*, p. 405.
60. *Ibid.*, pp. 411–412.
61. *Ibid.*, p. 417.
62. Interview, A. M. Johnson with Crawford Wheeler, New York City, February 2, 1966; interview, A. M. Johnson with Harrison Tweed, New York City, February 1, 1966.
63. Shepard Morgan to Winthrop W. Aldrich, July 22, 1932. Aldrich Papers.
64. 72 Cong., 1 Sess., Senate Committee on Finance, "Sale of Foreign Bonds or Securities in the United States," *Hearings*, 2039–2043; 73 Cong., 1 Sess., Senate Committee on Banking & Currency, "Stock Exchange Practices," *Hearings*, 2542–2544.
65. 73 Cong., 1 Sess., Senate Committee on Banking and Currency, "Stock Exchange Practices," *Hearings*, 2542.
66. *New York Times*, July 14, 1932; Chase National Bank, *Annual Report*, 1934, p. 15.
67. 73 Cong., 1 Sess., Senate Committee on Banking and Currency, "Stock Exchange Practices," *Hearings*, 2573–2574.
68. Chase National Bank, *Annual Report*, 1934, p. 15.
69. *New York Times*, July 12, 1932.
70. *Ibid.*, October 16–31, 1932.
71. *Ibid.*, December 2–15, 1932.

72. 73 Cong., 1 Sess., Senate Committee on Banking and Currency, "Stock Exchange Practices," *Hearings*, 2322.
73. *Ibid.*, 2311.
74. *Ibid.*, 4018.
75. *Ibid.*, 3872–3875.
76. Chase National Bank, *Annual Report*, 1933.

CHAPTER VII: The Crisis Year, 1933

1. *New York Times; New York Herald Tribune*, February 3, 1933.
2. 72 Cong., 2 Sess., Senate Committee on Finance, "Investigation of Economic Problems," *Hearings*, 521. Aldrich's complete testimony was reported in the *New York Times*, February 23, 1933.
3. 72 Cong., 2 Sess., Senate Committee on Finance, *Hearings*, 522–527.
4. Ray L. Wilbur and Arthur M. Hyde, *The Hoover Policies* (New York: Scribner's Sons, 1937), p. 181; Albert A. Romasco, *The Poverty of Abundance: Hoover, the Nation, the Depression* (New York: Oxford University Press, 1965), pp. 97–124.
5. 72 Cong., 2 Sess., Senate Committee on Finance, "Investigation of Economic Problems," *Hearings*, 554–555.
6. *Ibid.*, 552.
7. Wilbur and Hyde, *The Hoover Policies*, pp. 366–367, 447.
8. 72 Cong., 2 Sess., Senate Committee on Finance, "Investigation of Economic Problems," *Hearings*, p. 538.
9. *Ibid.*, 560.
10. Arthur M. Schlesinger, Jr., *The Coming of the New Deal* (Boston, Mass.: Houghton Mifflin Co., 1959), pp. 8–10.
11. 72 Cong., 2 Sess., "Investigation of Economic Problems," *Hearings*, 548–550.
12. *Ibid.*, 562.
13. *Ibid.*
14. McClure Syndicate, February 28, 1933. Aldrich Papers.
15. Winthrop W. Aldrich, "The Causes of the Present Depression and Possible Remedies," Chase National Bank Publication, 1933 [pamphlet].

16. 72 Cong., 2 Sess., Senate Committee on Banking and Currency, "Stock Exchange Practices," *Hearings*, 1766, 1775-1777.

17. *Ibid.*, 2027-2042. Ferdinand Pecora, *Wall Street under Oath* (New York: Simon and Schuster, 1939), p. 80.

18. Pecora, *Wall Street under Oath*, pp. 195-196; *New York Times*, October 12, 1937.

19. Wilbur and Hyde, *The Hoover Policies*, p. 361; Schlesinger, *The Coming of the New Deal*, p. 4; Raymond Moley, *The First New Deal* (New York: Harcourt, Brace & World, 1966), Chapter 1.

20. Schlesinger, *The Coming of the New Deal*, p. 5.

21. Rixey Smith and Norman Beasley, *Carter Glass* (New York: Longmans, Green and Co., 1939), pp. 340-342.

22. Winthrop W. Aldrich, Appointment Diary, March 4, 1933.

23. Schlesinger, *The Coming of the New Deal*, pp. 6-7; Moley, *The First New Deal*, p. 172.

24. Francis H. Sisson, "Men, Not Laws, Make Sound Banks," *Nation's Business*, Vol. XXI (January 1933), p. 13.

25. *New York Times*, March 8, 1933.

26. Mimeographed statement of Winthrop W. Aldrich, March 8, 1933. Aldrich Papers.

27. *Ibid.*

28. Quoted in *New York Tribune*, March 9, 1933.

29. Schlesinger, *The Coming of the New Deal*, p. 443; *New York Times*, March 9, 1933.

30. Quoted in *New York Herald Tribune*, March 9, 1933.

31. *New York Herald Tribune*, March 10, 1933.

32. *Wall Street Journal*, March 10, 1933.

33. *New York World Telegram*, March 13, 1933.

34. Franklin D. Roosevelt to Winthrop W. Aldrich, March 9, 1933. Clipping book, Aldrich Papers.

35. John D. Rockefeller, Jr. to Winthrop W. Aldrich, March 11, 1933. Clipping book, Aldrich Papers.

36. San Diego (Calif.) *Tribune*, March 21, 1933.

37. Smith and Beasley, *Carter Glass*, pp. 343-345.

38. *Ibid.*, p. 345; and Schlesinger, *The Coming of the New Deal*, p. 8.

39. Smith and Beasley, *Carter Glass*, p. 346.

40. Schlesinger, *The Coming of the New Deal*, pp. 20-21.

41. Groseclose, *Fifty Years of Managed Money*, p. 196.

42. Raymond B. Fosdick, *John D. Rockefeller, Jr.; a Portrait* (New

York: Harper and Brothers, 1956), pp. 251–261; Winthrop W. Aldrich to John J. Raskob, June 11, 1928. Aldrich Papers.

43. Groseclose, *Fifty Years of Managed Money*, p. 200.
44. Interview, A. M. Johnson with Winthrop W. Aldrich, May 12, 1966; Schlesinger, *The Coming of the New Deal*, p. 202.
45. Schlesinger, *The Coming of the New Deal*, pp. 196–197.
46. Interview, A. M. Johnson with Winthrop W. Aldrich, May 12, 1966.
47. *New York Times*, March 29, 1933.
48. 73 Cong., 1 Sess., Senate Committee on Banking and Currency, "Stock Exchange Practices," *Hearings*, 4031–4032.
49. *Ibid.*, 4028.
50. *Ibid.*, 4173–4174, 4178–4181.
51. *New York Times*, June 8, 1934; June 15, 1934.
52. Quoted in Chase National Bank, *Annual Report*, January 9, 1934, p. 19.
53. *Fortune*, Vol. XII (October 1935), pp. 80–83.
54. Chase National Bank, *Annual Report*, January 9, 1934, p. 20.
55. *Fortune*, Vol. XII (October 1935), p. 120.
56. *Moody's Manual of Investments, 1935* (New York: Moody's Investors Service, 1935), 1630; Chase National Bank, *Annual Report*, January 8, 1935, pp. 6–7.
57. Chase National Bank, *Annual Report*, January 9, 1934, p. 23.
58. Winthrop W. Aldrich, Appointment Diary, June 22, 1933.
59. Herbert Feis, *1933: Characters in Crisis* (Boston: Little, Brown and Company, 1966), p. 232; Schlesinger, *The Coming of the New Deal*, p. 222; *New York Times*, July 4, 1933.
60. The following section is based on an interview of Mr. Crawford Wheeler with Mr. Winthrop W. Aldrich, November 30, 1960. Copy in Aldrich Papers.
61. *Business Week* (April 12, 1933), p. 12.
62. 73 Cong., 1 Sess., Senate Committee on Banking and Currency, "Stock Exchange Practices," *Hearings*, 2281.
63. *Ibid.*, 2284–2285.
64. *Ibid.*, 2298.
65. *Ibid.*, 2294–2295.
66. *Ibid.*, 2300.
67. *Ibid.*, 2320–2323, 2356.
68. Quoted in Prescott, *New England Son*, pp. 156–157.

69. 73 Cong., 1 Sess., Senate Committee on Banking and Currency, "Stock Exchange Practices," *Hearings*, 2327.
70. *Ibid.*
71. *Ibid.*, 2879–2885. The technique is explained in Pecora, *Wall Street under Oath*, pp. 200–201, and Frederick L. Allen, *The Lords of Creation* (New York: Harper and Brothers, 1935), pp. 333–334.
72. Allen, *The Lords of Creation*, p. 334; Pecora, *Wall Street under Oath*, p. 152.
73. 73 Cong., 1 Sess., Senate Committee on Banking and Currency, "Stock Exchange Practices," *Hearings*, 2422–2428, 2875; Pecora, *Wall Street under Oath*, p. 151.
74. *Ibid.*, pp. 152–158.
75. 73 Cong., 1 Sess., Senate Committee on Banking and Currency, "Stock Exchange Practices," *Hearings*, 2979.
76. Quoted in *Fortune*, Vol. I (June 1930), p. 91.
77. 73 Cong., 1 Sess., Senate Committee on Banking and Currency, "Stock Exchange Practices," *Hearings*, 2947.
78. *Ibid.*, 2912.
79. *Ibid.*, 2856–2857.
80. For a typical instance, see *ibid.*, 2401–2402.
81. See Ray E. Hiebert, *Courtier to the Crowd* (Ames, Iowa, 1966), pp. 203–207.
82. 73 Cong., 1 Sess., Senate Committee on Banking and Currency, "Stock Exchange Practices," *Hearings*, 2311.
83. *Ibid.*, 3872–3879.
84. *Ibid.*, 4017.
85. *Ibid.*, 4019.
86. *Ibid.*, 3981–3990.
87. *Ibid.*, 4021.
88. *Ibid.*
89. *Ibid.*, 4026–4027.
90. *Ibid.*, 4027.
91. *Ibid.*, 4028.
92. *Ibid.*, 4030.
93. *Ibid.*, 4038–4039.
94. *Ibid.*, 4044–4046.
95. *Ibid.*, 4123–4125.
96. *Ibid.*, 4130–4134.
97. Pecora, *Wall Street under Oath*, p. 137.

98. John D. Rockefeller, Jr., to Winthrop W. Aldrich, December 1, 1933. Clipping book, Aldrich Papers.
99. 73 Cong., 1 Sess., Senate Committee on Banking and Currency, "Stock Exchange Practices," *Hearings*, 4164–4165.
100. *Ibid.*, 4186–4192.
101. *Ibid.*, 4184–4185.
102. *Ibid.*, 4178.
103. *Ibid.*, 4178–4181.
104. *Ibid.*, 4181.
105. Winthrop W. Aldrich, Appointment Diary, December 28, 1933. Interview, A. M. Johnson with Winthrop W. Aldrich, July 1967.
106. Thomas M. Debevoise to Winthrop W. Aldrich, December 18, 1933. Aldrich Papers.

CHAPTER VIII: The Early Leadership Years, 1934–1935

1. Interview, A. M. Johnson with H. Donald Campbell, New York City, April 22, 1966.
2. *Ibid.*
3. *Ibid.*
4. Frederic R. Coudert to Winthrop W. Aldrich, January 9, 1934. Aldrich Papers.
5. Root Committee materials, 1935. Aldrich Papers.
6. Bookbinder et al. *v.* Chase National Bank of New York City et al., amended complaint, Supreme Court of the State of New York, April 28, 1934. Aldrich Papers.
7. Memorandum on closed accounts, Chase National Bank, March 8, 1934. Aldrich Papers.
8. Interview, A. M. Johnson with H. Donald Campbell, New York City, April 22, 1966.
9. The trip is described by Winthrop W. Aldrich in an interview with Crawford Wheeler, September 28, 1962. Also see Western Trip, November–December, 1934. Aldrich Papers.
10. Interview, A. M. Johnson with H. Donald Campbell, New York City, April 22, 1966.
11. Winthrop W. Aldrich, "The Financing of Unemployment Relief," Chase National Bank Publication, 1934 [pamphlet].

12. *Ibid.*
13. *Dallas Morning News*, December 15, 1934.
14. Interview, Winthrop W. Aldrich with Crawford Wheeler, September 28, 1962.
15. *Dallas Morning News*, December 15, 1934.
16. Herbert H. Lehman to Winthrop W. Aldrich, July 24, 1935. Aldrich Papers.
17. Percy Johnston to Winthrop W. Aldrich, March 27, 1934; Memorandum, March 2, 1934, New York Clearing House, 1935. Aldrich Papers.
18. *Wall Street Journal*, December 6, 1933; January 10, 1934; Chase National Bank, *Annual Report*, January 9, 1934, p. 8.
19. Bascom N. Timmons, *Jesse H. Jones, The Man and the Statesman* (New York: Henry Holt and Co., 1956), p. 204; Schlesinger, *The Coming of the New Deal*, p. 430.
20. Winthrop W. Aldrich, Appointment Diary, February 20, April 19, 1934.
21. Schlesinger, *The Coming of the New Deal*, p. 499.
22. *The Commercial and Financial Chronicle*, American Bankers' Convention Section, Vol. CXXXIX, November 17, 1934, pp. 10–11.
23. Winthrop W. Aldrich, Appointment Diary, October 25, 1934.
24. Schlesinger, *The Coming of the New Deal*, p. 425.
25. Marriner Eccles, *Beckoning Frontiers, Public and Personal Recollections* (New York: Alfred A. Knopf, 1951), pp. 170–171.
26. *Ibid.*, p. 174.
27. *Ibid.*, pp. 192–193.
28. *Ibid.*, pp. 196–197.
29. *Ibid.*, p. 201. See also Robert V. Fleming to Crawford Wheeler, November 28, 1960, recorded in interview, Crawford Wheeler with Winthrop W. Aldrich, September 28, 1962.
30. 74 Cong., 1 Sess., House Committee on Banking and Currency, "Banking Act of 1935," *Hearings* (Washington, D.C., 1935), 514.
31. 74 Cong., 1 Sess., Senate Subcommittee of the Committee on Banking and Currency, "Banking Act of 1935," *Hearings* (Washington, D.C., 1935), 385.
32. 74 Cong., 1 Sess., House Committee on Banking and Currency, "Banking Act of 1935," *Hearings*, 515.
33. New Orleans, *Times-Picaynne*, March 30, 1935.
34. *American Banker*, Vol. C, March 28–29, 1935.

35. Washington *Post*, April 3, 1935.
36. 74 Cong., 1 Sess., Senate Subcommittee of the Committee on Banking and Currency, "Banking Act of 1935," *Hearings*, 386.
37. Eccles, *Beckoning Frontiers*, p. 202.
38. 74 Cong., 1 Sess., Senate Subcommittee of the Committee on Banking and Currency, "Banking Act of 1935," *Hearings*, 386, 389.
39. *Ibid.*, 390–391.
40. *Ibid.*, 392.
41. *Ibid.*, 392–393.
42. *Ibid.*, 395–399.
43. *Ibid.*, 423.
44. *Ibid.*, 399–401. See also 74 Cong., 1 Sess., House Committee on Banking and Currency, "Banking Act of 1935," *Hearings*, 181–183.
45. 74 Cong., 1 Sess., Senate Subcommittee of the Committee on Banking and Currency, "Banking Act of 1935," *Hearings*, 401–403.
46. *Ibid.*, 405–406.
47. *Ibid.*, 414–415.
48. Eccles, *Beckoning Frontiers*, pp. 205–206.
49. 74 Cong., 1 Sess., Senate Subcommittee of the Committee on Banking and Currency, "Banking Act of 1935," *Hearings*, 393–394.
50. Eccles, *Beckoning Frontiers*, pp. 218–219.
51. *Ibid.*, pp. 220–221.
52. *Ibid.*, p. 228.
53. Francis M. Law to Winthrop W. Aldrich, April 1, 1935. Aldrich Papers.
54. Rudolph S. Hecht to Winthrop W. Aldrich, August 31, 1935. Aldrich Papers.
55. Winthrop W. Aldrich to Rudolph S. Hecht, September 5, 1935. Aldrich Papers.
56. Interview, A. M. Johnson with Lawrence Bennett and Edward Love, New York City, June 10, 1966; see also *New York Times*, November 12, 1933.
57. Interviews, A. M. Johnson with Lawrence Bennett and Edward Love, New York City, June 10, 1966 and October 19, 1966.
58. Winthrop W. Aldrich, "Business Revival and Government Policy," Chase National Bank Publication, 1935 [pamphlet].
59. *New York Times*, November 23, 1935.

60. *Ibid.*, December 19, 1935.
61. Interview, A. M. Johnson with Hermann G. Place, New York City, April 14, 1966.
62. *Ibid.*
63. *Ibid.*; see also *Fortune*, Vol. XII (December 1935), pp. 85–93.
64. Interview, A. M. Johnson with Hermann G. Place, New York City, April 14, 1966; and interview, A. M. Johnson with H. Donald Campbell, New York City, April 22, 1966.
65. Interview, A. M. Johnson with Hermann G. Place, New York City, April 14, 1966; see also Chase National Bank, *Annual Report*, January 14, 1936, p. 15.
66. *Moody's Manual of Investments*, 1936 (New York: Moody's Investors Service, 1936), pp. 2,905–2,907.
67. Chase National Bank, *Annual Report*, January 9, 1934, pp. 14–18.

CHAPTER IX: The Transition Years, 1936–1939

1. Interview, A. M. Johnson with H. Donald Campbell, New York City, April 22, 1966.
2. *Ibid.*
3. Memorandum, Joseph Pogue to Winthrop W. Aldrich, October 28, 1947. Aldrich Papers.
4. Memorandum, B. H. Beckhart to Winthrop W. Aldrich, May 20, 1940. Aldrich Papers.
5. Winthrop W. Aldrich to Thomas McCarter, October 13, 1937. Aldrich Papers.
6. Foreign Department Memorandum, S. Stern to Winthrop W. Aldrich, March 3, 1938. Aldrich Papers.
7. Chase National Bank, *Annual Report*, January 11, 1938, p. 18; *ibid.*, January 10, 1939, p. 13.
8. Marjorie Wiggin Prescot, *New England Son*, p. 264.
9. *Ibid.*, pp. 262–263.
10. Chase National Bank, *Annual Report*, January 11, 1938, pp. 17–18.
11. Interview, A. M. Johnson with Hermann G. Place, New York City, April 14, 1966.
12. *Ibid.*

13. *Ibid.*

14. Chase National Bank, *Annual Report*, 1937–1939.

15. B. C. Forbes to Winthrop W. Aldrich, November 24, 1937. Aldrich Papers.

16. John Morton Blum, *From the Morgenthau Diaries: Years of Crisis, 1928–1938*, Vol. I (New York: Houghton Mifflin, 1959), pp. 355–356; Eccles, *Beckoning Frontiers*, pp. 289–290.

17. Winthrop W. Aldrich, "Foreign Trade and our National Interests," Chase National Bank Publication, 1936 [pamphlet].

18. Winthrop W. Aldrich, "An Appraisal of the Federal Social Security Act," Chase National Bank Publication, 1936 [pamphlet].

19. The Federal Social Security Act, Title III, section 902.

20. *Rocky Mountain News*, July 21, 1936.

21. Winthrop W. Aldrich, Remarks at the Stockholders Meeting of the Federal Reserve Bank of Boston, November 12, 1936 [typescript].

22. Winthrop W. Aldrich, "The Responsibilities of Business Leadership," Chase National Bank Publication, 1936 [pamphlet].

23. Winthrop W. Aldrich, "Business Recovery and Government Policy," Chase National Bank Publication, 1936 [pamphlet].

24. *Federal Reserve Bulletin*, Vol. XXIII (February 1937), pp. 95–97.

25. Blum, *From the Morgenthau Diaries*, Vol. I, pp. 381–383.

26. *Ibid.*, pp. 382–383.

27. Winthrop W. Aldrich, "The Stock Market from the Viewpoint of a Commercial Banker," Chase National Bank Publication, 1937 [pamphlet].

28. *New York Times*, October 16, 1937.

29. *Ibid.*, October 18, 1937.

30. *Ibid.*, October 21, 1937.

31. *Wall Street Journal*, October 15–18, 1937; Jerome Cuppia to Winthrop W. Aldrich, December 6, 1937.

32. Winthrop W. Aldrich to William O. Douglas, December 1, 1937. See also Fred Rodell, "Douglas over the Stock Exchange," *Fortune*, Vol. XVII (February 1938), pp. 64, 116–126.

33. Winthrop W. Aldrich to Russell Davenport, January 13, 1938. Aldrich Papers.

34. Trowbridge Callaway to Winthrop W. Aldrich, December 23, 1937; Winthrop W. Aldrich, Appointment Diary, December 30, 1937.

35. Winthrop W. Aldrich, "Causes of the Present Business Depres-

sion," Chamber of Commerce of the State of New York, *Monthly Bulletin*, Vol. XXIX (November 1937), pp. 181–184.

36. Chamber of Commerce of the State of New York, Press Release, January 3, 1938 [mimeographed]. Aldrich Papers.

37. 75 Cong., 3 Sess., Senate Special Committee to Investigate Unemployment and Relief, "Unemployment and Relief," *Hearings* (Washington, D.C., 1938), 521.

38. *Ibid.*, 526.

39. *Ibid.*, 536.

40. *Ibid.*, 523.

41. Blum, *From the Morgenthau Diaries*, Vol. I, pp. 387–388; Eccles, *Beckoning Frontiers*, pp. 304, 309–310.

42. *New York Times*, April 15, 1938; Eccles, *Beckoning Frontiers*, p. 311.

43. *Federal Reserve Bulletin*, Vol. XXIV (November 1938), pp. 960, 972.

44. John W. Hanes, Commissioner of the Securities and Exchange Commission, Address before the Commonwealth Club of Cincinnati, May 5, 1938 [copy in Aldrich Papers].

45. *New York Times*, April 27, 1938.

46. Franklin D. Roosevelt to John Hanes, April 27, 1938 [copy in Aldrich Papers].

47. Lenox R. Lohr, President, NBC, to Winthrop W. Aldrich, May 24, 1938. Aldrich Papers.

48. Winthrop W. Aldrich to Lenox R. Lohr, May 27, 1938. Aldrich Papers.

49. New York *Daily News*, May 4, 1938.

50. *New York Times*, May 5, 6, 1938.

51. *Ibid.*, December 15, 1937.

52. *Ibid.*, December 31, 1937.

53. 76 Cong., 3 Sess., Temporary National Economic Committee, "Investigation of Concentration of Economic Power," *Hearings*, 15209–15225.

54. Chamber of Commerce of the State of New York, *Monthly Bulletin*, Vol. XXX (May 1938), p. 30.

55. Winthrop W. Aldrich, "Sweden and the United States," Chase National Bank Publication, 1938 [pamphlet].

56. Winthrop W. Aldrich, Remarks at the First Meeting of the Committee on Monetary Policy and Credit of the International Chamber of Commerce, Paris, 1938 [typescript]. Aldrich Papers.

57. *World Trade* (April 1939), p. 23.
58. Winthrop W. Aldrich, Address to the Twenty-Fifth National Foreign Trade Convention, October 31, 1938 [typescript]. Aldrich Papers.
59. *The Consensus*, Vol. XXIII (January 1939), p. 23.
60. Quoted in *New York Times*, August 17, 1939.
61. *Ibid.*
62. *Ibid.*
63. *The Coupon*, Bulletin of the Bond Club of New York, No. 60 (August 1939), p. 29.
64. Transcript of interview, Winthrop W. Aldrich with Georges Bonnet, October 18, 1938. Aldrich Papers.
65. *Ibid.*, April 18, 1939.
66. Winthrop W. Aldrich to C. D. Hilles, December 5, 1936. Aldrich Papers.

CHAPTER X: The War Relief Years, 1939–1946

1. Senator Harry F. Byrd to Winthrop W. Aldrich, October 26, 1939. Aldrich Papers.
2. *New York Times*, January 26, 1940.
3. *Ibid.*, September 14, 1940.
4. *Ibid.*, January 5, 1941.
5. Anthony Eden to Winthrop W. Aldrich, January 31, 1941. Aldrich Papers.
6. *New York Times*, May 2, 1941.
7. *Ibid.*, July 6, 1941.
8. Winthrop W. Aldrich, Radio Address, October 15, 1940 [typescript]. Aldrich Papers.
9. Winthrop W. Aldrich, "The Public Debt and the Private Citizen," Chase National Bank Publication, 1940 [pamphlet].
10. *Ibid.*
11. Winthrop W. Aldrich to Andrew Price, July 10, 1941. Aldrich Papers.
12. Winthrop W. Aldrich to Franklin D. Roosevelt, June 3, 1941, and Franklin D. Roosevelt to Winthrop W. Aldrich, June 9, 1941. Aldrich Papers.

13. Report of Special Subcommittee on Program of Treasury Financing, May 28, 1942 [mimeographed]. Aldrich Papers.

14. William Richmond, Treasury Department, War Financing Committee, U.S. Savings Bond Division, to Winthrop W. Aldrich, February 7, 1946. Also, interview, A. M. Johnson with Winthrop W. Aldrich, New York City, May 26, 1966.

15. The account of this visit to Britain is in "Skeleton Diary of Winthrop W. Aldrich's Trip to England, July 23 to August 19, 1942." Aldrich Papers.

16. *Ibid.*, and interview, A. M. Johnson with Winthrop W. Aldrich, New York City, June 21, 1967.

17. "Skeleton Diary of Winthrop W. Aldrich's trip to England, July 23 to August 19, 1942." Aldrich Papers.

18. Stenographic report of Winthrop W. Aldrich's address to a luncheon of the British War Relief Society, August 27, 1942. Aldrich Papers.

19. *Ibid.*

20. *Time* (March 3, 1941), p. 15.

21. Telegram, Winthrop W. Aldrich to Thomas J. Watson, September 2, 1942. Aldrich Papers.

22. Charles P. Taft to Winthrop W. Aldrich, December 15, 1942. Aldrich Papers.

23. Winthrop W. Aldrich to Franklin D. Roosevelt, February 27, 1943. Aldrich Papers.

24. National War Fund, Statement of Recommended Procedure for Distribution of Funds, Approved by the Budget Committee, June 4, 1943 [mimeographed]. Aldrich Papers.

25. Winthrop W. Aldrich, Statement on the National War Fund, March 7, 1943 [typescript]. Aldrich Papers.

26. Report by the President of the National War Fund, October 9, 1944 [typescript]. Aldrich Papers.

27. *Ibid.*

28. Statement on the National Budget of the National War Fund (Draft), July 16, 1943 [mimeographed]. Aldrich Papers.

29. Report by the President of the National War Fund, October 9, 1944 [typescript]. Aldrich Papers.

30. Annual Report by the President of the National War Fund, April 30, 1945 [typescript]. Aldrich Papers.

31. *Ibid.*

32. Annual Report by the President of the National War Fund, February 4, 1946 [typescript]. Aldrich Papers.

33. Annual Report by the President of the National War Fund, April 30, 1945 [typescript]. Aldrich Papers.

34. Annual Report by the President of the National War Fund, February 4, 1946 [typescript]. Aldrich Papers.

35. *Ibid.*

36. Harold J. Seymour, *Design for Giving: The Story of the National War Fund, 1943–1947* (New York: Harper and Brothers, 1947), p. 79.

37. *Ibid.*, pp. 66–67.

38. Final Report of the National War Fund, July 9, 1957 [mimeographed]. Aldrich Papers.

39. This account is based on: United States of America *vs.* Leonard J. A. Smit, Anton Smit and Co., Inc., Elsantum, Inc., and the Chase National Bank. United States District Court, Southern District of New York, April 16–May 2, 1945 [stenographer's minutes]. 4 volumes.

40. Interview, A. M. Johnson with Winthrop W. Aldrich, New York City, May 26, 1966.

41. Timothy N. Pfeiffer and George W. Jaques, *Law Practice in a Turbulent World* (New York: Charles P. Young Co., 1965), p. 212.

42. Interview, A. M. Johnson with John T. Cahill, New York City, April 21, 1966.

43. *Ibid.*

44. Interview, A. M. Johnson with Winthrop W. Aldrich, New York City, May 26, 1966.

45. New York *Herald Tribune*, May 7, 1945.

46. *New York Times*, May 9, 1945.

CHAPTER XI: Years of Preparation for the
Postwar World, 1940–1946

1. Winthrop W. Aldrich, Address before the International Chamber of Commerce, May 7, 1940 [typescript]. Aldrich Papers.

2. *Ibid.*
3. Winthrop W. Aldrich, "The Public Debt and the Private Citizen," Chase National Bank Publication, 1940 [pamphlet].
4. Winthrop W. Aldrich, "The Economic Implications of Internal Debts," Chase National Bank Publication, 1943 [pamphlet].
5. Winthrop W. Aldrich, "The Problem of Postwar Monetary Stabilization," Chase National Bank Publication, 1943 [pamphlet].
6. *Ibid.*
7. *Ibid.*
8. Winthrop W. Aldrich, Address before the Economic Club of New York, November 23, 1943 [typescript]. Aldrich Papers.
9. Winthrop W. Aldrich, "The Importance of Liberal Foreign Trading Policies," *Printers Ink*, Vol. CCLX (October 20, 1944), p. 32.
10. Winthrop W. Aldrich, "The Problem of the Postwar World," *The Lee Traveler* (Camp Lee, Virginia), October 1944 [typescript]. Aldrich Papers.
11. Winthrop W. Aldrich, "Some Aspects of American Foreign Economic Policy," Chase National Bank Publication, 1944 [pamphlet].
12. *Ibid.*
13. *Ibid.*
14. *Congressional Record*, September 21, 1944, 8169–8171.
15. *Ibid.*, 8171.
16. I. Zlobin, "Meeting in America," *The War and the Working Class*, October 15, 1944 [mimeographed]. Translation in Aldrich Papers.
17. George L. Ridgeway, *Merchants of Peace; The History of the International Chamber of Commerce* (Boston: Little, Brown and Company, 1959), pp. 157–158.
18. Quoted in *ibid.*, p. 159.
19. *Ibid.*
20. Quoted in Press Release, November 10, 1944. International Business Conference [mimeographed]. Aldrich Papers.
21. John H. Williams, *Postwar Monetary Plans and Other Essays* (Oxford: Basil Blackwell, 1949).
22. Winthrop W. Aldrich, "The 'Key Nation' Approach to the Problem of Currency Stabilization," Address before the Rye conference, November 13, 1944 [typescript]. Aldrich Papers.
23. Winthrop W. Aldrich, "Currency Relations Among Nations: a

Report," Address before the Rye conference, November 1944 [typescript]. Aldrich Papers.

24. Final Reports of the International Business Conference (Rye, New York), 1944, pp. 17–18 [pamphlet]. Aldrich Papers.

25. George L. Ridgeway, *Merchants of Peace*, p. 168.

26. Draft of Report of the Committee on Special Activities of the American Bankers Association and the Special Committee of the Association of Reserve City Bankers on the Bretton Woods proposals, January 1945 [mimeographed]. Aldrich Papers.

27. American Bankers Association, "Practical International Financial Organization Through Amendments to Bretton Woods Proposals," February 1, 1945 [pamphlet]. Aldrich Papers.

28. Research Committee of the Committee for Economic Development, "The Bretton Woods Proposals," March 1945; 79 Cong., 1 Sess., House Committee on Banking and Currency, "Bretton Woods Agreements Act," *Hearings* (Washington, 1945), 739–740.

29. Winthrop W. Aldrich to Ralph Flanders, March 22, 1945. Aldrich Papers.

30. 79 Cong., 1 Sess., House Committee on Banking and Currency, "Bretton Woods Agreements Act," *Hearings*, 734–735.

31. 79 Cong., 1 Sess., Senate Committee on Banking and Currency, "Bretton Woods Agreements Act," *Hearings* (Washington, 1945), 402.

32. *Ibid.*, 420.

33. Winthrop W. Aldrich to Herbert Brownell, Jr., April 13, 1945. Aldrich Papers.

34. *Ibid.*

35. Richard N. Gardner, *Sterling–Dollar Diplomacy* (Oxford: Clarendon Press, 1956), p. 140.

36. 79 Cong., 1 Sess., Senate Committee on Banking and Currency, "Bretton Woods Agreements Act," *Hearings*, 324.

37. Gardner, *Sterling-Dollar Diplomacy*, pp. 201–202.

38. Winthrop W. Aldrich, "The Bases for World Trade," Chase National Bank Publication, 1945 [pamphlet].

39. Stenographic record of Mr. Aldrich's Speech at the Union Club, June 26, 1945 [typescript]. Aldrich Papers.

40. *Ibid.*

41. Trip Folder, Europe, 1945. Aldrich Papers.

42. Winthrop W. Aldrich, "The Objectives of the International

Chamber of Commerce," Chase National Bank Publication, 1945 [pamphlet].

43. Winthrop W. Aldrich to Lord McGowen, August 11, 1945. Aldrich Papers.

44. See, for example, Winthrop W. Aldrich to Emmanuel Monick, Bank of France, September 4, 1945. Aldrich Papers.

45. Winthrop W. Aldrich to Robert D. Murphy, September 3, 1945. Aldrich Papers.

46. "America Assists Vigorously to the Rehabilitation of the Netherlands," *Het Parool*, August 30, 1945 [translated typescript]. Aldrich Papers.

47. Winthrop W. Aldrich to Princess Juliana of Orange-Nassau, September 3, 1945. Aldrich Papers.

48. Winthrop W. Aldrich, "The Future Program of the International Chamber of Commerce," Chase National Bank Publication, 1945 [pamphlet].

49. 79 Cong., 2 Sess., Senate Committee on Banking and Currency, "Anglo-American Financial Agreement," *Hearings* (Washington, 1946), 342–365.

50. Gardner, *Sterling-Dollar Diplomacy*, p. 248.

51. Quoted in *ibid.*, p. 253.

52. Francis Cardinal Spellman to Count Enrico Galeazzi, July 11, 1945. Aldrich Papers.

CHAPTER XII: The Early Postwar Years, 1946–1948

1. Harry S. Truman to Winthrop W. Aldrich, June 17, 1946. Aldrich Papers.

2. George L. Ridgeway, *Merchants of Peace: The History of the International Chamber of Commerce* (Boston: Little, Brown, 1959), p. 131.

3. Press Release, June 26, 1946 [mimeographed]. Aldrich Papers.

4. Charles Symington to John W. Snyder, Secretary of the Treasury, June 27, 1946. Aldrich Papers.

5. Charles Symington to Arthur Page, June 27, 1946. Aldrich Papers.

6. *New York Tribune*, July 10, 1946.

7. Memo, President's Committee For Financing Foreign Trade, July 18, 1946. Aldrich Papers.
8. Minutes of Meetings, President's Committee for Financing Foreign Trade, September 25–26, 1946. Aldrich Papers.
9. Interview, A. M. Johnson with John J. McCloy, New York City, April 22, 1966.
10. *Ibid.,* also, interview, A. M. Johnson with Winthrop W. Aldrich, New York City, April 14, 1966.
11. The details of this trip are recorded in diaries kept by both Winthrop W. Aldrich and Harriet A. Aldrich, March 16–April 30, 1947. Aldrich Papers.
12. Interview, A. M. Johnson with Charles Cain, Jr., New York City, May 25, 1966.
13. *Ibid.*
14. Harriet A. Aldrich, Trip Diary, April 15, 1947. Aldrich Papers.
15. *New York Times,* September 14, 1947.
16. *Ibid.,* March 13, 1947.
17. *Ibid.,* May 9, 1947.
18. Winthrop W. Aldrich, "The Problem of European Reconstruction," Notes for Alumni Luncheon, Columbia University, June 4, 1946 [typescript]. Aldrich Papers.
19. Winthrop W. Aldrich, "International Economic Policy and the Future of Business," Chase National Bank Publication, 1946 [pamphlet].
20. Winthrop W. Aldrich, Statement to the Press, June 1947 [typescript]. Aldrich Papers.
21. *New York Times,* September 30, 1947. For more detail on this aid see U.S. Commission on Foreign Economic Policy, *Staff Papers* (Washington 1954), Chapter 2.
22. Winthrop W. Aldrich, "American Interest in European Reconstruction," Chase National Bank Publication, 1947 [pamphlet].
23. *Ibid.*
24. Frank McNaughton and Walter Heymeyer, *Harry Truman, President* (New York: McGraw Hill Book Co., Inc., 1948), pp. 96–97. See also, *New York Times,* December 20, 1947.
25. The text of Truman's Address to Congress, December 19, 1947, is quoted in Louis W. Koenig, *The Truman Administration: Its Principles and Practice* (New York: New York University Press, 1956), pp. 304–323.
26. Copies of the Harriman and Herter Committee Reports, No-

vember 8, 1947 [mimeographed] are with the materials of the President's Committee for Financing Foreign Trade. Aldrich Papers.

27. Gordon Rentschler to Winthrop W. Aldrich, January 23, 1948. Aldrich Papers.

28. Winthrop W. Aldrich to L. M. Giannini, January 27, 1948. Aldrich Papers.

29. R. A. Lovett to Winthrop W. Aldrich, January 15, 1948. Aldrich Papers.

30. Winthrop W. Aldrich to William L. Clayton, January 22, 1948. Aldrich Papers.

31. Winthrop W. Aldrich, "Inflation in Europe," March 18, 1948 [typescript]. Aldrich Papers.

32. Winthrop W. Aldrich, "The Foreign Assistance Act of 1948," Chase National Bank Publication, 1948 [pamphlet].

33. Louis C. Wyman to Winthrop W. Aldrich, May 25, 1948. Aldrich Papers.

34. Winthrop W. Aldrich to Ernest T. Weir, July 26, 1949. Aldrich Papers.

35. *Forbes*, Vol. LXI (January 15, 1948), pp. 18–19, 40.

36. Interview, A. M. Johnson with Louis Novins, New York City, May 26, 1966.

37. *Ibid.*

38. *Ibid.*

39. Winthrop W. Aldrich to Harvey Firestone, February 15, 1947. Aldrich Papers.

40. Interview, A. M. Johnson with Louis Novins, New York City, May 26, 1966.

41. Thomas D'A. Brophy to Irving S. Olds, July 29, 1947. Aldrich Papers.

42. Harry S. Truman to Winthrop W. Aldrich, May 10, 1947. Aldrich Papers.

43. Winthrop W. Aldrich to Charles Luckman, Lever Brothers, July 28, 1947. Aldrich Papers.

44. *New York Times*, June 21, 1947.

45. *Chicago Tribune*, September 11, 1947.

46. Thomas D'A. Brophy to Winthrop W. Aldrich, July 14, 1947; August 6, 1947. Aldrich Papers.

47. Winthrop W. Aldrich, Remarks in response to the Attorney

General, Philadelphia, Pennsylvania, September 16, 1947 [type-script]. Aldrich Papers.

48. Winthrop W. Aldrich, Remarks at Opening of Freedom Train, Philadelphia, Pennsylvania, September 17, 1947 [typescript]. Aldrich Papers.

49. Press Release, September 26, 1947. American Heritage Foundation [mimeographed]. Aldrich Papers.

50. Telegram, Walter White to Winthrop W. Aldrich, October 15, 1947; telegram, Louis Novins to Walter Winchell, October 15, 1947; letter, Louis Novins to Walter White, October 22, 1947. Aldrich Papers.

51. Reported in the Memphis *Press-Scimitar*, December 10, 1947. Aldrich Papers.

52. Memorandum Report submitted by Thomas D'A. Brophy, President, to the Board of Trustees, American Heritage Foundation, January 19, 1948 [mimeographed]. Aldrich Papers.

53. Winthrop W. Aldrich to DeWitt Wallace, April 29, 1948. Aldrich Papers.

54. Thomas D'A. Brophy, Memorandum on the Future Operations of the American Heritage Foundation, November 15, 1948. Aldrich Papers.

CHAPTER XIII: The Late Banking Years, 1941–1952

1. Interview, A. M. Johnson with Winthrop W. Aldrich, Providence, December 18, 1965.

2. Chase National Bank, *Annual Report*, January 9, 1945.

3. *Ibid.*; *New York Times*, September 26, 1944.

4. *New York Times*, August 8, 1945; October 15, 1945.

5. *Ibid.*, January 3, 1946.

6. Chase National Bank, *Annual Report*, 1946.

7. Winthrop W. Aldrich, "Economic Significance of Postwar Changes in Commercial Bank Portfolios," Chase National Bank Publication, 1948 [pamphlet].

8. The Committee on Money and Credit was established in 1958. See Commission on Money and Credit, *A Progress Report, February 1960* (New York: Committee on Money and Credit,

1960). Also, Commission on Money and Credit, *Money and Credit; Their Influence on Jobs, Prices, and Growth* (New Jersey: Prentice-Hall, Inc., 1961).

9. J. C. Rovensky and S. Stern to Winthrop W. Aldrich and H. D. Campbell, "Foreign Operations of Our Bank," November 8, 1943 [Foreign Department Memorandum]. Aldrich Papers.

10. *Ibid.*

11. The activities of the Chase foreign branches are recorded in the Chase National Bank *Annual Report*. See also two memoranda, Joseph Larkin to Winthrop W. Aldrich, June 14, 1943 [Foreign Department Memorandum]. Aldrich Papers.

12. Winthrop W. Aldrich to Dean Acheson, August 17, 1943, and Dean Acheson to Winthrop W. Aldrich, December 4, 1943. Aldrich Papers.

13. Interview, A. M. Johnson with Charles Cain, Jr., New York City, May 25, 1966.

14. J. C. Rovensky to Winthrop W. Aldrich, August 4, 1944 [Foreign Department Memorandum]. Aldrich Papers.

15. Chase National Bank, *Annual Report*, 1947.

16. See, Prescott C. Crafts, Jr., *A Management Re-Examination of Expansion Overseas by American Banks*, Graduate School of Banking, Rutgers University, June 1957, pp. 73–76 [mimeographed].

17. Interview, A. M. Johnson with Percy J. Ebbott, New York City, February 1, 1966.

18. Interview, A. M. Johnson with Charles Cain, Jr., New York City, May 25, 1966.

19. Alfred W. Barth to Winthrop W. Aldrich, December 15, 1950 [Foreign Department Memorandum]. Aldrich Papers.

20. J. A. Jacobson to Winthrop W. Aldrich, August 15, 1950 [Foreign Department Memorandum]. Aldrich Papers.

21. Alfred W. Barth to Winthrop W. Aldrich, November 16, 1950 [Foreign Department Memorandum]. Aldrich Papers.

22. Winthrop W. Aldrich to Dean Acheson, July 31, 1950. Aldrich Papers.

23. Memorandum, "The Establishment of An Investment Bank in Brazil," December 7, 1950 [Foreign Department Memorandum]. Aldrich Papers.

24. For details of this trip see Trip Schedule, April 14–June 21, 1950; also related trip correspondence. Aldrich Papers.

25. Spyros Skouras to King Paul and Queen Frederica of Greece, March 27, 1950. Aldrich Papers.
26. Interview, A. M. Johnson with Winthrop W. Aldrich, June 21, 1967.
27. This visit is credited with influencing ECA participation in Portugal. See Alfred Barth to Winthrop W. Aldrich, August 3, 1950 [Foreign Department Memorandum]. Aldrich Papers.
28. Chase National Bank, *Annual Report*, 1951.
29. *Ibid.*
30. Percy J. Ebbott to P. G. Dobson, November 28, 1951. Aldrich Papers.
31. Interview, A. M. Johnson with Winthrop W. Aldrich, June 9, 1967.
32. *New York Times*, August 21, 1951.
33. Interview, A. M. Johnson with Winthrop W. Aldrich, New York City, May 26, 1966.
34. *New York Times*, August 21–24, 1951.
35. Interview, A. M. Johnson with John J. McCloy, New York City, April 22, 1966.
36. Chase National Bank to Shareholders, Testimonial to Winthrop W. Aldrich by the Chase Board of Directors, January 7, 1953. Aldrich Papers.

CHAPTER XIV: The Ambassadorial Years: 1952–1955

1. *New York Times*, October 13, 1946.
2. Winthrop W. Aldrich, Appointment Diary, August 28, 1950. Aldrich Papers.
3. *New York Times*, August 31, 1950.
4. *Ibid.*, September 3, 1950.
5. Drew Pearson, *Washington Post*, August 31, 1950. [Copy is in Aldrich Papers.]
6. Winthrop W. Aldrich to W. S. Moore, September 6, 1950. Aldrich Papers.
7. Winthrop W. Aldrich to Frank Gannett, September 11, 1950. Aldrich Papers.

8. *New York Times*, September 27, 1950; October 9, 1950.
9. Dwight D. Eisenhower to Winthrop W. Aldrich, March 9, 1949. Aldrich Papers.
10. Winthrop W. Aldrich to General Dwight D. Eisenhower, December 28, 1950. Aldrich Papers.
11. Winthrop W. Aldrich to Mrs. Oliver D. Seevell, September 7, 1950. Aldrich Papers.
12. Winthrop W. Aldrich to General Dwight D. Eisenhower, November 26, 1951; December 10, 1951. Aldrich Papers.
13. Interview, A. M. Johnson with John C. Traphagen, New York City, June 10, 1966.
14. Washington, D.C., *Times Herald*, December 1, 1952.
15. Letter read at annual meeting of Chase National Bank stockholders and reprinted in the *New York Times*, February 4, 1951.
16. Interview, A. M. Johnson with Winthrop W. Aldrich, Dark Harbor, Maine, July 24, 1967.
17. *Ibid.*
18. London, *Daily Press*, November 30, 1952.
19. Winthrop W. Aldrich, Appointment Diary, January 1953. Aldrich Papers.
20. Interview, A. M. Johnson with Winthrop W. Aldrich, Dark Harbor, Maine, July 24, 1967.
21. *New York Times*, January 31, 1953; February 3, 1953.
22. Winthrop W. Aldrich, Remarks to the Press on Arrival in London, February 11, 1953 [typescript]. Aldrich Papers.
23. *New York Times*, February 21, 23, 1953.
24. The Pilgrim Dinner in Honour of Walter S. Gifford, Savoy Hotel, January 21, 1953 [pamphlet]. Aldrich Papers.
25. Viscount Jowitt to Winthrop W. Aldrich, December 18, 1952. Aldrich Papers. Also, interview, A. M. Johnson with Winthrop W. Aldrich, Dark Harbor, Maine, July 24, 1967. For the history and traditions of the Middle Temple see George Godwin, *The Middle Temple: The Society and Fellowship* (London: Staples Press Ltd., 1954).
26. *New York Times*, April 21, 1953.
27. *Ibid.*, February 28, 1953.
28. Winthrop W. Aldrich to Viscount Simon, March 25, 1953. Aldrich Papers.
29. John D. Rockefeller, Jr., to Sir Campbell Stuart, May 1, 1953. [Copy in Aldrich Papers.]

30. Winthrop W. Aldrich, Speech to the English Speaking Union, April 1, 1953 [typescript]. Aldrich Papers.

31. Winthrop W. Aldrich, Speech at the dedication of Kresge and Aldrich Halls, Harvard Business School, June 12, 1953 [typescript]. Aldrich Papers.

32. Dean Erwin Griswold to Winthrop W. Aldrich, June 15, 1953. Aldrich Papers.

33. Winthrop W. Aldrich, Speech to British National Committee of the International Chamber of Commerce, June 23, 1953 [typescript]. Aldrich Papers.

34. *Ibid.*

35. Winthrop W. Aldrich, Speech at Civic Dinner, July 24, 1953, Manchester, England [typescript]. Aldrich Papers.

36. Charles G. Cushing to Winthrop W. Aldrich, November 24, 1953. Aldrich Papers.

37. Winthrop W. Aldrich, Speech to the Cardiff [Wales] Business Club, February 15, 1954 [typescript]. Aldrich Papers. See also *New York Times*, February 16, 1954.

38. Randolph Churchill, *The Rise and Fall of Sir Anthony Eden* (London: MacGibbon and Kee, 1959), p. 233.

39. Secretary of State Dulles, "Report on the Near East," U.S. Department of State *Bulletin*, Vol. XXVIII (June 15, 1953), pp. 833–834.

40. Winthrop W. Aldrich, Remarks to the Birmingham Chamber of Commerce, May 10, 1954 [typescript]. Aldrich Papers.

41. *Ibid.*

42. *Ibid.* See also U. S. Commission on Foreign Policy, *Report to the President and the Congress* (Washington, D.C.: U.S. Government Printing Office, January 23, 1954).

43. Winthrop W. Aldrich, Remarks to the Birmingham Chamber of Commerce, May 10, 1954 [typescript]. Aldrich Papers. See also *New York Times*, May 11, 1954.

44. Winthrop W. Aldrich, Speech at the opening of the Commercial and Local Government Reference Library, Liverpool, England, January 27, 1955 [typescript]. Aldrich Papers.

45. See news clipping of Aldrich Speech, Liverpool, England, January 1955. Aldrich Papers.

46. Sir Arthur P. M. Sanders to Winthrop W. Aldrich, March 1, 1955. Aldrich Papers. See Winthrop W. Aldrich, Lecture at the

Imperial Defence College, London, England, March 1, 1955 [typescript]. Aldrich Papers.

47. E. P. Rugg to Winthrop W. Aldrich, March 24, 1955. Aldrich Papers. See Winthrop W. Aldrich, Off-the-Record Remarks at the Junior Carlton Club, London, England, March 22, 1955 [typescript]. Aldrich Papers.

48. Transcript, Question and Answer Session, Royal Empire Society, March 24, 1955. Aldrich Papers. See also Winthrop W. Aldrich, Speech before Royal Empire Society, March 24, 1955; and *New York Times*, March 25, 1955.

49. Winthrop W. Aldrich to Theodore Nicholson, March 5, 1956. Aldrich Papers. See also correspondence regarding Washington Old Hall, particularly the letters of Charles Sumner Bird to Winthrop W. Aldrich, various dates, 1955. Aldrich Papers.

50. The following is based on an interview, A. M. Johnson with Winthrop W. Aldrich, Dark Harbor, Maine, July 24, 1967.

51. *New York Times*, February 22–23, 1955.

52. Interview, A. M. Johnson with Winthrop W. Aldrich, Dark Harbor, Maine, July 24, 1967.

53. *New York Times*, August 4, 1955.

54. Churchill, *The Rise and Fall of Sir Anthony Eden*, pp. 207–208.

CHAPTER XV: The Ambassadorial Years:
The Suez Crisis, 1956

1. Herman Finer, *Dulles Over Suez: The Theory and Practice of His Diplomacy* (Chicago: Quadrangle Books, 1964), p. 33; Hugh Thomas, *Suez* (New York: Harper & Row, 1966), pp. 13–14.

2. Finer, *Dulles over Suez*, pp. 34–35; Thomas, *Suez*, p. 22.

3. Winthrop W. Aldrich, Appointment Diary, January 30–February 5, 1956. Aldrich Papers.

4. *Ibid.*, February 28; March 3, 6, 12; and April 11, 1956. Aldrich Papers.

5. Randolph S. Churchill, *The Rise and Fall of Sir Anthony Eden* (London: MacGibbon and Kee, 1959), p. 228.

6. Dwight D. Eisenhower, *Waging Peace, 1956–1961* (New York: Doubleday and Co., Inc., 1965), p. 31.

7. *New York Times*, July 20, 1956.

8. Eisenhower, *Waging Peace*, p. 35; Winthrop W. Aldrich, "The Suez Crisis," *Foreign Affairs*, Vol. XLV (April 1967), p. 542.

9. *Ibid.*, *Waging Peace*, p. 35.

10. *Ibid.*, p. 36; Anthony Eden, *Full Circle* (Boston: Houghton Mifflin Co., 1960), pp. 476–477.

11. Eisenhower, *Waging Peace*, p. 37; Robert Murphy to Winthrop Aldrich, March 4, 1968.

12. Winthrop W. Aldrich, Appointment Diary, July 26, 1956. Aldrich Papers.

13. Finer, *Dulles over Suez*, p. 88.

14. Eisenhower, *Waging Peace*, p. 39.

15. *Ibid.*

16. Eden, *Full Circle*, p. 484.

17. *Ibid.*, pp. 486–487; Finer, *Dulles over Suez*, pp. 88–97.

18. The letter is reproduced in Eisenhower, *Waging Peace*, pp. 664–665.

19. Eden, *Full Circle*, p. 487; Finer, *Dulles over Suez*, pp. 97–98.

20. Eden, *Full Circle*, p. 487.

21. *Ibid.*, p. 488.

22. Winthrop W. Aldrich, Appointment Diary, August 2–15, 1956. Aldrich Papers.

23. Winthrop W. Aldrich, Appointment Diary, August 15, 1956, Aldrich Papers; Finer, *Dulles over Suez*, p. 143.

24. Finer, *Dulles over Suez*, p. 145.

25. *New York Times*, August 22, 1956.

26. Finer, *Dulles over Suez*, p. 173.

27. Robert Gordon Menzies, *Afternoon Light: Some Memories of Men and Events* (London: Cassell & Co., Ltd., 1967), p. 156.

28. *Ibid.*, pp. 156–157.

29. Eden, *Full Circle*, pp. 504–506.

30. Eisenhower, *Waging Peace*, p. 48.

31. Anthony Nutting, *No End of a Lesson: The Story of Suez* (London: Constable & Co., Ltd., 1967), pp. 57–58.

32. Eden, *Full Circle*, pp. 509–510.

33. Eden quoted in *New York Times*, September 13, 1956; Aldrich, "The Suez Crisis," p. 543; Eisenhower, *Waging Peace*, p. 673.

34. Dulles quoted in *New York Times*, September 20, 1956.

35. Aldrich, "The Suez Crisis," p. 552; interview, A. M. Johnson with Winthrop W. Aldrich, Dark Harbor, Maine, August 28, 1967.
36. Eden, *Full Circle*, pp. 517–518.
37. Quoted in *ibid.*, pp. 518–521.
38. Eisenhower, *Waging Peace*, pp. 669–671.
39. Menzies, *Afternoon Light*, pp. 165–166; Eden, *Full Circle*, p. 524.
40. Interview, A. M. Johnson with Winthrop W. Aldrich, Dark Harbor, Maine, August 28, 1967.
41. Finer, *Dulles over Suez*, pp. 178, 240–241; *Facts on File*, Vol. XVI (September 12–18, 1956), p. 306.
42. Eisenhower, *Waging Peace*, p. 51.
43. Eden, *Full Circle*, pp. 536–537.
44. *Ibid.*, pp. 545–548.
45. *Ibid.*, p. 557.
46. Aldrich, "The Suez Crisis," p. 544.
47. Eden, *Full Circle*, pp. 549–550.
48. Eisenhower, *Waging Peace*, p. 52.
49. Nutting, *No End of a Lesson*, p. 68.
50. *Ibid.*, p. 77.
51. *Ibid.*, p. 79.
52. *Ibid.*, pp. 87–94.
53. *Ibid.*, pp. 97–99.
54. *Ibid.*, pp. 101–102.
55. *Ibid.*, p. 104.
56. *Ibid.*, p. 105.
57. Aldrich, "The Suez Crisis," p. 545.
58. *Ibid.*
59. *Ibid.*
60. *Ibid.*, pp. 546–547.
61. Finer, *Dulles over Suez*, p. 358.
62. *Ibid.*, pp. 358–359.
63. Eisenhower, *Waging Peace*, p. 77.
64. Finer, *Dulles over Suez*, p. 370.
65. *Ibid.*, p. 383.
66. Aldrich, "The Suez Crisis," pp. 547–548.
67. Eden, *Full Circle*, pp. 606–607.
68. *Ibid.*, pp. 616–620; *Facts on File*, Vol. XVI (November 14–20, 1956), p. 385.
69. Aldrich, "The Suez Crisis," p. 551.

70. Finer, *Dulles over Suez*, p. 448.
71. Aldrich, "The Suez Crisis," p. 551.
72. *New York Times*, November 25, 1956; Finer, *Dulles over Suez*, pp. 448–449.
73. Aldrich, "The Suez Crisis," p. 551.
74. Finer, *Dulles over Suez*, pp. 438–440; Eisenhower, *Waging Peace*, p. 73.
75. Finer, *Dulles over Suez*, p. 454.
76. Eden, *Full Circle*, pp. 622–624; Finer, *Dulles over Suez*, pp. 428–429.
77. Eden, *Full Circle*, pp. 640–641; Finer, *Dulles over Suez*, p. 454.
78. Finer, *Dulles over Suez*, p. 456; see also *New York Times*, December 3, 5, 1956.
79. *New York Times*, December 4, 1956; Finer, *Dulles over Suez*, p. 456.
80. *New York Times*, December 28, 1956.
81. *Ibid.*, January 8, 1957.
82. Winthrop W. Aldrich, Appointment Diary, January 15–28, 1957. Aldrich Papers.
83. *New York Times*, February 1, 1957.
84. Speeches at the Pilgrims Dinner in honour of the Honourable Winthrop W. Aldrich, G.B.E., Ambassador to the Court of St. James's, 1953–1957, January 31, 1957, p. 5 [pamphlet]. Aldrich Papers.
85. *Ibid.* p. 8.
86. *Ibid.*, pp. 10, 13–14.
87. *Ibid.*, p. 14.
88. *Ibid.*, p. 15.
89. *New York Times*, February 6, 1957.

CHAPTER XVI: The Vital Link

1. Edna Page Austin, *A Gallant Gentleman* (New York: John Day Co., 1932), pp. 168, 285.
2. William J. Schieffelin to Winthrop W. Aldrich, April 18, 1930. Aldrich Papers.

3. Interview, A. M. Johnson with George E. Warren, New York City, February 2, 1966.
4. *Ibid.*; interview, A. M. Johnson with Winthrop W. Aldrich, New York City, October 18, 1966.
5. Dr. F. D. Patterson to Winthrop W. Aldrich, November 29, 1943. Aldrich Papers.
6. Winthrop W. Aldrich to John D. Rockefeller, Jr., January 13, 1953; Paul H. Younger to Winthrop W. Aldrich, November 24, 1952. Aldrich Papers.

INDEX